The Influentials

SUNY Series,
Human Communication Processes
Donald P. Cushman and
Ted J. Smith III, editors

The Influentials

People Who Influence People

Gabriel Weimann

State University of New York Press

Published by
State University of New York Press, Albany

For information, address State University of New York Press,
State University Plaza, Albany, NY 12246

Production by Cindy Tenace Lassonde
Marketing by Dana E. Yanulavich

Library of Congress Cataloging-in-Publication Data

Weimann, Gabriel, 1950–
    The influentials : people who influence people / Gabriel Weimann.
        p.   cm. — (SUNY series, human communication processes)
    Includes bibliographical references and index.
    ISBN 0-7914-2141-4 (HC : acid-free). — ISBN 0-7914-2142-2 (PB :
acid-free)
    1. Public opinion.   I. Title.   II. Series: SUNY series in human
communication processes.
HM261.W42   1994
303.3'8—dc20   93-48383
                                                                       CIP

10 9 8 7 6 5 4 3 2 1

Contents

Tables

Foreword

There is (or used to be) an important genre of scholarship called "continuities in social research," in which a concept is critically reexamined and updated after making its mark. Gabriel Weimann's account of the career of the concept "opinion leader" is a contribution of this sort, from the vantage point of a third generation of scholarship. In this spirit, it would seem a fitting tribute to Weimann's effort if I were to attempt to look both forward and backward from the vantage point of a surviving member of the second generation.

In this foreword, therefore, rather than simply being ceremonial, I would like to reopen the substantive question of how Paul Lazarsfeld came to propose that modern society is sprinkled with go-betweens who filter the flow of information and influence to their intimate associates, thus to challenge the assumption that the media of mass communication reach everybody, directly, and simultaneously. That the opinion-leader idea is alive seems evident from the hundreds of studies incorporated in this book. That it implies a more important idea—for social research and for society—is the point I would like to make in this foreword.

The persistent interest in the idea that people who influence other people are sprinkled throughout society long predates empirical social science, as this book makes clear. But the idea that such influentials— might be empirically identifiable and, in turn, programmed to diffuse somebody else's message, probably dates to Paul Lazarsfeld's seemingly serendipitous discovery of opinion leadership in action. Lazarsfeld's finding excited marketers, advertisers, publishers, pharmaceutical companies, educators, the fashion industry, family planning agencies and almost anybody with something to sell. "If only research could tell us who they are and how to reach them, we could harness them to our cause"—whether it is selling soap or fundmentalism.

Yet, fifty years after *The People's Choice*, it still proves impractical to pinpoint and mobilize opinion leaders, even if we know from the amazing number of empirical studies assembled here, who is likely to influence whom in a particular institutional area. As one of these studies reconfirms, it remains true, apparently, that women influence men's fashion choices, that men influence women's political choices, and that men consult women, and vice versa, in making choices about which movies to see. But to activate this knowledge is not as easy. To target influentials in the realm of fashion, for example, means reaching selectively into the dense fabric of social networks that channel talk about fashion. To do so tends to be more expensive and more complicated than simply reaching everybody.

This is an opportunity to reiterate that Paul Lazarsfeld's interest in interpersonal influence, serendipitous though it seems, needs explaining of a different sort. He certainly did not set out looking for opinion leaders. His two-step flow hypothesis, rather, can be traced to a convergence among his long-standing interests in the micro-dynamics of individual decision making, in the macrodynamics of mass communication, and in the methods that make these processes empirically observable. Add to these the passionate interest of a European intellectual in how democracy and culture work in a mass society, and we shall have assembled all the ingredients necessary to explain how Lazarsfeld came to study the ways in which people make up their minds and diffuse influence in a presidential election.

Prior to studying voting decisions, Lazarsfeld had examined occupational choice and various kinds of marketing decisions, and supposed that there might be a generic process of decision making that would be equally applicable to choosing a product and choosing a president (an analogy that, misunderstood, continues to aggravate academic critics). Two original methods for reconstructing this process on a large scale are the key to Lazarsfeld's hypothesis: an interview guide that walks the respondent through the stages of his/her decision, and the so-called "panel method" of repeated interviews with the same respondent.

The interview guide focused, first of all, on the "changers"—those who had chosen differently than they had at an earlier time. And it distinguished clearly—as in "the art of asking why"—between the attributes of a chosen item, product or president, that attracted the decision-maker and the sources of information that brought word of these attributes or otherwise influenced the decision. Applied to voting, this back-to-front approach to the study of communication revealed that interpersonal influence was a factor to reckon with in election campaigns. The finding contrasted sharply with the expectation that the modern media have direct and immediate effect, and with the front-to-back methodology that follows from so believing.

The other methodological innovation, the panel, was designed to observe the process of making and changing decisions over time. The opportunity to return repeatedly to the same sample of respondents made it possible to explore new hypotheses as they surfaced during the course of the study. Thus, when the importance of interpersonal influence for changing votes became apparent, it proved possible, on subsequent waves, to attempt to identify the influentials, and then to establish—at each level of socio-economic status and of political interest—that these were the more active consumers of political communication.

Getting people to talk about what influenced them is hardly a positivistic enterprise; it is a reflexive approach. It could not be more different from traditional effects studies that seek to trace the influence of a medium or a message by relating exposure, on the one hand, to changed opinions and attitudes, on the other. Reflexivity also underlies the Lazarsfeldian approach to media "uses and gratificiations." In both effects and uses the reflexive method of reconstructing decisions is addmittedly replete with problematic assumptions—but neither does it lead us to the dead end of "no effect." It offers clues to the functions and dysfunctions of the media in modern mass society.

This is what interested Lazarsfeld about opinion leaders and the two-step flow. He was fascinated that he had stumbled on a dual challenge to the theory of mass society, which postulates the omnipotence of the mass media, on the one hand, and the vulnerability of the atomized mass, on the other. Critical theorists cannot abide these conclusions, considering them a naive distraction, at best, from attention to the hegemonic influence of mass communication on helpless individuals, whereas Lazarsfeld's contribution is an expression on a modicum of optimism for a "participatory democracy."

Opinion leadership research continues this argument, even if its main stream remains (overly) occupied with the characteristics of opinion leaders. Opinion leaders are interesting, in my view, because they imply that media influence is being intercepted and reexamined in conversation. Find an opinion leader and you find a conversation. Find a conversation and you find more considered opinions and better informed actions, and thus a brake on media power. Lazarsfeld's legacy, like Tarde's of a century ago and Habermas's today, directs us to keep watch on the changing prevalence, forms, and functions of conversation in the various institutional contexts in which it takes place. Inevitably, one is led to wonder what will happen to conversation and to public space in the era of individuation now being thrust upon us by the new media technology.

Elihu Katz
Philadelphia, 1993

Preface

The Influentials: People Who Influence People is about certain people among us, the people whose advice and guidance we seek. They are the "influentials," the people who influence people. Who are they? How do they influence us? Why do we turn to them? *The Influentials* summarizes research that extended over five years, four continents, was hosted by five universities, and supported by several foundations. It reviews the history of the concept of opinion leaders from its earliest conceptualization to the modern modifications and applications. This review is the product of a systematic survey of the literature in various domains, covering over 3,900 studies on influentials, opinion leaders, and personal influence. It also reports the analysis of data collected in the United States, Germany, and Israel. Thus, it provides both theoretical review and analysis, as well as methodological tools and statistical analysis for the identification of the influentials and the measurement of their impact or "influenceability."

Traversing various domains of influence from fashion to science, from health care to politics, or from agricultural innovations to family planning, *The Influentials* provides a true journey through the world of human decision making and personal influence. It takes the reader to rural villages in India, gay communities in New York, Israeli Kibbutzim, glittering shopping centers, American mental institutions, South African tribes, corn farms in Iowa, Finnish health care centers, American pharmacies, Mexican rural communities, international academic networks, American high school cheerleaders, German protest-prone communities, Norwegian voters, Turkish villages, family aid centers in Tennessee, Nobel Prize laureates, Canadian hospitals, and African magicians. It addresses various spheres of human decisions in many domains: birth control devices, new cars, mathematical innovations, rock music, clothing fashion, new drugs, farming technologies, donations, Cesarean sections, political votes, and movie selections are only a few illustrative examples.

The research reported here could not have been done without the contributions of a number of individuals and institutions. First to be thanked are the real influentials behind *The Influentials*: Professors Elihu Katz and Elisabeth Noelle-Neumann. Their ideas, guidance, and support paved the road to the project, its funding, and its completion. It should be noted that they both relate to their own mentor, Paul F. Lazarsfeld, who thus served as my indirect influential. Several foundations contributed to this project: the German Alexander von Humboldt-Stiftung, the American Fulbright Foundation, the Philip and Muriel Berman Center in Pennsylvania, and the Research Authority of Haifa University. Five universities hosted me and provided the required research facilities: the University of Pennsylvania in Philadelphia, Haifa University in Israel, the University of Mainz in Germany, Lehigh University in Pennsylvania, and the University of Chicago. The German research center, the Institut für Demoskopie Allensbach, directed by Professor Noelle-Neumann, also provided both generous hospitality and access to all its surveys and databases. I am grateful to Mr. Philip Berman, an influential himself in the domains of commerce and art, for his generous support and true friendship. The book was edited by Gretchen Kates whose devoted work went far beyond editing: her comments, ideas, and criticism considerably improved earlier versions of the manuscript.

Many of my colleagues and friends are to be thanked for their support and suggestions. There are always more people that have inspired the author than can be listed in a preface. Some, however, have played a role that deserves to be recognized. These are Hans-Bernd Brosius, Karin Flier, Robert Eisinger, Bob Cohn, Marsha Siefert, Gad Barzilai, Wolfgang Donsbach, Gideon Fishman, Gabriel Ben-Dor, Erica Nastasy, Hans Mathias Kepplinger, Arye Rattner, Muriel and Larry Silverstein, Daan Van Vuuren, and Charles Wright. I wish to express my appreciation and indebtedness to three anonymous reviewers for their excellent comments and to Clay Morgan, my editor at the State University of New York Press, for his friendly guidance. Finally, to my family: Nava, Oren, and Dana, who provided encouragement and support to a husband and parent who seemed at times more attentive to his research than to them.

Part 1

The Birth of the
Opinion Leadership Concept

Prologue: Opinion Leaders in the Wilderness

One of the earliest appearances of the two-step flow of communication is not to be found, as commonly cited, in the studies conducted by Paul Lazarsfeld and his colleagues at the Bureau of Applied Social Research of Columbia University, but thirty-three centuries earlier, in the thirteenth century B.C. in the Sinai Desert, with the Exodus of the Israelites from Egypt.

According to the book of Exodus, 600,000 people followed Moses into the desert, guided by God's message: "Depart, go up hence, thou and the people that thou hast brought up out of the land of Egypt, unto the land of which I swore unto Abraham, to Isaac, and to Jacob, saying: Unto thy seed will I give it" (Exodus 33:1). The narrative depicts Moses facing an impossible challenge: he was ordered to command a collection of slaves, a forming nation that lacked any political institution and tradition, across the desert, to a land they had never seen. He had to lead this expedition for forty years, replete with starvation, thirst, disaster, war, and crisis. For most of them the promised land was a promise never to be fulfilled. The long period of wandering was supposed to bring to the promised land a new generation that knew no slavery, a new and free generation.

The forty years in the wilderness was, by the biblical account, a period that the anthropologists call "liminality," a sort of in-between state (here between slavery in Egypt and a new existence through the covenant and the eventual new state in Eretz Israel).[1] Later tradition considered the passage a time of trial. The desert became the proving ground where God acquired a people.[2] The obstacles were many, creating constant grumbling and rebellion.[3] As soon as difficulty occurred, the people began to hedge their faith, question Moses's authority and even call for a return to the "fleshpots" of Egypt. The need to transform a community of ex-slaves into a nation was accompanied by the presentation of rules and laws that created an additional source of pressure and crisis. The introduction of the Ten Commandments was followed by rules outlining how the people whom God had chosen for himself ought to live.

A modern political leader would certainly be confused if not shocked by the obstacles facing Moses. But a modern leader will at least have one advantage: he will have modern means of communication to assist him. For Moses, in the desert, there were no media, no means of amplifying his and God's messages to the huge public. There was no television, no print, no commercials, no campaigns, and no broadcasting. Lacking any means of amplification Moses could not speak to a crowd of 600,000. Moreover, he had many complex messages and a highly diversified audience: the Israelites were divided into twelve tribes, each represented by a named elder. Each tribe was further divided by families and households.

The circumstances themselves required a constant flow of information and directions. It was not only the need to spread God's laws and rules: it was the daily execution of leadership during a persistent fight with nature and with human enemies. Moses was not an uncontested leader either. The grumbling and complaints often led to direct confrontation and series of rebellions (e.g., Korah, Dathan, and Abiram). Under these pressures it comes as no surprise that Moses almost broke down and expressed his frustration to God:

> Wherefore hast Thou dealt ill with thy servant? and wherefore have I not found favor in Thy sight, that Thou layest the burden of all this people upon me? Have I conceived all this people? Have I brought them forth, that Thou shouldest say unto me: Carry them in thy bosom, as a nursing-father carrieth the sucking child, unto the land which Thou didst swear unto their fathers? Whence should I have flesh to give unto all this people? For they trouble me with their weeping, saying: Give us flesh, that we may eat. I am not able to bear all this people myself alone, because it is too heavy for me (Numbers 11:11–14).

God answered with a suggestion that centuries later was termed by social scientists as the "two-step flow model of communication," highlighting the communicative role of the so-called "opinion leaders." Immediately after Moses's bitter complaint, God responded with the first introduction in history of the opinion leaders concept:

> And the Lord said to Moses: Gather unto Me seventy men of the elders of Israel, whom thou knowest to be the elders of the

people, and officers over them; and bring them unto the tent of meeting, that they may stand there with thee. And I will come down and speak with thee there: and I will take of the spirit which is upon thee, and will put it upon them; and they shall bear the burden of the people with thee, that thou bear it not thyself alone (Numbers 11:16–17).

Moses followed God's instructions and gathered the selected men who thenceforth were the personal channels of communication, in a multi-step flow of information from God to Moses, from Moses to the seventy chosen elders, and from them to the entire community. Moses himself describes the circumstances of the choice of the mediators: "How can I myself alone bear your cumbrance, and your burden, and your strife? Get you, from each one of your tribes, wise man, and understanding, and full of knowledge. . . ." (Deuteronomy 1:12–13). One should note the social characterization of these chosen men, so similar to the attributes related to opinion leaders in twentieth-century studies. And God often activates this step-wise flow by commanding Moses "Go and gather the elders of Israel together and say unto them. . . ." (e.g., Exodus 3:16). By activating the influential, selected persons Moses could have his messages spread, as described by the Bible: "And Moses gave commandment, and they caused it to be proclaimed throughout the camp" (Exodus 36:6). Thus, the Bible may be regarded as the first documentation of the multi-step flow of communication where personal networks and social positions are used for disseminating the messages from a single source (God in the Bible, the media in the Columbia studies) to the vast public.

Between 1940 and about 1960, from the first study entitled *The People's Choice*,[4] Paul Lazarsfeld and his troops at the Bureau of Applied Social Research were occupied with a series of panel studies on the role of mass communication in the making of decisions in various areas (voting, consumption, public issues, and others). The researchers focused on the impact of campaigns in the media (radio and print at that time) and were surprised to find that interpersonal communication had more effect upon the attitudes of the individual than the mass media alone. Moreover, they found certain individuals who were more central and influential in their groups, often acting as intermediaries between the mass media and the public: they acted as filters or mediators through which the persuasive messages of the mass media had to pass. These intermediaries, called opinion leaders,[5] could allow messages to pass through (backing them with their own personal authority), strengthen or weaken them, or block their passage.

Consequently, the flow of information and influence from the mass media to their audiences would be perceived as taking place in two steps: from the media to the opinion leaders and from them to the public. This became the two-step flow of communication model.

This book examines the history of the opinion leadership conceptualization, from early discoveries, through the emergence of the empirical evidence, to modern remodifications and methodological sophistication. Part one presents the first stage: the early studies of the flow of information and influence and the roles of personal networks and opinion leaders. It explains how the idea of influential individuals was first suggested and supported by empirical research. Part two is devoted to the "Golden Age" of the opinion leaders' research. It describes the various attempts to categorize and identify different types of opinion leaders in various spheres of social life, the various methods used to identify and measure opinion leadership, and the dominant characteristics of opinion leaders. It also examines the leaders' sources of information and influence, thus answering the question: who leads the leaders? Part three is a systematic review of accumulating empirical evidence of the opinion leaders concept in various areas. This part is categorizing hundreds of opinion leadership studies according to domain or subject area. The various domains include marketing and consumer behavior, fashion, politics and voting, family planning, science and scientific innovations, agriculture, and health care. In each area the main ideas, measures, findings, and practical implications of personal influence and opinion leadership are discussed. Finally, part four is devoted to the stage of the concept's fight for survival. It examines the growing criticism of the model, based on theoretical and empirical weaknesses of the original concept and measures. As a result of this criticism, new measures and modifications of the original model have emerged. This part presents some of the modification attempts, including a new measure of personal influence, namely the Strength of Personality Scale, introduced by the German public opinion researcher Professor Elisabeth Noelle-Neumann, and later developed into a validated method for measuring the influenceability and identification of the influentials. These influentials are compared with the original opinion leaders, a comparison that reveals the differences as well as similarities between the two concepts and measures of personal influence. The last chapters focus on the influentials, their social characteristics, media consumption, sources of information, and modes of operation. It reveals the relationship between the agenda-setting function and the communicative role of the influentials: are they the agenda-setters, mediating between mass media agendas and public agendas? The answers are based on a series of studies conducted during the 1980s and the 1990s in three countries—Germany, Israel, and the United States—and so facilitates testing the universality of the concept, the measurement, the findings, and their implications. The wide range of implications relate to theoretical as well as practical areas like persuasion, political and commercial communication, the formation of public opinion, the flow of mass communication, social networks and their communicative functions, media effects, and others.

The Early Studies

The concept of opinion leadership was first introduced in an era dominated by the powerful media and mass society theories. As the nineteenth century came to a close, the image of society that had emerged was one which was changing from a traditional and stable social system, where people were closely tied to each other, into a mass society in which individuals were socially isolated. This idea has been championed by some sociologists well into the twentieth century. Describing the nature of the urban, industrial society, Broom and Selznick argued that:

> Modern society is made up of masses in the sense that there has emerged a vast mass of segregated, isolated individuals, interdependent in all sorts of specialized ways yet lacking in any central unifying value or purpose. The weakening of traditional bonds, the growth of rationality, and the division of labor, have created societies made up of individuals who are only loosely bound together. In this sense the word 'mass' suggests something closer to an aggregate than to a tightly knit social group.[1]

Coupled with this view of the nature of modern society was the power attributed to the mass media during the early decades of the twentieth century. It was a frightening view that portrayed human populations as little more than irrational mobs that could be easily swayed and controlled by cleverly designed mass communication. Those who controlled the media, it was assumed, could control the public. This perception, labeled as the "magical bullet theory" or the "powerful media paradigm," implied that the media have *direct, immediate,* and *powerful* effects on their audiences. The theory assumed that media messages reach every eye and ear in the same way and

9

brought about the same cognitive and behavioral changes in the entire audience.[2]

Three factors contributed to the powerful, omnipotent media concepts. One was the fast rise and popularization of the electronic media.[3] The diffusion of the radio and then television into every living room in Western societies and the growing share of leisure time devoted to the consumption of these media were perceived as indicators of media power. The fast spread of television, its huge audiences and the assumed effects of certain television contents (violence, propaganda, and commercials, to name only a few), added to the notion of helpless, passive audiences controlled by powerful media industries. The second factor that led to the popular belief in the power of mass media was the emergence of the persuasion industries, namely advertising and propaganda. Even in the 1930s the annual advertising expenditures in American newspapers reached over $750 million. The figures went up during the 1950s to over $3 billion per year for newspaper advertising, $1.25 billion for television commercials, $750 million for mass-circulation magazines, and over $500 million for radio advertising.[4] The figures continued to rise in the 1960s (e.g., $4 billion for newspaper advertising and $2 billion for television commercials). As Lin argues: "The logical conclusion from such figures is that the mass media must be quite effective in inducing consumers of the mass media to change their behavioral patterns and commitments."[5]

Finally, some evidence also appeared to support the powerful media notion. The Payne Fund studies, for example, published in the early 1930s, were, at that early stage of media research, the best empirical evaluation of the impact of motion pictures on children. By today's standards of research many of these studies seem quaint, naive, and empirically weak. Still, the findings suggested that the movies had powerful impact on the daily behavior, thoughts, and attitudes of young Americans. The movies were suggested to be a source of imitation, unintentional learning, and emotional influence.[6] Other evidence was related to wartime experiences: the apparent success with which Hitler monopolized the mass media to unify the German public behind the Nazi party and exert enormous influence throughout Europe convinced many that the politicalization of the mass media could lead to governments completely indoctrinating their populations with devastating ideologies. The power related to propaganda was best illustrated by Lasswell's description, early in the 1920s:

> The fact remains that propaganda is one of the most powerful instrumentalities in the modern world. It has arisen to its

present eminence in response to a complex circumstances which have altered the nature of society. . . . In the Great society it is no longer possible to fuse the waywardness of individuals in the furnace of the war dance; a newer and subtler instrument must weld thousands and even millions of human beings into one amalgamated mass of hate and will and hope. A new flame must burn out the canker of dissent and temper the steel of bellicose enthusiasm. The name of this new hammer and anvil of social solidarity is propaganda.[7]

The set of beliefs about the nature and power of modern mass media was never formulated at the time into a systematic model or theory but in retrospect it has come to be called the magic bullet theory or other colorful names, such as "hypodermic needle theory" and the "transmission belt theory." The basic assumptions of these models, namely that media messages are received in a uniform way by every member of the audience and that immediate, direct responses are triggered by such stimuli, were completely consistent with general theory in both sociology and psychology as it had been developed up to that time. It reflected not only the stimulus-response theory, but also the dominant views regarding the social organization of society and the psychological structure of human beings who are exposed and stimulated by the mass media. It was against these theoretical and popular images of society, the mass media and the individual that the early studies on personal influence and mediated flow of mass communication emerged.

The People's Choice

The starting point for the interrelated ideas of opinion leaders and the two-step flow model is the 1940 voting study, which focused on the process of decision making during an election campaign. The researchers, interested chiefly in the impact of the mass media on political behavior, selected four groups of registered voters from Erie County, Ohio. This was a typical county in that it had voted in every presidential election as the nation had voted up to that time. The voters were interviewed at intervals throughout the campaign to determine what factors exerted the greatest influence in their decision making. The study applied the panel design procedure: four groups (with 600 voters in each) were interviewed every month from May to the elections in November, and then immediately following the elections. The design also used three control groups to check on any effects of the seven monthly interviews of the main panel.

As the researchers later explained, the Erie County study was designed to demonstrate the impact of the media in affecting and shaping voting decisions: "This study went to great lengths to determine how the mass media brought about such changes."[8] However, the findings, presented in *The People's Choice*,[9] suggest that the flow of mass communications may be less direct and powerful than was commonly supposed. According to Katz,[10] three distinct ideas were highlighted by the findings. The first revealed the *impact of personal influence*. Much to their surprise, the researchers found that people who made up their minds during the campaign, or those who changed their opinions during the campaign, were more likely to mention personal influence as the main source for their decision. The main sources mentioned were everyday groups, such as family and friends. Moreover, a greater number of people reported participating in personal discussion of the election than hearing a campaign speech or reading a newspaper editorial. This led the researchers to conclude that personal contacts appear to have been more frequent and more effective than mass media in determining voting decisions.[11]

The second set of findings relates to the *flow of personal influence*. Given the revealed impact of personal influence, the obvious next step was to ask if some people were more influential than others. The first attempt to identify those opinion leaders involved two questions: Have you recently tried to convince anyone of your political ideas? and has anyone recently asked you for your advice on a political question? Using these two questions as their somewhat oversimplified measure, Lazarsfeld and his colleagues were identifying the opinion leaders and then comparing them with the others. They found that opinion leaders were more interested in the elections and were almost evenly distributed in every social class and occupation. Therefore, the researchers suggested that the flow of personal influence was activated by certain individuals who were to be found on every level of society and, presumably, were very much like the people whom they influenced.[12]

The third and final set of findings concerned the *mass media and opinion leaders*. Compared with the rest of the population, opinion leaders were more exposed to the mass media (i.e., radio, newspapers, and magazines during the 1940 campaign). These results led to a new idea: if personal influence was so important, if it was executed mainly by certain individuals who were more exposed to the mass media than the people they influenced, then possibly there was a two-step flow process from the media to the opinion leaders and from them to their followers. As this was first presented in *The People's Choice*, "ideas often flow from radio and print to opinion leaders and from them to the less active sections of the population."[13]

The People's Choice is considered one of the most important studies in the history of mass communication research.[14] First, it introduced a new survey design, namely the panel design, a longitudinal research that allows for the study of social processes over periods of time. A second major contribution was the comparison between media and personal flow of information and influence. It certainly called into question most of the assumptions of the "powerful media" notion by revealing the limits of media influence while highlighting the role played by personal influence. These ideas caught the attention and imagination of a new generation of researchers who opened up a new theoretical and empirical vista. However, because the design of the study did not anticipate the importance of personal influence, both the two-step flow and the opinion leaders concept were the least documented by the data. The authors themselves point out that a far better method should be utilized in the identification of opinion leaders, a suggestion adapted by the subsequent research, namely the Rovere and the Decatur studies.

The Rovere Study

As the 1940 voting study in Erie County was being completed, another study in a New Jersey town (Rovere) was begun. A small sample of only 86 persons was asked to name the people to whom they turned to for information and advice regarding a variety of matters. Hundreds of names were given in response, and those who were mentioned four times or more were considered opinion leaders. These individuals were then sought out and served as the research population.[15] Based primarily on interviews with a small sample of 86 men and women drawn from diverse social and economic strata in Rovere (a town of 11,000 residents), it was essentially a case study rather than a statistical survey. As Merton noted, "the initial substantive aim of this pilot study was fourfold: 1. to identify types of people regarded as variously 'influential' by their fellows; 2. to relate patterns of communication behavior to their roles as influential persons; 3. to gain clues to the chief avenues through which they came to acquire influence; and 4. to set out hypotheses for more systematic study of the workings of interpersonal influence in the local community."[16]

The Rovere study was quite different from *The People's Choice* project: in Rovere the original sample was used only to locate the opinion leaders and then focused only on them. Moreover it applied a more valid measure of influence than the original, self-reported measure. Here, in Rovere, was the first attempt to locate influentials by asking people "Who influenced you?" and study the sociometric map of choices, locating the influentials as well as their followers. Moreover, this research design featured two significant differences from the 1940 voting study. The first was the conceptualization of opinion leadership. Whereas the voting study regarded advice-givers as opinion leaders if they influenced (or believed they did) even one person (e.g, a husband advising his wife how to vote), the leaders singled out by the Rovere study procedure were undoubtedly influential with a greater number of people. Additionally, these people were regarded as such not in their own judgment but by people influenced by them.

Secondly, the Rovere study, unlike the earlier study of *The People's Choice*, took the importance of personal influence for granted, and focused more upon the people who played an active role in this process. Once the opinion leaders were identified, all attention was given to classifying them into different types and studying the communication behavior of these types and the interaction among them. Very little attention was given to the relationships between the leaders and their followers, except for the initial interviews, used exclusively to locate the opinion leaders. This aspect was examined only in studies that later followed.

Merton's main contribution in the Rovere study was his development of the first typology of opinion leaders. In fact, he suggested several classifications: the distinction between *real* and *potential* opinion leaders, the distinction between *local* and *cosmopolitan* opinion leaders, and the distinction between *monomorphous* (influential in just one field, for example in the field of fashion) and *polymorphous* opinion leaders.[17]

The first classification dealt with phases in the cycle of personal influence. Thus, Merton suggested the distinction among the currently influential (occupying a supposedly stable position), the potentially influential (the rising star—still upward mobile), the waning influential (passed the zenith—now downward mobile), and the dormant influential (possessing the attributes of the influential but not exploiting these for the exercise of influence). However, this distinction was found to be relatively fruitless as it "resulted in a welter of discrete impressions not closely related one to the others. It did not enable us to account for the diverse behaviors of the influentials."[18] The second typology emerged during the analysis of the opinion leaders and was found to be more fruitful: a classification based on the influentials' orientation toward local and larger social structures or the distinction between local and cosmopolitan opinion leaders.

The main criterion for distinguishing between local and cosmopolitan opinion leaders is in their orientation toward their community and the larger society. The local largely confines his interests to his community and devotes little thought or energy to the national or international scene. He is, strictly speaking, parochial. The cosmopolitan leader is more oriented to the world beyond his own community. He has some interest in the local community and must, of course, maintain a modicum of relations within the community since he too exerts influence there. But he regards himself as part of larger social units, as involved and interested in the Great Society. Thus, if the local type is parochial, the cosmopolitan is ecumenical. This local/cosmopolitan classification was found to be related to four dimensions:

1. *The structure of social relations.* Local influentials are "local patriots": they never consider leaving their community and do not feel that they would be equally satisfied with life in any other community. On the other hand, the cosmopolitans do not feel rooted in the community. They are more mobile, consider the option of leaving the community, and do not feel wedded to it for life. The social networks of the two types differ sharply: the local influential is concerned with knowing as many people as possible and with establishing frequent contacts with many people. The cosmopolitans have markedly more selective pattern of social contacts.

2. *The avenues to influential status.* Merton found that "far more than with the cosmopolitans, their (locals') influence rests on an elaborate network of personal relationships. In a formula which at once simplifies and highlights the essential fact, we can say: the influence of local influentials rests not so much on what they know but on whom they know." The cosmopolitan's credentials are found in his/her prestige and authority while the local relies on his social ties, his social record and his ability to get social recognition.

3. *The exercise of influence.* Local and cosmopolitan opinion leaders also differ in the pattern of utilizing their positions. It appears that the cosmopolitan influential has a contingency because he knows; the local influential because he understands. Merton likens this difference to that between "the extremely competent but impersonal medical specialist" (i.e., the cosmopolitan) and

"the old family doctor" (i.e., the local).[20] Moreover, personal influence stemming from the cosmopolitans, as in the case of specialized expertise, involves some social distance between the advice-giver and the advice-seeker, whereas influence stemming from sympathetic, understanding locals entails close personal relations.

4. *The utilization of mass media.* Though both types were more exposed to mass communication than the non-leaders, their selection of media and contents differs sharply. Thus locals read less magazines as they rely more on their interpersonal sources, while the cosmopolitans, with their extra-local interests, devote themselves more fully to the kind of external information set forth in journals and magazines. Finally, listening to radio news was found to differ, locals tending to listen more to reported news and cosmopolitans preferring analytical news, particularly world news.

A final classification suggested by Merton was related to the number of spheres of influence. Some influentials were found to be active in one narrowly defined area (such as fashion or politics) and no more. These monomorphic opinion leaders are the "experts" in a limited field and their influence does not diffuse into other spheres of decision. The other type, the polymorphic influentials, exert influence in a variety of areas. The Rovere study did not look more closely at these types, and Merton actually suggested that future studies should focus on this distinction and reveal the conditions under which an opinion leader remains monomorphic and how stable these types are. The Rovere study, with its limited sample and case-study method, actually became a pilot study for a larger and more sophisticated project, known as the Decatur study. Still, Merton's contribution ranged from methodological innovation (e.g., mapping the flow of influence to identify the opinion leaders) to the introduction of typologies of opinion leaders. These were guiding ideas in many later studies of personal influence.

The Decatur Study

The most thorough and systematic study of the two-step flow model and the opinion leaders commenced only after World War II in what has come to be called the Decatur study (after the community in which it was conducted). This research was designed to follow up more systematically the ideas first noted in the Erie County and Rovere studies, applying better measures and closer examination of the opinion leaders and their relationships with their followers on one hand, and the media on the other hand. The study's procedures and findings were published in *Personal Influence*, one of the most impressive documentations of the opinion leadership concept.[21]

The research was conducted under the auspices of the Bureau of Applied Social Research of Columbia University, while financial support was provided by McFadden Publications (probably because of its implications for advertising and marketing),[22] and the Roper polling organization.

The choice of the research site, Decatur, Illinois, was dictated by the resources available and the special method employed. Decatur was judged the most consistently typical in the clusters of variables thought to be potentially significant for the research goals (such as demographic, social and economic structure, population composition, mass communication usage patterns, and the general quality of community life). Moreover, the size of the population (approximately 60,000) satisfied the desired ratio of no fewer than 1 interviewer to every 20 households with the sample size of 800 interviews.[23]

Within each household, women residents aged 16 and over were interviewed on two separate occasions, in June and in August. The interviews focused on the following four areas of decision making in daily life:

1. *Marketing*. Choices had to be made regarding foods, household products, and small consumer items.
2. *Fashion*. Choices concerned clothing, hair styles, and cosmetics.
3. *Public affairs*. Choices regard political and social issues.
4. *Movie-going*. One had to choose among the offered movies.

These four areas represented different decision-making fields and made it possible to study the actors that affected the process of decision making. The fact that each woman was interviewed twice allowed the tracing of any change in these four areas. Once any change had been verified, careful probing was employed to identify the sources that influenced the decision (purchasing a new product, change of opinion, selecting a movie, etc.). By isolating specific changes of opinion and digressing to the influences that allegedly produced them, the researchers located the individuals who were mentioned more frequently as sources of influence.

As this was a somewhat pioneering study, Katz and Lazarsfeld applied various methods and measures to locate and identify the opinion leaders. Briefly, there are two ways to locate opinion leaders in specific areas of influence. One is through the testimony of those whom they have influenced. The other is the self-designation procedure when the respondent is asked about his/her influenceability. This self-designation procedure was used in both interviews. Each woman was asked twice: "Have you recently been asked for your advice about (one of the four main topics: marketing, fashions, movies, or public affairs)?" In the second interview there was an additional question: "Compared with other woman belonging to your circle of friends, are you more or less likely than any of them to be asked your advice on (four topics)?" If a respondent answered yes to the first question, detailed information was collected regarding the person who asked for advice thus identifying both advice-giver and advice-seeker, the direction of the flow, and the topic of the influence. To verify the answers, the researchers asked for the confirmation of the people mentioned as advice-seekers. In fact, they obtained 1,549 designations of people who had sought advice but managed to contact only 634 of them. Of these, two-thirds confirmed the contact and the topic. Though the researchers were satisfied with this validation, it is far from being an acceptable measure of validity and indeed attracted later criticism.

The main subjects for the research were the 693 "self-detected" opinion leaders. Who were these opinion leaders? Katz and Lazarsfeld found three significant dimensions that related to the position and functioning of opinion leaders. These factors were:

1. *Position on the social ladder.* The economic and social status of the respondents was roughly divided into three groups (high, middle, low) by two factors: amount of rent paid and years of education.

2. *Position in the "life-cycle."* This variable is a combination of age, marital status, and number and age of children. It resulted in four basic groups in the feminine life-cycle: "girls" (single women under 35 years of age), "small-family wives" (married women, under 45, with one or no children), "large-family wives" (married women, under 45, with two or more children), and "matrons" (married women, over 45, most of whose children were over 15 years old).

3. *Gregariousness.* The extent of social contacts based on (a) the number of persons in the community the subject claimed to be "friendly with and talk with very often" and (b) the number of organizations and clubs to which she belonged. The combined measures formed a scale of gregariousness ranging from low to high. These three characteristics were used to study the opinion leaders in each of the four areas of decision making. Let us review the main findings in two areas: marketing and public affairs.

Marketing Leaders

About half of the women interviewed reported making some kind of change from a product or brand that they had regularly used to something new. They often consulted each other about the new products and the quality of different brands, and this allowed for an examination of who influenced whom. This analysis was made in terms of social status, life cycle, and gregariousness.

Social Status and Marketing Leadership

If the flow of influence is a vertical process, as has been assumed, then proportionately more opinion leaders should be found in the higher status. However, Katz and Lazarsfeld found marketing leaders to be equally distributed across the three social statuses. With statistically insignificant differences, the proportions of opinion leaders in each status were the same. Moreover, when comparing the social status of the opinion leader with that of her follower, a tendency toward a horizontal flow was detected. Only rarely did the influence cross the boundaries of social status, and it was usually between people of the same social status. According to the researchers, "women of each status level typically turn to marketing leaders of their own status level for advice," a preference to be explained by "seeking out a woman with similar budgetary problems and limitations" and "women are more likely to encounter status peers during the course of their marketing activities than to encounter status unequals."[24]

Life-cycle and Marketing Leadership

Marketing opinion leaders were found to concentrate among large-family wives. This finding is quite expected, though, because this is the group with more experience and more involvement in daily marketing issues. Unmarried girls are both less interested in marketing affairs and less experienced in this area while older women whose children have already left home (i.e., the matrons) have little current responsibility and interest in daily marketing. The question of the direction of influence, to be studied by cross-classification of the life-cycle category of the influential with that of her follower, was, unfortunately, unanswered in the Decatur study owing to missing data.

Gregariousness and Marketing Leadership

Highly gregarious women, those who have a large number of friends and belong to several organizations, are more likely to be marketing opinion leaders. This finding was very clear as the proportion of opinion leaders was found to increase with the level of gregariousness. This finding should come as no surprise since opinion leaders exercise their influence through their social ties when these ties are activated for the flow of advice, information and influence. Moreover, as revealed in a later study, the opinion leaders use their social networks to obtain information.[25]

Public Affairs Leaders

The study's findings on the flow of influence in the area of attitudes regarding public issues should be carefully interpreted within the special context of the Decatur project. As the researchers noted, women at the time of the study were generally less interested, less involved, and less informed than men about public affairs. These days such a distinction between men and women may not be valid, but then, in Decatur, the proportion of public affairs female leaders was very small. Nevertheless, there were female influentials in this field even in the Decatur community and the analysis focused upon their attributes.

Social Status and Public Affairs Leadership

This type of opinion leadership was found to increase with each step up the status ladder: the highest rate of influentials in this domain was found among the high status level (19 percent). For the middle and low status categories, the figures were lower (12 and 6 percent, respectively). This finding was explained by the fact that participation in the arena of public affairs requires contacts with politically active people, level of education, and enough leisure time to pursue such activity—all associated with higher social status.

Life-cycle and Public Affairs Leadership

The data provided some differences between the four life-cycle groups in terms of leaders' frequencies. The proportion declined somewhat with each stage, the girls leading (17 percent), followed by small-family wives, large-family wives, and matrons (13, 10, and 8 percent, respectively). Nevertheless, examining the flow of influence according to age, the data indicate that when influence travels among people of different ages there is a marked downward tendency: from older influentials to younger influencees. Though the girls as a group may influence each other more than other women do, the younger opinion leader is not likely to influence someone older than herself.

The authors attempted with speculative efforts to explain these differences but they could not test their explanations with the database available at the Decatur study.

Gregariousness and Public Affairs Leadership

Gregariousness was found to be positively and strongly correlated with this type of opinion leadership. Proportionately, the gregarious women include five times more leaders than do nongregarious women. This tendency is more significant in this area of public affairs than in any other area examined in this study. Moreover, the researchers tried to test the interrelations between social status and gregariousness and found that they were independent, each affecting the likelihood of being an opinion leader, but with gregariousness having a stronger impact.

The Drug Study

The next study introduced the notion of diffusion over time of a specific innovation through the social network of a community. The drug study was conducted to determine the way in which doctors make decisions in adopting new drugs.[26] Since the community of doctors was not very large (less than one and one-half per 1,000), it was possible to interview all members of the medical profession in four midwestern cities. Besides the usual demographic data (age, medical school attended, etc.) and data about attitudes, prescription of drugs, exposure to information sources, and influence, each doctor was asked to name the three colleagues he or she was most apt to talk with about cases, the three he or she was most apt to seek information and advice from, and the three he or she was most likely to socialize with.

In addition to "mapping" a doctor's network of interpersonal relations, the drug study also provided for the study of two additional factors: the acceptance of a specific innovation (a new drug) and a record of diffusion over time. This was accomplished by means of an audit of prescriptions on file in the local pharmacies of the cities studied, thus enabling the dating of each doctor's earliest use of a particular new drug. Altogether, compared with earlier studies, the drug project provided more accurate and objective measuresthan were previously available. The decision-maker was not the only source of information: objective data from the prescription records were used as well. Secondly, the role of different influences was assessed not only on the basis of the respondent's own reconstruction of the event, but also on the basis of the objective correlations from which inferences concerning the flow of influence can be drawn. It was possible to infer the role of social relations in a doctor's decision making not only from the doctor's own testimony regarding his or her sources and their influence but also from the doctor's location in the interpersonal network mapped by the sociometric questioning of the entire community. Doctors could be classified according to their integration into the medical community, their influence on peers, their personal networks, their adoption of a new drug and the timing of the adoption, and all these measures could be interrelated.

The drug study found that colleagues were more important sources of information and influence than media sources. Moreover, the factor most strongly associated with the timing of adoption of the new drug was the extent of the doctor's integration into the medical community. That is, the more frequently he appeared on other doctors' maps of personal networks, the more likely he was to be an innovative early adopter of the new drug. Extent of integration proved more important than the doctor's age, medical school, income of patients, readership of medical journals, or any other factors examined. The researchers attributed the innovativeness of doctors who were integrated into their respective medical communities to their being in touch and up-to-date with medical developments. They also noted that these were the doctors who could count on social support from their colleagues when facing the risks of innovation in medicine.

The drug study conforms with the earlier studies in highlighting the importance of personal influence, this time in a specific area and a defined group. Even when a scientific, professional decision is to be made, personal sources are more powerful than any other source, including the media and professional journals. Moreover, personal influence is not evenly distributed over the medical community but is concentrated among certain doctors who are best defined by their social centrality in the doctors' networks.

Early Characterization of Opinion Leaders

The early studies on personal influence and opinion leadership resulted in several attributes related to opinion leaders. Let us briefly review the main ones:

- Opinion leaders are found at every social level, and in most areas of decision making they influence people from the same social level.

- Opinion leaders are found in both of the sexes, all professions, all social classes, and all age groups.
- Opinion leaders tend to be more involved in various social activities and social organizations and occupy central positions in their personal networks.
- Opinion leaders are considered experts in their field but this is informal recognition by close friends, relatives, co-workers, colleagues, and acquaintances.
- Opinion leaders are more exposed to the mass media than non-leaders.
- Opinion leaders are interested, involved, and updated in the field in which they are influential.
- Opinion leaders tend to be monomorphous: they are usually experts in one area but rarely in various areas (i.e., polymorphous).
- Opinion leaders manifest a specific communication behavior: they are more involved in formal and informal personal communication than non-leaders.
- Opinion leaders are usually well aware that they are sources of information and influence for others.

In his review of the opinion leadership concept after the early studies, Elihu Katz suggested three criteria that distinguish leaders from non-leaders: 1. *who one is*—the personification of certain values by the opinion leader's figure; 2. *what one knows*—the competence or knowledge related to the leaders; and 3. *whom one knows*—the strategic location in the social network.[27] A more debatable characterization relied on the use of the mass media, or the so-called two-step flow model.

Opinion Leaders and the Media: The Two-step Flow

The original formulation of the two-step flow hypothesis may have been the most influential and problematic contribution of the early studies. As the discussion of the criticism of the opinion leaders concept (see chapter 14) will demonstrate, most of the debate on the concept and its measurement focused on the issue of the media and the opinion leaders. This should be considered as the significant consequence of the emerging two-step model: not only did it redirect communication research to the importance of primary groups, personal contacts, and informal, face-to-face influence, it also challenged the theories of mass society and powerful media that viewed an atomized, passive population as directed and manipulated by the omnipotent mass media.[28] How were opinion leaders related to the mass media and the flow of mass-mediated information and influence?

One of the findings of the early studies was that the flow of mass communications is mediated by the opinion leaders: influence and information stemming from the mass media first reach the opinion leaders, who in turn pass on what they read or hear to their followers. This description was called "the two-step flow of communication," given by Lazarsfeld and his colleagues in their voting study (*The People's Choice* states "ideas often flow from radio and print to opinion leaders and from them to the less active sections of the population"). Yet, as Katz noted, "of all the ideas in *The People's Choice*..., the two-step flow hypothesis is probably the one that was least well documented by the empirical data."[29] It was merely based on the only relevant finding that opinion leaders were more exposed to the mass media than non-leaders. The Decatur study corroborated this and went on to explore two additional aspects. First, it was shown that leaders in a given sphere (fashion, marketing, public affairs, etc.) were particularly likely to be exposed to the media appropriate to that sphere (for example, a movie or fashion magazine for these areas, or a national news weekly for public affairs). This joins the Rovere finding that the cosmopolitan leaders were more likely to be readers of national news magazines. Secondly, the Decatur study indicated that at least in the realm of fashions, the leaders were not only more exposed to the mass media, they were also more affected by them in their own decisions. This did not appear to be the case in other domains, where opinion leaders, though more exposed to the media than non-leaders, nevertheless reported personal sources as the major factor in their decision making. This suggests that in some decision-making areas considerably longer chains of flow may be applied, an idea that led to modifications of the two-step flow model into multi-step models.[80]

Other studies at this early stage of opinion leadership research have turned up similar evidence that those taken to be opinion leaders are more exposed to relevant media content, to technical or formal professional communications, or to commercial sources of information.[31] Considering the leaders' need to be informed, updated, and involved within their area of expertise, their heavier reliance on mass communication sources is almost obligatory. Thus, the media could be used in an attempt to influence them: Stycos suggested using the media-reliance characteristic of opinion leaders in the service of a government program on family planning.[32] In Turkish villages, he found, the political opinion leaders were more likely to own and use a radio than the religious leaders, and were more receptive than the latter to the concept of family planning. For both reasons, but particularly because of the leader's greater accessibility to formal communications via radio, Stycos recommended that the political opinion leader rather than the religious leader be made the channel of influence for winning popular acceptance of family planning.

Even at this early stage, the weaknesses of the oversimplified two-step model were exposed. Though opinion leaders attended more to the mass media, they were also more in contact with other opinion leaders or "experts." Contrasting this finding with the vertical flow of the two-step flow model suggests the need to add the possible horizontal flow. Moreover, as Katz later noted, "the greater exposure of opinion leader to the mass media may only be a special case of the more general proposition that opinion leaders serve to relate their groups to relevant parts of the environment through whatever media happen to be appropriate."[33] This more general formulation makes clear the similar functions of the media for the Decatur opinion leaders; of national news magazines for the "cosmopolitan" influentials of Rovere; of medical journals as well as out-of-town meetings and contacts for the influential doctors of the drug study; and of contact with the city for the farmer innovator in Iowa.

The end-result of the early stage of opinion leadership studies was the formulation of a new perspective on the mass communication process. It seemed clear that the flow of mass communication was not so direct, immediate, and powerful as had been previously assumed. It revealed the part played by personal communication and highlighted the role of certain more active individuals, labeled opinion leaders, who served as an additional step in the flow of mass communication. Yet these were not merely neutral transmitters of information but selective mediators who could screen, block, change, or support the messages originating from the mass media. These findings set off an intense and exuberant effort to investigate the nature of opinion leaders and their role in various aspects of social life. The results of this effort are detailed in the next part, on the Golden Age of opinion leaders' research.

Part 2

The Golden Age of
Opinion Leaders:
Methods, Typologies, and
Characteristics

The Methods of Studying
Opinion Leadership

Early communication research has almost exclusively focused upon the study of mass communication and the flow of information and influence from the mass media to their audiences. The audience has often been perceived as a passive mass, consisting of atomized individuals exposed to the omnipotent media. However, when the empirical evidence indicated that the media were overrated, the role of interpersonal influence was highlighted. The early studies of the two-step flow model, reviewed in chapter 2, created a growing interest in this concept. During the following decades, numerous studies sought to advance the understanding of the opinion leadership and personal influence ideas. Several hundred of these opinion leadership studies emerged in the 1960s and 1970s. These decades are referred to as the "golden age of the opinion leaders."[1] This chapter examines the methodologies applied to study and identify the opinion leaders, the accumulating evidence about their role in various areas, and the typologies and characterizations used to classify different types of opinion leaders during this era. Out of the many studies conducted, four main methods of identifying opinion leaders have emerged:

1. The Sociometric Method
2. The Informants' Ratings Method
3. The Self-designation Method
4. The Observation Method

The Sociometric Method

The sociometric method may be traced back to the early work of Moreno who used simple questions on social contacts to map the ties in small social groups. By asking individuals whom they meet and talk with, whose company they enjoy, and whom they like to have contact with, Moreno founded a method known as *sociometry*. This made it possible to map social ties, individual positions in the group, and social ranking according to number of preferences.[2] Applied to the study of opinion leaders, the method consisted of asking respondents whom they sought (or may seek) for information or advice about a given topic, and the opinion leaders are those members of a group or social system who are chosen the greatest number of times. Though Rogers argued that "Undoubtedly, the sociometric technique is a highly valid measure of opinion leadership, as it is measured through the eyes of the followers,"[3] one may question this face-validity: are all followers aware of their personal sources? Moreover, this method necessitates questioning all the members of the group in order to locate a small number of opinion leaders, and is, therefore, limited to the study of small, well-defined groups rather than large communities. By contrast, any sampling procedure may not reveal all the influentials and requires a more complex design, such as the snowball sampling in which an original sample of respondents leads to those who will be interviewed as a second sample, and so on.[4]

In an attempt to demonstrate its methodological advantage, the sociometric technique was applied to identify the opinion leaders in two South Indian villages.[5] The researchers interviewed 120 farmers and computed for each individual his or her "number of choices." In each village the three individuals with the highest sociometric scores were selected and their sociometric maps were drawn; that is, the sociometric choices directed to these opinion leaders were plotted in the form of a *sociogram* (one for each village). This made it possible to analyze the personal networks of the leaders, although for some reason the researchers preferred to compare the most popular leader (in terms of choices) with the other two opinion leaders in the village. They found that the spoked-wheel-type structure of ties best described the social networks of the villages, the opinion leader being the "sociometric star" (more in the nonprogressive village than in the progressive).

The sociometric method often relies on the use of a list of names, that is, a "roster study": each respondent is presented with the full list of all members of his group or community and is required to name those who are his sources of information, advice or guidance. One of the problems of such an approach is that it reveals the strong ties, or the more powerful sources, while failing to locate the weaker ties and sources. This disadvantage is more apparent in the widespread use of a limited number of choices. In this procedure each respondent is asked to name the three (or four, or five) members of the group with whom he or she consults most often. Accordingly, limited-choice mapping is likely to reveal only "strong ties." As Granovetter suggested, the importance of weak ties, especially in the diffusion of information, should not be overlooked.[6]

Granovetter suggested that weak ties may be more important than strong, close ties in the flow of information because they constitute the intergroup bridges, allowing information to flow between disconnected cliques. Why are weak ties so important? Because an individual's close acquaintances, relatives, and friends often know what the individual knows. The close friends form a closely-knit network or a social clique. Such a clique will serve as a poor source of new information causing the individual or the clique to rely on weak ties (more distant acquaintances) to import information that the group does not already possess. While strong ties usually exist within the clique, weak ties provide the intergroup bridges, the interconnectedness to the entire social system. More attention should then be paid to the less frequent, weaker social ties and this requires methods that weigh the sociometric choices rather than those that focus only on the strong and frequent ones.

This notion of "the strength of weak ties" was applied in Weimann's study of the personal communication networks in an Israeli kibbutz community.[7] By means of a pre-structured interview, each member was asked to list his or her conversational ties with other members (unlimited number of choices, including members of the family) and was then instructed to rate the strength of each tie on three scales: the importance attributed to the tie, the frequency of contacts, and the tenure of the tie. This operationalizes Granovetter's notion of the strength of social ties, assuming that the more frequent, important, and durable the tie, the stronger it is. As every tie was rated by two respondents, the scores given to each tie by both members of the dyad were summed, thus adding the element of mutuality (i.e., the tie is considered more important when both parties rate it as important). The sociometric data were arranged in a who-to-whom matrix, each column representing the individual chosen. Each entry in this matrix is a communication tie, characterized by the attributes of frequency, importance, and durability. The use of specific computerized procedure to analyze the structure of the network (i.e., the NEGOPY procedure),[8] made it possible to identify the cliques by sequential reordering of the matrix and to find the centrally positioned individuals in each clique by the number of choices received from the members of the clique.

The Informants' Ratings Method

An alternative way to identify opinion leaders without recourse to interviewing the entire group or community is to ask key informants who are especially knowledgeable about the communication and social ties in their group. Rogers argues that "Experience shows that often a handful of informants can identify the opinion leaders in a system, and almost as accurately as sociometric techniques, particularly when the system is small and the informants are well informed."[9]

The use of informants' ratings was illustrated and tested by Van Den Ban who studied opinion leadership in three Dutch rural communities.[10] He actually applied both the sociometric method as well as the informants' method: interviews were conducted with all the farmers in each of three rural communities (about 100 farmers each). Three sociometric questions were asked:

1. Which two farmers do you ask for advice when you are not sure of the merits of new farming methods?
2. Which two farmers do you consider to be good farmers?
3. Which two farmers do you talk to most frequently?

In addition, in each community six or seven "judges," (mostly influential farmers) were asked to give each farmer a rating from a low zero to a high ten to assess the farmer's influence on others in discussions on farm management.

The informants' ratings were averaged for each farmer in the three communities. Next, the three questions and the average informants' ratings were subjected to a factor analysis. The analysis revealed that each of the four measures belonged to the same factor or the same dimension. Van Den Ban then related the average leadership ratings to various relevant measures. The informants' ratings were found positively correlated with the number of farming papers read, the number of agricultural meetings attended, personal contacts with the local advisory officer, and demonstration attendance. The opinion leaders, as identified by the informants, differed from the non-leaders on all of these measures. This identification of opinion leaders was even better correlated with measures like "contacts with advisory service" than were the correlations with the sociometric questions.

A study of the use of opinion leaders to promote health innovations in North Karelia, Finland, applied the informants' ratings method.[11] Over 800 lay opinion leaders were trained to promote the reduction of heart disease risk factors. After four years a survey was conducted to assess the effects. The researchers' first challenge was to identify the opinion leaders in a large community that was spread over a huge area and divided into numerous villages. First, local informants from each village were selected, with the help of the heart association staff and local representatives. These informants, in turn, were interviewed to identify two opinion leaders in their villages. The latter were usually found to be active members of local organizations (e.g., farmers' union, housewives' club, village committee, and others).

The 800 opinion leaders identified by the informants were asked to participate in a training program that introduced them to the nature and background of cardiovascular problems, the risk factors involved, and the measures required to reduce these risks. Of the original 800 leaders, 399 were active in the project (mostly women). The long-term impact was methodologically hard to assess. (A more detailed discussion is presented in chapter 13.) The researchers concluded their ten-year project by stating that

> The overall evaluation of the project interventions in North Karelia from 1972 to 1982 showed a major impact on behaviors and risk factors related to cardiovascular disease, i.e., a 28 percent reduction in smoking when adjusted for simultaneous changes in a matched reference area, and the coronary mortality rates here were reduced significantly more than in the rest of the country.[12]

The activation of opinion leaders, it appears, can even save lives. Despite the advantages in saving money and time, this method may suffer from the need to choose informants (who may not represent the group) and to rely on their familiarity with the entire network (which may be partial and subjective). Another drawback is its suitability only for small groups with known boundaries. As with the sociometric method, the informants' rating method will not be applicable to sample designs. Therefore, it will be of limited usefulness in the study of large communities.[13]

The Self-designating Method

The self-designating method consists of asking respondents a series of questions to determine the degree to which they perceive themselves to be influential. The early studies of opinion leadership relied on the use of very simple scales, for instance the voting project conducted by Lazarsfeld and his colleagues[14] posited only two questions:

1. Have you recently tried to convince anyone of your political ideas?
2. Has anyone recently asked you for your advice on a political question?

The distribution of scores on these questions was then dichotomized into "leaders" and "followers." Later research suggested that opinion leadership is a continuous variable rather than a simple dichotomy,[15] thus requiring a much more sophisticated measurement and scaling. The potential of the self-designating technique was demonstrated in a survey using a single-step, 48-item questionnaire to isolate opinion leaders.[16] It included questions on personal influence within the cosmetics domain. The respondents were chosen from six sororities (248 members) along with a validation sample of two additional sororities (155 members). The researchers assumed that if their classification based on self-reported leadership was accurate, it would correspond with differences in other variables concerning information, interest, and communication behavior in the area of cosmetics. The questions used to test the identification of the opinion leaders were:

Item	Social Attitudes
X1	Attitude toward cosmetics
X2	Attitude toward giving advice on cosmetics
X3	Attitude toward social integration
X4	Attitude toward independence in decision making

Item	Advice experience
X5	Total advice-giving occasions
X6	Advice-giving on product type
X7	Advice-giving on application
X8	Advice-giving on appropriate cosmetics[17]

The opinion leaders and the non-leaders ("influencees" according to this study's terms) were compared on the preceding measures. The comparison revealed consistent differences on each scale, opinion leaders ranking higher than influencees. The researchers, therefore, suggested a discriminant function based on the variables and their discriminant weights. This function takes the following form:

$$I = 4.20 - 0.26 \times 1 - 0.005 \times 2 + 0.015 \times 3 - 0.326 \times 4$$
$$- 0.902 \times 5 - 0.188 \times 6 - 0.061 \times 7 + 0.203 \times 8$$

When this index or discriminant function was applied to the two groups (leaders and influencees), it successfully discriminated between the two. The influencees' mean score was 2.99, versus 3.60 for the opinion leaders. To prove the efficiency of their single-item classification, the researchers used the discriminant function and compared the classifications based upon self-reports to the linear discriminant function (using a cutoff point to assign respondents to the two groups). This procedure was used for the research population as well as two additional sororities that served as a "validity survey." Of the analysis sample, 90.4 percent were classified accurately by the discriminant function. Of the validation sample, 85.3 percent were accurately classified. Though this research compared two measures of opinion leadership (no "external" source of validity was applied), and so lacked any true measure of validity, its findings supported the researchers' aim: "to prove the predictive efficacy of a single-step questionnaire design in successfully segregating opinion leaders from influencees."[18] Nevertheless, it took many more studies and tests to empirically establish this discriminative validity.

A first modification of the Lazarsfeld's two-item scale, by adding four questions to the original ones, was introduced in a 1957 study of the diffusion of new farm ideas among Ohio farmers.[19] A self-designating opinion leadership scale consisted of six items:

1. During the past six months have you told anyone about some new farming practice?
2. Compared with your circle of friends are you (a) more or (b) less likely to be asked for advice about new farming practices?
3. Thinking back to your last discussion about some new farming practice, (a) were you asked for your opinion of the new practice or (b) did you ask someone else?
4. When you and your friends discuss new ideas about farm practices, what part do you play? (a) Mainly listen or (b) try to convince them of your ideas.
5. Which of these happens more often? (a) You tell your neighbors about some new farm practice, or (b) they tell you about a new practice.
6. Do you have the feeling that you are generally regarded by your neighbors as a good source of advice about new farm practices?[20]

The six-item scale proved to be more reliable than the earlier two-item version: it yielded a split-half reliability of .703 (compared with .486 in Katz and Lazarsfeld's split-half coefficient for public affairs opinion leaders and .563 for fashion opinion leaders). The test-retest reliability coefficients were even lower (.149 for public affairs and .238 for fashion). Moreover, the researchers tested the validity of their scale, comparing it to the results of a sociometric procedure applied to the same community. They asked the neighbors of each respondent whom they would approach for advice and information about farming innovations, and then contrasted the sociometric choices with the self-designating scale. Though the correlation was not high (.225), possibly because only few neighbors were interviewed, it was clear that those who received one or more sociometric choices had significantly higher scores on the self-designating opinion leadership scale. Several studies that applied the modified scale[21] found higher correlations (reaching .408) between the two methods.

A study of 145 dairy farmers in Central Ohio used all three methods of measuring opinion leadership—namely, sociometric, informants, and self-designation.[22] The self-designation scores correlated (.30) with the number of sociometric choices, and even more strongly (.64) with the ratings provided by the key informants. The sociometric scores correlated .87 with the informants' ratings. Though this evidence suggests that each method may be a powerful instrument for the identification and measurement of opinion leadership, the results called for the improvement of the self-designating technique.

The same modified scale was applied through a commercially oriented research. Fenton and Legget conducted a study of opinion leaders for the Continental Can Company in order to evaluate the company's communication program.[23] They tried to identify opinion leaders since it was felt they would be more responsive and predictive of the company's image than the general public. They used a sample of 556 individuals, drawn from the same socioeconomic area, and applied the six-item scale of opinion leadership identification (using the questions of Rogers and Cartano but replacing "agricultural innovations" with "public affairs"). They then divided the respondents by their scores on the self-designating scale, the higher scores indicating opinion leaders.

Comparison of leaders with non-leaders revealed significant differences on various dimensions. The leaders' participation in various organizations and offices was greater than the non-leaders'. Differences were particularly large in professional organizations where three times as many leaders than non-leaders were members and held offices. Opinion leaders were found to be more mobile in terms of the shorter length of time they held their current job title and the shorter period they lived at their current residence. Other differences were revealed in motivation for achievement, involvement in stock and trade activity, and personal aspirations. Opinion leaders rated higher than non-leaders in all categories. As the researchers concluded: "It seems that the technique is a useful tool when the researcher desires a sample of 'opinion leaders' because it allows random sampling procedures to be utilized; is less time consuming and less expensive to administer; and sharply reduces the possibility of interviewer error."[24]

Within the same area of marketing and consumer behavior research, Corey applied a simple self-report technique to distinguish between leaders and non-leaders.[25] He studied opinion leadership in two different projects: 1. a study of leaders in food preparation ideas (in 1964); and 2. a study of automobile leaders (in 1969). In each study he implemented a self-report technique, asking the respondents one question, which classified them into either a leaders or non-leaders group.[26] The study of food preparation was using on a sample of 299 respondents taken from a larger sample of 910 females in New York, Chicago, Los Angeles, Philadelphia, Houston, and Atlanta. The automobile study applied a sample of 755 males and females, in an area probability sample of Los Angeles–Orange County, California.

Though this measure of opinion leadership was rather simple, Corey found it efficient in terms of several variables that very strongly correlated with his grouping of opinion leadership. His analysis revealed significant differences between leaders and non-leaders (e.g., participation in activities related to the consumer topic, knowledge of new developments in the area, readership of printed media related to the topic). As Corey describes the scale's validity: "The data indicated that it satisfies an important criterion of validity: the consumers it classifies as opinion leaders have, as a group, the same characteristics as those attributed to opinion leaders by the theoretical and empirical literature."[27] This construct validity is far from being a satisfactory test of the scale's predictive validity. Do those identified as opinion leaders really influence others? Corey's answer, like those of many other scholars who introduced opinion leadership scales, was limited to the discriminative power of the scale in terms of relating other variables yet without testing the *actual* flow of influence between the self-designated leader and his or her followers.

A replication of Corey's method was reported by Bellenger and Hirschman, who applied the same procedure to a different product category (clothing) and also attempted to test the validity of the opinion leaders' identification.[28] Data for the study were gathered in a series of 495 telephone interviews conducted in Birmingham, Alabama, in August 1976. The sample was selected through a random digit-dialing technique and the self-report identification of opinion leaders was based upon the question used by Corey. (It queried, "Which answer most nearly characterizes you for ideas of fashion and clothing? 1. People come to me; 2. I go to other people.")

The researchers applied three sets of criterion variables: demographics (19 variables including life-cycle and social class), social activities (13 variables including hobbies, social activities and membership in organizations), and self-descriptive statements (5 variables related to self-perceptions on appearance, activity, innovativeness, etc.). A discriminant analysis procedure was applied to these measures, the sample being subdivided into two subgroups so that each procedure was repeated for each subgroup separately: the functions calculated for one subgroup were then applied to the second subgroup to cross-validate the analysis. After the discriminant functions were calculated, the resulting opinion leader profiles were compared to the self-reported identifications, thus providing cross-validation.

The cross-validation results indicated that the discriminant functions developed for each subgroup and each sex were reasonably successful in predicting opinion leaders and non-leaders. This, the researchers argued, "lends support to the validity of the self-report opinion leader measure."[29] However, one interesting finding should be noted: the discriminant functions in opinion leadership were different for men and women. The common variable that was a powerful discriminating factor for both sexes and in all subgroups was "I want to look different than others," a trait related to fashion, innovativeness, and even the risk-taking involved in innovativeness.

A somewhat different self-designating scale was suggested and tested by Troldahl and Van Dam.[30] Their seven-item scale was suggested to fit the area of public affairs and included items from the Decatur study, the Rogers's scale and additional questions. Data from an area probability sample of 202 residents of Detroit indicated that this scale reveals internal consistency: the inter-item correlations ranged from .17 to .46 and the correlations of each item along with the total score ranged from .58 to .73, with a median of .63. Again, this is not to be considered a true test of the scale's validity. However, the researchers still managed to demonstrate some of their scale's discriminatory power by correlating the scale's scores with various social variables. They found some significant correlations, such as between "perceived leadership" and number of news magazines read regularly, or between perceived leadership and amount of time spent reading news in newspapers, number of offices in social organizations, and attendance in social functions.

Within the marketing research tradition, the use of the self-designating technique was mainly based on the so-called King and Summers's opinion leadership scale. This scale was actually the adaptation of the Rogers's scale for marketing research purposes. It includes seven items and somewhat different wording of the original questions. The final King and Summers scale was:

1. In general, do you like to talk about _____ with your friends?
   a. Yes b. No
2. Would you say you give very little information, an average amount of information, or a great deal of information about _____ to your friends?
   a. Very little information
   b. An average amount of information
   c. A great deal of information
3. During the past six months, have you told anyone about some _____?
   a. Yes b. No
4. Compared with your circle of friends, are you less likely, about as likely, or more likely to be asked for advice about _____?
   a. Less likely to be asked
   b. About as likely to be asked
   c. More likely to be asked
5. If you and your friends were to discuss _____, what part would you be most likely to play? Would you mainly listen to your friends' ideas or would you try to convince them of your ideas?
   a. Mainly listen to friends' ideas
   b. Try to convince them of my ideas
6. Which of these happens more often? Do you tell your friends about some _____, or do they tell you about some _____?
   a. Tell them about it
   b. They tell me about it
7. Do you have the feeling that you are generally regarded by your friends and neighbors as a good source of advice about _____?
   a. Yes b. No[31]

The seven-item battery was prepared for broad product categories. (King and Summers applied it to six different product categories that included packaged food products, women's clothing fashion, household cleansers and detergents, cosmetics and personal grooming aids, large appliances, and small appliances.) The scale was administered to a sample of 1,000 housewives in Marion County, Indianapolis. However, the researchers focused on the measurement of the overlap of opinion leadership across product categories, thus leaving the issue of validity and reliability to future followers. In their conclusion they call for the "development of a precise definition of opinion leadership and standardized operational measures for identifying opinion leaders."[32]

In fact, several attempts were made to test the King and Summers scale years after its first introduction. Yavas and Rieken tested its reliability with a set of six different studies, covering nine product domains.[33] They used a special version of the alpha coefficient, the KR-20, to assess the internal consistency reliability of the scale, in each domain separately. The KR-20 values were quite high in all the studies and domains: they ranged from a high of .87 (for generic products) to a low of .67 (for volunteer organizations). The other coefficients were all high: .83 (clothing fashions), .82 (energy conservation), and .79 (career opportunities/jobs), to list only a few. Moreover, they argued that this indicates that the scale appears to be fairly robust with respect to the data collection mode and sampling method. The reliability coefficients were all high for responses generated through personal interviews, telephone interviews, and self-administered tests. Likewise, similar values were obtained from random samples, samples selected on a convenience basis, and across nine distinctive domains.

A year later the same researchers, namely Rieken and Yavas, retested the scale's reliability, this time applying it to the domain of college/university selection.[34] Data were collected through mail questionnaires sent to five relevant publics of universities: high school counselors, alumni, high school principals, community leaders (such as mayors, county commissioners, and heads of Chambers of Commerce), and college recruiters. The KR-20 coefficients, calculated for each subpopulation independently, were applied to assess the internal consistency reliability. Again, the KR-20 values were found to be very high, ranging from a high of .82 (for the community leaders' responses) to a low of .50 (high school counselors' responses). Other coefficients were .80 (both alumni and college recruiters' responses), and .65 (high school principals' responses). Though the authors concluded that "these coefficients indicate that the scale demonstrates at least satisfactory reliability,"[35] they also noted the variance across their samples (as revealed in their earlier study), thus suggesting that the scale's reliability and efficiency may change from one domain to another. Moreover, they suggested several changes in the wording of the scale when applied to a specific context (e.g., replacing "friends" with "co-workers" or "other teachers," which would be more suitable in the specific context of studying opinion leadership among individuals working together or among educators).

Although the King and Summers scale was adopted and used by several marketing researchers,[36] the scale's validity was tested only later (in fact, sixteen years after its first introduction), when Childers tested the scale in two studies using both the original scale and a modified version of it.[37] The subject investigated was the adoption of cable television services and the opinion leaders in this domain. Data for the first study were collected through a mail survey of 250 households selected at random from the subscriptions of a cable television franchise. A total of 110 (or 44 percent) of the households returned the questionnaire, which included the King and Summers seven-item scale, questions on the perceived risks of the adoption of cable television and the ownership of electronic/technical products, and a modified version of the use innovation scale.[38] The last consists of five items, three of which were used in this study: the creativity/curiosity component, a general risk-preferences scale, and the multiple-use-potential component.

When the scale's reliability and validity were analyzed, the results were not satisfactory. Alpha coefficient for internal consistency reliability was .66, and nomological validity was not impressive either. Childers examined validity by correlating the scale with the other measures (the use of innovativeness components, creativity/curiosity, etc.) and found that only two of the five variables correlated significantly with the opinion leadership scale. One possible reason for these limitations is the format of the scale's response alternatives. The scale consists of five dichotomous items and two trichotomous items. This format may affect the limited range of the summed scores, attenuating the correlations. Moreover, the dichotomous classification may reflect the early conceptualization of opinion leadership (consisting of two categories only: leaders and non-leaders), but not the more advanced perceptions of opinion leadership as a continuous variable. The scale was modified by providing each of the questions in the original King and Summers scale with five response categories (instead of two or three).

The modified scale was tested in a second study. Data was again collected by a mail survey, sampling 375 households from the same cable franchise of the first study. Of the distributed questionnaires, 176 (47 percent) were returned. The analysis revealed that the revised version of the opinion leadership scale appeared to improve its reliability and its validity. The reliability coefficient rose from .68 in the first study to .83 in the second study (with the revised scale). Nomological validity, tested by the correlations with other scales, was also improved:

significant correlations were found for four of the five measures (compared with only two in the former version of the scale). The modification of the scale to reflect a common number of response alternatives while maintaining the character of the scale's items was found to improve the efficiency of the scale in the study of consumer behavior and marketing opinion leadership.

A more recent study applied the modified King and Summers scale to examine the characteristics of opinion leaders.[39] The subjects were 262 American undergraduate students, who were asked to answer all the questions in a distributed booklet containing both the opinion leadership scale (modified, range from 1 to 49 as each of the seven items had a seven-response scale) and a battery of scales covering other personal characteristics, such as media exposure, public individuation, risk preference, dogmatism, product (wine in this study) familiarity, and others. The respondents' score on the opinion leadership scale served to classify them into leaders' and non-leaders' groups (29.8 percent classified as leaders and the remaining 70.2 percent as non-leaders).

To test the reliability and validity of the scale, the analysis included the reliability coefficients (Cronbach's alpha) and a t-test comparison between the two groups across all other scales. Again, the scale revealed high internal consistency reliability (alpha of .85) in addition to some significant differences on other scales: opinion leaders scored significantly higher than non-leaders on the scales of personal involvement with the product, product familiarity, risk preference, and public individuation. The direction of these differences were all consistent with the hypothesized characteristics of opinion leaders. Interestingly, although opinion leaders were found to be slightly less dogmatic than non-leaders, the difference was not statistically significant. The same pattern was found for print media exposure, the leaders' group average being only somewhat higher than the non-leaders' average.

The most thorough testing of the modified scale's validity was reported by Goldsmith and Desborde, who took Childers' version of the King and Summers scale and subjected it to measurements of reliability, validity, and dimensionality.[40] The sample consisted of 187 undergraduates who completed a questionnaire with the Childers' opinion leadership scale and various questions related to rock music record albums (awareness and purchase), and three scales used to test nomological validity: 1. a scale of innovativeness;[41] 2. a scale of self-esteem;[42] and 3. a scale of information seeking.[43]

The seven items of the scale were intercorrelated and factor-analyzed by the principal component method. The analysis yielded a single factor with the an eigenvalue greater than unity (3.66). The reliability tests revealed high internal consistency (alpha values were .81 for men, .84 for women, and .84 overall). Like previous studies, this too supported the scale's reliability in terms of its internal consistency, and also went on to test its validity as well.

As a measure of criterion-related validity, the respondents were tested for their knowledge of various rock music albums. The researchers argued that positive correlations between opinion leadership and knowledge (awareness and purchase) indicate the scale's criterion validity. Indeed, the coefficients presented in table 3.1 are all positive and significant, even when the effects of age, social desirability, and yes-saying are controlled.

Table 3.1

Validity Test of the Opinion Leadership Scale
(Correlations of Opinion Leadership with Dependent Variables)

Dependent Variable	Range	Mean	Zero-order Correlation	Partial Correlation
Awareness	0–6	1.92	.46***	.46***
Purchase	0–5	.27	.32***	.32***
Innovativeness	57–139	103.1	.22***	.24***
Self-esteem	29–70	57.09	.10	.13*
Information-seeking	12–35	36.86	.08	.10

Note: Partial correlations are computed with the effects of age, social desirability, and yes-saying controlled.
* p < .05
*** p < .001

To evaluate nomological validity, the correlations with the scores on the three scales of innovativeness, self-esteem, and information seeking were calculated. The values shown in table 3.1 attest only to the innovativeness-leadership relation, and even this is somewhat weak (partial correlation of .24). The explanation given for this finding may illustrate the complexity of validating the opinion leadership scale: the scales usually measure leadership for a specific product or domain (e.g., record albums, cosmetics, or movie selection). When the validation process involves criterion measures, they are also measured at a comparable level of specificity (and yield significant correlations). However, when the validity measures are at the global level (e.g., general innovativeness or general self-esteem), with no reference to the product area, the validity coefficients tend to be very low. As the researchers noted: "It should come as no surprise that the resulting validity coefficients are zero or very small. In fact, we should not expect to find strong positive correlations between measures at different levels of generality."[44]

Hence, one of the main limitations of the validation procedures of the opinion leadership scales concerns the level of measuring leadership and the other constructs: both should be studied at the same level of specificity. Measures of self-esteem, innovativeness, or information-seeking should be applied at the same level of the opinion leadership measurement: if the leadership is identified and measured within a specific domain (cars, for example), then the construct measures of innovativeness or of information seeking or any other measure, should be studied in the same domain (information seeking about cars, innovativeness about cars, etc.).

The use of these self-designating scales, despite their advantages, raises some questions regarding the extent to which they may be affected or biased by the response set. Abelson and Rugg note their reservations about using these questions because they "anticipated the responses would reflect a bias in the direction of inflating the number of self-designating influentials."[45] Bylund and Sanders detected patterns in the responses to three self-evaluation questions, including an opinion leadership item, which they suggested to be symptomatic of yes-saying.[46] Consequently, Silk attempted to check if the Rogers's scale was affected by problems of response set by measuring its convergent and discriminant validity and the response tendencies it yielded.[47]

The data came from a Los Angeles sample of 168 females, tested twice with the Rogers's self-designation scale, with reference to two different decision items—purchasing furniture and cooking. The internal consistency of the six-item scale when applied to these two topical areas appeared to be roughly the same as found by Rogers and Cartano (the split-half reliability coefficients previously mentioned). As to item convergence, the analysis of the Yule's Q values to test the association between every pair of the six items in the scale revealed high levels of intercorrelation.[48] Of greater interest was testing the scale's discriminant validity. This was done by the scale's ability to discriminate between the two areas of opinion leadership. The notion that there are "generalized" opinion leaders (as suggested by Marcus and Bauer[49]) would, of course, lead to some overlap between the two types of opinion leaders, but there is no reason to believe that such overlap would be anywhere near perfect. (In fact, most studies revealed a very limited frequency of overlap across areas.)[50] This analysis revealed, however, that the scale met this test of discrimination quite well, but somewhat better for the furniture leaders than the cooking leaders, which may suggest that there is an interaction between the specific topic or decision area to which the scale is applied and some source of method variance.

Intriguing findings were found when the scale was tested for the yes-saying factor. Silk computed the scores for each of his respondents on the Agreement Response Scale (ARS), measuring the tendency of respondents to agree, or the yes-saying factor. Then he computed the correlations between these ARS scores and the opinion leadership scores, and found an interesting pattern: yes-saying was positively and significantly correlated with opinion leadership in furniture, though not with opinion leadership in cooking.[51] Again, this may suggest that the self-designating scale, despite its revealed validity and qualities, may have varying empirical value across topic or areas.

The self-designating technique depends upon the self-awareness of the respondents and the accuracy of their perceived self-images. The fact that often the self-perceptions of leadership do not overlap completely with the perceptions of others (be they the informants or the sociometric questioning of the group), may be partly explained by the difference between the self-concept and the actual functioning of opinion leadership. This distinction was first suggested by Hamilton, who studied these two leadership measures separately.[52] Using a small cross-sectional survey of some 100 homemakers in Chicago, Illinois, Hamilton examined the two types of leadership: 1. self-appraisal of one's influentiality and 2. actual advice-giving. He, therefore, rated opinion leadership on both the self-concept scale and the functional role scale.

One interesting finding was that the two measures of opinion leadership did *not* overlap and were clearly independent of each other. In fact, only 39.3 percent of the opinion leaders identified by functional role were also classified as opinion leaders by the self-concept measure. This was the first evidence of multidimensionality of opinion leadership. Hamilton went further and tested the relationships between the two dimensions of leadership and other relevant variables (such as exposure to television, exposure to magazines, and interpersonal contacts measured by the frequency of talking with friends about shopping).

As the author concluded his report of the analysis: "The main empirical contribution of this paper, however, consists of the data on how each of these dimensions correlates with other variables. When a series of variables pertaining to the flow of influence and the location of opinion leaders in the social structure is examined, it is seen that the two dimensions relate differently to such variables."[53] Hamilton suggested that researchers involved with studying the pragmatic validity of self-designated measures of opinion leadership should be aware of the leadership's multidimensional nature and "it would clearly be appropriate to assure that the measure is as pure an index of such functional role as possible."[54]

The Observation Method

The fourth method of identifying opinion leaders and measuring their influence is through observation. This method requires an observer who monitors the given group's activities and records the communication behavior, the links used, and the main actors in the interpersonal flow of information and influence in the group. One advantage of this method is its directness: the trained observer does not have to rely on indirect measures, such as the respondents' self-reports, the followers' answers, or mapping the social system based upon respondents' answers. However, this method is limited to only small social units (a class, a village, a military unit, etc.), and requires a relatively longer time than the other methods based on surveys and questionnaires. As a result, Rogers found that "observation is seldom used to measure diffusion networks and opinion leadership."[55]

A recent example of the use of this method is found in an experimental study that used opinion leaders for an acquired immune deficiency syndrome (AIDS)-prevention program.[56] Personal influence was suggested as a possible factor that may be recruited for the introduction and adoption of behavioral changes to reduce risk of Human Immunodeficiency Virus (HIV). Because HIV-risk behavior levels were high among homosexual men in small cities, the project targeted the male homosexual communities in small cities (Biloxi and Hattiesburg, Mississippi, and Monroe, Louisiana). One community (Biloxi) was randomly selected to receive the intervention while the other two communities (Hattiesburg and Monroe) served as comparison cities. In the intervention city, a three-stage process was used to identify, train, and then contract with opinion leaders among gay men to endorse behavior changes among their peers.

The procedure of intervention and its results will be discussed later (see chapter 13). At this stage our focus will be the identification of the opinion leaders. To identify the leaders in this specific gay community, four club bartenders familiar with the community were trained to observe social interaction patterns in their gay clubs. Each made unobtrusive observations for one week, recording first names and a physical identifier for thirty people observed to socialize and be greeted positively most often by men in the clubs. Recording sheets were cross-matched for repeated mention; 36 of a total of 82 names received multiple nominations and were considered key persons. Twenty-two were located, entered into the program, and asked to suggest one other influential person in this community. These influential people were subjected to a training program, recruiting them to serve as behavior-change endorsers. The results provide interesting evidence of the impact of this intervention program (accelerating population behavior changes to lessen risk of HIV infection) and to the efficiency of the identification and training procedures.

A Comparison of Methods

It is clear that each of the methods has its own methodological advantages and disadvantages. Table 3.2 presents the basic description of these methods and their advantages and limitations.[57]

Several attempts were made to measure the cross-method correlations. Two or three methods of identifying opinion leaders were used with the same respondents, revealing consistent positive correlations.[58] The most systematic attempt was reported by Jacoby, who applied three methods: the self-designation, the sociometric and the informants' ratings methods, to the same individuals and with regard to the same domains.[59]

As the informants' ratings and sociometric methods require cohesive groups, Jacoby chose to study fraternities, sororities, and their pledge classes at Purdue University (two groups from the fraternities and two from the sororities). The fraternity groups were examined for opinion leadership in clothing, alcoholic beverages, and long-playing music records: the two sorority groups were studied with respect to clothing, cosmetics, and decoration. The self-designating method applied the modified Rogers's scale for each domain separately, while the sociometric method involved asking each member of the four groups to name the best personal sources he or she knew in his or her group, regarding a specific item. The answers were used to rate the members according to the number of choices. The informants' ranking method

Table 3.2

Advantages and Limitations of Four Methods of Measuring Opinion Leadership

Measurement Method	Description	Questions Asked	Advantages	Limitations
Sociometric method	Ask all members to whom they go for advice and information about an idea.	Who is your source of advice or information?	Easy to administer and adaptable to different types of settings and issues.	Complex data analysis. Requires full mapping of the entire network. Not applicable to sample designs.
Informants' ratings	Key informants in a social system are asked to designate opinion leaders.	Who are the leaders in this social system?	A cost-saving and time-saving method as compared with the sociometric method. Each informant must be thoroughly familiar with the system.	
Self-designating method	The degree to which each respondent perceives himself/herself to be an opinion leader.	Are you a leader in this social system?	Measures the individual's perceptions of his or her position.	Dependent upon the accuracy with which respondents can identify and report their self-images. Low validity.
Observation	Identify and record all the flow of information and influence.	None.	Unquestioned validity.	Obtrusive, best for very small groups. Demands time.

Reprinted with the permission of The Free Press, a Division of Macmillan, Inc., from *Diffusion of Innovations*, 3rd edition, by Everett M. Rogers. New York: The Free Press, 1983, p. 278, table 8-1. Copyright © 1962, 1971, 1983 by The Free Press.

was used by asking key people in the groups (e.g., the president or the social chairperson) to name the influentials in their groups, in each domain.

The next step involved testing convergent validity by looking at the multimethod-multitrait matrices for each of the four groups. The test applied requires that the correlations along the diagonal be significantly different from zero, and sufficiently large: approximately 80 percent of the diagonal coefficients (28 out of 36) reached acceptable levels of statistical significance. Table 3.3 presents the coefficients of convergent validity, for each group separately.

Next Jacoby tested the methods' discriminant validity. This requires satisfying three criteria. First, a validity measure for a scale or a variable should be higher than the correlation obtained between this scale or variable and any other variable having neither trait nor method in common. Across all groups, methods, and domains, approximately 72 percent of these comparisons (207 out of 288) satisfied the first discriminant validity criterion. (See table 3.3 for each group's coefficients.)

Table 3.3

Validity Tests for All Methods

Convergent Validity	Group 1	Group 2	Group 3	Group 4
median r	.622	.358	.414	.421
number significant	7 out of 9	6 out of 9	8 out of 9	7 out of 9
Discriminant Validity				
tests satisfying criterion 1	7 out of 9	1 out of 9	4 out of 9	5 out of 9
tests satisfying criterion 2	65 out of 72	26 out of 72	56 out of 72	60 out of 72
Kendall's coefficients criterion 3	.481 $p < .01$	.084 n.s.	.259 n.s.	.753 $p < .01$

From "The Construct Validity of Opinion Leadership," by Jacob Jacoby, *Public Opinion Quarterly*, 38, 1974, p. 86, table 1. Reprinted by permission of the University of Chicago Press.

The second criterion requires that the scale or variable correlate higher with an independent effort to measure the same trait than with measures designed for a different trait but using the same method. This is done by comparing each of the diagonal values in the matrices with the two other values related to the same method but applied to a different trait (i.e., domain or topic). Overall, 55.44 percent of these comparisons satisfied the second criterion. The third criterion for establishing discriminant validity is that the same pattern of trait interrelationships must be shown in all heterotrait triangles of both the monomethod and heteromethod blocks. Kendall's coefficients of concordance were computed for the rank-ordered nine coefficients in each group. The values of these coefficients were significant for two of the four groups. The results of the four validity tests for each of the four groups are summarized in table 3.3. "It would appear," Jacoby concluded, "that convergent validity has been adequately established,"[60] but the results regarding discriminant validity are less conclusive. (Changes over groups in discriminant validity measures may be the result of different groups' characteristics.)

The second analysis involved the intercorrelations among the opinion leadership ratings of the three methods: almost all of the coefficients (10 out of 11) were statistically significant (and the last nearly so, p=.06). All the coefficients were positive but varied in magnitude (and to some extent across groups), and they were, on the average, highest for the sociometric and informants' ratings correlation (average correlation of .69), somewhat lower for the sociometric and self-designating correlation (.63), and lowest for the informants' ratings and self-designating correlation (.45). Moreover, when the correlations were computed for each product or domain separately, the correlations between methods were even higher. This indicates that the use of each method may be appropriate when considering the specific circumstances (e.g., size of group; visibility of communication exchange; type of product, issue, domain, and others). Nevertheless, the methodological priority of any one method was not established.

Conclusion

The various methods reviewed in this chapter are not necessarily in competition and do not even serve as alternatives to each other. Rather, they should be considered complementary, a set of tools needed to handle a complex phenomenon. The various forms of opinion leadership, the different areas or domains of influence, the diversity in terms of community's size and structure—all result in the need of the social scientist who studies opinion leadership to be equipped with a full range of research procedures. The next chapter presents different typologies of opinion leaders; beginning with a classification of influence, and suggesting various forms of the latter from manipulation to contagion. Such typology and the subsequent classifications of opinion leaders will illuminate the need to apply different methods and procedures.

Typologies of Opinion Leaders

This chapter examines the various typologies of opinion leaders emerging from the hundreds of studies that attempted to reveal the roles, functions, and characteristics of opinion leaders. Some of these typologies were purely theoretical; some were followed by empirical findings; some were rejected by research, some were supported and well-founded; some were general; some related to a specific domain or issue. Nevertheless, all of them contributed to the impressive effort to examine this multidimensional social phenomenon.

Typology of Influence

When considering the classification of influentials, one should commence with a basic typology of influence flow. Such basic typology was suggested by Hamilton, who used a two-by-two matrix to illustrate types of influence according to the perceptions of the influential-influencee dyad.[1] Hamilton used two dichotomized variables to create the matrix presented in table 4.1: the influential's report on his or her influence and the influencee's report of such influence.

Table 4.1

Types of Influence

		Designated Influencee Reports Influence	
		Yes	**No**
Influential		Corroborated	"Manipulation"
Reports	**Yes**	"persuasion"	or unsuccessful
Influence		or advice	persuasion
	No	"Imitation"	"contagion"

From "Dimensions of Self-designated Opinion Leadership and Their Correlates," by Herbert Hamilton, *Public Opinion Quarterly*, 35, 1971, p. 274, figure 1. Reprinted by permission of the University of Chicago Press.

The combination of the influential's and the influencee's reports creates the various forms of influence flow. The first option is of corroborated persuasion: both influential and his or her follower are aware of the influence and are willing to acknowledge it. As we saw in the previous chapter, many of the research methods applied to the identification of opinion leaders related to this corroborated type of influence: they asked the individuals to report who influenced them or who turned to them for guidance or advice. Additionally, many of the validation procedures that were applied to the scales developed to measure opinion leadership were based upon the verification of the influential's report by his or her designated follower.[2] Nevertheless, this conceptualization of influence is limited to one specific form of influence, corroborated persuasion, or acknowledged advice-giving.

Another form of influence is that known to the follower but not to the source, and so labeled as "imitation." The model person may not be aware of his role as a model for potential follower or know that his or her opinions, suggestions, or ideas serve as guidance for others. This type of influence will not be revealed by the standard self-designating procedures that have become the most popular measures of opinion leadership.

The third option involves an influential who reports his or her influence and an influencee who denies it or is unaware of it. This combination may indicate one of three alternatives, namely:

1. *Manipulation*—when the influential tries to influence a target individual or target group without exposing his or her functioning as a source of potential influence. Methodologically, validation of this form of influence would appear to require not only the influential's report but some objective measure (e.g., change of behavior).

2. *Unsuccessful persuasion*—when both the influential's report of attempted influence and the influencee's failure to corroborate the influence are valid. This combination may result from two different perspectives of the individuals involved, when they do not agree on the performance of the influence. Nevertheless, the term "unsuccessful" should be used with some caution as the only reason to label it thus is the designated influencee's impression. It does not necessarily indicate an unsuccessful attempt but may reflect the influencee's denial or unawareness of it. At the same time, it may stem from an overconfident influential who is unaware of his or her true impact.

3. *Invalid report*—results from one of the partners involved, wittingly or not, wrongly identifying or denying influence. This problem may be very acute since the act of influencing or being influenced involves prestige and social status implications.

The fourth and last option involves an act of influence denied by both the influential and the designated influencee. This flow of influence, labeled contagion, suggests that both the self-designating and the sociometric technique will neither identify nor measure this form of influence: "We can readily see that valid measurement of opinion leadership functional role need not involve the reporting of such influence by the influencee, nor, indeed, even the report of the influential, since both can be seen as unaware of the influence transmission."[3]

The four forms of influence revealed by combining the impressions of the influential-influencee dyad only illustrate the rich variety of opinion leadership forms. Each of the previously mentioned forms of influence suggests also a different form of opinion leader: a source of advice, a model for imitation, a manipulative influential, or an unacknowledged leader acting through contagion. Each requires different definitions and specific methods of identification.

An illustrative use of classifying opinion leaders by the influential-influencee dyad is provided by Saunders, Davis, and Monsees in their study of family-planning opinion leadership in Peru.[4] The opinion leaders were identified by the self-designating questionnaire: respondents were asked if their advice had been sought regarding contraception. Those whose answer was negative were termed non-leaders. However, those who replied affirmatively were in turn asked whether the person seeking their advice had acted upon it by adopting a birth control practice or by attending a clinic for this purpose. This way the advice-givers were further divided into two categories: "opinion leader" (whose advice has been sought and adopted), and "ineffective" (whose advice has been sought but not adopted). The analysis of these types revealed interesting differences in terms of characteristics and functions. (For a detailed review of this study see chapter 10.)

Typologies of Leadership

Most studies of opinion leadership drew a basic distinction between leaders and non-leaders (or influencees, followers, advice-seekers, etc.), and the opinion leaders were usually classified by domain or area of expertise. Most conventional typologies of opinion leaders relied on the sphere of influence, such as marketing (subdivided by product area), fashion, politics, public affairs, movie selection, medicine and health care, agriculture, scientific innovations, and others. Relatively little effort was devoted to other dimensions of leadership considering the existing literature and research on leadership in general. One of the few exceptions was a typology of opinion leaders suggested by Kingdon.[5] This study of opinion leadership, unlike most previous studies, distinguished among types of leaders and discovered patterns among the types.

Using a nationwide sample, the Survey Research Center at the University of Michigan conducted a study of the 1966 election campaign. The identification of opinion leadership was based on two questions: one to ascertain whether or not the respondent went to someone during the campaign and tried to persuade him to vote for one or another party or candidate; and the other to discover if someone came to the respondent for suggestions (the questions roughly parallel those asked by Lazarsfeld in the Erie County study). However, Kingdon used the cross-classification of these two questions in order to suggest a typology of opinion leaders. The typology, together with the proportion of the sample falling into each category, is presented in table 4.2.

Table 4.2

Typology of Opinion Leaders

		"During the election campaign, did anyone ask you for your suggestions about which party or candidate was best?"		
"Did you talk to any people and try to show them why they should vote for one of the parties or candidates?"		**Yes**	**No**	Total
	Yes	"activists" 10%	"talkers" 12.4%	22.3%
	No	"passive leaders" 6.9%	"non-leaders" 70.7%	77.7%
	Total	16.9%	83.1%	100.0% (n = 1,285)

From "Opinion Leadership in the electorate," by John W. Kingdon, *Public Opinion Quarterly*, 34, 1970, p. 257, table 1. Reprinted by permission of the University of Chicago Press.

Three types of leaders emerge from the classification—"activists", "talkers", and "passive leaders"—comprising 29 percent of the sample.

The three types are derived from the leaders' perceived activity: the activists are targets for advice seekers and guides for others while talkers, though active by attempting to influence, are not asked for advice or guidance. Finally, the passive leaders are consulted for advice but do not attempt to influence: their leadership is sought by others but not activated by themselves. Kingdon tested his typology by applying several measures of political information. His index of political information was constructed from three items: 1. whether or not the respondent could name the candidate for Congress in his district; 2. whether or not the respondent could say which party had the most congressmen in Washington before the election; and 3. after the election, which party elected the most congressmen.

When the measures of the information index were computed for each of the four groups separately, a clear pattern emerged: opinion leaders are indeed better informed than non-leaders. Moreover, within the leaders the three types of leadership have distinct levels of information: the most informed are the activists, followed by the talkers, and the less informed passive leaders. Those leaders who are active by their own ambition as well as by others' expectations are also more familiar with political issues (their domain of leadership). One may argue that these differences are not a result of leadership types but merely reflect the impact of occupation and education. To test this possibility, the partial correlations between opinion leadership and information (using Kendall's tau-beta) were calculated, with controls for occupation and education. But as Kingdon concludes from these tests: "Controls for occupation and education do not materially affect the original relationship."[6]

In the area of medical advice, Booth and Babchuk suggested and applied a classification stemming from the frequency of influence.[7] They distinguished between "occasional opinion leaders" and "active opinion leaders." Occasional opinion leaders those who rarely influence others while the active opinion leaders are frequently acting as advice-givers. To examine this typology the researchers studied a probability sample of 800 adults in two midwestern urban areas. Each respondent was questioned about advising or influencing others regarding seeing a new doctor or medical service. After screening out the physicians and paramedical personnel, 148 persons were identified as advice-givers. They were further divided according to the frequency of influence: those who had advised only one person during the last year were classified as occasional leaders while those who reported more frequent influence were classified as active leaders.

When comparing the three groups (non-leaders, occasional leaders, and active leaders) in the area of medical advice, Booth and Babchuck found that occasional leaders did not differ significantly from the non-leaders. On the other hand, active medical opinion leaders differed in a number of respects from both the occasional leaders and the non-leaders. First, they were well-read individuals and had firsthand knowledge of the health facilities or personnel about which they offered advice. Second, a disproportionate number were women, which, according to Booth and Babchuck was consistent with the care-of-the-sick role often assigned to females.[8] And third, their self-image as leader was coordinated with their advisory role. Other important differences between occasional and active leaders related to social status, gregariousness, and the extent to which leaders exercised influence in other domains. For example, they found that the frequency of active leaders was positively correlated with social class (more leaders in higher class with a significant under-representation in the blue-collar class), while occasional leaders were found to be evenly spread over the classes.

Additional distinctions between the active and occasional leaders were in the identity of their influencees. Occasional opinion leaders were found to restrict their advisory activities to their spouse or close relatives. Active opinion leaders, on the other hand, were likely to influence a larger spectrum of followers, including co-workers, friends, relatives, and acquaintances. Finally, active leaders were found to have more social ties, more friends, and more social contacts than the occasional leaders. They were also more involved in formal voluntary associations and in every measure of social gregariousness. All of these comparisons revealed the need to distinguish between the more consistent, stable, and active leaders, and those who infrequently exercise their influence. As chapter 3 described, the growing sophistication of measuring opinion leadership and the use of continuous measures instead of leader/non-leader dichotomy, was the methodological answer to the suggested differentiation.

Another typology of opinion leaders is based on leadership styles, as demonstrated by Thomas and Littig.[9] They argued that although the literature reveals different styles of leadership, the notion of style was not applied in a typological manner. The Thomas and Littig typology utilizes a Leadership Opinion Questionnaire (introduced by Fleishman).[10] It measures two basic dimensions of leadership:

1. *Consideration*—reflects the extent to which an individual is likely to have job relationships characterized by mutual trust, respect for subordinates' (or followers') ideas, consideration for feelings, etc.

2. *Initiation of structure*—reflects the extent to which an individual provides direction and is likely to define and structure his or her role and those of subordinates (or followers).

These two measures were combined to create a fourfold typology of leadership, the individuals placed in one of the four types on the basis of whether they had scored above or below the median on both scales. These four types are: HC/HS (high on both scales, combining high consideration and high structure definition) and their opposite extreme, LC/LS (low on both measures). The two other categories combine a high score on one scale with a low score on the other. They either rely heavily on socioemotional support but not in directing followers (HC/LS), or are not very considerate but provide a highly defined direction to their followers (LC/HS). As the authors argue, "the use of a classification scheme, such as the one described in this research, increases precision in description of leadership behavior."[11] In fact, this classification is one of many potential categorizations of opinion leaders by applying measures of leadership styles.

Another study of opinion leaders' style was conducted in a psychiatric hospital community in Australia.[12] The study sought to elicit three leadership types, following Parsons' three types of leadership: the "knowledge-bearer," the "emotional, supportive leader," and the "instrumental, task-oriented leader."

Finally, opinion leaders may be categorized by the nature of their influence: whether they are supporting an innovation or blocking it. This distinction uses the "negative leaders" and "positive leaders" to distinguish between influentials who promote and support an innovation, idea or concept and those who are against it (the innovation rejecters). In the studies of Rogers and Svening,[13] and Rao and Rogers,[14] opinion leaders were found to be rejecting and fighting innovations. The leaders' negative or positive response was related to the community's norms: if the norms were very traditional, the leaders were found to be non-innovative. More recently, Leonard-Barton studied negative opinion leaders among dentists to reveal their role in the diffusion of a controversial technological innovation.[15]

The study focused on a specific innovation (the use of non-precious alloys as a gold substitute fused to porcelain in the construction of crowns and bridges) among dentists and prosthodontics. Data came from dentists in the Boston area (63 interviewed at home or at the offices) and a national probability sample of the members of the two largest organizations in this field,[16] using a mailed questionnaire yielding 182 responses. Opinion leadership was measured by asking the dentists to identify those individuals they regard as the most technically competent and to whom they would refer, given the opportunity. Both samples (nationally and in the Boston area) were asked the same question. The analysis revealed a surprising amount of convergence of leaders nationwide, considering that no constraints were put on the choice and the geographical spread. Yet, most of the dentists' choices identified the same four influentials. In the Boston area sample, as expected, the convergence of choices was even more evident with one influential getting over 54 percent of the choices.

The chosen leaders were identified also as negative or positive leaders, according to their attitudes toward the innovation (i.e., the use of non-precious metals as gold substitute in dental restorations). The impact of the leaders' attitudes was revealed by comparing the groups who chose a positive or a negative influential. (For a detailed description of the findings see chapter 13.) Clear differences were discovered between the dentists who "follow" a pro-innovation or an anti-innovation leader, the former expressing more positive attitudes than the latter. The impact was revealed not only in attitudes but in actual practice as well: nonusers of the innovative practice (or those who tried it but discontinued its use) were more likely to cite a negative opinion leader. Positive leaders were chosen more often by dentists who adopted the new practice and currently use it. It is not clear from this study's data and analysis whether the influentials actively shaped the choices of their followers or whether they served instead as rallying points around which pro and con opinion could cluster.[17] As the evidence in this study was merely correlational with no controls for establishing causality, the true impact of negative or positive leadership was not assessed. But even if anti-innovation influentials were assumed to reinforce and legitimize rather than to sway innovation adoption decisions, they would still serve an important function in the diffusion process. Regrettably, only few scholars have attempted to provide and test this typology. The most frequent categorization of opinion leaders, nonetheless, relies on their area or domain of leadership.

Spheres of Influence

Robert Merton was the first to suggest a typology derived from spheres of influence, distinguishing between two types of opinion leaders, the monomorphic and polymorphic: "the monomorphic influentials are the 'experts' in a limited field, and their influence does not diffuse into other spheres of decision. Others, and this includes a good number of the top influentials, are polymorphic, exerting influence in a variety of (sometimes seemingly unrelated) spheres."[18] Moreover, Merton suggested that some individuals may serve as monomorphic opinion leaders for some groups and polymorphic leaders for others.

Katz and Lazarsfeld tested the idea of "general leader." They compared the leaders in the areas of marketing, fashion, and public affairs and found no evidence for such a type: "the fact that a woman is a leader in one area has no bearing on the likelihood that she will be a leader in another."[19] For Katz and Lazarsfeld it appeared that an overlap of leadership across areas or domains was very unlikely. But this was based on a calculation of the expected frequencies of overlap with hypothetical frequencies expected by chance only. They found that these rates were almost identical, and so concluded that being an opinion leader in one area did not affect the probability of being an opinion leader in another. However, these computations and conclusions were to be later criticized and reanalyzed.

Marcus and Bauer argued that Katz and Lazarsfeld miscalculated the "hypothetical" values of expected frequencies.[20] They claimed that in order to calculate the hypothetical frequency of two-area-only overlap, one has not only to multiply the probabilities of leadership in these two areas but *also* to multiply it by the probability of *not* being an opinion leader in the third area.[21] Using the corrected formula, Marcus and Bauer recalculated the values from Katz and Lazarsfeld's data. They now found that the actual rates of overlap were somewhat higher than expected by chance. The overlap was not frequent (fashion and public affairs 2.4 percent; fashion and marketing 5.1 percent; marketing and public affairs 2.8 percent) but these were overlaps across *two* areas only. When the 3.1 percent of three-area overlap was added to each of them, the "corrected actual rates" were quite significant. This lead the authors to entitle their article with the argument: "Yes, there are generalized opinion leaders."

But despite the reemergence of the overlap idea, other studies at that early stage of opinion leadership research found no evidence for such generalized opinion leadership. In rural sociology, Emery and Oeser in a study of farm opinion leaders in Melbourne, Australia, reported no leadership overlap.[22] Wilkening, Tully, and Presser likewise found opinion leaders to be primarily monomorphic in the case of the diffusion of various farm practices.[23]

Silk studied the issue of leadership overlap across five specific dental products and services.[24] Using a modification of Katz and Lazarsfeld's single self-designating question, he identified opinion leaders (among 177 adult residents of West Los Angeles) in the areas of choice of dentist, electric toothbrush, mouthwash, toothpaste, and regular toothbrush. He found that the percentage of the multiple-product opinion leaders decreases sharply as the number of areas of influence increases. Moreover, the cases of overlap are few and concentrated in the two-area overlaps. Silk used the refined method of Marcus and Bauer to compare the actual occurrence of overlap with that expected by chance and found the actual frequencies very close to those expected by chance rates. The discrepancies between them were minimal and none even approached statistical significance. In spite of this study's relatively small sample and its focus on very closely related products, the findings provide no support for the overlap of opinion leadership.

The study of generalized opinion leadership required more than mere comparisons of overlap across areas, however. As Silk himself noted,

> there are at least three factors crucial to the definition of generalized opinion leaders: the number and similarity of areas of influence; the number of occasions on which an opinion leader is influential; and the period of time over which his activities are studied. All these factors might determine the likelihood that overlapping opinion leadership will be observed because they tend to determine what portion of an individual's social interaction is included in a particular study.

Indeed, the study of generalized leadership has become more sophisticated owing to the need to control variables, such as type of product or domain, time period, method of identification, type of network being studied, the measures of overlap, and others. King and Summers, for example, measured overlap of opinion leadership across six consumer products.[26] The data came from a survey of new-product adoption in Marion County (Indianapolis, Indiana) conducted by the New Product Adoption and Diffusion Research Program at Purdue University. The research instrument was an interview and question-naires that included King and Summers scale of self-designating opinion leadership (a modification of Rogers' scale, see chapter 3), measures of demographic and social profiles, mass media exposure, social activities, and product involvement and adoption.

The sample of 976 housewives (drawn from a population of 200,000 households) was classified according to opinion leadership in six product areas: packaged foods, women's fashions, household cleansers and detergents, cosmetics and personal grooming aids, large appliances, and small appliances. The first measure used to study overlap was the aggregate analysis. It reveals some evidence of overlap: 46 percent of the sample qualified as opinion leaders in two or more product categories, 28 percent in three or more categories, and 13 percent in four or more product categories. When the product areas of overlapping opinion leadership were examined, it appeared that "opinion leadership overlap across the six product categories is a common phenomenon, existing in every combination."[27] Further, the amount of actual overlap exceeded the expected amount assuming chance or statistical independence, and was statistically significant at the .001 level for each of the 57 possible overlap combinations!

Indeed, this was strong support for the notion of generalized leaders, though some reservations should be noted. The product categories used in this study were not totally independent; that is, some of them were related to the same domain, the same sphere of daily life. It is not surprising to find that King and Summers found that the most frequent overlap was of areas that are essentially interrelated. When two-product overlap was examined, the categories of small and large appliances recorded the highest overlap, followed by the overlap of women's fashion and cosmetics and personal grooming aids. This pattern of closely related areas as predicting opinion leadership overlap is better exposed in the correlation matrix of opinion leadership scores across product areas. (See table 4.3.)

Table 4.3

Correlation Matrix of Opinion Leadership Scores Across Products

Product Category	1	2	3	4	5	6
1. Packaged food	1.000					
2. Women's fashion	.316	1.000				
3. Cleansers/detergents	.497	.328	1.000			
4. Cosmetics/grooming	.267	.510	.346	1.000		
5. Large appliances	.288	.233	.314	.191	1.000	
6. Small appliances	.317	.240	.330	.240	.656	1.000

From "Overlap of Opinion Leadership Acress Consumer Product Categories," by Charles W. King and John O. Summers, *Journal of Marketing Research*, 7, 1970, p. 49, table 4. Reprinted by permission of the American Marketing Association.

The matrix of intercorrelations reveals the pattern of overlap across closely related categories: the packaged food-household cleansers and detergents overlap (correlation of .497) reflects the household domain, whereas the strong correlation between the small and large appliances (.656) represents this specific expertise. The intercorrelation between fashion and cosmetics (.510) should come as no surprise: both relate to the appearance or personal-grooming domain. The reverse tendency is revealed when overlap is measured across product categories that appear to represent very different domains. Food and cosmetics, large or small appliances and cosmetics, appliances and fashions all yield low correlations and rare overlap. These findings suggest that the phenomenon of generalized leadership should be more applicable to certain domains and certainly for interrelated areas of expertise. As DeFleur noted long ago: "It may well be that influencing ability can be readily extended from one subject matter to another where these subject matters are essentially similar, but such attempts at generality may prove more difficult in unlike contexts of ideas."[28]

A similar conclusion was reached by Jacoby, who, if you will recall from chapter 3, applied three methods, the self-designation, the sociometric, and the informants' ratings methods to the fraternities, sororities, and their pledge classes at Purdue University.[29] Jacoby chose to study these groups because both the informants' ratings and sociometric methods require cohesive groups. The fraternity groups were examined for opinion leadership in clothing, alcoholic beverages, and long-playing records: the two sorority groups were studied with respect to clothing, cosmetics, and decoration. The self-designating method utilized the modified Rogers's scale, for each domain separately, while the sociometric method involved asking each member of the four groups to name the best personal sources he or she knew in his or her group, regarding a specific item. The data, argues Jacoby, "offer moderate to strong support for the contention that overlap in opinion leadership does exist across product categories. Moreover, the more similar the products the greater the degree of overlap."[30] For example, there was greater overlap within the sororities between clothing and cosmetic opinion leaders than between clothing and room decoration opinion leaders, or between cosmetic and room decoration opinion leaders.

To test the notion of clusters of interest domains as affecting overlap of opinion leadership, Montgomery and Silk designed a study that relates overlap of interest to overlap of leadership.[31] The data were collected as a part of a larger study of media attitudes and habits that included the King and Summers's modified scale of opinion leadership for 16 topics (ranging from travel, raising children, and automobiles, to finances, furniture, buying food, and clothing), as well as questions measuring interest in these topics. A national sample of 3,837 American women responded to a mail questionnaire. The sample was split into an estimating subsample (n=1,918), and a validating subsample (n=1,919).

The researchers' hypothesis was that the stronger the correlation in interest between topics, the greater the amount of overlap between opinion leadership in the same areas. To test it, they computed the intercorrelations among the 16 categories in terms of interest, and, separately, the intercorrelations among opinion leadership scores for these 16 topics. The gamma coefficients were all positive, ranging from .046 to .803 for interest, and from .088 to .825 for opinion leadership. The mean interest and leadership correlations were .312 and .407, respectively, indicating that opinion leadership tends to be somewhat more intercorrelated than interest. To measure the relationship between interest and overlap, the gammas of opinion leadership were regressed on the interest gammas for the same pair of topics (a total of 120 gammas for interest and 120 gammas for leadership). This procedure revealed a very strong relationship (R square of .78). That is, for any pair of topics, the tendency for opinion leadership to overlap varies directly with the magnitude of association in interest (in the same topics).

Encouraged by the revealed association between interest and overlapping leadership, the researchers applied cluster analysis to expose those topics that constitute a domain, or a cluster. This enabled them to test the interest-overlap relationship in a different way: if the hypothesized relation existed, then the manner in which the 16 categories cluster together in terms of interest should be similar to the cluster patterns obtained for opinion leadership. This analysis revealed that the clusters formed were almost identical for interest and leadership. They included three-topic clusters, such as BPH (buying food, preparing food, and household work) or CHE (clothing, home furnishings, and entertaining); and a pair of two-category clusters, such as SC (science and culture) and TA (travel and automobiles), which were found to cluster similarly in both samples. Even the order in which these clusters emerged was similar for both interest and leadership overlap, including the two unclustered topics (raising children and hobbies, which in both measures were not related to any other topic).

The clusters of topics appear to represent both domains of interest and personal influence. It is not surprising to find that buying and preparing food and household work form a tight cluster since they all are part of the homemaker's routine. Clothing, home furnishing, and entertaining are all socially visible manifestations of taste, leisure, and status. The important contribution of this study, however, was the relationship between these clusters of interest and overlapping opinion leadership. This notion was further investigated by Myers and Robertson, who applied the same hypothesis to 12 different topics.[32] They sent questionnaires regarding twelve topics (see listing in table 4.4) to 400 households in the Los Angeles area. The response rate (65 percent) reduced the sample to 246 homemakers, all rated by a self-designating scale of opinion leadership, for each of the topic areas.

The intercorrelations among the domains reveal some strong associations among certain pairs of topics. For example, influence for women's clothing was highly related to that for cosmetics and personal care (coefficient of .78), and influence for household furnishings correlated highly with that for household appliances (.63). To reveal the pattern of similarity, or the structure of domains, a principle component factor analysis was performed, using highest row values as communalities estimates and performing varimax rotation on all factors with eigenvalues greater than +1.0. This analysis yielded two factors, presented in table 4.4.

Table 4.4

Rotated Factor Loadings for Opinion Leadership Overlap

	Factors		
Topics	Endogenous Interests	Exogenous Interests	Communality
1. Home entertainment	.32	.44	.29
2. House furnishings	.62	.27	.46
3. House appliances	.67	.16	.47
4. Home upkeep	.78	−.05	.61
5. Recreation/Travel	.15	.67	.47
6. Politics	−.05	.80	.65
7. Child upbringing	.38	.35	.26
8. Women's clothing	.73	.18	.57
9. Medical care	.60	.37	.49
10. Personal Care	.74	.26	.61
11. Cooking and food	.61	.06	.37
12. Automobiles	.21	.68	.51
Proportion of variance:	.36	.12	

From "Dimensions of Opinion Leadership," by James H. Myers and Thomas S. Robertson, *Journal of Marketing Research*, 9, 1972, p. 45, table 3. Reprinted by permission of the American Marketing Association.

The two factors revealed by the analysis were interpreted by Myers and Robertson as (a) "endogenous interests" (those centering around the home), such as home upkeep (loading of .78 on this factor), personal care (.74), women's clothing (.73), household appliances (.67), household furnishings (.62), and cooking and foods (.61); and (b) "exogenous interests" (those related to out-of-home activities), such as politics (loading of .80 on the second factor), automobiles (.68), and recreation and travel (.67). The researchers even suggested that when they applied an unrotated factor matrix, a third factor had emerged, with loadings on child upbringing and medical care, thus defined as "family care" domain.[33] The generalized opinion leadership concept was supported again, but only within a cluster of topics that belong to the same domain of activities and interests. Since interests and activities are divided (e.g., by their indoor or outdoor nature), personal influence cannot be generalized across all topic areas. Overlapping opinion leadership remains within the boundaries of a domain or sphere of interest.

An additional factor that affects overlap of leadership areas was introduced by Richmond: the nature of the community within which the opinion leaders function.[34] As societies become more complex in terms of division of labor, roles, and diversity of fields, there may be more decision-making domains, and a need for different sources (such as opinion leaders) who can give advice and information. Rogers and Shoemaker in summarizing the studies of Yadav,[35] Sengupta,[36] Attah,[37] and Sen,[38] suggest that there is "greater monomorphism in opinion leadership in more modern villages."[39] Studies of traditional communities mostly supported this notion. Dodd, who studied villages in Ghana, found that approximately 76 percent of the villagers surveyed showed a preference for the same person for advice on such diverse topics as farming, settling disputes, and religious questions.[40] This result is consistent with an earlier study by Ho, who suggested that in traditional societies people tend to perceive competence and expertise on various topics as maintained by one person.[41]

As Richmond noted, when reviewing the conflicting evidence on generalized opinion leadership: "The discrepant results across the previous studies might not have been a function of modern versus traditional societal norms. The determining factor could be whether the social system under study is relatively open or closed."[42] Her study tested the hypothesis that opinion leaders serve as polymorphic leaders when operating in a relatively closed system, within a modern society. Four hundred and four college students in an American university were given a questionnaire that included: (a) *the Polymorphic Opinion Leadership Test* (POLT)—a test developed by Witteman and Andersen, with reliability estimates above .86;[43] (b) *the Monomorphic Opinion Leadership Test* (MOLT)—measures opinion leadership in the specific area of school work (classes to take, instructors, homework, exams, etc.), which yielded test-retest reliability measure of .86 in a previous study;[44] (c) *communication apprehension*—the subjects' perceptions of their communication apprehension level as measured by the Personal Report of Communication Apprehension (PRCA), with reliability estimates above .90;[45] and (d) *innovativeness*, measured by the Individual Innovativeness Scale (IS), with reliability estimates above .86).[46]

In order to test the relationship between monomorphic and polymorphic opinion leadership and these two with communication apprehension and innovativeness, a correlation matrix was used. The reliability of each of the four measures was tested by split-halves correlations, presented with the cross-measure correlations in table 4.5.

Table 4.5

Correlations and Reliability Coefficients for Opinion Leadership Measures

	PRCA	MONO	POLI	INOV
PRCA	.93	− .24	− .53	− .58
MONO	− .19	.66	.70	.36
POLI	− .47	.53	.86	.62
INOV	− .52	.27	.53	.86

Note: Diagonal coefficients represent internal reliability estimates. Those below the diagonal are raw correlations, and those above the diagonal are disattenuated correlations.

From "Monomorphic and Polymorphic Opinion Leadership within a Relatively Closed Communication System," by Virginia Peck Richmond, *Human Communication Research*, 6(2), 1980, p. 115, table 1. Copyright © 1980. Reprinted by permission of Sage Publications Inc.

The reliability coefficients range from .66 to .93, all within the acceptable range. All the correlations in table 4.5 are statistically significant at the .001 level. As the results indicate, the monomorphic and polymorphic opinion leadership scores are highly correlated (r=.53, disattenuated r=.70). This result, the researcher argued, is contrary to what one would expect if the prediction was based only on the modern nature of the society studied. Previous research would point to a low relationship between the two types of opinion leadership in such a modern society. However, this student community is a closed one, preserving some elements of a traditional closely-knit network in a modern, open society. This may lead to a broader conclusion, provided by Richmond:

It would appear likely that there are many other groups existing within an overall modern society that function as relatively closed systems (e.g., company towns, one-industry communities, single-religion communities) where monomorphic and polymorphic opinion leadership should be expected to be highly correlated. On the other side of the coin, it is likely that within some traditional societies some groups function as relatively open communication systems and the reverse patterns should be expected.[47]

However, there are certainly some differences between the two types of leaders, as revealed by the correlation matrix of table 4.5. In terms of explained variance, PRCA could account for over 22 percent of the variance in polymorphic opinion leadership, but for less than 4 percent in monomorphic. For innovativeness, over 28 percent of the variance in polymorphic could be predicted, but less than 8 percent in the monomorphic. This supports the hypothesis that personality-type characteristics (such as innovativeness and communication apprehension) would be more predictive of polymorphic than monomorphic leadership opinion leadership. Moreover, it suggests that although these two types are sometimes highly related, they are not isomorphic, and they probably stem from somewhat different functional causes. Nevertheless, the issue of overlapping opinion leadership was found to be related not only to the topic areas, but also to the nature of the community, and especially its connectedness.

Finally, the amount of overlapping leadership was found to be affected by the type of leaders involved. Booth and Babchuk's classification based on the frequency of influence,[48] distinguished between the "occasional leaders" and the "active opinion leaders." Using this typology, they studied a probability sample of 800 adults in two midwestern urban areas. The 148 people identified as advice-givers were further divided according to the frequency of influence. The researchers expected the more active opinion leaders to be influential in several domains. They state, "our reasoning was that active opinion leadership would require strategies and skills not ordinarily drawn upon in day-to-day affairs."[49] Indeed, when they analyzed the spheres of influence according to the type of influentials, they found that a substantial proportion of active opinion leaders were involved as influentials in more than one domain, while occasional opinion leaders were not. Thus, the study of generalized leadership has shown that the amount of overlap is highly dependent upon other variables, such as type of product or domain, clusters of interests, time period, type of leadership or leadership style, type of network being studied, and others. All of these factors might determine the likelihood of overlapping opinion leadership and reject the earlier oversimplified concept of specialized opinion leaders.

The Characteristics of Opinion Leaders

The term "opinion leaders," which is used in most studies and also in this book, may be somewhat misleading. The problem stems from using the term leader, while the term influentials would have been more appropriate. Katz and Lazarsfeld themselves were the first to note the problems associated with the use of the leadership concept:

> What we shall call opinion leadership, if we may call it leadership at all, is leadership as its simplest: it is casually exercised, sometimes unwitting and unbeknown, within the smallest grouping of friends, family members, and neighbors. It is not leadership on the high level of Churchill, nor of a local politico; it is the almost invisible, certainly inconspicuous form of leadership at the person-to-person level of ordinary, intimate, informal, everyday contact.[1]

Before turning to characterize the leaders, let us first indicate what they are not. Opinion leadership is not really leadership in its common meaning and connotations. Opinion leader is not an authoritative, charismatic or leading figure but rather a position of an expert among his or her peers, a source of advice on a particular issue or subject. Most foregoing studies aiming at identifying the influentials did not employ any terms commonly associated with leadership: either by self-designation or sociometric techniques, the respondents or informants were asked about the people they sought for advice, or the individuals whose opinion influenced them. Therefore, leadership as such, was never measured but, rather, influenceability.

The early studies on personal influence and opinion leadership, conducted during the 1950s and 1960s, resulted in several attributes related to opinion leaders. These were reviewed in chapter 2, but let us only mention the three criteria suggested by Elihu Katz, in his review of the early opinion leadership studies: 1. *who one is*—the personification of certain values by the opinion leader's figure; 2. *what one knows:*—the competence or knowledge related to the leaders; and 3. *whom one knows*—the strategic location in the social network.[2]

This characterization combines both social and personal dimensions. It includes collective, group-related measures (e.g., network position, perceived competence or personification of certain social values) as well as individual measures (e.g., knowledge, authority, personality). The growing interest in the study of personal influence, the applicability of the opinion leadership concept to many areas (see part three), and the accumulating data on opinion leaders resulted in more sophisticated and complex profiling of those influential individuals. Part of the complexity stems from the variance across spheres of influence, domains of decision making, and attitudes. The political opinion leaders differed from the fashion leaders, thus providing different characteristics. The various chapters in part three examine the influentials within each domain and provide the exclusive features of the leaders within each area. Yet, there are many similarities that transcend the boundaries of domains, cultures, and societies. In fact, it is surprising to note the similarities between the medical influential who determines the use of a new drug or medical practice, the rural influential who guides fellow farmers, the fashion leader, the family-planning influential in primitive communities, the scientific leader who determines the adoption of scientific innovations, and the homosexual community's opinion leader. They come from unlike backgrounds, live in differing social and cultural climates, encounter different challenges and decisions, represent distinct values and norms and, yet, they all share some common key attributes.

The rich literature on opinion leadership, though covering thousands of publications on various aspects, forms, and areas of personal influence, has not yet explored these similarities, these common attributes of the opinion leaders. This chapter is an attempt to explore the synonymous features of the opinion leaders while the variance in their profiles will be revealed in the following chapters, devoted to each domain of their presence and activity.

Personal Traits and Personality Attributes

Intelligence, Knowledge, and Interest

One of the most promising personal measures related to leadership in terms of personal influence was intelligence. (For example, in a review of the personal leadership literature, Mann noted that "the best predictor of an individual's performance in a group is intelligence,"[3] a conclusion corroborated by later research.)[4] But the correlations found between intelligence and leadership were rather modest (average of .25), indicating that less than 10 percent of the variance in leadership can be accounted for using intelligence as predictor. This result inspired the suggestion that the relation between intelligence and personal leadership may not be linear, as some of the brightest individuals in the group may have no impact whatsoever on their fellows: "There may occur a nonmonotonic relation between how intelligent a person is and the impression that same person leaves on group decision making" argued Simonton who examined four nonlinear models relating intelligence to personal influence.[5] The four models were progressively developed to provide different curvilinear relations between intelligence (in terms of IQ score) and the individual's influence over other group members. The findings suggest that intelligence is not a sufficient and powerful predictor of personal influence: "On the contrary, we can surmise that other factors besides intelligence *must* participate in the determination of who becomes the leader of the group."[6] Thus this study joined the conclusions reached long before:

> One of the most interesting results emerging from studies of the relations between intelligence and leading is the suggestion that leaders may not exceed the non-leaders by too large a margin. Great discrepancies between the intelligence of one member and of others militate against his emergence into and retention of the leadership role, presumably because wide discrepancies render improbable the unified purpose of the members concerned and because the highly intelligent have interests and values remote from those of the general membership.[7]

Surprisingly, intellectual superiority does not characterize the influentials, even when controlling for other variables and testing curvilinear relationships. This, in fact, should be interpreted as suggesting *similarity* between the influential and his or her followers: such similarity facilitates common language, considerations, interests, values, and evaluations. An intelligence gap between leader and follower constitutes a barrier rather than a promoter of personal influence. Yet, one should not confuse the variables of intelligence and knowledgeability, for one of the most consistent predictors of opinion leadership was the familiarity, or knowledgeability of the leaders with the various aspects of their issue category.

Myers and Robertson focused on the knowledgeability of opinion leaders in twelve different areas.[8] They distributed questionnaires regarding twelve topics to 400 households in the Los Angeles area. For each topic, the respondents were rated by a self-designating scale of opinion leadership as well as measures of knowledge, discussion, interest, and innovativeness.[9] The correlations between the leadership scores and the various measure of knowledge and interest are presented in table 5.1.

Table 5.1

Correlations of Opinion Leadership with Knowledge/Interest

Topics	Discussion	Knowledge	Interest	Innovativeness
Home entertainment	.65	.59	.51	.58
House furnishings	.46	.52	.37	.42
House appliances	.76	.76	.52	.43
Home upkeep	.63	.52	.61	.33
Recreation/Travel	.66	.75	.63	.65
Politics	.73	.81	.73	.54
Child upbringing	.60	.55	.59	.38
Women's clothing	.65	.85	.61	.75
Medical care	.70	.54	.41	.29
Personal Care	.82	.87	.69	.56
Cooking and food	.74	.70	.78	.75
Automobiles	.66	.61	.72	.70
Average R	**.67**	**.67**	**.60**	**.53**

Note: all the correlations are significant, $p < .01$.

From "Dimensions of Opinion Leadership," by James H. Myers and Thomas S. Robertson, *Journal of Marketing Research*, 9, 1972, p. 43, table 1. Reprinted by permission of the American Marketing Association.

The correlations in table 5.1 are moderate to high, ranging from a low of .37 (interest in household furnishing) to a high of .87 (knowledge about cosmetics and personal care). Averaging the correlations indicates that all three measures—discussion about the topic, knowledge of it, and interest in it—are strongly correlated with opinion leadership. Moreover, the variance across topics or areas is not very large and all the coefficients are statistically significant. Thus, knowledge of an item, issue, or area is an excellent predictor of leadership in politics, medical care, automobiles and recreation, clothing, or cooking. Regardless of the subject area, an opinion leader must be interested, involved, informed, and updated about his or her area of expertise. The data from this study as well as from numerous studies from a wide range of leadership domains reveal the same pattern of correlations: it was found among farmers and rural leaders,[10] among fund-raisers,[11] among consumer product leaders,[12] among clothing fashion leaders,[13] financial opinion leaders,[14] influentials in family planning,[15] young rock music influentials,[16] and political issues leaders,[17] to name only a few.

Another indication of the leaders' interest and knowledgeability is their "cosmopoliteness."[18] In many studies the opinion leaders were found to be much more cosmopolitan than the followers. The rural opinion leaders, for example, travel more often to urban centers, are more exposed to a variety of media and personal sources, and are more dependent upon external sources (see chapter 12). The various dimensions of interest, knowledge and discussion are interrelated: they are facets of the single dimension of personal involvement. Several scholars within the marketing domain suggested the term "enduring involvement" or "personal involvement" as representing this important personal trait of the influential.[19] These studies provided evidence that enduring involvement plays a critical role in opinion leadership,[20] and was found to be highly correlated with the leaders' communicative activity:

> The implicit assumption in examining the personal influence of opinion leaders is that they are motivated to talk about the product because of their involvement with it...Product involvement remains the predominant explanation for opinion leaders' conversations about products.[21]

The research on opinion leaders' involvement offered two models, relating the two variables: moderating and mediating models.[22] The moderating relationship model suggests that enduring involvement moderates the relationship between opinion leadership and its characteristics (as communication activity, influence, information-seeking and giving), while the mediating model implies that opinion leadership mediates between enduring involvement and the characteristics of the leaders. Not many studies attempted to distinguish between these two alternatives but the few that did supported the mediating configuration: according to this model enduring involvement drives opinion leadership, which in turn accounts for behaviors such as exerting influence, gaining knowledge and sharing information and experience."[23] It is clear from the literature that across societies, cultures, times, and issues, opinion leaders combine the attributes of high interest, familiarity and knowledgeability. As these are strongly interrelated, reflecting the involvement in the issue (or product), they are often collapsed into a single, powerful predictor of personal involvement.

Risk Preference and Innovativeness

A consistent pattern emerged in many opinion leadership studies involved the close relationship between early adoption of innovation and opinion leadership. This led several researchers to investigate the variables of innovativeness, risk-taking, and individuation. As these studies have revealed, all of these are important elements of the opinion leaders' profiles. Yet, some reservations should be made. Many of the studies confused the terms "innovators" and "opinion leaders" thus often relating to opinion leaders the characteristics that actually described innovators or early adopters. Though opinion leaders are frequently found among the early adopters of an innovation or new fashion/product/idea, the overlap is far from being complete,[24] thus their interchangeability is to be avoided. Taylor, for example, listed all the attributes related to innovators as revealed in previous studies (venturesomeness, inner-directedness, lower dogmatism, innovativeness, and others), though his characterization was based upon those individuals who reveal innovative behavior and not personal influence or opinion leadership.[25] Similar confusion is evident in many other studies and reviews.

An early attempt to correlate opinion leadership with innovativeness was reported by Robertson and Myers.[26] Using peer reports of a person's reputed influence, they measured opinion leadership and then administrated the California Psychological Inventory (480 items), which measures 18 personality traits, ranging from dominance to flexibility. Innovative behavior was measured separately, by studying the purchases of new products in three categories. When regression analysis was applied to the independent variables of innovativeness and opinion leaders, only weak correlations emerged for each of the personality traits and their combinations: "None of the personality variables would predict opinion leadership."[27] Moreover, innovative behavior and opinion leadership were not strongly correlated, further supporting the need to avoid their interchange.

Nevertheless, more recent studies have reported significant relationships, questioning the Robertson and Myers' findings (e.g., their method of identifying the leaders or the focusing on three specific products). When specific personality traits were correlated with more sophisticated measures of leadership, significant results did emerge. Thus opinion leaders were found to be less dogmatic,[28] more innovative,[29] and more venturesome.[30] Look at the last column of table 5.1. Across the twelve topic categories, opinion leadership was positively and strongly correlated with innovativeness (average correlation is .53). A recent attempt, reported by Chan and Misra, is focusing on several measures, including dogmatism, risk preference, public individuation, personal involvement, and others.[31] Subjects were American undergraduate students, rated by both an opinion leadership scale and a battery of measures of other personal characteristics. The findings are detailed in chapter 7, however the main conclusion was that opinion leaders differed from non-leaders in personal involvement, familiarity, public individuation, and risk preference, but not in dogmatism. The two last measures require some explanation: public individuation is the degree to which the individual feels differentiated from other people. The tendency of opinion leaders to exhibit a greater degree of public individuation explains their innovativeness and is closely related to another trait: risk preference. The influentials are willing to take more risks and are able to handle the threat of public individuation.

As Rogers concluded, "There is a strong empirical support for the generalization that opinion leaders are more innovative than their followers," and furthermore that "The research findings do not indicate, however, that opinion leaders are necessarily innovators."[32] In fact, several studies in various domains, revealed this distinction. One of these, was the Schrank and Gilmore study of fashion.[33] The data, analysis, and findings will be discussed in chapter 8. Our concern at this point is the revealed distinction between leadership and innovativeness: first, by the different correlates of the two measures to other variables; and second, by their intercorrelation (.411, significant but not a full match between the two measures). Though this may be explained by the nature of fashion ("The fact that opinion leadership and innovativeness in fashion were frequently found among the same respondents in the present study might be explained by the speed with which clothing innovations are diffused compared to most other innovations"[34]), this pattern of intercorrelation was revealed in non-fashion items as well. This indicates that some opinion leaders are also the innovators while others are only mediating between innovators and adopters.

Thus, when the opinion leaders are also the innovators they tend to be more venturesome, less dogmatic, and more innovative, while the non-innovative leader, playing the role of the mediator, lacks these tendencies. This distinction explains the lingering controversy and inconsistent findings regarding these traits and opinion leadership. The inconsistencies stemmed from the fact that different types of leaders were studied (i.e., the innovator-leader and the mediator-leader) and the existence of large variance across domains or spheres of influence.

Conformity and Individuation

The frequent combination of individuation and conformity highlights another paradox noted by Rogers: "How can opinion leaders be most conforming to system norms and at the same time lead in the adoption of new ideas?"[35] For example, in almost all studies in the area of agricultural innovations, rural opinion leadership was found to be more innovative and more inclined to adopt new farming methods. Yet, on the other hand, the same opinion leaders were also found to be most conforming to village norms.[36] A similar pattern was revealed in other domains, such as science, fashion, marketing, and family planning. How can conformity and innovativeness be blended in the same person?

Several explanations emerged. First, opinion leaders are not always more innovative; that is, they may reject innovations or even exercise their influence to slow down the adoption of an innovation.[37] Thus, many opinion leaders do not experience the contradiction. Secondly, when the social norms favor social changes (i.e., modernization), opinion leaders are more innovative and, therefore, function in close conformity to the community's social norms. In traditional communities, opinion leaders are not especially innovative. In fact, Rogers found that the innovators are viewed in such social setting with suspicion and disrespect by other villagers. In the Columbian villages "opinion leaders in the modern villages were more innovative than their followers, but in the traditional villages the opinion leaders were only slightly more innovative than their followers."[38]

Furthermore, the nature of the leaders' conformity is quite different from that of their followers. Gur Arie, Durand, and Bearden examined the differences between opinion leaders and non-leaders in attitudinal and normative dimensions.[39] They suggested that the two groups differ in the factors that determine their behavioral intentions toward a product, a service, or an issue. The normative control is the case of intentions or beliefs being affected by social norms regarding the expectations of salient referents, while the attitudinal control involves the beliefs about the consequences of the use of a product or service. The researchers hypothesized that opinion leaders will be under strong attitudinal influence because others turn to them for advice and information, while the non-leaders will be affected by the normative consideration, because they rely upon others. With the use of multiple regression analysis, significant differences were found between the leaders and the non-leaders, in accordance with this hypothesis. Opinion leaders were more affected by attitudinal control while the normative control was more significantly affecting the non-leaders. This may suggest that though both leaders and non-leaders may be conforming to the same values and norms, their motivations for such conformity are very different.

The opinion leaders represent social values (or as Katz suggested, "personify" social values), conform to the existing system of social norms and values, and yet are able to be different. This trait, termed as "public individuation," is the state in which people feel confident enough to be different, to individuate themselves. The fact that opinion leaders tend to score higher on the scales measuring this trait,[40] should not be misunderstood as their being deviant or nonconformists. It is simply the ability to follow their own judgment, a trait easily understood when related to other characteristics of opinion leaders: familiarity with the issue, self-confidence, personal involvement, and knowledgeability. Thus the influential individuals combine the personification of social values and the conformity to the widely accepted social norms with an independent and individualistic approach based on their knowledge, status, and self-confidence.

Social Attributes

Gregariousness and Social Activity

A very consistent attribute of opinion leaders, from the early studies and across numerous areas of leadership and personal influence was their social activity and gregariousness. Opinion leaders in every domain are socially very active; they come into contact with many people both through their activities in various voluntary organizations and through their jobs; they speak at meetings, participate in discussions, and take part in many social events. They are well integrated into many social networks and have many friends and acquaintances. One exception to this trend in opinion leadership studies, however, was reported by Carter and Clark, who studied public affair opinion leaders.[41] They found no significant differences between the "high" and "low" leaders in terms of interaction with relatives, friends, neighbors, or co-workers, and in voluntary association membership. But their sample was rather unique (educational television viewers), their measurement of opinion leadership rather simple (the use of Katz and Lazarsfeld's two questions on influencing others), and their classification of the respondents rather strange (with 40 percent of the sample classified as "high" opinion leaders by answering positively to the two questions). All these reasons may explain why this study differed from numerous subsequent studies that found significant differences.

Let us briefly review some representative examples. Troldahl and Van Dam, in their pioneering study of public affairs opinion leadership, compared "opinion givers" to "opinion askers" and "inactive" members in an urban sample.[42] They found that opinion givers reported higher gregariousness on each of the items used: interaction with relatives, interaction with friends, membership in social clubs or organizations, activity in social organizations, and holding offices in social organizations.[43] In a study of opinion leaders in a South African township, Heath and Bekker compared opinion leaders to others in three areas: public affairs, educational matters, and family planning.[44] They found that in all three areas, the opinion leaders were more involved in personal communication about the issues related to their area. Rieken and Yavas, who studied donors and fund raising, found that the opinion leaders in this domain were clearly characterized by various sociographic measures: they were found to attend more concerts, plays, and movies, to be members in many types of social organizations including church, social services, special interest groups, professional associations and political organizations.[45] A study of the profiles of opinion leaders in public affairs also revealed significant differences between leaders and non-leaders on 8 out of 10 measures of participation and membership in social organizations and groups.[46] Finally, in a study of opinion leaders in high schools, McCleneghan found that the nineteen opinion leaders identified by the students and teachers tend to be active in campus activities, to be elected for campus leadership roles, to take part in sports and service activities in the campus, and know more students on campus.[47]

In the medical domain, several studies indicated a similar pattern. For example, Booth and Babchuk found that a dominant characteristic of the active opinion leaders in this area was social gregariousness.[48] These leaders were found to have more social ties, more friends, and more social contacts than the occasional leaders and the non-leaders. They were also more involved in formal voluntary associations and rated higher on every measure of social gregariousness. Active leaders were likely to communicate with and influence a wider range of followers including acquaintances, co-workers, relatives, and friends. The same applies to fashion opinion leaders: the leaders were found to differ from non-leaders in all measures of sociability: they scored significantly higher on the scales of organizational membership, organizational participation, organizational affiliations, participation in informal social activities, physical mobility, sporting activities, and others.[49]

Network Centrality and Accessibility

Modern studies of opinion leadership added another social dimension: the concept of social networks. While the early studies highlighted social activity and gregariousness in terms of small peer groups, the introduction of the social networks concept and methodology was soon related to personal influence and leadership.[50] In fact, two broad approaches to network research can be distinguished. The first was inspired by sociometric studies and works toward mapping the entire social system and analyzing it by means of various structural measures. A second approach focused less upon social structure and more upon personal networks. This approach followed the Columbia tradition by tracing an individual's sources of information and influence. The focus upon personal positions in the networks and their roles led to the study of more influential position in terms of network attributes. The feasibility of network analysis to study opinion leadership was suggested by Scheingold[51] and followed by several empirical studies.[52]

The various studies soon revealed the centrality of opinion leaders in their social networks. Weimann, who studied the communication networks in an Israeli Kibbutz, found that opinion leaders are the "sociometric stars" in a highly dense network.[53] Measurement of the communicative activity was rated by both frequency of communication and measures of efficiency (accuracy, speed, and credibility of the information) across six information items (gossip, general news, and consumer information—two items from each category). As to the flow of influence, two decision-making items were used to study the matrix of who-influenced-whom. In both flow of information and influence, the "centrals," or the opinion leaders, were more active: they were the most frequent disseminators of information items (except for gossip), the most active influentials, and their activity rated higher on each of the efficiency scales. That is, messages originating from them were regarded more accurate and credible and were diffused faster.[54] Though this study highlighted the role of "marginals" as the individuals who bridge different groups or cliques by their frequent intergroup communication, the intra-group flow was carried out mainly by the opinion leaders, enjoying their centrality within their cliques or social groups.

Similar findings were also revealed in studies of scientific opinion leaders. Chapter 11 details the various studies relating the network positions to the status of scientific influentials. The accumulating findings from numerous studies in various scientific areas indicated clearly the presence of an invisible college or network of scholars linked to central, influential scientists in each area. Crane, in her study of the "invisible colleges," the social networks of scientists, revealed the role of the centrally located scientists.[55] For example, innovations that were adopted by these central figures were more widely accepted by other members of the field than the innovations they did not adopt. A similar pattern was reported by Zaltman and Blau who studied 977 high-energy physicists from 36 countries.[56] They located a small group of 32 physicists who were frequently mentioned by other scholars. All of the members of this clique were linked by direct or indirect ties. Eighty-five percent of them were also mentioned by the respondents as being responsible for the most important research in this area. The authors labeled this group "a highly elite invisible college." Crawford's study of the sleep-and-dream-research scientists also exposed the important role of key individuals.[57] He found that the 36 most frequently mentioned scientists were also highly interconnected and surrounded by others who looked to them for information and guidance. This led Crawford to conclude that "information generated by scientists is communicated through central persons in one research center to central persons in another center, thus cutting across major groups in the large networks of scientists. Through the central scientists, then, information may be transferred to all other scientists in the network."[58]

The centrality of opinion leaders in their social networks should not be surprising: it provides them with the crucial social accessibility. The access factor is an essential attribute of personal influence and opinion leadership: it provides the leaders with the needed channels for disseminating their influence and for gathering information. As Rogers concluded: "In order for opinion leaders to spread messages about an innovation, they must have interpersonal networks with their followers. Opinion leaders must be accessible."[59] In one of the classic studies of opinion leaders and diffusion of innovation, Coleman, Katz, and Menzel found that social accessibility is the best predictor of opinion leadership among physicians and provides the best channels for the swift diffusion of a new drug.[60] They found that adopting the new drug was associated with several measures of social accessibility and inter-connectedness, such as more regular attendance at staff meetings, being named as a friend by other doctors, social contacts with colleagues, and others. A similar relationship was found in many other studies on the diffusion of new items, innovations, and fashions.[61] In the area of family planning, for example, Saunders, Davis, and Monsees found that "information transaction variables" were the strongest predictors of opinion leadership.[62] Using a multivariate analysis relating numerous variables and characteristics to opinion leadership in family planning, they found social accessibility, in terms of number of friends, information contacts, and exchanges, as the most powerful characteristic in the model.

The opinion leaders rely on their social contact to collect information, update their knowledge, and be informed on new trends, brands, fashions, and innovations. They import knowledge not only from the mass media (as the early two-step model suggested), but more frequently from personal sources. At the same time these personal ties and contacts serve as the channels that diffuse their information and influence. Thus, it is not surprising to find the opinion leaders more strategically located in their social networks, involved in more and larger networks. Schenk and Pfenning related measure of network characteristics to political leadership in German samples and found strong correlation between leadership and the networks size and multiplexity.[63] Multiplexity refers to the multidimensionality of the relationships in the network, thus indicating that opinion leaders are involved in networks that combine various dimensions of social ties. The social accessibility of the influentials is facilitated and activated by their network characteristics: pivotal positions, involvement in multiplex and large networks, and links to interlocking and radial networks.

Social Recognition

Opinion leadership requires social recognition: it is not enough to be well informed, one has to be recognized as such. The opinion leaders in every domain and issue were found to enjoy social recognition, comprising credibility, trustworthiness, and confidence. The various studies on opinion leadership often identified the influentials by studying a sample's answers to the question on the identity of their personal sources. All of these studies reported no difficulty in assessing the leaders or identifying them (see chapter 3). Though not recognized as leaders or influentials but as "reliable sources of advice and guidance,"[64] the opinion leaders are easily recognized by their followers.

The status of opinion leadership is based on this recognition and is determined by the leader's reputation as an expert in the area, who is better informed, and more updated than others.

The empirical focus was almost exclusively directed to the leader half of the influence dyad. Nevertheless, several studies did try to look at the recipients or followers. Wright and Cantor, for example, compared those who seek the advice of opinion leaders (opinion-seekers) with those who avoid seeking their advice (opinion-avoiders).[65] They also noted that opinion leaders are often also opinion seekers, motivated by their interest and involvement in the issue to seek information from others. But more important for the present discussion are the opinion-avoiders. Their existence and characteristics may indicate the conditions for the leader-follower dyad. Wright and Cantril found that the opinion-avoiders "not only avoid seeking the views of their peers, but they make relatively little use of other sources of information about the subject."[66] The opinion-seekers are interested in the subject, active in gathering information about it, and, consequently, consult with a friend or acquaintance whom they see as knowledgeable and informed.

The social recognition of an opinion leader is an issue-related, specific, and personal perspective. As discussed in the previous chapter, there is little overlapping of leadership across domains and issues. An opinion leader is usually regarded as an expert in one specific subject or in issues that are closely related. Moreover, the status of opinion leadership does not spillover to other forms of influence and social status. The reliance on the influential is restricted to information and guidance within the specific domain and not beyond it. Moreover, the range of the "followers group," though varying across the domains, is usually narrowed to a social circle of friends, acquaintances, relatives, and co-workers. Even with a large circle of followers, the opinion leaders are far from being political leaders, community or cultural stars, or public opinion makers. In fact, the close, personal contact between the opinion leader and the follower, is his or her source of credibility and confidence. Although prestige and social status in the community were not significantly related to opinion leadership, in some diffusion areas they joined the "expert's reputation" characteristics as necessary attributes.[67] The most commonly found attribute of prestige was the credibility, a precondition to any act of influence and persuasion, as revealed by Hovland and his colleagues.[68]

Socio-demographic Attributes

The earliest attempts to characterize opinion leaders were based on socio-demographic variables. Are opinion leaders more frequent in certain social classes, certain age groups, specific occupations or education levels, certain income groups, or among males or females? The early characterizations of the Columbia scholars suggested a different socio-demographic profile for different issues or domains. They found that opinion leaders are present at every social level, and tend to influence people from the same social level. Opinion leaders were found in both of the sexes and in all professions, social classes, and age groups. Moreover, they differed sharply from one subject area to another, thus making a standard profile almost impossible.

Following the Columbia studies, numerous studies in various spheres of influence and opinion attempted to define opinion leaders in socio-demographic terms. The procedure was repeated: opinion leaders and non-leaders were compared in their frequencies in various social groups, thus revealing any concentration of opinion leaders, which deviates from the rate expected by the general distribution of the population. The results are very confusing, to say the least. While some studies suggest that there are clear and unique profiles of the influentials, other argue that no relationship exists between background variables and opinion leadership. To add to the complexity, some studies highlight only certain attributes while others suggest others. This confusion stems from the combination of several factors:

1. The different definitions of opinion leadership.
2. The different methods and measures used to identify the leaders.
3. The different categorizations and comparisons (e.g., leaders to non-leaders, advice-givers to advice-seekers or inactives).
4. The different subject areas and domains.
5. The different socio-demographic measures used and their varying categorizations.
6. The different social, cultural, and organizational settings of the populations studied.

Some of the confusion will be removed in the following chapters, when studies in each domain will be discussed separately. This will reduce the variance also in definitions, methods, and categorizations, thus resulting in more consistent profiles. On the general level, however, this profiling of the opinion leaders is almost impossible. However, this may be a finding by itself, indicating that opinion leaders' profiles change considerably across areas and domains. Let us illustrate some of the relationships between socio-demographic variables and opinion leadership. These revealed relationships range from no correlation at all to very well-defined and discriminatory profiles.

In their study of the dimensions of opinion leadership, Myers and Robertson studied opinion leaders in twelve different domains (see listing in table 5.1), and concluded:

> In general, correlations of demographic variables (age, income, wive's education, husband's education, time at present address, ages of children, and number living at home) with opinion leadership in each topic area were low. Only 5 of 84 correlations exceeded the .01 level....The conclusion that opinion leaders cannot be identified by demographic factors is in contrast to the earlier findings.[69]

Indeed, this conclusion was in sharp contrast with many other studies. For example, Troldahl and Van Dam found significant differences in social status and formal education between the leaders and the non-leaders[70] while Corey reported a different set of discriminatory variables.[71] His analysis of automotive opinion leaders revealed "large and statistically significant differences between leaders and non-leaders on two characteristics related to social status, income, and occupation,"[72] while no significant differences were found in age and education. The contradictions between these studies may be the result of studying different types of opinion leaders: Myers and Robertson studied opinion leaders in various areas, Troldahl and Van Dam focused on opinion leaders in news and public affairs, and Corey studied automotive opinion leaders.

Moreover, the discrepancies may stem from *changes over time*. Let us take, for example, the changes in the role of women: Richmond and McCroskey argue that the slogan "You've come a long way, baby" is relevant also to the growing importance of *female* opinion leaders.[73] They sampled three subject populations to investigate possible variance in choice of general opinion leaders in terms of the sex of the subject and the sex of the potential opinion leader. The choice of "general leader" was operationalized as "the person you most often turn to for advice, other than a member of your family," while the specific opinion leaders were defined by different topics: choice of movies, fashion and politics,[74] following the original items from Katz and Lazarsfeld's study. A student sample was asked about the opinion leaders for course information.[75]

In the married adult sample, both the males and the females overwhelmingly chose general leaders of the same sex. In the single undergraduate sample, only the females chose same-sex leaders. But the complexity of the factors affecting the choice is highlighted in the analysis of specialized leaders. It is clear that the topic interacts with gender to affect the choice of an opinion leader. The pattern revealed is an interactive one: married adults preferred a leader from the opposite sex in the movie selection area, preferred female leaders in the case of fashion, and preferred male leaders in the case of politics.

Finally, the student sample revealed a tendency of same-sex preferences: the high school and college females preferred female leaders while the males preferred male leaders, in all three groups (college class information, high school information, and high school elective courses). The interpretation of the results is suggesting that "baby" has come a way:

> Although previous research suggests that females judge males to be more competent than other females across a wide variety of topics, this bias was reflected in the present study only on the topic of politics...As a whole, examination of the results provides an encouraging picture for the acceptance of women's views in contemporary American society. The problem of 'male topics' and 'female topics' may have declined over the past 30 years.[76]

This study illustrates the multidimensional nature of opinion leaders' characteristics. The findings indicate how the identity of the leaders is affected by the sex of the leader and the follower, by topic, by the interaction between these factors, and by the changes over time in the effects of these factors and interactions. It appears that today's influentials and those of the early 1950s and 1960s do not share the same characteristics. Not only did the status of women change but so did the status of many other groups and social categories. For example, Goldsmith, Stith, and White examined race and sex differences in fashion opinion leadership.[77] Previous research on black consumers had suggested that black consumers grew more fashion conscious and innovative, thus becoming more likely to be fashion opinion leaders than whites. However, Goldsmith, Stith, and White argued that such generalizations did not take into account sex, age, and socio-economic status. When these were controlled by the research design, a much more complex relationships emerged: "Differences among blacks based on income, education, occupation, sex, life style, and personality seem to be greater and of more use to marketers than global generalizations about black/white differences."[78] The analysis performed by Goldsmith and his colleagues (for a detailed review, see chapter 8) revealed that middle-class blacks and whites are similar in their fashion attitudes and interests but the real difference in terms of opinion leaders was gender:

among the males more black leaders were found while among the females the frequencies of black and white leaders was almost the same. Thus, this study too contributes to our notion that changes over time in social values, social statuses, or social categories, resulted in changing the socio-demographic profiles of opinion leaders.

Finally, the cross-cultural differences are enormous. If one compares the characteristics of opinion leaders in the same domain, at the same time, using similar measures but in different societies, the profiles will be totally different. Take for example the domain of public affairs and politics: a simple comparison of the characteristics of opinion leaders in South African community,[79] a Norwegian national sample,[80] and in several American studies,[81] reveals the variance in the discriminatory characteristics and their weight. A similar cross-cultural variance is revealed in the health care domain and the family planning domain (see chapters 10 and 13), where a wide range of societies and cultures were studied.

The almost single possible generalization on the socio-demographic level is the tendency towards similarity of the influential-influencee dyad. The trickle-down model, suggesting a vertical flow from upper classes to lower classes, from more educated to less educated, or from higher income groups to lower income groups, was rejected in almost all domains. The more frequent flow was from leader to follower from the same social group. This tendency resulted in a homogeneity of the leader-followers groups in terms of most socio-demographic measures. People turn to seek advice from their peers, from individuals of the same background, interests, and values. The flow of information and influence is likely to be rather horizontal, thus requiring a spread of leaders across classes and social groups. This is basically a confirmation of the early studies, which suggested that opinion leaders are found at every social level and tend to have similar characteristics to those they influence.

To conclude, the search for common characteristics of opinion leaders continues. Despite the variance in the attributes of opinion leaders in various areas and domains, a careful comparison of the thousands (!) of studies in these areas reveals some universal patterns or consistent profiles. On the personal level several personality traits were found to characterize opinion leaders across societies, cultures, times, and domains. These were the attributes of innovativeness (though not all opinion leaders are innovators), and individuation combined with social conformity. Opinion leaders also reveal higher knowledgeability, familiarity, and interest in their area of expertise.

These were often grouped into one dimension of personal involvement or enduring involvement.

The social characteristics of opinion leaders in all domains were high levels of gregariousness and social activity, centrality in social networks, and social accessibility. The opinion leaders in every domain and issue were found to enjoy social recognition, comprising credibility, trustworthiness, and confidence. In terms of socio-demographic profiles, opinion leaders' characteristics were found to differ according to social setting, subject area or domain, and even over time when modern leaders differ from the leaders in the same domain. These changes reflect the dynamic nature of opinion leadership as affected by the dominant social values, social structure, and cultural climate. Nevertheless, as this chapter suggests, there appear to be several attributes of influenceability that cross both time and social boundaries, and remain powerful predictor of opinion leadership. These are:

Personal Attributes
- innovativeness
- individuation combined with social conformity
- knowledgeability, familiarity, and interest in subject/domain
- cosmopoliteness
- personal involvement or enduring involvement

Social Attributes
- gregariousness
- social activity
- centrality in social networks
- social accessibility
- social recognition
- credibility

Socio-demographic attributes
- profiles change according to domains
- within domains profiles change across cultures and societies
- within domain and society, profiles change over time
- tendency to similarity of influential/influencee profiles

Finally, an additional dimension should be mentioned—the opinion leaders' sources of information and influence. These sources, or the actors and factors that influence the influentials, will be the subject of the next chapter.

6

Who Leads the Leaders?

The early studies conducted by Paul Lazarsfeld and his colleagues revealed that political choices, consumer decisions, and diffusion of fashions were dominated more by active personal influence and face-to-face communications than by the mass media. When studying the flow of interpersonal information and influence, the more active and influential individuals were identified. These were termed "opinion leaders," the people whose advice, opinions, and guidance are sought by others. Consequently, numerous studies focused upon these influentials and their impact within various domains and areas. But who leads the leaders? Who influences the influentials? What are their sources of information and influence?

To the Columbia researchers, the answer seemed clear: a two-step flow model from the mass media to the opinion leaders, and from them (after a selection and processing) to their followers. However, the two-step flow model was based on a rather weak empirical basis: Katz and Lazarsfeld found that women who were opinion leaders in one of the four areas they studied (marketing, fashion, public affairs, and movies) read more magazines or books than did the non-leaders. In addition, they were more likely to read a type of magazine relevant to their area of leadership (for example, a fashion or movie magazine for these areas, or a national news weekly for public affairs) than were the non-leaders. However, in comparison with non-leaders, only the fashion leaders were more likely to mention the media as a source of influence. Public affairs leaders were even less likely to mention the media as the source of a recent change of opinion and more likely to mention personal influence.

This chapter examines the various sources utilized by opinion leaders. It explores the differences between leaders and non-leaders in their exposure and reliance on mass media, forms of consumption and processing media contents, and personal sources including social ties and networks and information exchanges. It is our purpose to suggest that only a multi-source and multi-step flow model can accurately describe the influentials' sources and their use of these sources. But first let us examine the basic distinction, the exposure to mass media.

Opinion Leaders and Media Exposure

The differences in media exposure in the Katz and Lazarsfeld's study were questioned by many critics of their model. Yet, other studies have turned up similar and even more convincing evidence that the influentials are more exposed to the mass media and especially to relevant media contents. We will review some of this evidence according to various domains or subject areas, ranging from traditional rural communities (family planning and agricultural innovations) to fashion, public affairs, and political issues in modern urban settings.

Opinion Leaders in Rural Communities

Van Den Ban studied three agricultural communities in the Netherlands and tried to relate the leaders/non-leaders distinction to various sources.[1] When comparing the sources of opinion leaders and followers in these villages, Van Den Ban found that indeed opinion leaders were more exposed to certain media than their followers (mainly to farming papers), but also that they relied on personal sources more than the followers.[2] A similar finding was recorded among villagers in Turkey: Stycos suggested using opinion leaders in the service of a government program on family planning.[3] In the Turkish villages studied, the political opinion leaders were more likely to own and use a radio than the religious leaders, and were more receptive than the latter to the concept of family planning. However, a study of opinion leaders in rural Egypt found a distinct pattern.[4] This study found that mass media messages (daily papers and radio) reached the majority of the public directly and effectively. Opinion leaders, therefore, serve as mediators only to a smaller group of the public, mostly those who have less access to the mass media. Only for these followers can the leaders make use of their exposure to the media and become significant agents of information and influence.

A study conducted in a black South African township (Atteridgeville) attempted to identify the attributes of the local opinion leaders in the areas of family planning, public affairs, and education.[5] Media exposure was studied by the amount of newspaper reading, radio listening, television viewing, and magazine reading. The respondents were classified into four groups by way of a self-designating interview.

They were (a) opinion leaders, (b) opinion seekers, (c) opinion avoiders, and (d) inactives. Opinion seekers were those who reported someone else's advice in one or more of the three topics. Opinion avoiders were those who did not seek any advice. Inactives were those individuals who had not talked with anyone about the topic recently, making no attempt to influence or to ask for advice. Table 6.1 presents the comparisons of these groups by measures of media exposure.

Table 6.1

Differences in Measures of Media Exposure (South Africa)

	Averages of daily time spent reading newspapers		
Group	Domain: Public Affairs	Domain: Education	Domain Family Planning
Leaders	1.09	1.03	1.11
Avoiders	0.52	0.38	0.51
Seekers	0.72	0.81	0.64
Inactives	1.06	0.91	1.16
F value and significance	$F = 26.83$ $p < .0001$	$F = 32.5$ $p < .0001$	$F = 33.11$ $p < .0001$

	Averages of weekly time spent watching TV1 (Channel 1)		
Group	Domain: Public Affairs	Domain: Education	Domain: Family Planning
Leaders	7.26	6.70	7.78
Avoiders	3.26	2.51	3.44
Seekers	5.51	5.78	4.34
Inactives	7.83	7.25	7.84
F value and significance	$F = 11.32$ $p < .0001$	$F = 10.56$ $p < .0001$	$F = 10.52$ $p < .0001$

	Averages of weekly time spent watching TV2/3 (Channels 2 and 3)		
Group	Domain: Public Affairs	Domain: Education	Domain: Family Planning
Leaders	10.55	8.11	9.01
Avoiders	4.95	4.62	5.19
Seekers	5.78	5.94	6.28
Inactives	8.31	8.50	7.91
F value and significance	$F = 7.33$ $p < .0001$	$F = 5.12$ $p < .001$	$F = 4.24$ $p < .01$

The rates and averages are taken from various graphs and tables, Heath and Bekker, pp. 45–52.

The results presented in the upper part of table 6.1 indicate that opinion leaders spend more time reading newspapers than opinion seekers and avoiders, though not more than the inactives. The pattern remains the same across the three domains. Moreover, the comparisons of watching television (center and lower parts of table 6.1) reveal that in all domains the opinion leaders are more exposed to both television channels. The report included a log-linear analysis of radio listening, comparing the total listening hours of the four groups. This analysis was concluded by the statement: "It is possible to infer from the tables that opinion leaders for public affairs, educational matters, and family planning on average spent more time listening to radio programs than non-leaders."[6]

But the researchers went one step further: they analyzed the impact of all the sources on the opinion leaders to find their primary source of information and found that reading newspapers served as the dominant source of the opinion leaders, both by their own reports as well as by an analysis of the predictive value of each source. (The variation in population in each domain serves as the dependent variable.) All of these indications correlate opinion leadership with higher exposure and use of mass media, including radio, television, and newspapers, across domains. Likewise, similar conclusions were reached by a study of family planning leadership in Peru.[7] The opinion leaders were found to be more engaged in information gathering about contraception than the others. They were significantly more active in all forms of information gathering, including the use of personal sources, the mass media, and other sources (see chapter 10).

Opinion Leaders in Politics

Almost all studies of political opinion leaders that included a comparison of media exposure, reported higher levels of exposure among the leaders. As an illustrative example, let us examine the findings of a study that focused on media consumption among the political leaders. Andersen and Garrison studied the information sources from which opinion leaders and non-leaders heard about political candidates in the 1974 race for the United States Senate.[18] A sample of 339 residents of Tallahassee, Florida, were measured by an opinion leadership scale,[19] media exposure questions, knowledge of the political candidates for the Senate, and the source of this knowing (radio, television, magazines, newspapers, and interpersonal communication).

Opinion leadership positively and significantly related to mass media sources: the higher the leadership degree, the more the media was reported as the source of information. The strongest relationship was found with television exposure, followed by newspapers and radio. The usage of magazines was not found statistically significant (mainly because 97.9 percent of the respondents reported hearing about neither of the candidates in magazines). The significant role of television exposure for opinion leaders is an important finding because many studies of political opinion leaders were conducted *before* the widespread adoption of television and its emerging role in political campaigns.

Robinson suggested and tested several models of media/interpersonal influences on voters during an election campaign.[10] He analyzed the surveys conducted by the Center for Political Studies (CPS) of the University of Michigan, focusing on communication behavior of a national sample of 1,346 American adults after the 1968 elections (Nixon vs. Humphry). Robinson compared the "opinion givers"[11] with the "opinion receivers" and the "nondiscussants" in terms of their sources of information and various forms of political behavior during the campaign. Opinion givers were clearly more exposed to mass media than the others (opinion receivers and nondiscussants). In every medium, and especially with regard to print media, the opinion givers utilized the media as the source of information to a larger extent than the other groups. A similar preference of press media usage (magazines and newspapers) was reported also by Troldahl and Van Dam.[12] They correlated public affairs leadership with exposure to various media and found the highest correlation with exposure to newspapers and magazines, while radio was not significantly correlated and television was even negatively correlated.

The variance in the influentials' reliance on different media within the same domain or subject area may again be a question of changes over time. While the studies of the 1950s and 1960s reveal the importance of the print media, the following decades witness the rise of the electronic media and especially television as a political actor. Its importance is clearly rising among the opinion leaders. For example, early in the 1970s Ostlund conducted a study on interpersonal communication on a political event:[13] the announcement of George McGovern's decision to drop Thomas Eagleton from the 1972 Democratic national ticket following the disclosure of Eagleton's past mental illness. A survey focused, among other variables, on the sources of information of opinion leaders and non-leaders. The broadcast media, radio, and television were the leading sources for both leaders and non-leaders. The opinion leaders were informed more by radio than the non-leaders (42 and 30 percent, respectively) and far less by interpersonal communication (4 and 22 percent, respectively). These findings support, to some extent, the two-step flow model: opinion leaders rely more on the media, and the non-leaders rely more on interpersonal sources (mainly the leaders, as other analyses in this report indicate).

Consumer Opinion Leaders

The tendency of opinion leaders to be more exposed to mass media and use them as sources of information was also revealed in numerous studies conducted upon consumer opinion leaders. Again, we will present only some typical findings as illustrations. A study conducted by Corey compared the leaders and non-leaders in automotive topics.[14] The comparison revealed that the leader/non-leader distinction yielded significant differences expected under the two-step model (see detailed findings in chapter 7). The opinion leaders were more interested in magazines devoted to their area of expertise (36.6 percent among the leaders and 15.3 percent among the non-leaders read automobile magazines). A similar comparison, conducted by Martilla on industrial opinion leaders,[15] compared the leaders in 106 paper-converting firms in the United States with the non-leaders among the buying decision-makers in these firms. The opinion leaders in the industrial markets were found to satisfy two of the basic notions of the two-step model: they were more active in giving advice to others and they were more exposed to every type of mass media information and mainly sample books, product literature, and advertisements in trade journals.

Schiffman and Gaccione, who studied opinion leadership within 263 nursing homes in six northeastern American states, applied a similar comparison to the leaders/non-leaders categories.[16] Opinion leaders were found to be more exposed to professional publications, to salespeople, and to professional and social ties in the nursing area than non-leaders.[17] A study of consumers who are "financial opinion leaders" revealed the impact of the informal influentials in this area.[18] Stern and Gould compared the leaders with non-leaders by numerous measures of financial attitudes and behavior, media exposure, and sources of information. In terms of media exposure, they found that opinion leaders are more likely to follow their investments daily in the newspaper, read financial books and magazines, watch TV shows about finance, read more magazines and newspapers related to finance (e.g.,

Money magazine, the *Wall Street Journal*, the *New York Times'* Financial Section), watch "Wall Street Week" on TV, and listen to radio programs about finances.[19] Chan and Misra found consumer opinion leaders to be more exposed to mass media in general, but the differences are larger in specific product-related media. Thus, the opinion leaders are more exposed to magazine and newspaper sections devoted to their area of expertise.[20] A similar pattern was reported by Armstrong and Feldman, who conducted a study on automobile opinion leaders.[21] They found these opinion leaders to be more exposed to specific magazines (devoted to cars, sports and adventure, and men's magazines) but not to general newspapers, general interest magazines, or general radio listening and television viewing.

Fashion Opinion Leaders

Fashion leaders are more exposed to mass media than their followers although their exposure is rather selective. Summers studied the women's clothing fashion opinion leaders and found their media usage to be very fashion oriented.[22] Table 6.2 presents the frequency of opinion leaders in various groupings according to media consumption.

Table 6.2

Frequencies of Fashion Opinion Leaders According to Media Exposure

	Percentage of Opinion Leaders*			
Media exposure	**Low**	**Medium**	**High**	**p<****
Radio listening	28	26	31	n.s.
Television watching	25	28	30	n.s.
Book readership	24	30	30	n.s.
News magazine readership	34	30	39	.05
Home magazine readership	25	35	36	.001
Women's magazine readership	31	25	36	.001
Women's fashion magazine readership	40	53	63	.001
Romance magazine readership	25	24	34	n.s.
Total magazine readership	21	26	37	.001

* Percentages in table should be read as follows: 28 percent of all the respondents scoring "low" on radio listening were opinion leaders.
** Significance of differences were tested by the chi-square test.

From "The Identity of Women's Clothing Fashion Opinion Leaders," by John O. Summers, *Journal of Marketing Research*, 7, 1970, p. 182, table 4. Reprinted by permission of the American Marketing Association.

Radio listening, television viewing, and book readership did not differ for fashion leaders and non-leaders. The press and especially magazine readership were strongly related to leadership in this domain. It is clear that fashion leaders are more frequent among the "heavy" consumers of specific fashion-related magazines. Women's fashion magazines represent the category in which opinion leaders were dramatically more concentrated in the highest exposed group, "supporting previous research in which opinion leaders tended to be more exposed to mass media in general and substantially more to media specializing in their area of influence."[23] It should also be noted that the leaders are more exposed to *several* sources of fashion information, including home magazines, women's magazines as well as fashion magazines. Similar findings were reported by Baumgarten in his study of fashion opinion leadership.[24] Compared with others, the opinion leaders in this study were significantly more likely to read newspapers and magazines such as the Sunday *New York Times* and *New Yorker* magazine, and fashion-oriented magazines such as *Esquire, Gentlemen's Quarterly*, and *Playboy*.

The opinion leaders are clearly heavier consumers of mass media and especially the media sources in their area of expertise. However, the choice of media and the degree of reliance upon various media depend on the subject area as well as the cultural setting. The changes across societies and cultures and across time within the same society, indicate that opinion leaders are affected by the supply of various sources and the changing nature of the media (e.g., the growing reliance on broadcast media among "modern" opinion leaders). But exposure to mass media is only one dimension of media usage. Let us now turn to a different dimension, that of processing media contents.

Opinion Leaders and Processing Media Contents

One of the main characteristics of opinion leaders, based on the available research, is their knowledge and competence in their subject area. The conventional explanation for the informational superiority of opinion leaders over followers was a combination of motivation (being involved and interested) and mass media exposure. There is, as we saw, a convincing body of supportive research data for both attributes. However, an alternative or complementary explanation is that opinion leaders *process information differently* than non-leaders. Simple exposure does not guarantee learning or retention of information. Opinion leaders may not just be more exposed to the mass media but also more efficient in processing their messages. Regrettably, only few studies set out to examine this aspect of opinion leadership. Nevertheless, those that did, provided support for this suggested trait of the influentials.

Richmond tested the following hypotheses on the information acquisition skills of opinion leaders:[25] (a) opinion leaders will acquire more information than non-leaders under the condition of free, voluntary exposure; and (b) opinion leaders will acquire more information than non-leaders under the condition of forced exposure. Using a self-designating scale of opinion leadership, Richmond classified 343 students from the University of Nebraska into one of three levels of leadership (low, moderate, and high). Information acquisition was measured by means of an experiment involving the distribution of a mimeographed handout. Thirty words were omitted from the text to form a Cloze test. The experiment was conducted twice, according to the hypotheses, under both voluntary exposure and forced exposure conditions.[26]

The results of the analysis indicate significant effects for both exposure condition ($F = 31.32$; $p < .0001$) and level of opinion leadership ($F = 7.84$; $p < .001$). Correlational analyses also reflected the relationships suggested by the hypotheses: under forced exposure, the observed correlation between opinion leadership and information acquisition was .63. When exposure was voluntary, the correlation was .37. This suggests an important attribute of opinion leadership: "it was found that under either voluntary or forced exposure conditions, individuals reporting high opinion leadership acquire more information than people reporting either moderate or low opinion leadership."[27] Indeed, the high opinion leaders retained 41 percent more information than those designated as low opinion leader under forced exposure, and 17 percent more under voluntary exposure, which indicates that opinion leaders are clearly better equipped with information-processing skills. Not only are they more exposed to mass media, but they can absorb and retain more of their messages.

The findings of a study conducted by Levy on opinion leadership and the use of television news highlighted another dimension of media exposure and opinion leadership.[28] Levy found that public affairs leaders do not differ from non-leaders in their amount of television news consumption but rather in the *uses* of their exposure. He correlated various measures of television news viewership with public affairs opinion leadership, and questions on the uses of viewing television news. These motives or uses were of two dimensions: "cognitive orientation" and "surveillance-reassurance."[29] He found very weak correlations between the amount of television news viewing and opinion leadership but a direct and strong relationship between opinion leadership and endorsement of cognitive orientation. As opinion leadership increased, the viewing of television news was explained by cognitive needs and mainly the need of information acquisition and cognitive orientation. As Levy suggested, these findings make it more important to examine possible *qualitative* differences between opinion leaders and non-leaders in terms of their forms of consumption and not mere amount of exposure. Only few studies focused on this aspect of the media-opinion leadership relations.

Recently, a new conceptualization of the influentials reveals interesting patterns of media content processing among the influentials. In chapter 15 the reader will find a detailed presentation of this project.

Opinion Leaders and Interpersonal Sources

The two-step flow model highlighted the role of the media as the leaders' main sources. However, though opinion leaders attend more to the media, they also have more contact with other personal sources, including other opinion leaders and non-leaders. Thus, while Katz and Lazarsfeld focused on the role of the mass media, they also reported personal influence as affecting the opinion leaders themselves. For example, they found that in comparison with non-leaders, public affairs opinion leaders were less likely to mention the media as a their source and more likely to mention personal sources. Similarly, studies of the adoption of innovations have shown that in science, agriculture, medicine, or fashion the influentials are integrated into social networks that serve as information-gathering channels as well as conduits for the diffusion of information and influence.[30] Moreover, as demonstrated by several studies, opinion leaders relied upon personal sources sometimes more than on the mass media. Let us examine some of the empirical evidence.

In their study of media consumption and political opinion leaders, Andersen and Garrison focused mainly on the mass media.[31] As discussed earlier, the influentials were found to rely on mass media more than their followers. However, the same study included one more source, that of interpersonal communication. The results of the cross-classification of degree of opinion leadership with information on political candidates revealed an interesting pattern: political opinion leaders were more informed by personal communication than non-leaders. Thus, the opinion leaders combined various sources, including mass media and personal contacts, in order to acquire information. A similar pattern was reported by Hamilton who examined the sources of opinion leaders and non-leaders, using various measures to identify the leaders.[32] Using a small cross-sectional survey in Chicago, Illinois, Hamilton examined two types of leadership: self-appraisal of one's influentiality (self-concept) and actual advice-giving (functional role). Then he compared their sources (television exposure, magazine readership, and talking with friends). The results revealed that for both measures of leadership, the influential individuals were more exposed to the media as well as to personal communications.[33] However, there were differences according to the leadership measure: correlations with interpersonal communications were higher for the self-concept leadership than for the functional role measure.

The South African study, reported earlier in this chapter as highlighting the higher exposure of black opinion leaders, also examined personal communications.[34] The analysis revealed that in each of the three domains (namely, educational matters, family planning and public affairs) the opinion leaders were more active in interpersonal communication than all other groups (opinion seekers, opinion avoiders, and inactives). The questions presented in this study did not distinguish between personal discussion for getting information or for giving it, but rather about interpersonal communication with respect to a problem or unclear situation in any of the three domains. This higher involvement of opinion leaders in interpersonal exchanges of information was also reported by Saunders, Davis, and Monsees in their study of family planning and opinion leadership in Lima, Peru.[35] Patients attending a family planning clinic in Lima were sampled and categorized into three following groups. The first was opinion leaders—people who reported their advice was sought and whose advice regarding birth control was adopted. Non-leaders were further categorized into "followers," women whose advice had not been sought but who manifestly acted on the advice of others, and "ineffectives," those whose advice was sought but not followed.

Opinion leadership was examined in relation to several variables: background characteristics, motivation, fertility, information transactions, mass media exposure, and social interaction. The analysis (see chapter 10) found that the strongest predictor of leadership was "information transaction": seeking and exchanging information. The leaders were not only more often seekers of information than were the others, but also more active in disseminating the information in an influential manner. To do so they relied on their higher social accessibility, numerous social ties, and their eagerness to exchange information on family planning issues. A similar conclusion was reached by Palmore and his colleagues in a study of family planning opinion leaders in rural Malaysia.[36] They found that the critical variable for opinion leadership in this community was participation in personal discussions. The opinion leaders were informed about specific family planning methods mainly by friends, relatives, and neighbors and influenced others using their personal contacts. These results led the researchers to suggest that at least in the family planning area there is more evidence to the second step in the two-step model (i.e., from leaders to followers) than for the first step (i.e., from media to leaders).

The dual role of opinion leaders as "information exchangers" was best demonstrated by an Australian study of a sample of homemakers and their product communication patterns.[37] A sample of 125 homemakers was asked to report their communication activities, using a time diary. The diary contained sections on (a) time spent reading, listening to radio, watching TV; (b) time log for each half hour of a 24-hour period; and (c) for each of the seven designated products, communication given and received. The communication patterns were classified as mass media messages (MMM) and interpersonal communication (IPC) and used to construct four types of communicators:

1. *Opinion Leaders*—receive MMM and then transmit the information to others by IPC.
2. *Opinion Exchangers*—receive and transmit by IPC, or do not receive MMM but give IPC.
3. *Opinion Followers*—Only receive with three subtypes: singular (receiving either MMM or IPC), dual: (receiving both MMM and IPC), and mixed: (using MMM for some products and IPC for others).
4. *Isolates*—receive no MMM and no IPC.

The time diaries were completed for a single weekday and the data was subjected to a factor analysis (using a principle components analysis followed by a Varimax Rotation of vectors). The factor emerging as accounting for the greatest variance was an opinion exchanger factor. In most of the products studies, communication activity and personal influence tended to be dominated by the modified opinion leaders, the exchangers. The influentials relied mainly on getting information and giving it by interpersonal sources. The classic opinion leadership was found only for one product. As for the followers, the frequent mode was that of the dual type, combining advice and information from the mass media and personal sources.

This modification of the opinion leadership concept was supported also by Robinson, who suggested additional directions of flow to the opinion leaders.[38] Following Troldahl and Van Dam's proposition of "opinion-sharing,"[39] Robinson suggested the horizontal flow, occurring between opinion leaders. A similar suggestion was advanced by Wright and Cantor.[40] Robinson proposed:

> The considerable conversational activity *within* the ranks of the opinion leaders deserves far more recognition, and perhaps primary attention, in the model; any "influence" that takes place between one opinion leader and another would hardly constitute a relay of mass media information, as the second stage of the original model implies. These conversations might also take place prior to, and consequently modify, any downward step in the flow that occurs.[41]

Moreover, opinion leaders may not only rely on horizontal flow of opinion-sharing among leaders but also on "upward" flow from their followers. Their sources of information may include non-leaders, followers, and even "marginal" individuals. Weimann's study of social networks in a kibbutz community and the flow of communication provided support to this flow from followers to leaders.[42] He found that the opinion leaders, centrally located in their social networks, often rely on marginally located individuals to "import" information from other groups. There are structural advantages of the marginals in terms of intergroup communication:

> "Centrals," by definition, have more ties but they tend to have higher rates of strong ties among them. On the average two-thirds of the ties of the "centrals" are strong, whereas "marginals" tend to have mostly weak ties (72 percent). Adding the direction of the tie into the analysis, the tendency of "marginals" to weak ties is more salient: their weak ties are mainly intergroup, while "central" weak ties are mainly directed to members of the same group.[43]

Thus, marginals serve as "communicative bridges," using their weak ties and tendency to have more intergroup ties.[44] This finding suggests a new version of the multi-step flow: the marginals serve as the importers of new information from external sources, while the dissemination of the information *within* the group is carried out by the centrals. As Weimann concluded:

This model implies that "centrals" rely on "marginals" for "imported" information, while "marginals" require the enlistment of "centrals" for spreading the information in the group. Thus, the original two-step flow model, assuming the existence of a downward vertical flow from the media to opinion leaders and from them to their followers, is to be modified as far as information flow is concerned; the model should include personal sources of information, other than the mass media, thus adding a new horizontal step.[45]

The various modifications of the original two-step model will be discussed later (see chapter 14); however, at this time attention need only to be drawn to the contributions of these modifications. They highlighted the role of the various personal sources of opinion leaders, including other leaders, followers, and marginal individuals in their networks.

Conclusion

So who leads the leaders? The answer is a rather complex one, based on the opinion leaders' multi-source exposure and patterns of information processing. The opinion leaders are guided by a combination of several factors and actors:

1. *The opinion leaders themselves.* The opinion leaders are well-informed of, updated on, and involved in their subject area. Their familiarity, interest, and self-confidence combine to make them experts in their area and, as studies indicated, they are well aware of their status. But one must make a distinction between "influence" and "information": while the influentials rely on their own judgment based on their expertise, their interest and need to be constantly updated lead them to be active seekers of information. They are less likely to be influenced by "external" actors but more likely to be seeking information from a variety of sources.
2. *The opinion leaders' heavier media exposure.* The forms of exposure and the selected-for-exposure media differ significantly across domains, times, and cultural settings; in general, however, opinion leaders are more exposed to mass media and especially to those media closely related to their field of expertise. This

tendency is mostly explained by their "enduring involvement," interest, and need to keep updated.

3. *The opinion leaders' information processing skills.* The opinion leaders were found in several studies to differ from others in their information processing: they acquire more information from the media, process and retain more details, and are able to use this information in their functioning as influentials.

4. *The opinion leaders' personal sources.* Well integrated into social networks, socially active and involved in many social ties, the opinion leaders are able to use these social channels not only to diffuse their influence and advice but also to gather information. Interpersonal sources of information involve other opinion leaders, followers, and others.

It appears that the opinion leaders are guided by their own judgments, based on deep comprehension and enduring involvement with the subject, constant search for information and reliance on multi-channel sources involving the mass media and interpersonal communications.

Part 3

The Spheres of
Opinion Leadership

Since the introduction of the opinion leadership concept, numerous studies have sought to advance both the understanding and applicability of this idea. By the early 1970s several hundred studies were listed[1] and the number has continued to grow steadily.

Part 3 reviews the various areas and disciplines in which the concept was utilized. Such a review involves two problems: *categorization* and *representation*. Hundreds of studies and reports had to be classified and there are several alternative methods of classification. The one chosen for this book is based on domain (or area), assuming that readers interested in a specific domain (e.g. politics, marketing, or fashion) will find it more convenient. Yet, possible categorizations could be based on flow of information vs. flow of influence, on the social setting (e.g, modern vs. traditional societies), or on the various methods used for the identification of the influentials.

The second problem involves a representation of hundreds of studies from a vast realm of theories and research. It is nearly impossible to evaluate the entire collection of literature on opinion leadership; instead, the method of review employed was based on a sampling. In each domain, several studies were chosen to represent the concept, methods, and findings. Therefore, though the majority of opinion leaders studies is included, numerous studies were left out. Furthermore, the studies selected were not necessarily the most prominent or most significant studies. Studies were chosen based upon an attempt to present the various aspects of the opinion leadership concept, including studies from various societies and cultures. Finally, the analysis within each domain involves statistical data and analysis. For the reader less familiar with statistical methods, each table or datum is followed by an explanation highlighting the main findings.

Opinion Leaders in Marketing

In no other area has the concept of opinion leaders enjoyed so much attention, follow-up research, and applications as in the marketing domain. Several reasons combine to explain this attraction: the long tradition of research on consumer behavior, which highlighted the important role of personal influence long before the emergence of the Columbia studies; the instrumentality of the concept for practical, marketing-oriented researchers and commercial bodies; and finally, its practical testing and validation in real-life situations with accurate measures. The marketing industry and scholarship were more prone to accept the notion of influential individuals whose advice guides others' consumption decisions and were more open to examine its applicability to various marketing issues. After all, in the marketing research area, it is not only the independent variables that are more visible and measurable but so are the dependent variables and the reward for a successful marketing innovation. Thus, unlike in other areas, the interest of commercial organizations was easily translated into research funding, a translation that was less frequent and harder to activate in other, less instrumental areas.

In this chapter we will examine the role of social forces in shaping consumer behavior, the impact of group pressures, the agents of personal influence (namely, the opinion leaders) in marketing, and the various implications of the opinion leadership ideas in marketing.

Studying Consumer Behavior

The objective of studying consumer behavior is to understand, explain, and predict human actions in the consumption area.[1] The emergence of consumer behavior research is commonly associated with the 1960s. It was a result of several factors including the growing recognition of behavioral sciences as providing usable models to describe and explain human behavior.[2] Consequently, the 1960s witnessed not only the emergence of the field of consumer behavior research but also a strong reliance on interdisciplinary bases. The first attempts were the series of formal models, which dealt with a broad range of consumer behavior aspects. Many of these early models focused on relatively limited aspects and tried to base the explanation of consumer behavior on a specific behavioral concept, such as social class or reference group. But the bulk of consumer studies and models at this stage was based on *individual* behavioral concepts. Such a model was the microeconomic model, emphasizing the maximization of utility, or more generally, satisfaction from consumption as the motive guiding consumers. This model proved to be disappointing because of its limiting assumptions of rational behavior and its focus on aggregate measures. It was replaced by another model, based on a different behavioral science—motivation research with its roots in Freudian psychoanalytic concepts. The motivation research model posited that particular consumption behavior is a direct result of the product's psychological meanings to individual consumers. These meanings are related to basic motivational and personality components of human beings. When the predictive validity of such analytical concepts applied to consumer behavior was found rather questionable, this model faced decline and criticism.

The realization that no single theory of a uni-variate model could provide a sufficient explanation and prediction of consumer behavior led to the multi-theoretical approach. It involved the combination of factors, variables, and theories taken from different disciplines. It resulted, as expected, not only in more complex and sophisticated multi-variate models but also in more valid and efficient models. Three different disciplines served as theoretical sources:

1. *Psychological theories*—focus on cognition, perception, learning, personality, motivation, and attitudes as affecting human behavior, including consumer behavior.
2. *Sociological theories*—focus on social factors, such as reference groups, peer influence, group membership, opinion leaders, and social conformity as shaping consumer behavior.
3. *Sociocultural theories*—relate social aggregates or social categories, such as social classes, cultures, and subcultures, to individual behavior.

Recent consumer behavior research suggested that psychological, sociological, and sociocultural factors form a compatible and inter-dependent set of influences on consumer decisions, choices, and behaviors. As a result, various complex models were developed to explain and predict consumer decision-making processes. The complexity of these models rose with the recognition that this decision-making is a multi-step, hierarchical process.[3] It was generally agreed that the process involves a cognitive step (awareness, interest, and information), an affective step (evaluation), and a behavioral step (trial and adoption). First, the consumer becomes aware of the product or brand. If awareness is followed by interest, the consumer acquires some knowledge about the product by searching for additional information. This search involves a review of internal sources stored in the consumer's memory and an active search for external information sources, such as the experience and opinions of friends. Based on this information, the consumer evaluates the product and forms a positive or negative attitude. This evaluation leads to a decision either to try or not to try the product. During this trial stage, the consumer may use the product on a small, experimental scale to determine whether or not the product is useful and worth its price. This trial, combined with additional information obtained during this stage, leads to a decision of adoption or rejection.

In each phase of the adoption process different communication sources are sought and used by the consumer.[4] Advertising may create initial awareness (or word-of-mouth), while personal advice may be sought for the evaluation stage. A typology of information sources, presented in table 7.1, illustrates the variety of sources used by consumers in various stages of their decision-making.

Table 7.1

Categorization of Consumer's Information Sources

Type	Personal	Impersonal
Marketer controlled	salesperson telemarketing trade shows seminars	advertising displays packaging sales promotions
Nonmarketer controlled	word-of-mouth professional advice	media coverage editorial, reviews

The typology of sources illustrates their variety and also suggests a distinction between personal sources and impersonal sources. A review of the measured effectiveness of these sources suggests:

In general, personal sources of information are reported by consumers to provide more information and to have more impact on consumers than impersonal sources...Personal sources are more effective because of the two-way flow of information between the source and the consumer. Salesperson, friends, and family are able to tailor information to satisfy the recipient's needs...On the other hand, impersonal information sources only provide one-way communications. Information delivered via print or other mass media is developed to satisfy the typical needs of large groups of consumers. Because individual needs cannot be considered, the information provided is not ideally suited for any one customer.[5]

In fact, a study that followed the design and questions of the *Personal Influence* research, with only three types of consumer items, revealed the relative effectiveness of the various sources. Robertson surveyed consumers and asked them about their information sources regarding small appliances, clothing, and food.[6] Three questions were used:

1. "Could you tell me how this product came to your attention for the very *first time?*"
2. "How *else* did you hear about this product before you bought it?"
3. "Which of these was your *most important* source of information in your decision to buy this product?"

The survey results indicate an interesting "division of labor" between mass media sources and personal influence: consumers typically became aware of a product (that is, heard about it for the first time) from advertising. Forty-five percent were first informed about small appliances by advertising along with 35 percent in clothing items and 45 percent in the food products category. When decision-making is the criterion, the sources are reversed: personal influence is more powerful than any other source. When asked what was the most important source when deciding about a purchase, personal influence emerged as the most influential source in every product category. The media are more effective in early stages of the consumer's decision-making process (i.e., creating awareness and interest, and informing) while personal sources appear to be more influential at the later stages (of evaluation, trial, and final decision). The revealed role of personal influence and the contribution of various sociological theories to consumer behavior research led to a growing recognition of buying as a social act.

Consumer Behavior as a Social Act

Consumers' decisions along the stepwise process of decision-making is a complex combination of many factors and considerations. Kerby attempted to provide a detailed model of these factors, including the consumers' needs, tensions, attitudes, motivation, purposes, habits, and requirements.[7] But, as many other marketing researchers realized, the individual is also affected by many social motives, making the simplest purchase a complex social act. Surprisingly, long before modern consumer behavior models detailed these influences (in fact so long ago that it was in the former century), Thorstein Veblen developed a social conceptualization of consumption. In 1899 Veblen, a remarkable and innovative sociologist, published a book entitled *The Theory of Social Class*.[8] In this book and subsequent publications, Veblen developed the thesis of "conspicuous consumption." This thesis highlights the social value of consumption in terms of social status:

> The basis on which good repute in any highly organized industrial community ultimately rests is pecuniary strength; and the means of showing pecuniary strength and so of gaining or retaining good name, are leisure and a conspicuous consumption of goods. . . . No class of society, not even the most abjectly poor, forgoes all customary conspicuous consumption. The last items of this category of consumption are not given up except under stress of the direst necessity. Very much of squalor and discomfort will be endured before the last trinket or the last pretence of pecuniary decency is put away.[9]

Veblen has undoubtedly observed his own social and cultural environment and based his concepts on such observations. He observed that economic wealth was translated into social status by means of leisure and consumption. According to Veblen, the tendency toward conspicuous consumption is universal and ubiquitous, extending from the highest levels of society to the very lowest. Important elements in Veblen's concept of conspicuous consumption are the notion of waste and the social meaning of consumption. To Veblen these are two interconnected components: waste is the demonstration of one's ability to purchase things that are not really needed. But it is not a real "waste" because it has the social gratification, the social reward for the ability to waste. Though written in the previous century, Veblen's concepts are valid today. Kerby, who argues that "conspicuous consumption may appear to be even more prevalent and of greater importance today than it was when Veblen first drew attention to it," provides publicized examples of the modern "waste-makers," the conspicuous consumers who follow Veblen's patterns, a century later.[10]

Consumer behavior is a social act in many other ways than described in the conspicuous consumption pattern. Modern studies and concepts of the social factors affecting consumers can be classified into five groups of social factors:

1. *Emulation.* This is the tendency to follow the consumption pattern set by others. One aspect is known as "keeping up with the Jonses" while another is the embarrassment or discomfort experienced when one's behavior is different or contrary to the behavior of those with whom one associates or wishes to associate. Emulation may be copying or imitating a certain buying behavior of a group, a "social model" or an influential person. As conceptualized in the Bass model, for example, imitation is a key parameter in determining the speed of a new product's diffusion.[11] This approach is based on the "social learning theory" that was applied to various human behaviors. It involves three stages or effects: suggestion, modelling, and imitation. Suggestion refers to the individual following a possible mode of action (i.e., consumption); modelling is presenting a person or a pattern of behavior as worthy of imitation; and imitation is the actual following of a pattern of behavior. The social learning framework for consumer behavior analysis has been utilized extensively by marketing researchers who have found the theories, concepts, and methods of the learning paradigm very useful and efficient.[12]

2. *Social class.* Consumption varies across social classes especially when considering the strong link between economic resources and social class. In some cases, a particular social segment accounts for the consumption of an entire product category. In other cases, the product or service can be consumed by a range of social segments, with variance in terms of form or frequency of consumption, or with certain brands appealing to specific social segments. Moreover, although the same product may be used by members of different social classes, the motivation underlying use varies by class. Various market segmentations apply social class categorization in order to predict consumer behavior. Such segmentation focuses on the variation in values and lifestyles that determine consumption. Consequently, a recent trend in market segmentation research is based upon

profiles called "Values and Lifestyles" (VALS). Arnold Mitchell and his colleagues at the Stanford Research Institute (SRI) conducted a series of "values-oriented" studies to examine how an individual's values influence his or her spending patterns.[13] These studies resulted in VALS categories, grouping consumers by their guiding values. An outdated VALS matrix consisting of nine lifestyles developed in the late 1970s was replaced with refined versions by the 1990s. The latest matrix groups consumers into eight categories: actualizers, achievers, makers, fullfilleds, experiencers, strivers, and strugglers.[14]

3. *Reference groups*. The sociologist Herbert Hyman coined the term "reference group" to refer to those groups with the ability to modify or reinforce an individual's attitudes and behaviors.[15] The common definition of reference group is a group that serves as a point of reference to whom individuals compare themselves (thus comprising negative and positive reference groups). Reference groups can be those that serve as groups to which individuals aspire to belong, or those whose norms and standards for behavior are adopted by the individual. The individual may have multiple reference groups. One need not be an actual member of all these groups. Merely considering these groups as a potential source of guidance delineates them as a reference group (affiliative groups to which one belongs, aspiratory groups to which one does not belong but would like to, and dissociative groups to which one does not belong and prefers not to). Bearden and Etzel provide a detailed list of studies that related the concept of reference groups to consumer decisions and behavior.[16] Dozens of studies revealed the impact of consumers' reference groups on product and brand purchase decisions though this impact varies across product categories (e.g., between publicly and privately consumed products, between luxuries and necessities), across types of reference groups, and across types of influence (e.g., informational, utilitarian, and value-expressive influences).[17]

4. *Cultural environment*. Individuals live in a cultural and social environment that comprises all the norms and customs that characterize a society. Within cultures there is a great diversity of subcultures, or "a subdivision of a national culture, composed of a combination of factorable social situations such as class status, ethnic background, regional and rural or urban residence, and religious affiliation."[18] Various studies highlighted the impact of subcultures on their members' consumption

patterns (for example, studies of the Amish subculture's values and consumption patterns,[19] or the Jewish subculture as affecting values as the need for achievement and, indirectly, consumer behavior).[20] Similar findings were found when studying white, black, and Hispanic consumers in the United States. The impact of subculture on buying behavior may be explained by its relationships to ethical codes of behavior, socio-economic status, social values, and traditional guidelines for daily life.

5. *Personal influence.* The effectiveness of personal influence on the consumers' decision-making process was revealed in numerous studies.[21] We will discuss some of them in the following section; at this stage, however, we should highlight the role of "word-of-mouth" as an additional, powerful social factor. It can be illustrated by either the amount of individuals reporting personal sources as their most important sources or by case studies. For example, in a study on a new coffee product, it was found that of the persons who reported exposure to favorable word-of-mouth, 54 percent purchased the product, while only 18 percent of those receiving unfavorable word-of-mouth purchased the product.[22]

The individual consumer operates in a "social climate." The information, motivation considerations, evaluations, and decisions involved in the consumer decision-making process are all affected by a myriad of social factors. They include social reference groups, social models, social classes, cultures and subcultures, personal contacts, and social networks. Often they interact in a single decision-and-purchase act, affecting various stages of the process or simultaneously affecting the same stage. The developing body of theory and research on individual behavior and social influences has provided a basis for a productive series of applications undertaken in the marketing field. The most frequently applied notion was of personal influence or word-of-mouth. Interpersonal communication was found to play a crucial role in determining consumer choices. As the studies indicated, word-of-mouth communication can be a significant source of information as well as influence. One should, therefore, distinguish between the interpersonal flow of information and the flow of personal influence.

The Interpersonal Flow of Consumer Information

Several illustrative examples can highlight the role of word-of-mouth communication in purchasing decision-making:

1. Almost 50 percent of male and female students at Florida State University reported discussing with their friends clothing brands, styles, retail outlets, and prices.[23]
2. A study of the diffusion of new food products in married students' apartment complexes revealed that exposure to favorable word-of-mouth increased awareness and the probability of purchase, while unfavorable personal communication had the opposite results.[24]
3. A large-scale study of Indianapolis homemakers revealed that nearly two thirds of them told someone else about new products they had purchased or tried.[25]
4. A study of purchasing decisions found that the source of information most frequently consulted by durable goods buyers were friends and relatives. More than 50 percent of the buyers turned for advice to acquaintances and in most instances also looked at products owned by them.[26]

Many other studies found interpersonal communication to be an important source of consumer information in a wide range of products, such as food items, soaps, cleansing items, hair styles, fashion, movie selections, makeup techniques,[27] general fashions,[28] dental products and services,[29] new fabrics,[30] home computers,[31] solar energy systems,[32] and durable goods,[33] to mention only a few. Applying the diffusion of innovation conceptual framework, Gatingon and Robertson explained why interpersonal communication is so significant in the flow of information and ideas about new products: "It is our thesis that consumer diffusion theory has considerable further potential as a theory of communications and an important framework for new product marketing." Their impressive review of the consumer diffusion research literature provides numerous examples of the functions of interpersonal communications in the diffusion model.[34]

Why is interpersonal flow of information so important for consumer decisions? "Although considerable research has been conducted on the importance of interpersonal communication" argue Engel, Kollat, and Blackwell, "research on the transmitter-receiver dyad is scarce."[35] Yet, King and Summers concluded that there are several factors revealed to cause the reliance on personal sources of information.[36] They listed the following four causes, all based on the characteristics of the dyad involved in the exchange of information:

1. *Homogeneity.* The interacting dyad is usually very homogeneous. Studies comparing the social status and age of the participants

in the exchange indicated that people tend to rely on information sources from the same age and social status.

2. *Credibility.* The information seekers search for referents who are better informed and "more qualified" than themselves. The perceived credibility and expertise of personal sources (compared to the biased commercial and mass-mediated messages) promote the reliance on these sources.

3. *Socialization.* We are socialized by social agents, such as the family and social groups. The reliance on them as sources of information is a part of the general reliance on the support and guidance of these important socialization agents.

4. *Proximity.* This variable is actually a two-dimensional factor, including physical proximity and social proximity. Personal influence often involves one or both types of proximity, thus making the influential and the influencee share social status, social values, interests, life style, etc.

Personal information is found to be significant not only in the consumer market but in the industrial market as well. The role of word-of-mouth communication in the industrial adoption process was the subject of a study conducted by Martilla.[37] The study investigated paper-buying practices of 106 converting firms. The buying process in these firms was studied by means of personal interviews and written questionnaires. The respondents in each firm were questioned about their sources of information during each of the three different consumer stages: the *introduction* stage (gathering information about a new grade of paper and its manufacturer); the *consideration* stage (decision about trying the new paper); and the *post-purchase evaluation* stage (decision to continue or not to continue the purchase of the new paper). Martilla distinguished between "personal sources" (people in one's own firm and other firms, salespeople, and mill representatives) and "impersonal sources" (literature, journals, advertisements, and trade shows).

At every stage of the adoption process, personal sources were the most frequently used sources of information. However, this tendency varied across the stages with greater reliance on personal information at the later stages: the proportions reporting personal sources rise from 51 percent at the introduction stage to 70 percent at the consideration stage, and 74 percent at the post-purchase evaluation stage. The sources were further divided, distinguishing between within-firm personal communication and between-firms personal communication. Personal sources within the firm were the most frequent channels, while between-firm flow was found to be more situational, appearing to vary with the level of innovation and market structure. Thus, like individual consumers, the industrial consumers rely mainly on personal influence for their information gathering.

The Interpersonal Flow of Consumer Influence

Personal ties may be used not only as sources of information but also as sources of influence. The use of personal influence in consumer decision-making was found to correlate with certain characteristics of the product. Personal influence was found to increase (in terms of reliance and impact) with:[38]

1. *Involvement*—the purchase of products that require the individual's involvement (e.g., cars, clothing, and appliances) is more likely to be lead by personal influence.
2. *Visibility*—the purchase of products with high visibility (e.g., clothing and air conditioners)[39] is more susceptible to personal influence than products with low visibility (e.g., laundry detergents).
3. *Testability*—the purchase of products that cannot be tested or whose testing requires use over a long time period (e.g., electrical appliances) is strongly related to personal influence, while the ability to test products quickly (e.g., food items) reduces the need for personal advice and guidance.
4. *Complexity*—the purchase of highly complex products (e.g., personal computers and investment programs) increases the consumer reliance on personal influence when compared to simple products.
5. *Perceived risk*—when consumers associate a risk or threat with a product, they seek personal guidance. The perceived risk may be physical (e.g, the use of a new drug) or social (e.g., fashion).

The susceptibility to personal influence is also a personal trait, revealed to exist to varying degrees in different individuals. This notion is derived from McGuire's concept of influenceability,[40] and is consistent with numerous studies demonstrating how individuals differ in their response to social influence.[41] Personal susceptibility to influence was related to other personal characteristics, such as self-esteem and intelligence, and was found to vary across items.

Several attempts to construct empirical instrument for the measurement of consumer susceptibility were reported.[42] Based on some of these early attempts, Bearden and his colleagues developed the consumer susceptibility to interpersonal influence scale (SUSCEP) and tested its validity in several studies.[43] The scale was developed to measure three different manifestations of interpersonal influence (i.e., informational, value expressive, and utilitarian), resulting in a twelve-item scale, in the form of twelve statements (e.g., "to make sure I buy the right product or brand, I often observe what others are buying and using" or "If I want to be like someone, I often try to buy the same brands that they buy"). The scale was found to be reliable and valid across multiple samples of both student and nonstudent subjects. Correlations with other constructs (i.e., self-esteem, consumer behavior indices, attention to social comparison information and others) demonstrated convergent and discriminant validity. Finally, the scale was correlated with external judges' ratings of the subjects in terms of susceptibility to interpersonal influence. The correlations were all positive and significant, ranging between .37 and .47. The later validation test compared the SUSCEP scale with other scales by their correlations with various measures of consumer behavior. The results provided additional evidence regarding the scale's validity and the individual differences in susceptibility to personal influence.

The multitude of factors affecting the consumer's reliance on personal influence led Bristor to propose a complex model that outlines several dimensions of factors. She suggested a three-dimensional solution: on the first dimension are the individual factors that include susceptibility and influenceability; the second include the product factors such as perceived risk level, product newness or complexity; and the third dimension include the situational factors such as the stages of the consumer's decision-making process. Trying to explain the power of personal influence on consumer behavior, Bristor suggests three explanations:

> The first is that there are so many factors that motivate word-of-mouth that it is very pervasive phenomenon. The second is that it can convert lower order cognitions and affect to higher order cognitions and affect, which in turn can lead to committed behaviors. The third is that through multiple dyads and retransmission, one message can reach and potentially influence many receivers.[45]

In fact, several theories of personal influence were suggested as accounting for the power of personal influence. The first theoretical focus was on problem solving, the second on social comparison process, and the third on interpersonal flow of influence. The problem-solving perspective was introduced as related to personal influence by Bauer.[46]

He proposed that people engage in two different kinds of "games": the psychological game and the problem-solving game. In the psychological game, the individual attempts to gain social status or acceptance (by following the leading clothing fashion, for example). In the problem-solving game, the individual uses information gained from others as a reference point in defining the circumstances and choosing the best action or decision (choosing among products, for example). Both games involve the reliance on personal influence. Undoubtedly, many consumer decisions are problem-solving situations in which both psychological and social considerations interact with the rational choice of the best option.

Another theoretical direction was suggested by Leon Festinger in his theory of social comparison processes.[47] Festinger's basic assumption is that individuals seek to evaluate their opinions and actions. To do so, they will turn to other people for advice and information. This social comparison process is more frequently used when nonsocial means of evaluation are nonexistent or are untrustworthy. Thus, in the case of consumer decision-making, the nonsocial sources are confined to advertisements perceived as biased, one-sided, and less dependable than the social sources. Under such circumstances, the individual will be more dependent on the social means of evaluation and comparison. Moreover, the motivation for social comparison is supported by the need for social acceptance. The social comparison process provides the consumer with both social means of evaluation as well as testing the potential social acceptance (or rejection). Consequently, this theory leads to emphasizing the role of personal influence, perceived as a social mean of evaluation and comparison.

Another theoretical and empirical tradition focused on the interpersonal flow of influence. It involved a gradual development of different theories and models, commencing with the "trickle-down" theory, continuing into the "two-step flow" model, and finally resulting in the "multi-step flow" models. The trickle-down theory is rooted in the works of Veblen and Simmel. Veblen's *Theory of the Leisure Class* introduced the concept of "conspicuous consumption" and the notion that the wealthy seek reputability by the display of products perceived as symbolizing wealth.[48] Such consumption is then emulated by the lower classes. Simmel, whose work on fashion is reviewed in chapter 8, offered the trickle-down model for fashions:

Social forms, apparel, aesthetic judgment, the whole style of human expression are constantly transformed by fashion, in such a way, however, that fashion—in all these things—affects

only the upper classes. Just as soon as the lower classes begin
to copy their style the upper classes turn away from this style
and adopt a new one, which in its own turn differentiates them
from the masses; and thus the game goes merrily on.[49]

The trickle-down theory that was used to describe the diffusion
of clothing fashion was less successful in the general marketing domain:
its "vertical flow" assumption was criticized by several studies, which
asserted mainly the contrary, "horizontal flow."[50] These studies
suggested several explanations to the weakening of the trickle-down
process: social changes that created a less rigidly stratified society, the
advent of mass production and mass distribution, and the growth of
the wide middle class. The growing evidence of the horizontal flow led
to the two-step flow model. According to this model, people look to
their peers (people of their own status) and not vertically, to higher
social class referents. The two steps comprise the flow of information
from the media to the more involved and influential individuals (the
opinion leaders) at stage one, and from these influentials to their
followers, usually of the same social strata, at stage two (see chapter
2 on the basic assumptions of this model). Further research, however,
has not conclusively demonstrated the occurrence of such a two-step
process and the criticism (see chapter 14) has resulted in the
development of more complex models, the multi-step flow models.
    The multi-step model of personal influence is built upon the two-
step flow. It recognizes that most influence is transmitted horizontally
at the peer-group level. However, it goes beyond the initial two steps
by proposing multiple patterns of flow. For example, the multi-step
model suggests other directions or level: it includes vertical and
horizontal flow, upward flow (from marginals to more prominent
individuals),[51] opinion sharing (among influentials or among followers),
direct media effects, chains of flow (along weak and strong ties),[52] and
others (see review in chapter 14). Yet, the growing sophistication and
complexity of the models only added to the revealed impact of personal
influence on consumer behavior. Consistent with this emphasis was
the recognition that not all consumers wield equal influence. Some who
are more active in influencing others, the so-called opinion leaders, have
received special attention in numerous marketing theories and studies.

Is There a Two-step Flow?

The attraction of marketers and marketing researchers to the
concept of influentials is clear: it provides them with a target group

that may serve to influence others; it focuses the notion of personal influence on particular, more important individuals; it allows for empirical and applied implications of scientific concepts; and it is a promising theory that may cut down expenses and improve efficiency and impact of marketing strategy. Thus, the early findings of the Columbia studies found eager followers in the marketing domain. Considerable research has focused on the consumers' opinion leaders and the validity of the two-step flow model to marketing theory and practice. Early studies in marketing indeed found evidence to the existence and significance of opinion leaders: Glock and Nicosia pointed out that the marketing opinion leaders "act not only as channels of information but also as a source of a social pressure toward a particular choice, and of social support to reinforce that choice once it has been made,"[53] thus arguing that opinion leaders have three functions: information, social pressure, and social support. Are they really performing these functions, mediating between the media and the consumers? There are numerous studies attempting to answer this question in various areas of consumer behavior. We will examine only a sample of these studies, presenting examples from the wide spectrum of studies, methods, and findings.

One of the earliest attempts was Stewart's study of opinion leadership on consumer topics and awareness of new grocery products.[54] He first identified the opinion leaders in the grocery product topics among 2,399 female respondents from Fort Wayne, Indiana, using a self-designating question. His findings were quite limited to identifying the opinion leaders and measures of their proficiency. Yet, he found significant difference between the leaders and the non-leaders: opinion leaders were more aware of two new grocery products tested in the study. In a very similar study conducted by Corey, the leaders and non-leaders in automotive topics were compared.[55] Data came from a probability sample of Los Angeles-Orange County, California (n=755), using a self-designating measure of leadership.

Opinion leaders were found to differ from the non-leaders in all three measures used to represent the two-step flow model: they were far more involved in events related to their field of expertise (74.8 percent of the leaders attended races compared to only 44.7 of the non-leaders); they were more aware of new developments (65.6 percent among the leaders and 37.1 among the non-leaders knew of the new speedway); and they were more interested in magazines related to their expertise (36.6 percent among the leaders and 15.3 percent among the non-leaders read automobile magazines). A similar comparison, conducted by Martilla on industrial opinion leaders,[56] compared the leaders in 106 paper converting firms in the United States with the non-leaders among the buying decision-makers in these firms.

Opinion leaders in the industrial markets were found to satisfy two of the basic notions of the two-step model: they were more active in giving advice to others. Also, they were more exposed to every type of mass media information and, mainly, sample books, product literature, and advertisements in trade journals. Moreover, a comparison of the *form* of exposure (that is, the depth of exposure) by asking about the reading material thoroughly or just skimming through it, revealed that opinion leaders were more serious in their exposure. For each of the five sources, they reported a deeper exposure than the non-leaders.[57] Significant differences were found in the categories of readership of articles in trade journals and product literature. Schiffman and Gaccione, who studied opinion leadership in 263 nursing homes in six northeastern American states, applied a similar comparison to the leaders/non-leaders categories.[58] Opinion leaders were found to be more exposed to professional publications, to salespeople, and to professional and social ties in the nursing area than non-leaders.[59] Moreover, they found that the presence of opinion leaders at the nursing home predicts adoption of new products, a real evidence to the role of the influentials: nursing homes in which influentials were present adopted new products faster than those homes without such opinion leaders. This finding provides additional support to the important functions of the institutional influential, similar to the role of his or her counterpart in the private consumer domain.

The notion of the two-step model was substantiated in the cultural consumption area as well. A study of cultural activities and opinion leadership in a city in southern France applied the two-step measure to cultural activities, such as theater, movies, and reading books.[60] Using a self-designating questionnaire sent by mail, the researchers studied a sample of 1,200 subscribers of the local theater program, a sample of 202 nonsubscribers and a general population sample of 205 residents, both samples interviewed at home. The comparison of leaders to non-leaders revealed that "cultural opinion leaders are more exposed to cultural events or more committed to cultural activities than non-leaders...look for more information in the mass media than non-leaders, and...are disseminating more cultural information than non-leaders."[61]

From theater to banking and finances, a study of consumers who are "financial opinion leaders" revealed the impact of the informal influentials in this area.[62] Stern and Gould reviewed many studies conducted on how individuals choose banking services and what the sources for such decisions were. They concluded that the most effective communication sources were personal ties, word-of-mouth, friends, and acquaintances. This resulted in their focus on the opinion leaders. They administered a questionnaire, which included a self-designating measure of opinion leadership modified for financial items, to a sample in a northern New Jersey metropolitan area (n=173). Through the use of numerous measures of financial attitudes and behavior, media exposure, and sources of information, the opinion leaders and non-leaders were compared. This comparison revealed that opinion leaders in the financial realm are more likely to:

- follow their financial situation carefully
- use a computer to track their finances
- follow their investments daily in the newspaper
- read financial books and magazines
- talk about investments with other people
- watch TV shows about finance
- read more magazines and newspapers related to finance (e.g., read more *Money* magazine, the *Wall Street Journal*, the *New York Times* Financial Section).
- watch "Wall Street Week" on TV
- listen to radio programs about finances
- write for information from a brokerage house or a bank
- call a brokerage house or bank for information
- read information sent by banks or brokerage houses.[63]

Informal financial opinion leaders are clearly involved and knowledgeable in the investment/savings/banking domain. Not only are they active as information-seekers but also in influencing others:

The ability of opinion leaders to exert influence is considerable because their word-of-mouth conversations extend beyond current offerings to new services in the introductory stage. Augmentation of a bank's financial product line with brokerage services, financial planning, or computerized home banking can be speeded up if the opinion leader actively spreads information about the new services. . .Opinion leaders are important links in the distributive communication channel because other consumers consider them credible information sources.[64]

Finally, the opinion leadership concept is based on the need for such influentials, on their functions and instrumentality. "It takes two to tango," and it takes at least one opinion seeker to have an opinion leader. In *The People Who Use People: The Other Side of Opinion Leadership,* Feick, Price, and Higie provided the last dimension, that of the opinion seekers.[65] Opinion seekers were defined as individuals who sought information or opinions from interpersonal sources in order to find and evaluate products, services, current affairs, or other areas of interest.[66] The researchers applied this notion of opinion seeking to consumer decision-making by utilizing a self-designating scale that referred to various products in a telephone interview sampling 1,531 Americans. The results suggested a relatively high incidence of opinion seekers in the population. Opinion seeking was not found to be restricted to particular types of products, but ranged from nondurable to major durable products. The frequencies of opinion leaders and opinion seekers were found to be highly correlated across product categories. This was a result of two factors: the fact that some opinion seekers are also opinion leaders (who look for information from interpersonal sources, too); and the fact that the need for advice (i.e., opinion seeking) creates the advice givers, the influentials.

From nursing homes to theaters, movies to grocery products, and home appliances to clothing fashions, the important role of updated and well-informed influentials has been consistently revealed. The various studies, of which just a small sample was reviewed here, has supported the two-step model, however, only to some extent: they found convincing evidence of both steps, the heavier media reliance of the influentials and their effective influence over their followers' choices and decisions. But these studies have revealed additional dimensions thus exposing the weaknesses of the somewhat oversimplified two-step notion. They revealed, for example, that many opinion leaders rely on personal sources of information, that much of the information flow is also vertical and even upward (when leaders learn from other leaders or even from followers),[67] involving multi-step rather than two-step flow,[68] and that the media-to-consumer flow may be a one-step process when certain products are concerned or during the first stages of consumers' decision-making (namely, creating awareness and interest). Yet, in most instances, products and stages of the decision making process, the opinion leaders were a significant source of information and influence, leading marketing researchers to focus on identifying them and their characteristics.

Who Are the Consumers' Opinion Leaders?

Several distinguishing characteristics were used to identify the opinion leaders in the marketing domain:

1. Scope of influence
2. Demographic characteristics
3. Personality measures
4. Social measures
5. Life-style characteristics
6. Product-related characteristics

Scope of Influence

Early studies suggested that opinion leaders are rather specialized in one product area (monomorphic leaders).[69] Later studies, however, revealed some overlap of leadership areas, across product categories (see chapter 4 for a detailed review of the overlap issue). King and Summers, for example, found a high degree of overlap across six product categories: about 46 percent of the respondents qualified as leaders in two or more product categories, 28 percent in three or more categories, and 13 percent in four or more categories.[70] The overlap was more frequent across product categories involving similar interests. Thus, the highest overlap was between large and small appliances, the second highest between women's fashions, cosmetics, and personal grooming aids. The lowest overlap was found between "remote" categories, such as cosmetics and large appliances. In another study, Montgomery and Silk found overlap in opinion leadership across certain categories.[71] They revealed that the patterns of overlap appeared to parallel the manner in which the consumers' interests in these categories clustered together. Further work by Montgomery and Silk found that patterns of association in leadership for sixteen topics corresponded to the clusters of interest in the same topics.[72]

Demographic Characteristics

As noted in many opinion leadership studies, the interpersonal dyad tends to be homogeneous in terms of social status, age, income, education, and life styles. Chapter 5 provides a general socio-demographic profile of the influentials, but the general pattern of their prevalence throughout the social strata is evident also in the consumer and marketing domain. However, as expected, their demographic concentration varies considerably according to the product category. While in fashion the younger generations provide most of the influentials, the leaders in institutional purchasing are usually older (74 percent of the leaders in paper-converting firms are from 40 to 55 years old).[73] Consequently, any demographic characterization of the influentials is product-dependent. For example, Goldsmith, Stith, and White reported that both black and white females were more likely to be fashion leaders than their male counterparts.[74] Other studies, in other product categories have indicated that opinion leaders are younger, better educated, earning higher income, and showing greater social mobility.[75] In sum, it may be concluded that opinion leaders do not appear to form a particular demographic segment by themselves; but their impact is more evident when they are socio-demographically similar to their followers.[76]

Personality Measures

Several personality characteristics were related to consumer opinion leadership. Myers and Roberts were probably the first to measure personality characteristics with regard to the opinion leaders.[77] Focusing upon eighteen different traits (using the California Psychological Inventory), they concluded that none of the basic personality variables related substantially to opinion leadership for any of the product areas studied. However, later research did provide some significant relationships: Summers found that women's clothing fashion opinion leaders are more emotionally stable, assertive, likeable, less depressive/self-deprecating, and more self-confident than non-leaders.[78] Opinion leaders were found to be less dogmatic,[79] more innovative,[80] more venturesome,[81] more likely to be confident in their appraisal of the product category, and more socially active.[82] A recent attempt, reported by Chan and Misra, is focusing on several measures, including dogmatism, risk preference, public individuation, personal involvement, and others.[83] The subjects were 262 American undergraduate students, who were asked to answer all the questions in a booklet that contained both the opinion leadership scale and a battery of other scales that covered several personal characteristics (e.g., dogmatism, risk preference, and others). The respondents' scores on the opinion leadership scale served to classify them into leaders' and non-leaders' groups (29.8 percent were classified as leaders and the remaining 70.2 percent as non-leaders). Table 7.2 presents the results of these comparisons.

Table 7.2

Comparison of Characteristics for Opinion Leaders/Non-leaders

Characteristic	Leaders	Non-leaders	t	p<
Personal Involvement	105.72	80.82	10.78	.000
Product Familiarity	6.45	2.21	8.41	.000
Print Media Exposure	4.74	4.26	1.25	n.s.
Risk Preference	29.96	28.34	2.84	.005
Dogmatism	109.95	111.13	− .57	n.s.
Public Individuation	43.12	40.34	3.16	.002

Note: The various scales are detailed in the original report.

From "Characteristics of the Opinion Leader: A New Dimension," by Kenny K. Chan and Shekhar Misra, *Journal of Advertising*, 19, 1990, p. 57, table 2. Reprinted by permission of the *Journal of Advertising*.

Opinion leaders differed significantly from the non-leaders in four of the measures. As expected, they were more involved with the product class and more familiar with it. However, the analysis also revealed that the leaders had greater risk preference and greater public individuation. These two measures require some explanation: public individuation is the degree to which the individual feels differentiated from other people. The tendency of opinion leaders to exhibit a greater degree of public individuation explains their innovativeness and is closely related to another trait—risk preference. The influentials are willing to take more risks and to be threatened by public individuation, more than their followers. These traits are based on their social positions and innovativeness. These results suggest that psychological constructs could be applied to the opinion leaders' characterization and yield better and more accurate profiles.

Social Measures

The opinion leaders combine two social traits that appear contradictory: gregariousness and individuation. Yet, the combination of the two are not only the frequent attributes of opinion leadership but also their mode of operation. All studies on social characteristics of opinion leaders have found gregariousness to be the main attribute of leadership and have explained the phenomena as the need to gather and disseminate information by the use of social ties.[84] Leaders rely on their social activities as channels of communication. Yet, as the studies on leadership and public individuation indicate, despite their social activities, the leaders are more willing to individuate themselves, thus minimizing pressures to conform to group norms. This tendency may be explained by various factors. First, as innovativeness is strongly correlated with leadership, opinion leaders must be willing and able to risk exposure to social pressures. "Hence, the willingness to publicly individuate oneself may be viewed as necessary, though not sufficient, trait of an effective opinion leader."[85] Secondly, the status of opinion leadership requires self-confidence, based on knowledge and interest in a particular product or issue. These, in turn, lead to the ability to differ and use this difference in order to influence others by advice-giving.

Life-style Characteristics

Opinion leaders were characterized also by a profile of their life styles. Tigert and Arnold constructed life-style profiles of American and Canadian opinion leaders.[86] Using attributes, such as activity, interest, and opinion measures, they were able to construct a portrait of opinion leaders in a broad variety of product categories. The various attributes of life styles were factor-analyzed, a procedure that revealed eight factors: leadership, information exchanges, innovativeness, community and club involvement, independence, price consciousness, occupation, and fashion consciousness. These eight factors explained 27 percent of the variance in opinion leadership. However, Tigert and Arnold did not distinguish between product areas. Their analysis profiled the general opinion leader in consumer decision-making. A profiling of the leaders according to specific product categories would have raised the amount of explained variance and provide a more accurate description. Nevertheless, the concepts of life styles and opinion leadership were found to be intercorrelated thus providing additional method of characterizing the influentials.

Product-related Characteristics

Opinion leaders were found to differ from the non-leaders in various product-related variables. First, they are more knowledgeable about the product and more interested in it. This led to attempts to characterize them by "enduring product involvement," or "the on-going concern with a product that transcends situational influences."[87] These studies found that product involvement plays a critical role in opinion leadership but only the enduring type of involvement. Richins and Root-Shaffer used the product category of automobiles and by a mail survey studied adult consumers in a medium-sized sunbelt city. Measurement of opinion leadership was performed by means of the King and

Summers scale. Enduring involvement was measured by a nine-item scale and situational (or short-term) involvement was measured by the timing of the last purchase of a car.

The results of the path analysis of the relationships among measures of interpersonal communication on purchasing cars and opinion leadership in this area strongly supported the involvement-leadership-communication model: "Involvement does appear to be an important antecedent to opinion leadership, but it is necessary to specify that only *enduring* involvement results in opinion leadership. Situational involvement bears no relationship at all with opinion leadership."[88] Situational involvement does lead to word-of-mouth activity but more frequently in the form of sharing personal experience rather than advice-giving. Advice-giving is strongly related to opinion leadership which, in turn, is best predicted by enduring involvement. Thus, the best model, stemming from the path analysis, was enduring involvement leading to opinion leadership (path coefficient of .33), and leadership leading to communication activity: dissemination of product news (.34) and advice-giving (.37).

Product familiarity also plays an important role in establishing consumer opinion leadership. In order to maintain leadership status in this area, one must be attentive to information about the product or the product area. "It requires willingness to expend a great amount of cognitive effort to acquire and comprehend the extensive knowledge of the product or product category," argued Chan and Misra,[89] after reviewing the literature on opinion leadership and product familiarity. Familiarity is relevant to media exposure: opinion leaders were found to be more exposed to mass media, in general; but the disparities are greater in the specific media that are product-related. This confirms the general pattern of the leaders' media consumption (see chapter 6). Opinion leaders are more exposed to media and contents devoted to their area of expertise.

Practical Implications for Marketing

When Chrysler Corporation was planning the introduction of its new 1993 model, the LH car, instead of the conventional advertisements and promotion campaign, it had an innovative idea. The marketing plan included three-day test drives offered to a selected segment, labeled by Chrysler as "thought leaders."[90] These were defined as prominent individuals who may influence others to buy the car, or in other words, opinion leaders in the automotive market.

Marketing researchers were the first to realize the instrumental value of the opinion leaders concept. Thus, the early findings indicating their role in the flow of consumer information and influence were soon translated into practical implications and uses. Corey noted, "Identifying opinion leaders as market segment may be an effective way of using their personal influence in reaching defined markets."[91] Likewise, Robertson, Zielinski, and Ward concluded that "to affect personal influence, the most logical strategy is to reach opinion leaders and to let them influence their followers."[92] For example, in their study "Seeking Donations via Opinion Leadership," Rieken and Yavas investigated the feasibility of using opinion leaders in order to stimulate donating from the public.[93] The practical uses of opinion leaders in marketing involve many more options:

1. Identifying opinion leaders
2. Creating opinion leaders
3. Activating opinion leaders
4. Simulating opinion leaders
5. Learning from opinion leaders

Identifying Opinion Leaders

The key to any use of opinion leaders is the accurate identification of the influentials within a product category. Consumer behavior researchers argued that "for the consumer-goods marketers, locating and identifying opinion leaders very seldom is worth the cost, since this is indeed a difficult and expensive undertaking."[94] Yet, when dealing with specific and narrow markets, the cost of the identification effort may be surmounted by the benefits of an economical, "narrow" campaign targeting the influentials. Focusing on those individuals who will persuade the others may eliminate the need for expensive, broad promotion campaigns. Indeed, much of the effort of translating the opinion leadership concept into practical implications was devoted to methods that locate and identify the opinion leaders (see chapter 3). This impressive effort included the development and testing of various scales and measures, their validation, and their experimental use in various areas, which range from fashion to dental products. Nevertheless, despite the widespread acceptance of these measures, the marketing industry has been limited by the immense difficulties and costs associated with the initial identification of the opinion leaders. Consequently, this application characterizes limited product categories, with defined and narrow markets, making the identification study easier and less expensive.

Creating Opinion Leaders

If the identification of existing influentials is so complex but their value is so significant, why not create opinion leaders? In fact, the idea of creating opinion leaders was suggested and applied successfully in the electronics industry, the metal-working industry and the rock-and-roll music market.[95] In the case of rock music, Mancuso developed and tested a method of creating "rock-and-roll opinion leaders" in a competitive market where 200 new records are introduced every week. The process involved several steps. The initial step was to seek out candidates. These were social leaders among the relevant buying public (high school students). Class presidents, sports captains, cheerleaders, and others were selected from various high schools and then contacted by mail with an invitation to join a select panel to help evaluate new records. Following their evaluations and selection, the panel members were encouraged to discuss their choices with their friends and provided with information on the selected records. The total cost of the experiment was less than $5,000, but the results were impressive: in the trial cities several records reached the top ten charts while the same records did not reach the top ten selections in any other city. Thus, without any conventional campaign, the rock records were promoted by the recruited opinion leaders and became best sellers. When summarizing the process, Mancuso argued that the key was the selection of those who had the potential to become opinion leaders:

> The underlying belief about the process of creating opinion leaders is basically simple. First, select a subject already possessing to the greatest degree possible the variables that the creation technique are least able to strengthen. Second, to the degree possible, strengthen the remaining variables, so that the subject receives as high a rating as possible in the areas of mobility, status, and confidence.[96]

Mancuso's experiment highlights the potential leader as combining three independent variables, all are critical parameters of existing opinion leaders. The first, *mobility*, refers to amount of acquaintances and frequency of social contacts. *Status* was a combination of three attributes: group norms, life-cycle position, and degree of influence (all revealed by the Columbia studies and applied to marketing research). Finally, *confidence* is a measure of the knowledge one has and his or her familiarity with the product. Mancuso, in fact, selected individuals with high mobility and status scores and improved their confidence by creating involvement, providing information, and thus triggering influence. Yet, there are other alternatives to "creation" of opinion leaders:

> In the example cited earlier [the rock records], the initial step was to select high mobiles with a relatively high degree of status. The next step was to increase the subjects' confidence, and to a lesser extent, their status. Conceivably, with a different creation technique, a choice could have been made to select highly confident subjects, with a resulting attempt being made to increase their mobility and status.[97]

A similar implication is suggested by Rieken and Yavas in their study of promoting donations: "Nonprofit organizations should create opinion leaders. One approach is to recruit those people who by virtue of their status in the community would be in a position to affect the attitudes of their peers."[98]

Activating Opinion Leaders

Either by identifying existing opinion leaders or by "creating" them, the marketer may be interested in activating their influence. Stimulating opinion leaders to promote a product, brand, idea, or service is not that easy, considering the familiarity of the influential with the issue and his or her desire to maintain a status as more knowledgeable and updated. Yet, a sophisticated campaign targeting the leaders' group using both the appropriate tone and arguments, may stimulate the interest, involvement, and, consequently, action of the leaders. Stern and Gould studied the financial opinion leaders and concluded their study with strategic suggestions for banks and financial services firms.[99] They found that though financial opinion leaders appear to be active and important in determining others' financial decision-making, "to date, financial institutions have not made much use of the consumer opinion leader: they have been remiss in failing to capitalize on a valuable advertising media—their own customers."[100]

The strategic implications regarding the activation of the financial influentials included a list of communication methods, appeals, and messages, designed to convince the leaders and stimulate them to influence others. Needless to say, activation is based upon the prerequisite of persuading the opinion leaders themselves. Thus, a "two-step activation" is required: communicating information and influence to the leaders, followed by inducing them to exert their influence on others. For example, Stern and Gould suggest several methods of communicating with the financial opinion leaders, because, they argue, "information, given free to the opinion leader, can become a revenue item rather than a cost item. The financial firm that gives away information, albeit at considerable cost, probably receives a high return in terms of satisfied customers who spread positive word-of-mouth messages and attract new users."[101] They suggest advertising campaigns should target the financial opinion leaders by contacting individuals who are potential influentials. The suggested communication program is based on consumer messages specially designed for the opinion leaders, "to go beyond attracting the opinion leaders as customers and further persuade them to attract their friends, relatives, neighbors, and co-workers."[102] Similarly, in the area of fund raising and donations, Rieken and Yavas suggest the following communication strategy:

> First, nonprofit organizations need to stimulate word-of-mouth communication among the opinion leaders and opinion recipients...This can be achieved by advertising designed to prompt opinion leaders to talk to their peers, friends, and neighbors...Administrators of nonprofit organizations, besides appealing to the general public via mass media, should make an attempt to communicate directly with opinion leaders. One means of implementing this would be to provide information through direct mail to members of organizations.[103]

Considering the implications for the advertisers, Munson and Spivey suggested special advertising campaigns targeting the opinion leaders, using the appeals, arguments, and values prevalent within this group:

> The implications for advertisers is clear. Given this propensity of opinion leaders to filter media messages, to interject their personal evaluations, and to screen the message content for its compatibility with their audiences, advertisers should create messages that are consistent with both the values and life styles of the targeted opinion leader.[104]

Simulating Opinion Leaders

The revealed impact of the influentials led not only to their identification and activation but also to simulating their activity. As noted by consumer behavior researchers, "advertising can perform the function of *simulating* personal influence. The marketer simulates opinion leadership through setting up people as 'opinion leaders.' "[105] Yet, this may not be so simple, for the "simulated influential" must be viewed as a valid and trustworthy source of information. For instance, the popular use of celebrities, media stars, or famous athletes in advertisements and commercials is not always the right answer. Though these figures may attract attention and serve as models for imitation, they are not viewed as personal sources of advice and guidance: "Much testimonial advertising probably goes astray because the endorser is not seen as a credible source of information."[106] Modest, true-to-life endorsement may be more effective: "Ads can also simulate opinion leadership: slice-of-life scenes that depict people informally chatting about products in a realistic way are in this category."[107] The presentation of a simulated act of information-seeking and information-giving in a normal, daily setting, may create a substitute for the "real" act of consulting an opinion leader.

Learning from Opinion Leaders

Opinion leaders may serve as a valuable source of information for marketers, advertisers, and producers. Corey suggested three areas to which this learning might be applied: *product development, copy testing,* and *attitude research*.[108] New-product development can be improved by relying on suggestions and advice of opinion leaders. The fact that most of the "early adopters" are opinion leaders[109] may further support the need to learn the reaction of the influentials to a new product. Corey cites a case of a campaign for a motor speedway in Los Angeles in which fifty of the first purchasers, or "early adopters" were studied. Sixty percent of them were found to be automotive opinion leaders, compared to the 17 percent rate found in the general population. Thus, new-product research, including concept studies and market survey, should focus on the influentials as their evaluation may indicate the product's potential.

Copy testing is another potential use of the opinion leaders. Because opinion leaders are often the most frequent users of any media content regarding their expertise and since they serve as transmitters of this information to others, their evaluation of the any publicized information is important. In fact, they could be a perfect test group for studying the effectiveness of various communications ranging from advertisements to marketing arguments. Their evaluations are more crucial as they indicate the likelihood of acceptance and credibility among the leaders themselves and consequently, among the general public. Finally, marketers can learn from these sophisticated consumers about the attitudes toward a product category, a brand or a company. The influentials, who are both reflecting and shaping public attitudes, can serve as valuable sources of information on what determines consumers' choices, images, and considerations. Moreover, they will provide the marketers with the attitudes that opinion leaders "pass on" to their circle of influence.

Conclusions

• The concept of opinion leaders was enthusiastically adopted, tested, and applied by consumer behavior researchers. As shown, the marketing industry and scholarship were more prone to accept the notion of influential individuals whose advice guides others' consumption decisions and were also more eager to examine its applicability to various marketing issues.

• Consumer behavior was found to be a rather complex, multi-stage process of decision-making. Recent consumer behavior research suggest that psychological, sociological, and socio-cultural factors form a compatible and interdependent set of influences on consumer decisions, choices, and behavior.

• Consumer behavior is a social act in many ways. Modern studies and concepts of the social factors affecting consumers can be classified into five groups of social factors: emulation and social learning, social classes, cultures and subcultures, reference groups, and personal influence.

• Personal influence is a significant source of consumer information and influence, as a result of four factors: homogeneity, credibility, socialization, and proximity (social and physical). The reliance on personal influence was found to be related to individual differences (e.g., in susceptibility), certain product's attributes (involvement, visibility, testability, complexity, and perceived risk), and situational factors (e.g., stage of the adoption process).

• Opinion leaders in both the industrial market and private consumer purchase were found to satisfy two of the basic notions of the two-step model. They were more active in giving advice to others they were more exposed to every type of mass media information in their area of expertise.

• Marketing opinion leaders were characterized by several indicators: scope of influence, demographic characteristics, personality measures, social measures, life-style characteristics, and product-related characteristics.

• The concept of opinion leadership in marketing has many practical implications, including: identifying, activating, creating, simulating, and learning from opinion leaders.

Opinion Leaders in Fashion

Fashion as a Sociological Concept

The opening sentence in Herbert Blumer's paper on fashion was: "This paper is an invitation to sociologists to take seriously the topic of fashion."[1] Not only did Blumer feel that only a handful of scholars have given more than casual concern to this topic, but he was convinced of the social value of studying fashion:

> Fashion should be recognized as a central mechanism in forming social order in a modern type of world, a mechanism whose operation will increase. It needs to be lifted out of the area of the bizarre, the irrational, and the inconsequential in which sociologists have so misguidingly lodged it. When sociologists respond to the need of developing a scheme of analysis suited to a moving or modern world, they will be required to assign the fashion process to a position of central importance.[2]

Blumer echoed the argument suggested by Bell twenty years earlier:

> ... in sociological studies fashion plays the role which has been allotted to *Drosophila*, the fruit fly, in the science of genetics. Here at a glance we can perceive phenomena so mobile in their response to varying effects, so rapid in their mutation that the deception force of inertia, which overlays and obscures most other manifestations of human activity, is reduced to a minimum.[3]

At the beginning of the twentieth century, Simmel discussed the social functions of fashion with brilliant observations that led sociological thought in this area for a century. In his only work on fashion, dated 1904,[4] Simmel argued that fashion arose as a form of class differentiation in a relatively open class society. Fashion was suggested to be a form of clothing styles that demarcate an elite group. These styles are copied by those who wish to emulate the elite, thus forcing the elite group to devise new distinctive marks of their superior status. Several features of Simmel's work should be noted. One of the them is that fashion requires a certain type of society in which to take place. Another was the idea of fashion process, highlighting the fast-changing nature of fashion, and its introduction, adoption, emulation, and replacement by a new fashion.

Simmel's views of fashion focused on its social functions for the individual, for certain social groups, and for society at large. He pointed the various paradoxes of fashion: its integrative and yet distinctive nature, its incessantly changing character and yet its stabilizing and equalizing functions, and its individualistic emphasis and yet submission to group dynamics and approval. Regarding the continuity-change and the individual-group dualism, Simmel noted:

> The whole history of society is reflected in the striking conflicts, the compromises, slowly won and quickly lost, between socialistic adaption to society and individual departure from its demands. . . Fashion is the imitation of a given example and satisfies the demand for social adaption; it leads the individual upon the road that all travel, it furnishes a general condition, which resolves the conduct of every individual into a mere example. Thus fashion represents nothing more than one of the many forms of life by the aid of which we seek to combine in uniform spheres of activity the tendency towards social equalization with the desire for individual differentiation and change.[5]

Simmel was also aware of the changing character of fashion, its transitory nature: "Few phenomena of social life posses such a pointed curve of consciousness as does fashion."[6] But, he oversimplified the flow of fashion: Simmel saw it as a "trickle-down" flow, when only the upper class establishes new fashions. Once a new object is adopted by the upper class, it is imitated by each succeeding lower class until it has been trickled down to the lowest class. This simple presentation was later replaced by many other models (for a review, see Sproles),[7] including the "collective behavior" model. This model is highlighted as a "collective" or "mass" movement or a wave of social conformity that sweeps over a population. The efforts of an elite class to set itself apart in appearance takes place inside the movement of fashion instead of being its cause. The shift to collective behavior as determining the fashion process, not only revised the trickle-down theory,[8] but also highlighted the role of communication.

The Fashion Process and Personal Communication

Fashion is a social process. It is often defined as a socially derived valuation of an idea, practice, or product, or as a form of collective behavior; it, therefore, has many implications for various facets of social life. The social needs behind fashion and its consumption, the social values and functions of fashion, and the social channels used for its dissemination, evaluation, and approval are some of the reasons to consider fashion as a sociological concept, rather than merely a product, marketing item, and an individual form of behavior. As early as 1903, the French sociologist Gabriel Tarde had argued that fashion spreads as a social water tower from which "a continuous waterfall of imitation" descends.[9] Tarde saw fashion as a social process of imitation, an imitation of the superior by the inferior, but an imitation motivated by a social need. "Before imitating the act of another we begin by feeling the need from which this act proceeds."[10]

Fashion as an answer to social needs was the main motive in Anspach's analysis of *The Why of Fashion*.[11] Using a historical analysis of the rise of fashion, Anspach argues that "fashion arises where differentiated social groups exist. . .The initiating spark is the social need of people to be like others and yet to be distinct from others."[12] Thus, the need for fashion correlates with the amount of stratification and sub-divisions of society and is aided by the need to symbolize mobility and class identity in modern, open systems.

The fashion process, as a collective behavior, is a social mechanism of change, through which a potential fashion object is transmitted from its creation and first introduction to discernible public acceptance, and eventual obsolescence. This is commonly presented as a six-phased process:[13]

1. *Invention and introduction.* A source of fashion objects, such as a fashion designer, entrepreneur, or innovator, creates and introduces a new object.
2. *Fashion leadership.* A small proportion of the most fashion-conscious consumers adopts and introduces the new fashion to its followers. In most instances, the public may be aware of

the new fashion; the decision to adopt or reject it, however, relies on the influentials.

3. *Increasing social visibility.* The fashion receives increasing attention and recognition, supported by the opinion leaders, the media, and the commercial promoters of the new item.

4. *Social conformity.* The new fashion achieves social legitimacy; the compelling forces of conformity, communications, and mass marketing propagate widespread adoption of the fashion.

5. *Social saturation.* The new fashion is routinized and, in fact, may become overused, thus setting the stage for its decline.

6. *Decline.* New fashions are introduced as replacements of the old fashion, leading to its decline and disappearance.

This model points to the important role of various communicators in the life cycle of a fashion: the communicators who first introduce it to potential adopters; the fashion leaders who upon adoption introduce it to the public; the mass media that promote and legitimize the new fashion; the social communication that serves to spread it and create collective conformity to adoption and use, and finally to its replacement by a more modern and innovative fashion item. Several approaches applied communication models to the study of fashion: the symbolic communication approach, the diffusion approach, and the social network approach. As we will see, these are actually complimentary rather than alternative models, each highlighting other communicative aspects of fashion.

According to the symbolic communication model, fashion is a language of styles, a communication of symbolic meanings. This approach highlights the visual language of fashion and its latent social codes as guided by symbolic interaction theory. (See, for example, *The Language of Clothes* by Lurie[14] or *Appearances and the Self* by Stone.)[15] A special illustrative effort in this vein is the application of semiotic analysis and the concept of a "communicative code." A structuralist definition sees a code as "the underlying set of laws, within a given system of signs, by which these signs are combined into meanings."[16] Umberto Eco considers the concept of code on four different levels: (a) a set of signals ruled by combinatory laws, or the syntactic system; (b) a set of possible communicative contents conveyed by signals, or the semantic system; (c) a set of possible behavioral responses that indicate how the message has been received; and (d) a rule that couples the various systems.[17]

Society members share a perception on "how to read" different clothing fashions, styles, and combinations. This is the clothing code, one that encompasses all the four levels of Eco's conceptualization. Clothing is a language in the array of garments, available to the individuals and anchored to conventional values, social divisions, and normative meanings. It has its signals, its contents, its behavioral responses, and its changing meanings. Simone-Miller concludes this analogy by comparing the clothing code to a language and fashion to a speech act: "Clothing is the equivalent of a language—an institution, a set of conventions with structured, pre-established meanings; a fashion statement, on the other hand, is the equivalent of a speech act through the selection and combination process it entails."[18]

Another communication model used for the study of fashion process was the diffusion of innovation model. Applied to fashion, this approach suggests that fashion "change agents" (innovators, influentials, or "fashion-conscious consumers") play complementary roles in displaying new styles and verbally influencing others' choices.[19] The use of a new fashion is perceived as any other form of adopting an innovation and thus is analyzed in terms of diffusion stages, formal, and informal communication, and influential individuals or opinion leaders.

A cross-cultural study of fashion, applying the diffusion of innovation model, revealed the role and impact of personal sources.[20] When samples of Americans, English Canadians, and French Canadians were questioned about their information sources regarding fashion, the most common sources were "visiting the stores" and "observing other women," which rated higher than fashion magazines, newspaper fashion advertisements, catalogs, or fashion on television and radio. This pattern was consistent across cultures and time. (The surveys were repeated).[21] Several studies conducted within the perspective or methodology of the diffusion model,[22] revealed the role of personal influence: "Thus individuals adopt fashions based on exposure to communications, and diffusion becomes a result of communications, often from one person to another within immediate social networks."[23] Indeed, the diffusion of innovation concept became closely related to another communication model used to study fashion process, the social networks approach.

The social networks approach highlights the informal communication regarding fashion, through person-to-person channels. These personal networks are the transmitters of new fashions, in the give-and-take, usually face-to-face contacts.[24] The networks may be composed of family members, friends, neighbors, co-workers, or relatives; they constitute the channels of social dissemination and approval. In their classic work, *Personal Influence*, Katz and Lazarsfeld pointed to the important role of social networks in communication flow and explained it by several functions: (a) the instrumental function of conformity's benefits; (b) the group as providing meanings or interpretations of social realities; (c) convergence as a result of interaction within a group or network; and (d) the attraction of shared values or "value homophily."[25] However, within the networks of personal communication, certain individuals were found to be more effective, more involved in disseminating information and influence. These were the fashion opinion leaders.

The Role of Fashion Opinion Leaders

Though most reviews relate the first use of the opinion leadership in fashion to the work of Katz and Lazarsfeld, earlier evidence to the idea of leadership is found in the works of Gabriel Tarde and Georg Simmel. Katz and Lazarsfeld themselves acknowledge the observations of Tarde on nineteenth-century France and the role of the French salons on shaping public opinion. But the first description of the influential fashion leader is to be found in Simmel's work on fashion, published half a century before the Columbia studies profiled the fashion leaders. In his 1904 paper on fashion, Simmel wrote about "he who leads the way":

Thus he represents something distinctly individual, which consists in the quantitative intensification of such elements as are qualitatively common property of the given set of class. He leads the way, but all travel the same road. Representing as he does the most recently conquered heights of public taste, he seems to be marching at the head of the general procession. . .as a matter of fact, the leader allows himself to be led.[26]

Simmel noted not only the importance of the influential figures but also how they conform with social norms, serving as the mediators between changing culture to established social values. These individuals are personifying social values and translate them to influence thus further reinforcing the existing values. Blumer also highlighted the role of the opinion leaders in the flow of fashion:

A fifth condition for fashion is the presence of prestige figures who expose one or another of the competing models. The

prestige of such persons must be such that they are acknowledged as qualified to pass judgment on the value or suitability
of the rival models. If they are so regarded, their choice carries
weight as an assurance or endorsement of the superiority or
propriety of a given model. A combination of such prestigeful
figures, exposing the same model, enhances the likelihood of
adoption.[27]

Fashion leaders serve as sources of advice, assurance, and
endorsement for others. More than in any other area, the adoption of
a new fashion item relies heavily on the perceived social acceptance.
The price of an unsuccessful choice may be social embarrassment while
a successful choice may bring rewarding popularity and acceptance.
Thus, fashion decision-making requires some careful testing and
evaluation. Nobody better than the updated, well-informed, socially
integrated opinion leaders can provide such social support and
endorsement.

As the Decatur study found (see chapter 2), fashion opinion leaders
were the most effective sources of influence. Later, Anspach suggested
a somewhat different conceptualization of the fashion leaders.[28]
According to her, the innovators in fashion are seldom the opinion
leaders. The innovators are the first to adopt the new fashion, they
"provide the spark that introduces change," but they must be followed
by opinion leaders. Anspach, therefore, has suggested a sub-division
even within the opinion leaders category. She argued that in fashion
there are the "community opinion leaders" who are celebrities, reacting
first to new fashion and exposing them to the masses.[29] Only then do
the "local leaders" act, accessible to their followers, who judge and
endorse (or do not endorse) the new fashion. Note that such distinction
does not follow the traditional definition of opinion leaders: Anspach's
definition regards leaders as prestigious personalities, and even
celebrities, whose impact lacks the personal, face-to-face contact related
to "conventional" leaders. One may question whether Anspach did not
confuse social celebrities with opinion leaders. At the same time such
analysis may suggest that, at least in fashion, the process of personal
influence may involve two-step flow *within the leaders*: from community
leaders to local leaders and from them to their friends and
acquaintances.

Schrank and Gilmore used a special scale for identifying fashion
opinion leaders and applied it to study the correlates of fashion
leadership.[30] The scale contained twenty statements, which were all
related to behavior in the realm of clothing. A split-half reliability

coefficient of .93 indicated its high internal consistency. The researchers were interested not only in the construction of the leadership scale but also in studying the leaders' functions in the fashion process. To do so, they used a fashion innovativeness measure that identified those with tendencies of early purchase and use of new fashion items. This measure was based on a list of clothing and accessory items with the extent and timing of adoption indicating innovativeness. (The clothing and accessory item list of each individual was scored and weighted according to the timing of acquisition in relation to the total group's timing with greater weight given to early acquisitions, before the "mode.")

The correlates and functions of fashion leadership were examined by a set of other traits, such as attitudes toward conformity in dress and clothing, interest in clothing, a measure of social insecurity, and socioeconomic level.[31] Data came from a sample of 145 American college women: the researchers chose this sample because they wanted to maximize the possible number of fashion leaders and expected the young, single women to be more influential in this area (based on the findings of the Decatur study). The respondents completed questionnaires that included all of the previously discussed scales (the five measures). Then their scores were correlated. The coefficients of partial correlation (controlling for socio-economic level) are presented in table 8.1.

Table 8.1

Correlates of Fashion Opinion Leadership

Variable	Innovativeness	Opinion Leadership
Fashion Leadership	.411*	—
Social Insecurity	−.237*	.132
Conformity	.055	.434*
Clothing Interest	.335*	.764*
Socioeconomic level	−.166	−.045

* p < .01, all correlations, except for those with the socioeconomic level, are partials with socioeconomic level partialled out.

From "Correlates of Fashion Opinion Leadership," by Holly L. Schrank and D. Lois Gilmore, *The Sociological Quarterly*, 14, 1973, p. 538, table 1. Reprinted by permission of JAI Press Inc.

Fashion leadership was strongly correlated with interest in clothing (.764), innovativeness (.411), and conformity (.434). The high correlation with interest in fashion were no surprise: opinion leaders are more interested, involved, and informed about their area. The significant correlation with conformity supports Simmel's notion of the leaders' conformity to social norms and also "the leadership as personification of social values" suggested by Katz.[32] However, the fact that no correlation was found with the socio-economic level contradicts the trickle-down idea and the "imitation of the upper class by lower class" as proposed by Simmel. It appears that Katz and Lazarsfeld's finding regarding the evenly distributed frequency of leaders across social strata (see chapter 2), describes better the relation between social class and leadership.

Fashion Opinion Leaders and Fashion Innovators

Are opinion leaders the fashion innovators or are they merely mediating between the innovators and the public? This question was tested by several studies that related opinion leadership and fashion innovativeness. The main conclusion of Schrank and Gilmore's study was the distinction between innovativeness and opinion leadership in fashion. Earlier studies and reviews often confused the two terms. For example, Tigert, King, and Ring studied "the fashion change agent" in four cultural settings. They perceived these agents as consumers who monitor the changing fashion environment on a regular basis and keep their wardrobe up-to-date with current fashions.[33] Rogers was the first to argue that the innovators may not be those who influence the others,[34] while Robertson and Myers, who studied opinion leadership and buying behavior, found that the overlap between innovativeness and leadership was not significant enough to equate the two.[35] The Schrank and Gilmore study provided additional support to such distinction: first, by the different correlates of the two measures (compare the coefficients in the two column of table 8.1), and second, by their intercorrelation (.411, significant but not a full match between the two measures).

The partial correlation between opinion leadership and innovativeness indicates some association between the two, explained by the researchers as a fashion-related factor: "The fact that opinion leadership and innovativeness in fashion were frequently found among the same respondents in the present study might be explained by the speed with which clothing innovations are diffused compared to most other innovations."[36] Yet, the two do not fully overlap. This indicates that some opinion leaders are also the innovators while others are only mediating between innovators and adopters. Schrank and Gilmore concluded that some individuals play a *dual* role of endorsement, by not only adopting, but also by verbally influencing others to adopt. In contrast, the lack of perfect correlation indicates that some individuals play a singular role as visual or verbal leaders. Furthermore, since the variables associated with innovativeness differed from those associated with opinion leadership, it appears that individuals with different characteristics serve different functions in the diffusion process of new fashion. This possibility requires a closer look at the characteristics of fashion opinion leaders.[37] A special insight into the dual-role leaders in fashion was provided by a Baumgarten who focused in his study on those who are both innovators and opinion leaders. Baumgarten referred to them as the "innovative communicators," methodologically defined as the overlap between those who are high on both measures (leadership and innovativeness). In a study of 389 unmarried male undergraduates at Purdue University, these dual-role leaders were identified and tested (one should note that the use of *male* samples in fashion studies is quite rare). Opinion leadership was measured by Rogers' modified six-item, self-designating scale (see chapter 3), identifying 27.7 percent of the respondents as high on the scale thus classified as opinion leaders. Innovativeness was measured by timing the adoption of certain clothing items (e.g., suits, shoes, neckties, sports jackets, and others). Sketches of various styles in each of these clothing categories were shown to the respondents. They were asked if they own them or intend to purchase them in the near future. Comparing the answer to the aggregate popularity resulted in the early adoption index with 26.3 percent of the sample being identified as high early adopters. The next stage involved cross-classifying the two variables.

Assuming that the two measures are independent, we would expect the overlap to be about 7.3 percent of the sample (26.3% × 27.7%). In fact, a total of 47 respondents or 12.1 percent of the total sample qualified as the dual-role leaders, or "innovative communicators." The correlation between the two measures (.34) is far from being perfect, though. It does support the notion of relationship between early adoption of fashion and fashion leadership but not to the extent of a full overlap or equation. Yet, it reveals a group of opinion leaders who are also fashion innovators. Who are those innovative communicators?

Baumgarten focused the analysis on these *dual-role leaders* and attempted to determine their distinctive profile in comparison to the rest of the population. To do so, he used demographic and sociological characteristics, social activities, media exposure, fashion characteristics, and psychological traits. Not surprisingly, fashion-oriented variables were the most significant discriminators between innovative communicators and others. On every indicator of fashion characteristics (e.g., style familiarity, clothing expenditures, brand familiarity, and style variety ownership), the innovative communicators scored higher than the others. They spent more money on clothing, knew more about clothing styles and brands, and owned a wider range of clothing styles.

Another feature of these innovative leaders was their readership of magazines and newspapers. Compared with others, they read more cosmopolite sources such as the Sunday *New York Times* and *New York Magazine,* and such "technical" sources of fashion information as *Gentlemen's Quarterly* and *Esquire*.[38] Furthermore, the level of readership of all magazines and newspapers (nine publications were used for the comparison) was significantly higher among the innovative leaders than among others. Similar differences were revealed in measures of sociability: the innovative leaders were found to be more involved in various social activities, including sports, dating, and social events. Finally, several psychological tests applied to the sample revealed interesting patterns. Of the 21 psychological self-description factors, only 4 were statistically significant in differentiating innovative leaders from others.[39] Baumgarten concluded: "While some few personality characteristics are significantly associated with innovative communicativeness, innovative communicators do not exhibit a markedly different general personality profile than their peers."[40]

Who are the Fashion Opinion Leaders?

The first attempt to characterize fashion leaders after the Decatur study was that of Summers, who applied demographic, sociological, attitudinal, communication, and fashion involvement measures to the leader-follower distinction.[41] A random sample of 1,000 homemakers was studied by a personal interview and four self-administered questionnaires. Opinion leadership was measured by Rogers's modified six-item, self-designating scale. The first analysis focused on the demographic profiles of fashion leaders.

Opinion leaders were found to be more highly concentrated among those segments that 1. were younger, 2. had more years of education, 3. had higher income; and 4. had higher occupational status. Yet, despite the significant differences in frequency, there were influentials in every given category of each variable. (Even in the category with the lowest concentration, there were at least 18 to 22 percent of leaders.) This suggests that although fashion leadership is more concentrated in certain demographic categories, it is frequent in other categories as well.

Fashion leaders were also found to differ from non-leaders in all measures of sociability: they scored significantly higher on the scales of organizational membership, organizational participation, organizational affiliations, participation in informal social activities, physical mobility, sporting activities, and other areas. Fashion involvement provided the strongest differentiating factor. In all four measures used to determine the extent of fashion involvement, opinion leaders scored significantly higher than the others: they were more interested in women's clothing fashion, enjoyed more "testing and experimenting with new clothing fashions just out," were more knowledgeable regarding a total of nine specific women's fashions, and more involved in communication of fashion-related issues.

Communication is certainly a powerful predictor of fashion influenceability. First, the fashion leaders were found to be more involved in general personal communication (serving them as channels for gathering information as well as for disseminating it). Moreover, Summers reported that they scored higher on the "social gregariousness" measure and revealed stronger "tendencies toward being progressive, outgoing (less shy), and susceptible to change... [that] may render fashion opinion leaders more 'interesting' conversationalists, which may provide them with larger and more attentive 'audiences' for fashion information."[42] The second aspect of their communicative activity relates to media exposure. In fact, Summers's findings barely support the two-step model in the case of fashion: radio listening, television viewing, and book readership did not differ for leaders and non-leaders. The only significant difference was found with regard to magazine readership, and only then in specific categories of magazines. Women's fashion magazines were the only media category to which opinion leaders were more exposed (that includes readership of home and women's magazines, which have substantial fashion content).

A somewhat more precise measurement of the discriminatory power of various characteristics was provided by Darden and Reynolds, who studied three different samples with a set of seventeen independent variables.[43] The three samples were all males, with one sample drawn from upper-middle-class suburban areas (n=104), one sample of college fraternities (n=76), and one sample of nonfraternity college males (n=102, both college samples taken at the University of Georgia). The set of independent predictors consisted of seventeen variables, grouped into three types: demographic (e.g., age, education), sociological variables (e.g., social participation, offices held in organizations), and predispositional characteristics (e.g., interest in fashion, fashion venturesomeness, cognitive clarity, information seeking). A stepwise regression was run on each sample, with opinion leadership as the dependent variable (measured by a self-designating, five-item scale). Table 8.2 presents those variables that significantly contributed to predictions of fashion leadership.

Table 8.2

Stepwise Predictions of Fashion Opinion Leadership

Variable	Stepwise R²	Beta	P<
Suburban sample (multiple correlation .77, p<.001)			
1. Fashion interest	.416	.447	.005
2. Fashion venturesomeness	.487	.252	.005
3. Cognitive style	,526	−.178	.005
4. Information seeking	.548	.170	.05
5. Relative popularity	.561	−.127	.05
6. Relative self-confidence	.575	.110	.10
7. Number of children	.581	−.149	.05
8. Age	.590	.116	.10
Fraternity sample (multiple correlation .81, p<.0001)			
1. Fashion venturesomeness	.395	.337	.001
2. Fashion interest	.486	.340	.001
3. General self-confidence	.546	.158	.05
4. Relative self-confidence	.575	.258	.005
5. Cognitive clarity	.602	−.180	.01
6. Number of children	.613	−.174	.05
7. Age	.633	.167	.05
8. Number of offices	.643	.119	.10
Independent sample (multiple correlation .74, p<.0001)			
1. Fashion venturesomeness	.310	.437	.005
2. Fashion interest	.415	.288	.005
3. Cognitive clarity	.487	.274	.005
4. Information seeking	.515	.179	.01
5. Number of offices	.535	.156	.05
6. Color-consciousness	.542	−.085	.10
7. Attitude toward change	.552	.098	.10

Note: Variables are listed in order of entry into forward stepwise regression. R² values represent the proportion of total variance explained at that step.

From ''Predicting Opinion Leadership for Men's Apparel Fashions,'' by William R. Darden and Fred D. Reynolds, *Journal of marketing Research*, 9, 1972, p. 326, table 2. Reprinted by permission of the American Marketing Association.

A relatively high proportion of the variance was explained by seven to eight predictors in each sample, ranging from 55 percent in the independent sample to 65 percent in the suburban sample. Despite inter-sample differences, several predictors consistently appeared in the regressions for each sample, indicating that these characteristics were relatively context-free attributes of male fashion leadership. The two most consistent predictors were *fashion interest* and *fashion venturesomeness*. In each sample, these variables were the best predictors and their combined predictive power accounted for 42 to 48 percent of the variance. The differences across samples suggest that fashion leaders should be characterized differently according to their social environment. Thus, we may expect different types of fashion leaders to operate in various social groups. There seem to be some common characteristics for all fashion leaders (e.g., fashion interest, fashion venturesomeness, information seeking, and communication activity), but some attributes will be different according to the leader's social affiliation.

The changing character and role of fashion leaders in different social contexts should be related to another aspect of leadership: the "situational influences." Szybillo conducted a study to examine the effects of perceived fashion scarcity (as a measure of situational influence) on the relationship of opinion leaders to the attractive new fashion.[44] Three fashion items were presented as having varying degrees of distribution to a sample of ninety female subjects in Lafayette, Indiana. The sample was introduced to evaluate a set of nine suits, each suit presented with its distribution condition in terms of numerical data indicating the suits' distribution level in area stores (classified as limited, no information, and extended). They were asked to rate the attractiveness of each suit (on a 100-point, fashion-attractiveness scale) and were themselves rated by the King and Summers opinion leadership scale (see chapter 3).

The 3×3 experimental design cross-classified the three levels of product distribution with three levels of leadership (high, moderate, and low). The attractiveness ratings served as the dependent variable. The results of a two-way analysis of variance revealed a strong leadership by distribution effect ($F=2.75$, $p < .05$), indicating different evaluations by various levels of fashion leadership at different levels of product distribution. When only the simple main effect of product distribution was tested, a very significant difference was found ($F=255.52$, $P < .0001$). The suits assigned to the limited distribution condition yielded the lowest ratings (average of 21.58); the suits assigned to no information condition received medium rating (average of 57.11); and the extended distributed suits were perceived as most attractive (average of 76.19).

Does the distribution condition affect the influentials? The effect of fashion-leadership at each level of the product distribution was significant only for the limited distribution condition. Relative to others, fashion leaders found new fashions that were characterized as having limited distribution to be more attractive. Yet, in other distribution conditions, no significant impact of leadership was detected. It appears that fashion leaders differ from others in their evaluation of new fashion only under the situational influence of limited distribution. Based upon these findings, the researcher concluded that "the relationship between fashion opinion leadership and new product attractiveness can be moderated by situational influences."[45]

Psychological Profiles of the Fashion Leaders

In recent years, information processing has emerged as a theoretical perspective in research on consumers' behavior. It highlighted the active engagement of individuals in acquiring, selecting, excluding, assimilating, structuring, and retaining information. However, it also emphasized individual differences in processing information. Such individual differences were related to differences in cognitive complexity, differences in perceptual skills and personality:

> Assuming that how a person behaves is determined by the interaction of his personality, his environment, and his perception of these, it was hypothesized that the opinion leader in fashion might be identified via an analysis of his/her perceptual style and personality.[46]

Several studies focused on the psychological profiles of fashion leaders, applying a variety of measures designed for the measurement of personality traits and information processing skills. One of the first attempts related three measures to opinion leadership: the locus of control measure,[47] a field dependence test,[48] and two measures of achievement anxiety.[49] A random sample of 102 female students at the University of Alberta were subjected to these measure plus Rogers' opinion leadership scale modified for fashion issues. Opinion leadership in fashion was significantly correlated with only two of the measures: facilitating anxiety ($r=-.37$, $p<.001$) and debilitating anxiety ($r=.28$, $p<.01$). No correlation was found either with locus of the control nor field dependence. Though the correlations with anxiety scales were only modest, they indicated an unexpected trait: fashion leaders tended to score higher on the negative type of anxiety, and score lower on the positive type of anxiety. The researchers tried to explain this surprising finding with a somewhat speculative argument, suggesting that the fashion leader influences others "to bolster her self-concept and compensate for the interference of anxiety."[50] This suggestion is not supported by any data, and the weak correlations do not justify such interpretation. Nevertheless, the study's main contribution is the highlighting of the weak correlations: opinion leadership was found to be independent of such personality traits as field dependence and locus of control, thus directing subsequent research to other aspects.

Such an attempt was the Davis and Lennon study on self-monitoring and fashion opinion leadership.[51] Based upon a review of several studies on fashion and self-conception, they argued that individuals select and wear clothing that they feel reflects their self-concept, self-esteem, and self-perceptions. They focused on one of these constructs of self, the monitoring of one's self-presentation. An individual's self-monitoring involves the disclosure of his or her self-image to others by means of verbal and nonverbal overt behavior. Thus, they hypothesized, one's opinion leadership in clothing fashion may be related to one's general self-monitoring orientations.[52] Grounded upon the findings of the previous studies on self-monitoring (especially the revealed relationship to communication and interpersonal influence),[53] Davis and Lennon expected opinion leaders to rate higher on the self-monitoring scale.

A sample of fifty female undergraduate students completed the self-monitoring scale and a self-designating fashion opinion leadership scale (range of 0–12). By a median split, subjects were classified into high self-monitoring and low self-monitoring groups. Then an average opinion leadership score was computed for each group. The comparison of these averages revealed that the self-monitoring groups differed significantly in the degree of fashion leadership, with high self-monitors displaying opinion leadership characteristics to a greater degree than low self-monitors (averages were 8.04 and 6.40, respectively; $F=6.28$, $p < .01$).

This led the same researchers to another attempt, focusing this time on cognitive complexity. Lennon and Davis suggested this construct, reflecting the extent and style of information search.[54] At the lower end of the continuum of cognitive complexity are those individuals who are concerned with behaving in a socially acceptable manner. They may express anxiety about incorrect actions and fear social sanctions. At the upper end of the continuum are the individuals who will not compromise their values to please others or to conform; however, they are tolerant of uncertainty, ambiguity, and differences of opinion. In fact, this measure combines cognitive traits with attitudes toward social acceptance. Lennon and Davis argued that innovativeness was correlated with cognitive complexity,[55] thus it may relate to personal influenceability.

They tested this idea by studying a sample of fifty female undergraduates with a self-designating scale of opinion leadership and the Hirschman and Adcock scale of fashion innovativeness.[56] The level of cognitive complexity was assessed by a special method (the Paragraph Completion Method).[57] Pearson coefficients were computed for each pair of variables. Since fashion opinion leadership and innovativeness in fashion were known to be related, partial correlations were also computed for each pair of measures with the effects of the third removed. The coefficients are presented in table 8.3.

Table 8.3

**Correlating Fashion Opinion Leadership with
Cognitive Complexity and Innovativeness**

Measure	2	3
1. Fashion leadership	.52*** (.56***)	−.22 (−.33**)
2. Innovativeness		.13 (.29*)
3. Locus of control		

*p<.05, **p<.01, ***p<.001
The coefficients in parenthesis are the partials, controlling for the third measure.

Table based on table 1, Lennon and Davis, op. cit., p. 329.

As expected, opinion leadership and innovativeness were moderately correlated, confirming the previous studies on the partial overlap of these two measures. An inverse relationship was found between fashion leadership and cognitive complexity (r=−.21). When the effects of innovativenss were removed, the correlation became more significant (partial r=−.33). This indicates that unlike fashion innovators, opinion leaders are lower in cognitive complexity. This relation is revealed only when controlling for innovativeness, thus indicating we will not find lower cognitive complexity when leadership and innovativeness are combined in the same person. Lower cognitive complexity among the fashion leaders (controlling innovativeness) suggests, according to Lennon and Davis, their higher conformity to social norms, "since individuals of lower cognitive complexity tend to be concerned about acting in a socially acceptable way."[58] In fact, the revealed tendency is of social conformity (a finding supported by many other studies) and not of any perceptual skill.

Conclusions

• The fashion process, as a collective behavior, is a social mechanism of change, through which a potential fashion object is transmitted from its creation and first introduction to discernible public acceptance, and eventual obsolescence.

• Various communicators are involved in the life cycle of a fashion: the communicators who first introduce it to potential adopters; the fashion leaders who upon adoption introduce it to the public; the mass media that promote and legitimize the new fashion; and the social communication that serves to spread it and create collective conformity to adoption and use and finally to its replacement by more modern and innovative fashion item.

• Several approaches applied communication models to the study of fashion: the symbolic communication approach, the diffusion approach, and the social network approach. These are actually complimentary rather than alternative models, each highlighting other communicative aspects of fashion.

• In the case of fashion, more than in any other area, the adoption of a new fashion item relies heavily on the perceived social acceptance. Nobody better than the updated, well-informed, and socially integrated opinion leaders can provide the needed social support and endorsement. Accordingly, all studies have found that the fashion opinion leaders were the most effective sources of influence in the adoption of fashion items.

• Fashion opinion leadership and fashion innovativeness are not synonymous. Though several studies found some relationship between the two they did not fully overlap. This indicates that some opinion leaders are also the innovators (the dual-role leaders), while others are only mediating between innovators and adopters.

• Fashion leaders were found to differ from non-leaders by measures of sociability, exposure to mass media (limited to magazines and fashion-related media), interest in fashion, fashion venturesomeness, information seeking, and communication activity. Yet, the profiles and functioning of fashion leaders vary according to their social environments and situational influences.

• The notion of individual differences in personality traits, and cognitive and perceptual skills was applied to fashion opinion leadership. It has revealed only partial support for such differentiation, mainly in terms of conformity, individuality, security, and self-monitoring.

Opinion Leaders in Politics

Opinion leadership and personal influence were first introduced by Lazarsfeld and his colleagues at Columbia University's Bureau of Applied Social Research, in their classical studies of the 1940's presidential campaigns and the voters' decision-making.[1] Paradoxically, though the political domain was the first to be studied with regard to the opinion leadership concept, for decades this area has not witnessed the pursue of the methods and concepts of the Columbia research tradition. While the opinion leadership concept was frequently and fruitfully applied to such areas as marketing and fashions, health care, and diffusion of innovations, it has not enjoyed such scholarly attention in the political arena. Only recently was there a "resurrection" of the Columbia research agenda: several studies applied the social network analysis to voters' decision-making process and re-explored the value of personal flow of information and influence in politics.

In this chapter, we will examine the basic arguments of the Columbia studies and those of the challenging Michigan research tradition, the role of social networks, and the key influentials in determining voting behavior.

Traditions of Research on Voting Behavior

The study of voters' decisionmaking followed different directions and focused on various processes and factors. Yet, two distinct research traditions emerged—the Columbia research tradition and the Michigan research tradition.[2] Given the financial resources required to mount sophisticated voting research projects and the intellectual trends in the area, Sheingold suggested that only these two research institutes became the leading and dominant traditions of voting behavior research. The analytical focus of the two traditions differ significantly. The Columbia studies, concerned with *individual* decisionmaking, focused upon sociological independent variables, namely the personal sources of information and influence. The primary emphasis of the Michigan studies, on the other hand, has been attitudinal variables, mainly on the *aggregate* level, focusing upon elections and electorates rather than individual voters. Let us briefly review the two traditions' different approaches to voting research.

The Columbia studies of the 1940 and 1948 presidential campaigns marked a new conception in the study of voting decision making.[3] These early studies, conducted by Columbia University's Bureau of Applied Social Research, raised more questions than gave answers but directed scholarly interest to the role of personal influence in general, and opinion leaders in particular. The first two studies focused their attention on the findings about the stability of voters' choices and preferences. Most of the voters do not change their opinion or choice: the actual proportion of stable voters was 87 percent in 1940 and 75 percent in 1948. This led the researchers to explain the voting stability by various social mechanisms. They argued, for example, that voting intentions were not simply the result of campaign effects or changing mood, but the cumulative product of social affiliations, group pressures, and personal contacts. The limited impact of election campaigns, namely in the more frequent reinforcing of existing attitudes and preferences than in changing them, was explained by several social factors:

1. *The power of primary groups and their political homogeneity.* Lazarsfeld and his colleagues argued that most people interacted during the campaigns with other members of their primary groups who usually shared the same attitudes, preferences, and predispositions.[4]
2. *Selective exposure, selective perception, and selective projection.* Most people paid primary attention to information that reinforced their original intentions and perceived issues and arguments in a selective way that suited their pre-existing images and preferences.[5]
3. *The role and impact of opinion leaders.* Most voters were affected by personal sources and mainly some influential persons. These influential opinion leaders eliminated or modified information inconsistent with the political predispositions and prejudices of the group.[6]
4. *The role of organizations.* Politically involved organizations devoted most of their effort to mobilizing the faithful rather than converting the uninitiated.[7]

The major conclusion of the Columbia research was that voting is a group process, a combined impact of social actors that limits the effects of mass-mediated campaigns by channeling them in a way that reinforces existing preferences and attitudes. Yet, the Columbia studies pre-dated the introduction of television and televised conventions, debates, and campaigns. Pool, as early as 1959, was predicting the significant role of the new medium: "There is little doubt that the effect of television will be profound. With the use of radio and television, and the decline of party machines and political fervor, the direct impact of the media is increasing and that of opinion leaders declining."[8] Ten years later, Mendelsohn and Crespi confidently summarized some of the documented effects of television on American politics:

> Television has spawned four major changes in traditional American politics: 1. It has altered the process of nominating candidates at party conventions; 2. it has altered campaigning; 3. it has altered traditional party structures and functions; and 4. it has helped to encourage questioning of the traditional ways of choosing and electing candidates, and as a consequence, will aid in ushering in the new politics of the future.[9]

The power of television as a political instrument was soon revealed by numerous studies.[10] The growing importance of television was only one of the weaknesses of the Columbia paradigm. Other problems were related to methodological procedures. For instance, a major limitation derived from its dependence on self reports as measures of influence and decision making. This raised serious doubts as to the accuracy of certain key findings.[11] "Furthermore," argued Sheingold, "these self report data did not and could not reveal the social structure context of decision making."[12] The growing criticism of the Columbia studies will be reviewed in chapter 14. We can conclude that it led to the Columbia tradition's decline and rare follow-up efforts as well as the rise of alternative approaches. Among these alternative voting research schools, the most prominent one was associated with the University of Michigan's Survey Research Center (SRC).

The Michigan tradition traces its intellectual heritage to V. O. Key, the salient critic of the Columbia voting research.[13] The SRC researchers, following Key, were more interested in the study of political aspects of voting, such as political attitudes, political knowledge, and ideology. Contrary to the Columbia tradition, this line of research suggests that the personal attributes an individual brings to the campaign with him or her effectively determine voting behavior. Key presented the idea that voters are swayed by their own policy views and by their own evaluations of the candidates' performance. The SRC researchers have systematically studied the attitudinal bases of voting behavior. They highlighted the role of individual attitudes with respect to party identification, issue orientation, and candidate orientation. The major criticism they directed against the Columbia voting research was that it has "taken the politics out of the study of voting."[14] Moreover, the Michigan critics also argued that political attitudinal variables would provide better explanation of voting behavior than the sociological variables used by the Columbia researchers:

> The experience of the last two presidential elections has shown us, however, that the simple classification of voters into sociological categories does not have the explanatory power that at first appeared. It has been demonstrated that the application of the Lazarsfeld index...resulted in a prediction of the vote not remarkably better than chance.[15]

The Michigan research agenda, which was focused upon partisanship and individual attitudes, shifted the scholarly attention from social predictors to personal, political factors. With growing sophistication of their measures and analyses, the Michigan researchers emphasized key variables, such as party identification and realignment,[16] party loyalty,[17] and partisanship.[18]

The criticism of the Columbia research tradition,[19] the challenging research agendas, and the relatively small amount of follow-up studies in the political domain created a scientific vacuum. Sheingold complained that "the failure of students of voting to follow up on the Columbia research has created a vacuum of considerable analytical and practical significance."[20] Similarly, Burnham argued that "...great many lacunae in our understanding of American politics....appear to be particularly concentrated at the level of macro-analysis, where the concern is with the quantitative study of an aggregate system of behavior rather than with the behavior of individuals within the system."[21] And yet, recently, there has been a resurrection of the research agenda suggested by the Columbia studies. Several political scientists have expressed renewed interest in social, environmental factors. For instance, Pomper wrote:

> Perhaps the major fault of the Michigan studies has been the comparative neglect of the political environment as an independent variable. The methodology of survey research has brought an overemphasis on the individual behavior of isolated respondents. The influences upon these respondents have been

studied only indirectly, through the voters' personal perceptions and actions. But voters in fact are not isolated, for they are affected by their environment, the mass media, the economic system, and the prevailing ideology. More attention must be devoted to these shaping influences.[22]

Two factors may explain the revival of the Columbia tradition or at least some of its ideas: (a) *The shifting focus of interest from the voting act to the voters' process of decision making during the campaign.* Sheingold noted that "What such critics [of the Columbia research] missed was that the Columbia researchers—particularly in their analyses of group process—were not primarily interested in explaining the vote itself. Their dependent variable had shifted, albeit implicitly, from the partisan outcome of voting to the within-campaign movement of voting intentions."[23] (b) *The emergence of network analysis theory and methods, and their applicability to the study of voting behavior.* Weatherford was one of the first to suggest the applicability of interpersonal network analysis and the Columbia concepts to the study of political behavior: "Even the more recent advances in network theory and methods have taken place outside the province of political studies and have not been integrated into current research. As the rich vein of individual-level analyses of political behavior is exhausted, a return to the social context of political decision making promises not only the completion of an unfinished research agenda but also the production of new insight."[24] Let us turn now to the role of personal networks in voting decision making.

Social Networks and Voters' Decision Making

Recent decades have witnessed a growing interest in the study of social networks.[25] Yet, the notion of social networks is not very new. As Laumann argues, "Close examination reveals that network analysis is, at least in part, some rather old ideas that have been refurbished and made more attractive by being combined with sophisticated mathematical and quantitative tools."[26] Modern network analysis may owe some of its prosperity to modern technologies of data processing, namely high-speed computers, special programs for sociometric data analysis, and sophisticated mathematical procedures like matrix algebra and sociometric topology. It was not only technology and improved methodology that led to the revival of network analysis. As Alba and Kadushin noted,[27] the revival of network analysis is attributable to an increasing recognition of the importance of networks in relating micro to macro analysis. Fischer highlighted this promise well:

> Society affects us largely through tugs at the strands of our networks—shaping our attitudes, providing opportunities, making demands on us, and so forth. And it is by tugging those same strands that we make our individual impact on society— influencing other people's opinions, obtaining favors from 'insiders', forming action groups. . . In sum, to understand the individual in society, we need to understand the fine mesh of social relations between the person and society; that is, we must understand social networks.[28]

Network analysis provided a promising bridge between small groups and individuals at the micro level and the large-scale social process at the macro level. Granovetter argued that "the analysis of processes in interpersonal networks provides the most fruitful micro-macro bridge. In one way or another, it is through these networks that small-scale interaction becomes translated into large-scale patterns, and that these, in turn, feed back into small groups."[29]

Two broad approaches to operative network research may be distinguished. The first was inspired by sociometric studies and works toward mapping social relations and applying structural measures. Some of these studies focus on the structural patterns of small groups with the entire sociomatrix being studied.[30] This necessitates full mapping of all the contacts among all the members of a small and clearly bounded group, thus limiting its applicability to the study of large social units. A second approach focuses less on social structure and more on "personal networks." This approach follows the Columbia tradition by tracing the individual's sources of information and influence. Such a design addresses several of the problems that make the production of sociomatrices impractical for large and open populations. The focus on egocentric networks enable inferences beyond individual properties and may be easily applied to the political domain: "such aspects of interpersonal political contact as the social status and partisanship of acquaintances, frequency of political discussion, levels of involvement, and chain length can be charted with such data."[31]

An attempt to apply social networks to political behavior was reported by Weatherford. He studied data from a two-wave national sample survey conducted by the Center for Political Studies for the National Election Studies in 1980.[32] Weatherford focused upon local networks, the neighborhoods' networks: their politicization, climate of political discussion, and partisan composition. He found that the neighborhood in which a politicized social network is likely to arise is relatively parochial and localistic, peopled by residents who center other aspects of their lives in the local area. The next step involved determining the impact of the local networks on their members. Evidence that political networks exist, however, does not show that network interactions are influential in shaping individual attitudes. Thus, Weatherford's hypothesis suggested that there was a main effect on individual partisan opinion, attributable to network partisanship. This effect was studied by measuring the impact of the network on its members' attitudes in three political domains: attitudes toward economic management, minority programs, and presidential performance.

Of the eighteen tests of the hypothesized effects of network properties on individual attitudes, there are fourteen confirmed expectations: network partisanship shows a significant impact upon opinionation. Only issue agreement and frequency of contact in the network failed to support the hypothesis. On the other hand, the networks' politicization, party similarity, intimacy, and duration all had strong influence on individual attitudes in each of the three attitude categories. This can be partly explained by the within-group agreement on political partisanship and political issues supported by the intimacy and duration of contacts. Despite this study's limits in terms of sampling and the use of "neighborhood networks," it provided a primary support for the "social contextual effects" approach to the study of political behavior. Furthermore, as Weatherford concluded: "Network studies are important, however, not so much as a methodological adjunct to the contextual effects approach, but primarily because the formation of political networks and the transmission of political influence are ill-understood—especially when compared with our knowledge of the individual-level antecedents of political choice."[33]

The flow of personal influence in social networks within the political context was further studied in a more thorough investigation, which focused on the flow of political information.[34] Huckfeldt and Sprague followed the social contextual vein, arguing that "Political behavior may be understood in terms of individuals tied together by, and located within, networks, groups, and other social formations that largely determine their opportunities for the exchange of meaningful political information."[35] The database combined a 1984 election survey of citizens in South Bend, Indiana, with a subsequent survey of people with whom these citizens discussed politics (the "discussants"). The data were collected in a three-wave panel survey of approximately 1,500 respondents prior to, during, and after the 1984 presidential election.

Networks were measured from two vantage points: first, that of the main respondent in the survey; second, that of the political discussant named by the main respondent. Based upon the responses, a sample of 900 discussants were interviewed. The analysis revealed that individuals do purposefully construct information networks corresponding to their own political preferences. Most of the respondents could correctly identify their discussants' voting choice (Reagan, Mondale, or nonvoter). Perceptual accuracy increased in politically congruent relationships, the more frequent the relationships were.

A similar finding regarding personal influence and political behavior was reported by Finkel, Muller, and Opp.[36] They proposed two models to study why individuals participate in collective political action—a personal influence model and a collective rationality model. These models were tested for predicting two forms of political behavior—participation in legal and illegal protests. Data were collected from three German samples, a national sample and two samples from protest-prone communities. The analysis revealed the explanatory power of the personal influence model, which was efficient in both forms of political behavior, while the collective rationality model was less efficient and supported only for legal protest.

A more recent attempt to study voters' information sources in terms of social environments examined American voters in the 1988 presidential campaign.[37] Beck based his study on the need to return to the Columbia agenda:

> For most Americans, these personal intermediaries are a critical source of information about politics and of political evaluations, as they probably always have been...In view of the acknowledged importance of these intermediaries, it is surprising that over the years so little research has focused on their role in individual political behavior. The seminal research on the topic by Paul Lazarsfeld and his colleagues at Columbia University is drawn from data now four decades old...Since the Columbia studies, research on political behavior has been rooted in intellectually competing social structural and individualistic approaches, neither of which focused directly on the social process of intermediation.[38]

Beck's study focused on the voters' sources of information or intermediaries. Data were collected through a telephone survey of the Ohio electorate after the 1988 presidential election (n=652). About three quarters of the respondents reported discussing the election with someone, usually with their spouses or co-workers. In all, 62 percent of married respondents discussed politics with their spouses, and 55 percent of those working outside the home discussed politics with fellow workers. Individual characteristics affected the exposure to personal sources. The political attentiveness variables were the most important correlates of exposure to personal intermediaries. Political attentiveness, measured by interest in the campaign, concern about who would win, and how well-informed about politics the respondent was, provided strong and positive correlations with exposure to personal sources. These relationships suggest a motivational basis for communication activity with the most attentive individuals typically more involved in personal political communication. Other interesting differences were found between men and women: women reported more reliance on personal sources within the family than did men.[39]

Another finding consistent with the early Columbia studies, as well as with the more recent Huckfeldt and Sprague study previously reported, was the concordance between individuals and their personal intermediaries. The hardly unexpected finding of this analysis is how rarely respondents see themselves in discordant personal networks. The overwhelming tendency is towards shared choices and attitudes, especially within the family. This does not necessarily indicate the homogenizing impact of personal influence but probably does reflect the initial similarities in basic viewpoints in addition plus the tendency to choose discussants with similar political views. The notion of political homophily suggests that "personal networks of political discussants provide protective cocoons for an individual's political preferences... This cocoon is more likely to be penetrated, however, as one's network expands beyond the walls of home and family into the broader home."[40] Moreover, Beck discovered that concordance is negatively correlated with political attentiveness. The people most interested, involved, and informed about politics are the most exposed to dissonance in their personal networks. Presumably, this is because they are most capable of resisting the influence of dissonant information and can rely on their own judgments and information. Nevertheless, when only the most important discussant was examined, even the highly attentive respondents reported concordant relations with this person.

Beck also measured the role of the mass media in the capacity of political intermediaries. Though many respondents reported the mass media as sources of political information, the rates were lower than those reported for personal sources. Moreover, there was no indication of concordance of media-individual preferences as revealed in the personal networks. The media were almost three times as likely as personal networks to challenge an individual's preferences. To many, the media provide the only dissonant source in an otherwise supportive social environment. Thus, social networks were found to be active and popular channels of political information. However, the information flow in these networks tended to reinforce pre-existing political preferences (as opposed to altering them), because generally people prefer exposure to like-minded personal sources. Under certain circumstances, though, personal intermediaries may play important roles in challenging preferences and perhaps even inducing partisan change. People whose political networks extend beyond their families are exposed to more dissonant information. This conduct contact can overcome the inertial force of political homophily and plays a significant role in electoral change.

The return to the Columbia tradition is illustrated by another recent study that focused on the "interpersonal gateways to political information and influence."[41] Straits joins the emerging interest in the flow of political information and influence in personal networks. While previous studies of this flow sampled specific segments of personal networks (such as parents,[42] spouses,[43] male friends,[44] neighbors,[45] and other political discussants),[46] Straits extended the scope to include all types of personal ties and discussion partners. The network data for his study were from the 1987 General Social Survey (GSS) in which respondents were asked information about political discussions, the partners for these discussions and frequency of discussions, as well as background characteristics, political orientation (interest in politics and partisanship), and media exposure. The data were subjected to regression analysis with the frequency of political conversations with various discussants serving as the dependent variable. This analysis revealed the importance of close, strong personal ties: closeness of personal relationships and frequency of contacts were the significant determinants of political intercourse. The respondents engaged more frequently in political conversations with spatially proximate associates (spouses and co-workers):

> The findings underscore the importance of including close relatives and other strong ties in studying social contexts of political behavior. Even though spouses may be quite similar in education, age, and other social characteristics, their network gateways through which political information and influence flow may be quite different. The results suggest, for example, that a married-couple's exposure to political information is

enlarged by co-worker links to workplace environments. Also, individuals uninterested in politics nevertheless may receive considerable exposure to political information from politically motivated close associates.[47]

The realization that there is a reliance on personal networks, face-to-face discussions, and social ties in an individual's political decision-making process results in several attempts to map these social networks. Laumann used network data in the Detroit Area Study to determine how network factors influenced political variables.[48] He suggested that different types of homogeneity would affect different attitudes. For instance, attitudes about moral and religious issues should correlate with ethno-religious network homogeneity; but attitudes toward occupational status should correlate with occupational homogeneity. He continued and demonstrated that, in fact, homogeneous networks "foster and sustain more 'extreme,' clear cut and consistent attitudes then heterogeneous groups."[49] Subsequently, Laumann also established that network density had an effect on attitudes, including political opinions. He referred to loose-knit "radial" networks and to close-knit, "interlocking" networks. His study revealed that "interlocking networks serve as more effective social anchors for an individual's attitudes leading to more well crystallized attitudes on various issues."[50]

Marsden examined the discussion networks of Americans.[51] Using the survey data from the 1985 General Social Survey (GSS), he studied several aspects of the personal networks in which Americans discuss "important matters." He found that these networks are small, kin-centered, relatively dense, and very homogeneous. The size of the network was found to vary with the individual's characteristics: network range was greatest among the young, the highly educated, and metropolitan residents. The same database was used by Bienenstock, Bonacich, and Oliver who followed Laumann's suggestions regarding networks' impact on the individual's political attitudes.[52] They used the 1985 GSS data to determine if network homogeneity and density magnify the individual differences in terms of polarization of social and political attitudes. Their analysis revealed that structural characteristics of social networks (homogeneity and density) have a powerful impact on their members' attitudes regarding various social and political issues (such as racism, feminism, morality, and free speech). The findings led the researchers to conclude that "understanding the characteristics of social networks could be used by political behaviorists to increase their understanding of factors that contribute to attitude formation and maintenance."[53]

The mapping of personal networks and their revealed impact on personal attitudes led to scaling the network positions according to their influenceability or importance (for example, Laumann and Pappi applied network analysis to a German community where they focused on the community leaders, their functions, and their characteristics).[54] Are there opinion leaders, active and influential, in the political attitudes domain?

Influentials and Followers in the Political Domain

While the early Columbia studies are commonly considered the first formulation of the opinion leadership concept, it is interesting to note that at least one other study, during the same time period, used the notion of "informal leaders" to personal influence in an election campaign. This was the study of the 1950 senatorial election campaign of 1950, conducted by Lowe and McCormick.[55] Without any relation or reliance on the Columbia studies, Lowe and McCormick set out to measure the influence of formal and informal leaders in Madison, Wisconsin. Formal leaders were well known public men while informal leaders were friends or relatives whose advice regarding political issues was commonly sought by others. Before and after the 1950 elections 743 interviews were conducted. It was found that most respondents had three formal leaders (mainly local politicians) and one informal leader. To learn about the informal leaders named by respondents, the researchers interviewed a sample of these leaders (58 percent of them, or 223).

The data showed that informal political leaders, compared with the individuals who named them, tended to be male (84 percent),[56] older, more educated, members of white-collar occupations, and members of many social organizations. Additionally, the informal leaders were also found to be more interested in political issues and more politically active than their followers. The analysis of the attitudes of leaders and their respective followers revealed strong correlations: correlating the attitudes regarding three issues (government spending, health program, and farm program) yielded a significantly positive coefficient of .7, implying "a considerable amount of agreement between the respondents and their leaders."[57] Moreover, the analysis also found evidence of the leaders' effectiveness: the researchers found that the voters tended to change their opinion to what they considered their leaders' opinions to be. One should, nonetheless, be aware of the nature of the measurement of influence: "In all of the statistical tests the respondents' opinions behaved as if they were influenced by the leaders' opinions; ...Leader influence may then probably be inferred from positive correlations between respondent-leader discrepancies and respondents' later changes of opinion."[58] However, most importantly, unrelated to and independent of the Columbia arguments and findings, Lowe and McCormick concluded that: "These informal leaders apparently stood between the public leaders and the voters, translating, modifying, supporting, or opposing campaign issues and candidates, according to their judgment."[59]

The first test of Katz and Lazarsfeld's opinion leadership idea[60] in the political arena was conducted in Sweden. Anderson[61] studied opinion leaders in four Swedish communities, between 1956 and 1960, soon after the publication of *Personal Influence*. Samples of the adult populations in Malmo (n=799), Kolsva (n=175), Vasteras (n=363), and Bralanda (n=254) were interviewed and asked to name one or more individuals whose opinions on some current political issues were considered important and whose advice was heeded. Personal interviews were conducted with the 112 influentials identified in the four communities. One of the most distinct features of these 112 leaders was their involvement in various social and political organizations. The influentials were found to be more active in each social organization, ranging from labor unions to athletic associations. However, the greatest influential-follower participation discrepancy was within the political organization category: 83 percent of the influentials are active in these organizations whereas only 7 and 4 percent among the male and female followers, respectively. Not only did the influentials participate in more organizations; often they held offices in those organizations (especially in union associations and political organizations) and were more active members than the followers.

In the same, study opinion leadership was also related to attempted influence: Anderson's survey included a number of questions about attempts to influence other people politically. These questions were: 1. Does the respondent ever show articles in newspapers and magazines to friends and acquaintances and suggest that they read them? 2. Has the respondent ever asked a friend or acquaintance to go with him or her to a political meeting? 3. Do the respondent and his or her friends and acquaintances ever discuss political matters after having heard radio programs about political issues? 4. Does the respondent ever suggest to other people that they should listen to political radio programs? 5. Has the respondent tried to convince someone else to vote for the political party for whom he or she votes?

Some of these items involved the two-step flow model (items 1, 3, and 4), that is, different ways in which the opinion leader can help to transmit a message from the mass media to his or her followers. The other items involved direct influence regarding political activity and voting. Table 9.1 presents a comparison of the influentials with the general sample in the four communities, according to self-reported attempts to exert influence.

Table 9.1

Attempting to Influence: Influentials Compared to Others

Type of Activity Reported	Percent of Influentials	Percent of General Sample in			
		Malmo	Vasteras	Kolsva	Bralanda
1. Show articles and suggest reading	71	22	22	25	23
2. Ask to go to political meeting	71	11	10	16	22
3. Discuss contents of political radio programs	92	50	44	38	46
4. Suggest to listen to political radio programs	61	18	14	18	23
5. Tried to convince others to vote for a party	60	12	11	23	21
Averages of the above activities	71	23	20	26	27
Sample size	n = 112	n = 799	n = 363	n = 175	n = 254

From "Opinion Influentials and Political Opinion Foramtion in Four Swedish Communities," by Bo Anderson, *International Social Science Journal*, 14)2), 1962, p. 326, table 8. Reprinted by permission of Blackwell Publishers.

It is clear from the data in table 9.1 that the influentials are considerably more active on all five counts than the sample of general populations in each of the four communities. Moreover, Anderson found that not only do the influentials report more attempts to influence and give opinion but their followers verify it: the influentials are often asked for advice and opinion on various political issues ranging from voting to pension plans. The political influentials, according to the Swedish study, are very similar to their characterization in the early American studies:

They are politically active; they come into contact with many people through their activities in various voluntary organizations and through their jobs; they speak at meetings, participate in discussions, . . . they follow the political debate in the press closely and frequently discuss the contents of mass media with other people; they are often asked for their opinions about current political affairs and often try to mold the opinions of other people.[62]

The opinion leaders' attempts to influence others was also the subject of another early leadership study in the political domain: Ostlund's study of interpersonal communication upon a political issue.[63] This study was concerned with the diffusion and persuasive role of interpersonal communication due to the announcement of George McGovern's decision to drop Thomas Eagleton from the 1972 Democratic national ticket following the disclosure of Eagleton's past mental illness. A survey, conducted four days after the announcement, yielded 108 completed interviews, measuring the awareness of the event, sources of information, change of opinions, and other variables. Only 15 percent stated that they first learned of McGovern's decision from personal sources, yet nearly all respondents reported discussing the subject with others within four days after the event. Nevertheless, despite the rather high level of interpersonal communication, little opinion change was reported by the respondents. Ostlund explained this finding: "While respondents may have overstated their resistance to influence as an ego-defense mechanism, it seems likely that conversations about McGovern's announcement served largely to reinforce initial reactions, . . . voters may have tended, unintentionally, to converse with others of similar political persuasion, as some previous studies have argued."[64]

Although little opinion change apparently occurred, many respondents sought to influence others: 46 percent of the respondents claimed to have made some attempt to convince others to adopt their opinion, while 54 percent made no such attempt. Ostlund classified these two types of respondents as leaders and non-leaders, though this classification hardly relates to the measure of opinion leadership. (He actually classified the individuals according to their self-reported attempt to influence others, a measure far from providing a satisfactory leadership scale.) Consequently, almost half of the sample were categorized as leaders. Yet, when he compared the leaders with the non-leaders according to their sources about McGovern's decision, an interesting pattern emerged: 42 percent of the leaders reported the radio as their source compared to only 30 percent among the non-leaders. Interpersonal communication served as the source for only 4 percent of the leaders, compared to 22 percent of the non-leaders. Television was mentioned slightly more by leaders than by non-leaders (42 and 38 percent, respectively). Given the restricted sample and the crude categorization of opinion leadership, this analysis revealed some supporting evidence to the two-step flow model in the political domain.

Another aspect of political opinion leaders was studied by Bockman and Gayk who were interested in the leaders' political efficacy and trust. They selected a community in proximity to the Los Angeles metropolitan area (designated the pseudonym Spectra) and employed a random and snowball sampling in order to identify two types of leaders: (a) opinion leaders, according to the Columbia studies' conceptualization, using similar question to the one used by Katz and Lazarsfeld.[66] There were 234 opinion leaders identified by the respondents; 73 of them were interviewed either as part of the snowball sample or random sample; and (b) "communication leaders," operationally defined as individuals who received many sociometric choices as sources of political information. Eighty-four such leaders were identified, 50 of them interviewed. The leaders and the general sample were tested by scales, designed by Campbell et al., to measure the individual's efficacy and trust in the political system.[67] The two leader-type groups were then compared to a sample of local decision-makers (chosen by local organization leaders as "top decision-makers in the community," n=29), and a sample of citizens (n=282). The comparison was based on the trust and efficacy levels of these samples. Table 9.2 presents the results of this comparison.[68]

Table 9.2

Political Orientation of Leaders and Other Groups

Political Orientation	Opinion Leaders	Communication Leaders	Decision-Makers	Others
Low trust/low efficacy	15.1%	18.0%	17.2%	31.6%
High trust/low efficacy	8.2%	2.0%	0.0%	26.2%
Low trust/high efficacy	41.1%	42.0%	31.0%	17.4%
High trust/high efficacy	35.6%	38.0%	51.7%	24.8%
Total	100%	100%	100%	100%
	(73)	(50)	(29)	(282)

Though this comparison was not originally produced and analyzed by Bockman and Gayk (who preferred the comparison within leaders), it nevertheless produced interesting differences and similarities. The two types of leaders do not differ and it appears both have high efficacy (about 70 to 76 percent being high on the efficacy scale) and resemble the decision-makers (82 percent being high efficacy). The others, the "regular" respondents, are quite different: only 42 percent of them are high efficacy individuals while the majority are low (58 percent). The same pattern appears with regard to trust: the two types of leaders and the decision-makers are for the most part low in trust, while the ordinary respondents are usually high in trust. The most common combination among the leaders is low trust/high efficacy, the decision-makers are most frequently high trust/high efficacy, and the "others" are most frequently low trust/low efficacy. These results indicate that the communication and influence leaders are more informed about but also and less trusting of the political system. They share with the decision-makers the high level of efficacy, based on familiarity and information though, unlike the decision-makers, they appear to distrust the political elites. The non-leaders, as expected, are low on efficacy and are divided between high trust and low trust. Finally, the similarities between the two types of leaders suggest that these are, in fact, two sub-types of the opinion leaders, comprising those who are information leaders and those who are influence leaders.[69]

A test of the actual bearing of opinion leaders on their followers' political attitudes was applied by Black, whose report was entitled: "Opinion Leaders: Is Anyone Following?"[70] Using a questionnaire with self-reported leadership items, Black classified a sample into three groups: "recent advisors" (the opinion leaders, those who are more likely to be asked for their opinion on national issues and were recently consulted for advice on these issues), "potential advisors" (who may be more likely to be consulted but were not asked recently), and "non-advisors" (who are never consulted). When these three groups were compared in their political participation,[71] the recent advisors, or the opinion leaders, scored higher on all measures of political activity ranging from participation in political conversations to actual attempts of persuading others on voting issues. But Black went beyond identifying the political opinion leaders: he endeavored to measure their influence upon change of opinions. To trace such a change, he conducted series of panel surveys, four times a year, from 1975 to 1978, on various governmental activities (such as health measures, space exploration, defense, or employment). A change of opinion was measured by a comparison of quarterly changes, computed separately for each of the three groups.

This comparison showed that the opinion leaders (recent advisors) altered their opinions earlier than nonadvisors for five of the six issues studied. Potential advisors, on the other hand, changed later than the opinion leaders, but earlier than the nonadvisors for all the issues. When the comparison was repeated within each demographic group, the pattern did not vary: opinion leaders were always the first to change while the rest followed their decisions. The finding that opinion leaders are the first to change opinions and attitudes does not, however, prove they are the source of change for others. As Black himself noted, "Those nonadvisors who changed the later may have been influenced by those who changed their opinions earlier, but they may simply be responding to the media at a slower pace."[72]

A similar problem is found in Omura and Talarzyk's study of opinion leaders as shapers of public opinion.[73] The issue under study was the impending impeachment of Richard M. Nixon, 1974, following the Watergate scandal. The researchers examined the interpersonal flow of influence of those who favored versus those who were against Nixon's impeachment. A national sample of 1,000 households was asked to return a mail questionnaire. The questionnaire included the King and Summers's modified opinion leadership scale (see chapter 3), as well as questions regarding opinion about Nixon's impeachment and exposure to mass media. Significant differences were found across opinion leadership levels. High opinion leadership was found to be associated with supporting the impeachment: the majority of the supporters came from the high and medium leadership groups while most of those opposing the impeachment came from the medium and low leadership groups. The same differences were found also in each of the six opinion leadership items: those who answered the "leader's answer" were supporting the act more than those who gave the "non-leader answer." This analysis revealed that a small group (16.6 percent of the sample) are high on the leadership scale as well as supporting the impeachment. Because they were also the earlier supporters of the opinion that later united most of the Americans, the researchers deducted that they "may be viewed as the population segment that could have shaped public sentiment toward impeaching then President Nixon."[74] This is a somewhat questionable deduction as it associates early change of opinion with influencing those who change later. One of the potential sources may be, for example, the mass media. Let us examine the impact of media versus personal influence on political attitudes and choices, a relationship that led to several remodifications of the original opinion leadership concept within the political domain.

Remodifications of Original Concepts

At this stage, the roles of mass media and personal influence remain unclear. We know that some individuals, the opinion leaders, are more involved in and better informed about political issues. We know that they report attempting to influence others while others identify them as sources of advice and guidance on these issues. Yet, there are instances in which the public relies upon the media (see, for example, Robinson's findings on "the press as kingmaker"),[75] when national surveys revealed that only few respondents identified "other people" as an important source of news on certain issues and events.[76] In other cases, public opinion was not following the directions endorsed by the mass media.[77] What are the actual influences of the media and personal influence? Robinson suggested and tested several models of media/interpersonal influences on voters during election campaign.[78] Some of his models served as suggested remodifications of the original two-step flow model (see chapter 14), but at this stage let us focus on the findings relevant to sources of information and political persuasion. Robinson's data came from the surveys conducted by the Center for Political Studies (CPS) of the University of Michigan. These surveys examined mass communication and interpersonal communication behavior of a national sample of 1,346 American adults after the 1968 elections (Nixon vs. Humphry). Robinson compared the "opinion givers"[79] with the "opinion receivers" and the "nondiscussants" in terms of their sources of information and various forms of political behavior during the campaign. The results of this comparison are presented in table 9.3.

Opinion givers were clearly more exposed to mass media than the others (opinion receivers and nondiscussants). In every medium, and especially with regard to print media, the opinion givers used the media as source of information to a greater extent than the other groups. These differences support the previous studies' findings on opinion leaders' use of the mass media. Table 9.3 also compares the political behavior of the three groups: the opinion givers are more active in all forms of political behavior. They tend to attend political meetings or rallies and belong to political organization, work for a party and donate money, display their party's button or sticker—far more than the other two groups. Thus, the opinion givers are more involved, more interested and more active in the political daily life. Are they also successful in their attempted influence? Unlike former studies, Robinson did not rely on simply asking respondents to say if they were influenced or not but examined the actual vote and the sources of influence (media and opinion givers).

Table 9.3

Comparison of Opinion Givers and Others in the 1968 Campaign (U.S.)

Mass Media Usage	% Opinion Givers	% Opinion Receivers	% Nondiscussants
Television	94	85	87
Newspaper	85	67	68
Magazine	51	29	25
Radio	49	33	40
Political Behavior			
Attended meetings/rallies	8	4	2
Belonged to organizations	7	3	1
Worked for a party	14	3	1
Was asked for money	35	23	14
Donated money to parties	16	7	4
Displayed button or sticker	28	14	6
Voted in 1968 election	88	79	66
Sample size	n=432	n=229	n=685

From "Interpersonal Influence in Election Campaigns: Two Step Flow Hypotheses," by John P. Robinson, *Public Opinion Quarterly*, 40, 1976, p. 312, table 1. Reprinted by permission of the University of Chicago Press.

Robinson's analysis involved a Multiple Classification Analysis (MCA), which included party identification, pre-election intention, and twelve other predictors. He found that the personal influence accounted for 14 percent differentials (Humphry minus Nixon), while newspaper endorsement accounted for 6 percent differential. However, media and interpersonal influences differed from one group to another. When the sample is broken into the three sub-groups the opinion givers seem far less influenced than others by any influence attempts. The opinion receivers, on the other hand, were influenced by the personal contact whereas the nondiscussants show an 11 percent differential in voting behavior with relation to newspaper endorsements. (As nondiscussants they are not exposed to personal influence.) The findings are thus suggesting two different influence patterns for different groups: the advice seekers who are exposed to personal contacts are more influenced by their opinion givers; and those who avoid personal contacts and do not discuss these issues are more influenced by the mass media. The two-step model appears to be correct only in specific circumstances: "when interpersonal sources and mass media sources are compared or are in conflict, interpersonal sources wield greater influence."[80] Opinion leaders are indeed effective sources but only when there is a demand for their guidance.

Finally, another remodification of the opinion leadership concept in the political domain was suggested by Hellevik and Bjorklund who studied opinion leaders with relation to political extremism.[81] The relationship between political activism and political extremism in terms of opinion leaders' presence and activity had never been questioned prior to this study. It appeared that, being well established in their social settings, opinion leaders would be more conservative. The fact that they personify widely accepted social norms[82] and were found to be more conservative in various areas,[83] led to the inevitable assumption that they will be politically conservative or at least not extremists. And yet, one might hypothesize an increasing level of attempts to influence the opinions of others as one moves from the center (of the political continuum) toward either extreme. The intensity of opinion was found to increase with extremity and the interest in politics was higher among those at the extremes. In a German survey conducted by the Allensbach Research Center, August 1990, the 5,038 respondents were classified on a scale of political left to right and asked about their level of interest in politics. The percentages of the interested individuals on the left-to-right scale (grouped into five levels) were: 63, 57, 48, 60, and 68. More interested individuals were concentrated at the extremes. On the other hand, the extreme positions are held, usually, by few, while the majority of people are located in more central, moderate positions. The general frequencies do not represent the opinion leaders, so the interesting question remains: where are the opinion leaders on the political map?

The answer, given by Hellevik and Bjorklund after an analysis of a survey with 14,000 respondents from Norway, is based on a surprising finding. Utilizing the monthly omnibus surveys held in Norway representing the adult population, the respondents were asked to locate themselves on a self-placement, left-right scale with ten positions (one representing extreme left and ten extreme right). They were then asked three questions of their own evaluation of political participation, activity, and influence. These questions served as an index to identify the political opinion leaders. The next step involved the computation of the frequencies of opinion leaders on the political continuum (and compare it to the general public's distribution). Table 9.4 presents the distributions of the general sample and the opinion leaders, in various domains, on the left-right scale.[84]

The general public, as expected, revealed a bell-shaped, almost normal curve: most of them placed themselves in the center or near-the-center positions. But the political opinion leaders's curve was

U-shaped! That is, more political opinion leaders were found in the extremes, and the proportion of opinion leaders increased the more extreme the position is, to both right and left sides.[85] The opinion leaders in other domains (health, fashion, shopping) were almost evenly distributed across the political categories while only the political influentials were found to be extremists. How can we explain the surprising differences between the general public and the political opinion leaders' political distribution?

Table 9.4

Opinion Leaders' Political Positions: The Norwegian Case

| | Left | | | | | | | | | Right |
	1	2	3	4	5	6	7	8	9	10
General Sample (N)	213	357	1237	1855	2453	1809	1636	1597	540	328
Political Opinion Leaders (%)	26	42	36	32	25	27	31	36	39	43
Health Opinion Leaders (%)	33	31	30	30	30	31	31	32	27	32
Shopping Opinion Leaders (%)	36	35	36	38	41	40	41	40	40	36
Fashion Opinion Leaders (%)	25	18	19	21	23	23	22	25	26	23

Note: Percent of opinion leaders is the proportion of influentials within each political position.

From "Opinion Leadership and Political Extremism," by Ottar Hellevik and Tor Bjorklund, *International Journal of Public Opinion Research* 3(2), 1991, p. 176, table A1. By permission of Oxford University Press.

One can easily dismiss the findings by limiting them to the Norwegian political setting. Lacking, at this stage, any follow-up studies in comparable societies, this is a potential argument but it leaves us with the same surprise, limited only to the Norwegian population. Another possibility, suggested though not tested by the researchers, is the relative durability of opinion leaders under the social pressures of the "climate of opinion" and the "spiral of silence."[86] Noelle-Neumann was aware of the relationship between her ideas about the "spiral of silence" and the opinion leadership concept. When examining the sources of the individual's estimation of the "climate of opinion," Noelle-Neumann highlighted the role of the media and personal influence, especially by opinion leaders.[87] Moreover, opinion leaders may be more independent and more resistant to the climate of opinion, as suggested by Hellevik and Bjorklund: "Political interest and intensity of opinion [both measures of political opinion leadership] associated with an extreme position thus seem to outweigh any effect that lack of support for ones political views may have."[88] The Norwegian database was not sufficient to test this explanation, thus it remains a challenge for future research.

Finally, the analysis of the Norwegian data provided strong support for additional remodifications. The examination of five campaigns in Norway revealed a strong correlation between the activity of opinion leaders and the success of the parties they supported. The trends for the level of opinion leadership activity, in both political right and left, paralleled the changes in electoral strength for the various parties. One explanation for this correlation is that the activity of an opinion leader is indeed a powerful mechanism. But, altering the causal relationship suggests another explanation: the support gained by a party may affect the desire of the opinion leaders to be active. This returns us to the issue of the perceived climate of opinion and its impact on opinion leaders' activity. The correspondence between opinion leadership and political behavior should be analyzed within the climate of opinion and spiral of silence framework. Such perspective would explain whether opinion leaders are indeed more resistant to social pressures, such as the fear of isolation, whether they are the agents of the perceived climate of opinion, and whether they are the cause of rising support or the followers of existing trends in popular support. After years of neglecting the study of opinion leaders in the political domain, the recent revival of scientific research in this area will undoubtedly provide some answers to these questions.

Conclusions

• The early studies conducted by Columbia University's Bureau of Applied Social Research on the 1940 through 1950 campaigns directed scholarly interest to the role of personal influence in general, and opinion leaders in particular. Recently, there is a resurrection of the research agenda suggested by the Columbia studies. Several political scientists have expressed renewed interest in social and environmental factors applying network analysis.

• Network analysis revived the interest in social environments as affecting political behavior by providing both the needed bridge between micro and macro levels of analysis and the methodological tools for mapping and analyzing the flow of personal influence.

• Social networks were found to be active and popular channels of political information, but the information flow in these networks tended to reinforce existing political preferences because people preferred exposure to personal sources with whom they agree. Under certain circumstances, though, personal intermediaries may play important roles in challenging preferences and perhaps even inducing partisan change.

• Certain structural characteristics of social networks (such as homogeneity and density) have a powerful impact on their members' attitudes regarding various social and political issues. Several characteristics of social networks were used by political behaviorists to study the process of attitude formation and maintenance. Among these factors re-emerged the role of the influentials or the opinion leaders.

• Opinion leaders in the political domain are politically active; they come into contact with many people through their activities in various voluntary organizations and through their jobs. They speak at meetings, participate in discussions, closely follow political debates in the media, and frequently discuss the contents of mass media with other people. They are often asked for their opinions about current political affairs and often try to mold the opinions of other people.

• Opinion leaders in the political domain are effective sources but only when there is a demand for their guidance. The advice-seekers— those who are exposed to personal contacts—are more influenced by their opinion leaders. Yet, there is a large section of the population that does not discuss these issues with other people and is more influenced by the mass media.

10

Opinion Leaders in Family Planning

Personal Influence in Family Planning

The sociological research tradition that dealt with the diffusion of various innovations, found several followers among researchers and educators interested in promoting family planning. Like other innovations within the areas of politics and public affairs, marketing, fashion, and agriculture, to name only a few, family planning was another domain where, it was thought, innovative items could be diffused by personal networks, and especially by the central individuals in these networks. It was Bernard Berelson who stated early in the 1960s:

> I have come to think that there are three factors, or clusters of factors, that are involved in the effective spread of family planning...They are (a) the nature of the society, from traditional to modern or modernizing; (b) the nature of the contraceptive method, from hard to easy; (c) the nature of the communication approach.[1]

Once family planning was recognized as a communication-dependent innovation, more attention was directed to the various channels of communication utilized for its successful introduction. Soon the importance of informal communication became evident and documented. For instance, in a Kentucky family planning program, one third of the clients for a new birth control program heard about it through friends, relatives, or neighbors.[2] In Tennessee, 27.4 percent of all new patients admitted to family planning clinics said their referral source was a friend or a relative.[3]

The evidence supporting informal communication effects came from studies conducted in various societies and different cultural settings. In Taichung, where an extensive formal family planning campaign was conducted, half the intrauterine device (IUD) users within Taichung, and two-thirds of those from outside the city, said they heard about the IUD from friends, relatives, or neighbors.[4] Comparing the various sources of information led to the conclusion that informal diffusion by personal communication was more instrumental than formal channels (radio, posters, formal home visits, direct mailing, etc.). The role of personal communication and influence in family-planning programs was also highlighted by studies in India,[5] Chile,[6] Puerto Rico,[7] Thailand,[8] Japan,[9] Pakistan,[10] and other societies.

Revising the Two-Step Model for Family Planning

Following the revealed importance of personal influence, the next step in family planning research was to identify the influential individuals. The earliest attempt to do so was reported by Stychos, who studied the role of opinion leaders in Turkish villages in an introductory family planning program.[11] Interviews were conducted in 240 villages (2,744 wives and 2,373 husbands were interviewed) and distinguished between two types of leaders: the political leader (*muhtar*) and the religious leader (*imam*). The findings point to the instrumentality of only one type of leader for family planning programs:

> While we identified *a priori* two types of potential leaders— political and religious—we emerge with the recommendation that attention be focused on only one, the political leader, or *muhtar*. First of all, we found the *muhtars*, whether young or old, relatively educated or uneducated, to be more favorable than the average village male to the idea of family planning and a government education program on family planning. Second, they are relatively powerful, prestigeful, and accessible to the villagers.[12]

These suggestions were supported by another study of community leaders in Turkish villages. In 1959, a special research project was conducted by the Turkish government, aided by consultants from Massachucetts Institue of Tecnology (MIT), interviewing 6,480 villagers and about 1,500 elite villagers in 443 villages. The reports high lighted the role of the political opinion leaders for the purpose of modernization:

> Our personal impression is that the overall position and characteristics of the *muhtar* indicate that he might well be

utilized as the focal figure in the modernization of Turkish villages. He is clearly an individual of formidable power and authority. He plays a central role between the village and outside agencies as well as in the internal communications structure of the village. He would seem generally to be more interested in and responsive to modernization than most male villagers.[13]

Yet, at the very early stage of adhering the opinion leadership idea to family planning, critical and sometimes negative suggestions were presented. For example, Bogue argued that the theory of opinion leaders may be less applicable in family planning than it is in other issues.[14] As he noted, it may be that the final decision to adopt a family planning practice or not may not be a result of personal influence of any major influential person in particular but may depend on the combined reactions of the spouse, intimate friends, or relatives. This is not to deny, Bogue argued, that these influentials are important. For if the leaders in the community oppose the suggested family planning, the program will most likely encounter difficulties.

The two-step flow model was another source of criticism in this area. According to this model, opinion leaders should be more informed by the media than their followers. Palmore's study questioned the validity of the two-step idea and suggested that it may need to be revised.[15] Applying the notion of the multi-step process from awareness of an innovation to final decision, Palmore argued that the first step—information flow—may reach more people, and not necessarily the opinion leaders: "under appropriate conditions there may be a large impact of a mass media message on the populace."[16] Furthermore, Palmore examined three steps in the adoption process of family planning, namely the "awareness stage," the "information-gathering stage," and the "trial stage."[17] He tested the various sources of 1,227 women in Taichung, Taiwan, regarding seven methods of birth control (Ligation, Ota ring, foam tablet, condom, IUD, vasectomy, and rhythm). The analysis revealed that various sources were used in different stages of the awareness-to-adoption process, with variance across the type of contraceptive.

In another study conducted by Palmore and his colleagues, a sample of married West Malaysian women was studied. The researchers were interested in the women's sources of information in various stages of their decision-making process regarding family-planning methods. The data revealed that the distributions of sources were identical for opinion leaders and other women at the first stage of awareness. Hence, it appears that family planning leaders and other women do not rely on different information sources. The only variance is in the amount of sources: opinion leaders rely on more sources than the non-leader (averages of 2.7 and 0.9 sources, respectively). When social and demographic variables were controlled, the pattern remained the same. Within each sub-group (for example, of age or education), the family planning leaders and others had the same source distribution.

Because of these findings, Palmore and Bogue suggested that the two-step hypothesis is really two hypotheses, namely that (a) the mass media tend to have cognitive contact with only a small portion of the eligible persons exposed; and (b) persons affected by the mass media influence others in a second stage of the process, by face-to-face communication. Data from Palmore's studies provided evidence that the first hypothesis did not seem to hold in the family planning area while the second hypothesis was strongly supported. It has even been suggested that the second stage in the family planning domain involves more activity on the part of opinion leaders than in other domains.[19] Thus, one unique attribute of opinion leadership in the family planning area is their lesser involvement in creating awareness to new birth control practices and their more significant role in influencing the final decision regarding trial or adoption.

A study that attempted to examine the use of media and opinion leaders for family-planning programs was conducted and reported by Placek.[20] The data were collected by personal interviews with a random sample of 300 recipients of Aid to Families with Dependent Children (AFDC) in Tennessee. About three weeks before the interviews, a random half of the sample was mailed information booklets regarding birth control and a list of public clinics providing family planning services. The letter attached to the material encouraged the receivers to discuss these issues with their friends, relatives, and neighbors. The group that received the direct mail constituted the experimental group: the other one, without any direct mail, the control group.

Opinion leadership was measured by the use of self-designated questionnaire, regarding four areas of family planning practices: the pill, IUD, birth control clinics, and other methods of birth control. The same amount of opinion leaders was found in the experimental and the control groups. Two other measures were used in the analysis: (a) *knowledge index*—the total number of correct answers given to a set of five open-ended questions about contraception, and (b) *diffusion index*—the amount of people the respondent talked to about birth control in the last months, or the amount of people a person advised about birth-control practices.

When the two groups were compared by their knowledge and diffusion scores, the experimental group (the one that received the direct, mailed information) was found to score higher on both the knowledge and diffusion scales. This finding suggested that the use of direct mail increased knowledge about contraception, and also increased the number of family planning discussions. However, this is not a sufficient measure of the role of opinion leaders: this was accomplished by calculating zero-order, multiple, and partial correlations among the measures of knowledge, diffusion, and opinion leadership for the total sample and for the experimental and control groups separately. These coefficients are presented in table 10.1.

The top part of table 10.1 presents the correlations for the total sample. The statistically significant correlation between diffusion and direct mail (.271), diffusion and opinion leadership (.151), and diffusion and knowledge (.210) suggests that these three variables are associated with personal communication regarding family planning. The partial correlations $r_{41.23}$, $r_{42.13}$, and $r_{43.12}$ were all significant, indicating that direct mail, opinion leadership, and knowledge are reliable predictors of diffusion, even after controlling for the effects of the other two variables. Opinion leadership in the entire sample strongly correlated with knowledge ($r_{23}=.227$), and this relationship remains unchanged even when controlling for the effects of the direct mail ($r_{23.1}=.223$). Opinion leaders were more informed about birth control practices, regardless of the material mailed to them.

Next, it was necessary to study the correlations for the two groups, presented in the lower part of table 10.1. In the control group, the strongest relationship was found between opinion leadership and diffusion; this relationship is maintained when controlling for knowledge. However, the zero-order correlation between diffusion and knowledge is weak and is reduced to insignificance when controlling for opinion leadership. "This leads us to conclude that in the absence of experimental intervention, opinion leadership, rather than knowledge, is the significant independent predictor in the diffusion process."[21]

A different pattern was revealed in the experimental group. In this group, which was exposed to the direct mailing, the strongest correlation of diffusion was knowledge and not opinion leadership; this relationship remained significant even when opinion leadership was controlled. Thus, in the presence of direct mailing, knowledge, rather than opinion leadership predicts diffusion. Yet, in both groups there is a strong correlation between knowledge and opinion leadership: it may suggest that the leaders do know more about family planning issues and even seize the opportunity to learn more from the direct mailing. (The correlation between leadership and knowledge is stronger in the experimental group.)

Table 10.1

Correlating Knowledge, Diffusion and Opinion Leadership Regarding Birth Control Practices

	Total Sample (n = 300)			
	1	2	3	4
1. Direct mail	-	.046	.179***	.271***
2. Opinion leadership		-	.227***	.151***
3. Knowledge			-	.210***
4. Diffusion				-

Partial correlations: $r_{41.23} = .244{***}$ $r_{23.1} = .223{***}$
$r_{42.13} = .110{*}$ $r_{21.3} = .005$
$r_{43.12} = .144{**}$ $r_{31.2} = .174{***}$

Multiple Correlation: $r_{4.123} = .334$

	Control Group (n = 150)			
	1	2	3	4
2. Opinion leadership		-	.177**	.261***
3. Knowledge			-	.135***
4. Diffusion				-

Partial correlations: $r_{42.3} = .244{***}$
$r_{43.2} = .093$

Multiple correlation: $r_{4.23} = .276$

	Experimental Group (n = 150)			
	1	2	3	4
2. Opinion Leadership		-	.263***	.074
3. Knowledge			-	.196**
4. Diffusion				-

Partial correlations: $r_{42.3} = .024$
$r_{43.2} = .183{**}$

Multiple correlation: $r_{4.23} = .197$

* = p < .05, ** = p < .01, *** = p < .001

From "Direct Mail and Information Diffusion: Family Planning," by Paul J. Placek, *Public Opinion Quarterly*, 39, 1975, p. 558, table 4. Reprinted by permission of the University of Chicago Press.

These results support the modification of the two-step flow model when applied to family planning: it appears that opinion leadership is more effective in later stages of the adoption process. In early stages that involve awareness and information gathering, many sources may be used effectively, including mass media and direct mail. Yet, the final decision is reached by consulting with and being affected by influential personal sources.

The Attributes of the Family Planning Leaders

The attributes of opinion leaders in family planning differ from those of opinion leaders in other domains. In fact, Palmore argued that opinion leaders in the family planning area share only six common characteristics with leaders in other areas.[22] These were:

1. Participating more in social situations in which relevant information is transmitted
2. Having a greater sensitivity to "external" information sources
3. Having additional and more varied information sources
4. Being better informed in their area
5. Adopting innovations faster, being more innovative
6. Giving advice and guidance to others

Palmore argued that only these six characteristics are common attributes of opinion leaders in various areas and those in the family planning domain. Rosario, in his review of opinion leaders in family planning studies,[23] suggested that there are four specific characteristics of leaders in this domain. He cited many studies, including the projects conducted by Palmore, to show that these four attributes were the best predictors of the family planning leadership. These were:

Sensitivity

Opinion leaders are more sensitive to any source of information regarding family planning, birth control, and related matters. Their reliance on numerous sources pre-supposes greater exposure to mass media and a high degree of cosmopoliteness. Yet, Palmore noted that in the domain of family planning the mass media may have limited value as these issues are not widely covered and discussed (at least in some societies). Consequently, the influentials may be exposed to other sources of relevant information, including personal contact, change agencies, and specific publications.

Knowledgeability

The influentials in this area were better informed and more knowledgeable regarding birth control practices and their comparative value. Opinion leadership in family planning was highly correlated with awareness, information, and understanding of the various methods. (Palmore found such correlation among the Malaysian opinion leaders,[24] while a study in Lima, Peru, found that the strongest predictor of leadership was "information transaction": seeking and exchanging information.)[25]

Accessibility

Opinion leaders in the family planning area were found to be more outgoing and sociable. They participate in more social activities, are more centrally located in their networks, and have many social contacts with friends, acquaintances, neighbors, co-workers, and relatives.

Credibility

Palmore suggested that the knowledgeability of the family planning leader is not only objectively higher but also a socially recognized trait. The credibility of the influentials in this specific domain is regarded more important because of the personal consequences of adoption, the need to internalize the change and adapting it to moral and personal values. In birth control issues, the meaning of adoption stresses the need to rely on a credible and trustworthy source. Thus, these specific family planning leaders are required to be more credible than those active in areas like fashion or marketing.

These four attributes do not include those related to opinion leadership in other areas. Rosario compared the characteristics and noted that several common traits are atypical to the family planning leader, such as cosmopoliteness, prestige, social perceptiveness, and achievement orientation.[26] A more sophisticated measurement of the family planning opinion leaders provided support for this characterization, as well as additional attributes and their weighting.[27] The study of family planning leadership in Peru focused on the profile of the influentials and provided a more accurate measurement of the factors included in this profile.

Patients attending a family planning clinic in Lima were interviewed (587 women or 40 percent of the patients). A self-designating technique was used to identify the opinion leaders: people who reported that their advice was sought and whose advice regarding birth control was adopted were termed opinion leaders. The non-leaders were further categorized into "followers" (women whose advice had not been sought but who manifestly acted on the advice of others) and "ineffectives" (those whose advice was sought but not followed). Opinion leadership was examined in relation to several variables: background characteristics, motivation, fertility, information transactions, mass media exposure, and social interaction.

Background Variables

Several background variables were tested: education, socio-economic status, and length of residence in a currently occupied home. Education significantly differentiated leaders from ineffectives and followers, with leaders being more educated than the others. Combining education with income to measure socio-economic status was also associated with opinion leadership, though income alone yielded no significant difference. It appears that education was the most powerful discriminating variable. Finally, the length of time the respondent had lived in the house she was occupying at the time of the study was positively associated with opinion leadership. According to the researchers, "this suggests that residential stability provided greater opportunities for the development of informal social networks through which leadership could be exerted."[28] No other background variables were related to leadership.

Motivation Variables

Motivation was measured by the use of several indicators: pre-consideration of the use of contraception (prior to visiting the clinic), regularity of attendance in the clinic, and timing of adoption. Earlier adoption, regular attendance and pre-consideration were all regarded as manifestations of greater motivation. Motivation was found to correlate strongly with opinion leadership, since the leaders are usually more motivated than the ineffectives and, particularly, the followers.

Information Gathering

Leaders were found to be more engaged in information gathering about contraception than others. They were significantly more active in various forms of information gathering, including the use of personal sources and consulting the clinic, the mass media, and other sources.

Personal Communication

The leaders were not only more often seekers of information than were the others, but also more active in disseminating the information in an influential manner. To do so, they utilized their social accessibility, social ties, and eagerness to exchange information on family planning issues.

To determine the overall influence of all these variables on family planning opinion leadership, a multi-variate analysis was used. Table 10.2 presents the results of testing the effects of nine independent variables on opinion leadership. The results are presented by means of the proportion of variance explained by each variable separately (Eta^2) and the squared coefficient of partial determination ($Beta^2$).

Table 10.2

Multiple Correlation Analysis of Opinion Leadership

Independent Variable	Eta²	Beta²
Background		
Education	.007	.006
Monthly income	.022	.005
Length of residence	.005	.004
Motivation		
Regularity of attendance	.043***	.024**
Mass Media		
Media exposure	.021*	.003***
Fertility		
Number of children	.017	.024
Information Transactions		
Information seeking	.041***	.012**
Information exchanging	.158***	.095***
Number of friends	.059***	.035***

$* = p < .01$, $** = p < .005$, $*** = p < .001$

From "Opinion Leadership in Family Planning," by John Saunders, J. Michael Davis, and David M. Monsees, *Journal of Health and Social Behavior*, 15, 1974, p. 226, table 6. Reprinted by permission of the authors and the American Sociological Association.

The strongest explanatory variables were those related to information transactions: the strongest and most significant coefficients in table 10.2 are all in this category. These include information gathering, information seeking (the strongest among the three), and number of friends. In addition, mass media exposure, motivation, and fertility also contribute a moderate amount to the explained variance in leadership.

Finally, the applicability of opinion leaders to programs of introduction and promotion of family planning practices was recognized, following the previous studies. As Saunders, Davis, and Monsees concluded their project:

> This knowledge has practical implications for attempts at planning the diffusion of contraceptive use. Clinic patients who fall into the pre-leader category, particularly, may make the most effective outreach workers and conduits for the diffusion of contraceptives. They possess the personality characteristics that result in higher motivation, in a greater number of friendships, and in more active seeking and exchanging of information regarding family planning.[29]

Conclusions

• The importance of personal communication and influence in family planning programs was highlighted by studies in various societies, cultures, and communities.

• Compared to other areas and issues, opinion leaders in the family planning area are less dominant in creating awareness to new birth control practices but are more significant in influencing the final decision regarding trial or adoption.

• Four attributes were found to characterize the family planning leadership: sensitivity, knowledgeability, accessibility, and credibility. These combine personality traits, social recognition, and social gregariousness.

• The findings of studies on the diffusion of family planning and personal influence resulted in practical implications: the opinion leaders in this area are the most effective outreach workers and conduits for the diffusion of contraceptives. Their identification and activation may promote family planning practices more effectively in terms of reach, speed, and influence.

11

Opinion Leaders in Science

The Sociology of Science

The sociology of science is a relatively young and recent development. Several theoretical approaches in this field can be identified. There are two leading approaches.[1] The first is concerned with the relationships between science and other social institutes. For example, Marx's basic theme contributes to this approach his views on the impact of social relationships (based on the economic system) upon the system of ideas and knowledge in that society. He argued that an individual's position in the social class structure will determine which ideas he or she will accept and produce. Weber, on the other hand, suggested the opposite direction of influence: in his view, ideas and values affect the economic structure, the social stratification, and the production of knowledge. Merton's early study of the scientific development in Western society was an attempt to extend Weber's ideas.[2]

A second approach is identified as the social history of science. Historians of science have been concerned with identifying the characteristics of scientific knowledge that bring about change and development in scientific ideas. One of the best known examples of this approach is Kuhn.[3] Kuhn presented a model of scientific change that sees the growth and development of scientific knowledge as a result of the development of paradigms. A paradigm sets guidelines for research and interpretation of findings. After a period of hegemony, during which the implications of the paradigm are explored, instances or facts that the paradigm cannot explain become inescapable. This may lead to a period of crisis during which a new paradigm emerges and is eventually accepted. Finally, a third approach has emerged:

> The third and more recent approach is concerned with science as a social system. Science is treated as a social organization, as...the organized social activity of men and women who are

concerned with extending man's body of empirical knowledge through the uses of these techniques. The relationships among these people, guided by a set of shared norms, constitute the social characteristics of science.[4]

Recently, more and more sociologists of science have focused on the study of the social system of science. These studies focus on the social norms of the scientific community, the scientific ethos and codes of conduct, the socialization of scientists, and the social networks and social circles of scientists. Underlying all these approaches is the basic assumption that, unlike its popular image, science is not an entirely rational, logical, continuous process.

Fashions in Science

In his book *Fashions in Science: Opinion Leaders and Collective Behavior in the Social Sciences*,[5] Sperber examines science as a "fashion process," based upon the studies of social scientists such as Georg Simmel, Alfred Kroeber, and Herbert Blumer. According to Sperber,

The fashion process refers to the preoccupation with keeping in step with the times; second, to following the example of prestigious opinion leaders who crystalize and reinforce the vaguely expressed collective tastes of the public; admiring proposals for adoption when they are in 'good taste' and new, and discarding them when they are in 'bad taste' and old; opposing the weight of tradition in general while rediscovering and modifying old proposals as though they were unprecedented, daring and modern; ignoring or downgrading the importance of explicit criteria by which competing proposals for adoption can be rationally evaluated. The fashion process facilitates major forms of change, continuity, and control in modern society: those who resist new and popular proposals are condemned as being old-fashioned or 'too straight.' Once a proposal is in fact widely adopted, it is defended as though it were sacrosanct because 'it's the latest thing,' only to be subsequently repudiated in favor of a newer one that is 'more in step with the times.'[6]

Although clothing is the most frequently used arena for fashion, science was often analyzed in terms of a fashion process with a considerable emphasize given to role of social agents and sociological forces that shape scientific fashions. In fact, it was Simmel who first (in 1904[7]) related the notion of fashion to a broader range of social phenomena, including science. He argued:

> In fashion the different dimensions of life, so to speak, acquire a peculiar convergence, that fashion is a complex structure with all the leading antithetical tendencies of the soul are represented in one way or another. . .Thus fashion can to all appearances and in abstracto absorb any chosen content: any given form of clothing, of art, of conduct, of opinion may become fashionable.[8]

For Simmel, then, a theory of fashion is applicable to a study of human history, science and all the "antithetical tendencies of the soul." Moreover, Simmel recognized that not only the operation of the fashion process in a wide variety of domains, but also the functions of social factors, such as social class and social groups:

> Fashion is a product of class distinction and operates like a number of other forms, honor especially, the double function of which consists in revolving within a given circle and at the same time emphasizing it as separate from others. . .Fashion on the one hand signifies union with those in the same class, the uniformity of a circle characterized by it, and *uno actu*, the exclusion of all other groups.[9]

Although Simmel felt that "fashion occasionally will accept objectively determined subjects, such as religious faith, scientific interests, even socialism, and individualism,"[10] he suggested several social forces with impact on the fashion process that was later related to areas he considered "objectively determined" (such as science).

The Social Networks of Scientists

The notion of scientists' networks or the "hidden colleges" is commonly associated with the work of Crane, and Price's *Little Science, Big Science*[11] before her. But its origin can be traced back to the beginnings of the Royal Society of London, founded in 1668, whose members likened their group to the "visible" colleges of Oxford and Cambridge. This concept highlighted the informal interpersonal networks of scientists, based upon shared scientific interests and personal friendships rather than on geographic proximity. We will later examine the impact of these "hidden colleges" on the growth of science but first we should turn to the networks themselves and explore how they were studied. Lievrouw, Rogers, Lowe, and Nadel provided a review of various studies that focused on scientists' personal networks in different scientific areas.[12] Their review includes a classification of these studies according to the scientific community or discipline being studied (rural sociologists, radio astronomers, mathematicians, physicists, Nobel laureates, molecular biologists, and chemists), the method employed to map the networks (questionnaires, co-citation analysis, participant observation, bibliometrics, co-authorship analysis, and interviews), and the major conclusions of these studies.

Most of the studies interested in scientific networks revealed evidence of the existence of the "invisible colleges" and even of their influence on scientific growth and decline. However, Lievrouw, Rogers, Lowe, and Nadel suggested a more sophisticated research method, the "triangulation strategy," designed to serve as a data collection and analysis tool for identifying the networks of scientists. The method involves three different stages, each employing specific database and mode of analysis. To illustrate the advantages of their multi-technique strategy, the researchers applied it to a study of a social network of biomedical scientists specializing in lipid metabolism research. Let us briefly review each stage and its results.

Stage 1: Clustering

An analysis of the National Institutes of Health (NIH) database of funded grants was employed to reveal clusters of scientists. Approximately 5,000 research grants awarded to biomedical scientists by the NIH were checked and analyzed to reveal grant clusters. This analysis produced 12 coherent clusters of scientists. To verify the clustering, 6 of the 12 clusters were selected for validation by interviewing scientists working in the subject area.

Stage 2: Co-citation Analysis

One of the clusters derived in the first stage (the field of lipid metabolism), was chosen for co-citation analysis, yielding clusters of articles that were most frequently co-cited.

Stage 3: Sociometric Matrix

Using questionnaires, interviews, and a roster-type sociometric instrument, the members of the cluster were asked about communication ties with other scientists in the area. The data served to construct a sociometric matrix, which revealed the structure of the personal ties in this community.

This three-step method was found to be an efficient tool for the identification of social networks: the findings revealed the communication patterns within a scientific community, namely personal contacts and calls, reflecting their social ties. The researchers argued: "We feel confident that the triangulation strategy for identifying and contextualizing communication networks among research scientists is an internally consistent and reliable approach."[13] The use of computerized electronic mail services (such as Internet or Bitnet), which link academic institutions and research facilities worldwide, provide an additional, fast and efficient, mode of communication among members of the same "invisible college."

The impact of scientists' social networks on the growth or decline of scientific knowledge was documented by various studies. Schott, for example, studied mathematicians in Denmark and Israel measuring interpersonal influence among the scientists.[14] He conceptualized an individual's influence as a combination of his or her general influentiality (influencing others), general susceptibility (receiving influence from others), and particular influence (influencing a particular individual). Schott surveyed the mathematical communities in these two countries, using questionnaires relating to the identity of influential scientists in the area. On average, a Danish mathematician acknowledged 3.1 direct influencers and the Israeli acknowledged 3.2 direct influencers. Most of the named influentials were of the same community, indicating that the mathematicians in each country constitute a relatively dense network.

Schott hypothesized that a scientist's susceptibility is affected mainly by the extent of his or her ties with others, while the influentiality is promoted by his or her own resources in combination with ties with others. These hypotheses were corroborated by the findings in both the Danish and the Israeli communities. Collegial ties were found to play a crucial role in the flow of influence among the mathematicians, affecting their general influentiality, general susceptibility, and also particular influence. The social ties are crucial because they "facilitate the conversion of resources into influence." This leads us to the question of individual differences: if personal networks of scientists are so important, are there strategic positions in the networks, or influential individuals in the scientific community?

Are There Opinion Leaders in Science?

One of Simmel's original ideas was the notion of the opinion leader. Long before the Columbia studies, Simmel characterized the opinion leader and although it is derived from observations regarding the fashion leader in the clothing domain, Simmel's notion is applicable to many other domains beyond that of costume adornment:

> He leads the way, but all travel the same road. Representing as he does the most recently conquered heights of public taste, he seems to be marching at the head of the general procession. In reality, however, what is so frequently true of the relation between individuals and groups applies also to him: as a matter of fact, the leader allows himself to be led.[16]

The applicability of the fashion process to the domains of science and knowledge was demonstrated by Sperber, who used Simmel's ideas to study the opinion leaders in the social sciences. In order to illustrate the role of opinion leaders in the fashion process of sociological thought, Sperber relied upon case studies of the most influential sociologists and leaders in social theory and research, such as Robert Friedrichs, Pitirim Sorokin, Robert K. Merton, and Jeffrey Alexander. He argues that "prominent leaders in the sociological profession tend on one hand to appear entirely original in their work as perceived by their many followers and on the other hand to accept the prevailing orthodoxies about the nature of sociological inquiry."[17] A leader, hence, both leads and allows himself to be led. Paradoxically, he notes, most of these opinion leaders share the tendency to neglect or trivialize the operation of the fashion-like process in the scientific community. Merton, as an exception, at least indirectly recognized its existence by studying the patterns of evaluation based on the referee system, the function of "status judges" occupying key positions for evaluating competing models, and acknowledging of the role of personal and social conflicts affecting the controversies among sociologists.

An empirical study of scientific communities and the diffusion of scientific innovations was provided by the impressive research conducted by Crane, deservedly entitled *The Invisible Colleges*. Crane argues that scientific development should be regarded as a social process, and mainly as a diffusion process, thus not only as a cognitive one:

If scientific growth represents the accretion of many small innovations, and if, in producing these innovations, authors are indeed building upon each other's work (as analyses of their citations to each other's publications suggest), then it would appear that such authors are adopting some of each other's innovations. In this sense, the growth of scientific knowledge is a kind of diffusion process in which ideas are transmitted from person to person.[18]

The diffusion of innovations was found to follow the logistic growth curve[19] with the exponential increase in numbers of adopters explained as a social influence process. Hence, the probability that a member of a certain social organization or system will adopt an innovation increases over time, because it is related to the number of people who have already adopted the innovation. As a result, the number of adopters also increases exponentially for a time. "Thus the exponential growth of scientific knowledge can be interpreted as 'contagion' process in which early adopters influence later adopters" argues Crane, suggesting that "the rate of expansion will vary depending upon the number of people with whom each scientist has personal contact."[20]

Since scientists in research areas may have varied sorts of social relationships with one another, it is necessary to map the entire network according to all possible links and ties before examining the flow of communication and innovations. For example, scientists are involved in joint research projects, in joint publications, in teaching and training, in reviewing and examining research reports, manuscripts and conference presentations, and many other forms of interaction and interpersonal communication. Thus, the personal networks of direct and indirect ties among scientists in a specific research create a "social circle."[21] These social circles can be characterized by their connectivity (the proportion of relationships that actually occurred in relation to all of those that possibly could have occurred) and structure (the sociometric networks of direct and indirect links).

To test the hypothesis that scientific growth is a result of the personal networks and the diffusion process in scientific communities, Crane studied two scientific areas: (a) rural sociology (the diffusion of agricultural innovations in rural sociology); and (b) applied mathematics (the mathematics of finite groups). Crane mapped the social networks in these areas by means of sociometric questionnaires (for example, information that respondents give regarding the identities of the people with whom they discussed their ongoing research, or regarding people that influenced the respondents' selection of research problems).

Arguably, the validity of this technique may be questioned: respondents may not recall their contacts accurately, or may tend to include people of higher status than themselves and omit people who are of the same or lower status. Moreover, this particular analysis may not reveal the flow of indirect or third part influence: scholars, linked by a third-person, who influence each other, indirectly. Thus, Crane applied a second method of data collection by analyzing the citations appearing in the scientific literature of the mathematics area, which provided a validation procedure for the sociometric data. As Crane concluded: "The network linking members of that area on the basis of the references to each other's work that appeared in their publications was very similar to that produced by the direct and indirect links generated from the names mentioned by members of the area."[22]

The "Invisible Colleges"

Crane was not the first to expose the networks of scientists or the so-called "invisible colleges." Crawford questioned 218 scientists engaging in research on sleep and dreams to name those with whom they communicated frequently concerning their research.[23] He found that one large network dominated the area: 72 percent of the scientists were linked to one another by either direct or indirect communication ties. He also found a high correlation between the sociometric data and the data obtained from an analysis of citations appearing in the literature of the area.

Gaston, who studied high-energy physicists in Britain, discovered that a sub-group of approximately 30 percent of the entire community were communicating with one another, linked directly or indirectly to one another, constituting the social circle within this area.[24] However, it appears that the forms of the networks vary from one scientific area to another. Lingwood found such cross-area differences within a group of scientists involved in educational research.[25] Griffith and Miller, who examined communication ties among psychologists, found that in some areas members chose each other frequently, while in other areas they did not.[26] Moreover, Crane's analysis revealed not only the different networks in these two areas (rural sociology and applied mathematics) but also the most influential people, the scientific opinion leaders. When the networks of these two communities were studied, an interesting pattern emerged: analysis of the networks showed that anyone choosing even one of the most productive members of the research areas studied by the author could have been in contact with a large network of individuals. In other words, the high proportion of choices directed toward these individuals meant that members of these groups were not so much linked to each other directly but were linked to each other indirectly through these highly influential members.

The structure of the network, based on the communication ties (derived from the mapping of choices)[27] highlighted the role of certain influential scholars. In the rural sociology area, 6 percent of the scientists received 58 percent of the choices (that is, named by other scientists). A similar pattern was found among the mathematicians: 6 percent of these scientists received 38 percent of the choices. Furthermore, those who were consulted frequently were also the most productive scientists in their area. Analysis of the relationship between productivity (measured by the number of publications in the area) and social centrality (measured by number of direct choices) revealed that those who were most frequently consulted were the most productive scientists in their area. The same pattern was found in the rural sociology. The distribution of scholars according to their social centrality (number of choices) was highly correlated with productivity: 62 percent of the high producers received over 20 choices (25 percent of them over 50 choices!) while none of the low and moderate producers received over 20 choices.

Similar findings were found by Zaltman and Blau, who studied 977 high-energy physicists from thirty-six countries.[28] This constitutes approximately 45 percent of the world population of scientists in this area. They located a small group of thirty-two physicists, who were frequently mentioned by other scholars. All of the members of this clique were linked by direct or indirect ties. Eighty-five percent of them were also mentioned by the respondents as being responsible for the most important research in this area. The authors labeled this group "a highly elite invisible college."

Crawford's study of sleep and dream research scientists also exposed the important role of key individuals. He found that thirty-six of the most frequently mentioned scientists were also highly interconnected and surrounded by others who looked to them for information and guidance. Thus Crawford concluded that "Information generated by scientists is communicated through central persons in one research center to central persons in another center, thus cutting across major groups in the large networks of scientists. Through the central scientists, then, information may be transferred to all other scientists in the network."

Who Are the Scientific Opinion Leaders?

The accumulating findings from numerous studies in various scientific areas indicated clearly the presence of an invisible college or network of scholars, which is linked to the central, influential scientists in each area. Who are the scientific opinion leaders? Are they important actors in the diffusion of scientific innovations? Crane, in her study of the rural sociology and mathematics area found that their role is crucial. For example, in the rural sociology area, innovations that were adopted by these central figures were more widely accepted by other members of the field than innovations they did not adopt. The "high producers" in this area were influential in terms of innovation adoption: if they cite an innovation it is likely to be cited by many other scholars in their area. Forty-one percent of the high producers had cited an innovation that was also cited by at least six other scholars, while the rate for moderate and low producers were 4 and 6, respectively. A similar pattern was revealed in the mathematics area: publications cited by the prominent scholars in this field were more frequently cited by others as opposed to publications the leaders did not cite.

Another interesting relationship was found between the scientific leadership and innovations. Crane found that 51 percent of the 203 authors in the rural sociology area were the authors or co-authors of a publication in which an innovation had appeared. Only 27 percent of the authors had produced more than one such publication, and only 6 percent had produced more than five. Thus, while most scholars in this area had not produced any innovations, six members (3 percent) had produced 52 percent of the innovations![30]

Those innovators were also the prominent, influential scholars in their area, which was revealed in the credits accorded to the innovations. The prominent, highly productive scientists were more likely to be credited with having influenced members of the field, even if their contribution did not exceed that of less prominent scholars. Only twelve authors had produced more than five innovations, and all of the prominent, highly productive members among this group of twelve were mentioned at least five times by respondents as a source of influence. On the other hand, only a third of the moderately productive innovators were mentioned more than five times as a source of influence. Though "it appears that some members of the area may not have realized the original source of some of the innovations"[31] they certainly tended to attribute them to the productive.

We may sum up these findings by stating that within the two scientific areas studied, a small group of scientists was identified as the opinion leaders (a term used by Crane herself). They were more centrally located in the social network in this area, more productive, more associated with influence and innovations, and their adoption of an innovation determined its adoption by other scientists. As Crane concludes: "The factors affecting the diffusion of innovations in science appear to be similar to the factors affecting the diffusion of other types of innovations."[32]

Conclusions

• The personal networks of direct and indirect ties among scientists in a specific research are create a "social circle."

• The structure of the networks, based on the communication ties derived from the mapping of social ties, reveals the central position of certain influential scholars in each area.

• There is a positive, strong relationship between centrality in the social network of scientists and productivity. These centrally positioned scholars, the scientific opinion leaders, determine the process of scientific progress: innovations that were adopted by these central figures were more widely accepted by other members of the field than innovations they did not adopt.

• The opinion leader in a certain field tend to be inter-connected thus creating a powerful "invisible college" that dominates the adoption or the rejection of new scientific models, ideas and methods.

Opinion Leaders in Agriculture

The Social Diffusion of Agricultural Innovations

Rural sociologists have conducted many studies to understand the process of change in rural communities and to use such knowledge for the introduction and promotion of innovations. They soon realized the importance of personal communication, face-to-face interaction and social networks that serve as informal channels of information and influence. In rural communities where formal channels of communication are either not developed or not trusted, the innovator or "modernizer" is not able to approach the community directly. He or she must rely largely upon traditional social networks in order to activate the local influentials and to use these means to both introduce and promote an innovation. No wonder that in rural sociology the concept of opinion leadership found so many followers who applied it not only in their empirical research but also in the practical management of the diffusion of agricultural innovations.

The earliest documented research in this area is probably the Ryan and Gross study of the diffusion of the hybrid corn in Iowa in 1941.[1] Hybrid seed was developed by agricultural scientists at Iowa State University and was released to Iowa farmers in 1928. It soon became an important innovation that led to a myriad of agricultural changes in the 1930s through the 1950s amounting to an "agricultural revolution in farm productivity."[2]

In 1941 Ryan and Gross, two rural sociologists at Iowa State University, personally interviewed 259 farmers living in two small communities, and asked them about the adoption of the hybrid corn and the sources used to learn about it. The farmers were assigned to various "adopter categories" according to the timing of their adoption.[3] It was discovered that the early adopters differed from the later adopter. As this study predated the opinion leadership concept, the researchers used their categorization of adoption but pointed to the existence and functioning of influentials and personal networks. Thus, for example, they found the small group of early adopters more cosmopolitan, more educated, and having larger farms and higher income than late adopters. The study highlighted the role of personal networks and even focused upon certain individuals who appeared to be more receptive to innovations and would later influence others to follow: "the behavior of one individual in an interacting population affects the behavior of his fellows. Thus, the demonstrated success of hybrid seed on a few farms offers a changed situation to those who have not been so experimental. The very fact of acceptance by one or more farmers offers new stimulus to the remaining ones."[4] This notion was later conceptualized as the opinion leadership model.

The Rural Opinion Leadership

The opinion leadership idea and the interpersonal flow of communication model were applied to the agricultural domain in a slightly different version, entitled "The Trickle-Down Process."[5] When examining the role of government agricultural agencies in the promotion of agricultural innovations, Rogers found that the governmental extension workers who were in contact with the farmers reported the existence of the trickle-down process: "the process by which: 1. certain farmers (often called adoption leaders or influentials) have direct contact with extension workers, and then 2. pass the technological information to their neighbors who are less likely to have direct contact with their county agent."[6] As Rogers suggested, the trickle-down process is a special case of the general two-step flow of communication model in which the extension workers represent one source for information and influence, and the adoption leaders one type of opinion leaders. Consequently, the practical implementation of such process involves change agents working intensively with the influential farmers who then will pass the information along to their friends and neighbors.[7]

A very thorough and pioneering study of the adoption process of farm innovations among farmers, conducted by Lionberger in two rural Missouri communities, further related the concepts of opinion leaders and agricultural innovations.[8] In both communities, Lionberger found that most farmers rely on advice and guidance from influential members of their communities. These influentials were highly accessible to other farmers for information and advice, and they were distinctively more active in formal groups and social activities that provided opportunities for contacts and exchanges of information. In fact, Lionberger lists the revealed attributes of these influentials in a strikingly similar way to those of the classical opinion leadership studies.

Lionberger found that the influential farmers in Missouri were "...much more receptive to new developments in farming,...using more improved practices,...more inclined to use all sources of information...The broad social orientation of local influentials is further conductive to the acquisition of new information about farming...One measure of this outward orientation from the immediate locality may be obtained by participation in extra-localistic groups."[9] Furthermore, Lionberger pointed to the significant functions of these influentials within their communities:

> Since the influentials in the Missouri study were frequently mentioned as sources of information and of influence, they performed an important communicative function. Like key communicators, they can select and interpret the information they transmit and to incorporate positive or negative recommendations with their messages to others. They are in a position to give advice and to serve as reinforcers of decisions already made. Being more exposed to almost all reliable sources of information than those who seek them for information or advice, they can pass on what they read, hear, or see to others. Farmers who are inclined to be late adopters of farm practices are often willing to accept advice from fellow farmers when the same or better advice may be wholly unacceptable from less trusted communication agents.

And he adds another function:

> Another important function performed by persons most sought for advice and as a sources of information is that of legitimation. When influentials put their stamp of approval on an idea, product, or practice, it is regarded as acceptable by most people. When these functionaries adopt a new practice, the adoption curve takes the characteristic sharp upward turn.[10]

The data collected by Lionberger in two Missouri communities, containing over 1,000 decisions to adopt new farm practices, revealed the important role of the opinion leaders in this domain. Most farmers reported personal contacts as their most important sources while the mass media and professional agencies were considered less important. Lionberger did not distinguish between information and influence so the results actually combine both stages of the decision-making process. As we will see later, when such distinction is made, the role of the influentials in the final stage of the adoption decision is clearer.

Opinion Leadership Studies in Rural India

Many early studies of agricultural opinion leadership were conducted in India. A major project on the diffusion of innovation was undertaken by the Indian National Institute of Community Development under the guidance of Everett Rogers. It resulted in many research reports and manuscripts, which documented the attempts to apply the opinion leadership notion to agricultural communities in India.

One of the earliest studies in India was reported by Dasgupta, who applied the diffusion of innovation model to Indian villages in the early 1960s.[11] His somewhat oversimplified categorization of the farmers into three groups (innovators, early adopters, and average farmers) correlated with numerous variables, such as socio-economic status, education, outside contacts, etc. He found that the innovators scored high on each of these scales and were likely to influence others: "It appears that in the village those who are social leaders also lead in the field of agriculture. Such [people] have a high level of education and more outside contact. By that they develop a broad outlook, which makes them change-oriented."[12]

Three years later, a more carefully designed portrayal of the opinion leaders in an Indian village was presented by Bose and Saxena.[13] When the answers of the farmers regarding their sources of advice and information about the innovation were transformed to a sociogram, the opinion leaders were easily identified. Most of them were early adopters of the new method (classified in the categories of "innovator" or "early adopter") and only a third of them were "late adopters" or "laggards." The opinion leaders were found to be the most important source for others (though not for themselves as they rarely sought information from other opinion leaders). Their influence was more significant than that of the mass media. In terms of the leaders' characteristics, this study portrayed them in a way that would be repeated in many other studies in other societies. They were found to be more innovative, more literate, have greater social participation and cosmopoliteness,[14] and be more competent farmers.

Other studies of agricultural innovations in India (e.g., the use of new type of rice in West Bengal[15]) revealed the active role of opinion leadears. In the highly segmented society of rural India, with complex social stratification based upon the cross-cutting caste system, religion, family, and wealth of the individual, the identity and characteristics of the opinion leaders are, as expected, unique. Sen noted that:

> The direction of influence from leaders to followers is then vertical, from high to low strata of the village society. Opinion leaders in Indian villages are not the 'molecular' leaders of Lazarsfeld, Berleson, and Gaudet, but the power-holders of the community.[16]

The Center for Management in Agriculture at the Indian Institute of Management, Ahmedabad was responsible for a several studies, conducted in three villages in Raipur district.[17] Using the sociometric technique, the opinion leaders in each village were identified (the leadership in agricultural issues was measured separately for five issues: fertilizers, pesticides, improved seeds, agricultural implements, and improved agricultural practices). Each village, irrespective of its community size, had four to six leaders. The analysis revealed that most people consulted leaders from their caste, a finding explained by the structural significance of the caste system in the Indian villages. Regarding the adoption of agricultural innovations, such as fertilizers, opinion leaders were found to be more aware of the innovations than the followers, and to adopt them earlier than the followers with the diffusion process taking six to eight years. It is interesting that while most farmers were informed of the innovation (fertilizers, new seeds) from many sources, the critical decision involving adoption depended upon the leaders' advice and guidance.[18]

Who Are the Rural Leaders?

The ideas of personal influence and influentials as determining the fate of an agricultural innovation had to face the challenge of other explanatory models. Such models could, for example, focus on the personality traits of the individuals, the various attributes of the innovation itself or other alternative explanations. The best comparison of the competing models when applied to rural communities and agricultural innovations is testing these models' explanatory potential for the same problem, the same population, and the same innovation or decision. Such a comparison was provided by a study Wilkening, Tully, and Presser conducted in Australia.[19]

This study set out to explore the way in which information about farm matters and new practices is transmitted, how decisions are made, and how various social and psychological characteristics of the farmers affect the adoption of new farm practices. The study area was a dairy farm district in northern Victoria, Australia. The farmers in this area were relatively homogeneous in origin, religion, and education with a very modest form of stratification within the communities. One hundred farmers were chosen at random and interviewed at their farms regarding farm practices. Within each area, the researchers discovered the same pattern: farmers sought advice mainly from other farmers and their choices were focused on certain individuals, the opinion leaders. When comparing the influentials across the areas, the overlap was limited "indicating that, in general, information seeking is selective by type of information sought. . . information seeking for this sample of farmers is selective in that they usually go to different [people] for information on different types of problems. Pastures and irrigation are related, and hence the same farmer is often sought for information on both these topics."[20]

Who was sought for advice in these Australian dairy farms? The analysis compared the proficiency ratings of each farmer in three areas. (Ratings were based on dairy supervisors and were validated by comparing different supervisors' ratings to the same farmer and correlating it with the farmers' ratings of other farmers' proficiency.) Of the total choices, 60 percent were upward, that is choosing another farmer rated as better than the advice-seeker. Rated as equivalent were 33 percent, and only 7 percent were downward choices with the influential rating less proficient. Moreover, the researchers found that when the selection of the influential is based upon proficiency, the geographical area within which the influential will be sought is widened. Farmers sought advice and guidance even from very remote individuals if they were considered reliable and proficient sources.

The decision-making process of the farmers in this project was divided into three different stages: initial knowledge of an innovation, further knowledge, and decision whether to try it out. Note that such distinction differs from the earlier studies that combined the stages of information and decision. When the roles of different sources of information regarding three recent innovations in dairy farming were compared, the different functions of various channels were revealed: 1. The mass media were the most important sources of first knowledge about each of the new practices; 2. Further information is obtained from several sources, including media and personal contacts; and 3. The most important source at the stage of deciding whether to try a new practice is another farmer, usually the opinion leader.

The distinction between various stages in the process was also adopted by following studies, including one conducted in Dutch rural communities. This study of three agricultural communities in the Netherlands set out to find the opinion leaders, their sources, and their effectiveness.[21] The three communities differed in terms of contact with urban culture and the modernity of farm management. The opinion leaders were identified by means of a sociometric questionnaire as well as the choices of six or seven informants in each village. The analysis of the farmers' answers regarding adoption of new agricultural innovations revealed an interesting "division of labor" between the mass media and the opinion leaders. For initial information about farming methods, 75 percent of the farmers mentioned the mass media as their most important source of information; but the media have hardly any significant role with the decision to adopt the new method. During this decision-making stage of the adoption stage, personal sources (other farmers, meetings, or advisors) were the most frequently mentioned sources, mentioned by 75 percent of the farmers.

When comparing the sources of opinion leaders and followers in these villages, Van Den Ban found that opinion leaders were indeed more exposed to certain media than their followers (mainly to farming papers), but also that they relied on personal sources more than the followers. Hence, Van Den Ban concluded that "opinion leaders as well as their followers are influenced both by mass media and by other people, but during different stages of the adoption process."[22] Opinion leadership within agriculture affects primarily the final decision of adoption; however, it does not seem to affect the dissemination of information process.

A similar pattern was revealed in several Columbian villages, studied by Rogers.[23] Using the sociometric measure (validated by three other measures: self-designating scale, judges' ratings, and a self-anchoring ladder technique), Rogers identified the opinion leaders in five Columbian villages. When analyzing the areas of leadership, Rogers found evidence of the "overlapping" domains of leadership. Many leaders were found to be influentials in several areas, all related to the daily life of farmers. This pattern was also noted by Lerner who studied Turkish villages and reported the following from an interview with one of the opinion leaders:

Leader: This is my main duty, to give advice.
Interviewer: About what?
Leader: About all that you or I could imagine, even about their wives and how to handle them, and how to cure their sick cow.[24]

Rogers also noted a high degree of polymorphic opinion leadership in the five Columbian villages but the range of the topics was limited (e.g., agriculture, health, politics). Moreover, the expected relationship with modernity, that is, the more modern the village the more mono-morphic are the leaders, was not supported by the findings. Yet, the variance in modernity across this five communities was not significant enough to affect the degree of polymorphism of opinion leadership.

More recently, a study of opinion leadership in a remote area of Bangladesh attempted to compare the leaders and their followers in measures of adoption of agricultural practices.[25] Employing a snow-ball sampling procedure the researchers identified the opinion leaders and then compared them to their followers. The comparison revealed that these opinion leaders were not earlier adopters of innovations. Overall extent of adoption between the leaders and the followers did not differ significantly. The adoption of the high-yielding variety of wheat by most of the opinion leaders was the only exception. Opinion leaders were not found to be innovators or early adopters of farm practices. Their main attribute was their perceived influence on others, the status of influentials.

Opinion Leaders in Various Communities

The characteristics of the opinion leaders in the agricultural domain appear to be rather stable across societies and studies. Rogers's studies, as well as other reports,[26] portray the influentials in rural communities as characterized by more formal education, higher levels of functional literacy, larger farms, higher level of innovativeness, higher social status within their small communities, more mass media exposure, and more political knowledgeability.[27] Nevertheless, the opinion leaders vary from traditional to modern villages in consistent patterns. Let us review briefly some of the main findings regarding the relationship between the community's modernization and the nature of its influentials.

Rogers reported that whereas opinion leaders are older than their followers in more traditional villages, they are younger than their followers in more modern villages. Lerner found the same relationship in the Middle East and attempted to explain it: "the traditional rule that age brings wisdom probably worked well in immobile isolated villages, where change was slow and experience was the only teacher. The longer one lived, the more experience he gained and the greater his title to wisdom. Now the young men no longer await their patrimony. . ."[28]

Another clear and consistent distinction based on the modernity of the village is in the leaders' cosmopoliteness. In modern villages, the opinion leaders are much more cosmopolitan than the leaders in traditional villages: they travel more to urban centers, are more exposed to a variety of media and personal sources, and are more dependent on external sources. This finding was explained by the fact that traditional villages are not as open to new ideas and innovations thus requiring and supporting less cosmopoliteness from their influentials.[29] This relates to another dimension of differences across villages—the innovativeness of their leaders.

Almost all studies in the area of agricultural, rural opinion leadership found that the leaders were more innovative, and more inclined to adopt new farming methods. On the other hand, opinion leaders were found to be the greatest conformists to village norms.[30] How can conformity and innovativeness combine? First, opinion leaders are not always more innovative; that is, they may reject innovations or even exercise their influence to slow down the adoption of an innovation.[31] Secondly, where village norms favor social changes (i.e., modernization), opinion leaders are more innovative and, therefore, function in close conformity to the community's social norms. In traditional communities, opinion leaders are not especially innovative. In fact, Rogers found that the innovators are viewed in such social settings with suspicion and disrespect by other villagers. In the Columbian villages "opinion leaders in the modern villages were more innovative than their followers, but in the traditional villages the opinion leaders were only slightly more innovative than their followers."[32]

The last dimension of opinion leadership associated with the community's level of modernization is the issue of influential-follower homophily or heterophily. This is a measure of the homophily in the dyadic relationship between the leader and the follower or the influential and the influencee. Rogers found that there is a general tendency for opinion seekers to turn to influentials who are more innovative and more competent than themselves. Yet, this heterophily is affected by the nature of the community: greater homophily was found in the traditional villages while in more modern villages the leader-follower dyads were more heterogenous.[33] A similar pattern was found by Pontius in his study of Thai farmers in four villages of the Central Plain of Thailand.[34]

The influentials in rural communities may serve as agents of change; however, they can as well be those that "block" or slow modernization. A study conducted in a Mexican village investigated the relationship between opinion leadership, social participation, and the degree of innovativeness.[35] The village, an Ejido community, had 247 villagers and was approached by an agricultural change agent who attempted to introduce the use of chemical fertilizers. After a detailed presentation of costs and potential benefits of increased crop yields, the community decided to reject the innovation. One plausible explanation was that the leadership in this community was responsible for the rejection. Thomas' hypothesis was that "leadership in traditional communities is by nature conservative and reflects a general value orientation that is resistant to innovation."[36] Thus, the leaders were suggested to be more pivotal than their followers, yet not more innovative.

Thomas found that opinion leadership was most strongly correlated with social centrality. A weaker correlation, though significant, was found between leadership and innovativeness thus providing only partial support for the study's hypothesis. However, it might be argued that the correlation found between leadership and innovativeness is nevertheless spurious. It may be the result of the correlations between these two variables and centrality. To test this possibility, Thomas calculated the partial correlation between opinion leadership and innovativeness, maintaining centrality constant. The result was a partial correlation coefficient of .036, indicating that the simple correlation between these variables (.372) is actually spurious. When social centrality was controlled, leaders were not more or less innovative than the other farmers. One may question the value of measuring leadership when controlling for centrality; yet the weak correlation between innovativeness and leadership in this village supports Thomas' hypothesis. Such confirmation suggests that in traditional communities, opinion leaders may play a significant role in "blocking modernization." Therefore, in the Mexican village the change agent who attempted to convince villagers to adopt fertilizers did so without regard to the functions and positions of the community's influentials.

Practical Implications

These findings resulted in practical implications. When the role of opinion leaders in rural communities was disregarded, their influence was activated to block or at least to moderate the adoption of innovations. Furthermore, when activated properly, opinion leaders could be recruited for promoting modernization:

> A modicum of success in the delivery of aid might be gained if change agents were to pay more attention to and work with village leaders. Programs may have a better chance of success

if influential individuals are first convinced of their utility and given the opportunity to adapt the program to existing local economic and social conditions.[37]

Similar conclusions were reached by many other studies of rural opinion leaders and their potential as promoters of innovations and modernization. Fiah, in his study of training programs used in rural areas of Gambia,[38] found that identifying and training opinion leaders are significantly improving rural development. Trivedi, who studied eight villages in Northern India,[39] also found that the process of modernization in such communities requires the recruitment and activation of the local influentials: "they have to serve as intermediaries and interpreters of new ideas to their followers...and to mediate the values and demands of modernization [in order to] transmit modern culture and technology to people who are rooted in traditional values and beliefs."[40]

Conclusions

• Different sources of information and advice regarding recent innovations in farming practices are used by farmers in various stages of their decision-making process. The mass media are more frequently used for first knowledge about new practices. However, the most pivotal source, at the stage of deciding whether to try a new practice, is another farmer, usually the opinion leader.

• Opinion leaders are found to play a dominant role in the diffusion of agricultural innovations, new farming practices, and improved methods. Their functions and importance are found in many societies, nations, and cultures.

• The functions of opinion leaders in various rural communities involve the dissemination of information regarding new practices or technologies, their early adoption, their being a source for advice, influence, and social legitimation for the new products or methods.

• The characteristics of the rural opinion leaders usually involve higher formal education, higher levels of functional literacy, larger farms, more innovativeness, higher social status within their small communities, more mass media exposure, and more political knowledgeability.

• The characteristics of the opinion leaders, their cosmopoliteness, innovativeness, and heterophily/homophily with their followers are highly dependent on the nature of their community, especially in terms of modernity. There are significant differences between the influentials of traditional and modern villages and rural communities.

• Opinion leaders are not only agents of change and adoption. In certain circumstances, they may be blocking modernization and innovations. This is especially evident in more traditional communities in which the leaders personify the values of a conservative, traditional-oriented community.

13

Opinion Leaders in Health Care

Personal communication with regard to health care issues applies to two levels: exchange of information and influence among (a) medical professionals; and (b) among the "clients," or the non-professionals. Both forms have been extensively studied and documented by numerous research projects. We will initially examine the communication flow within the professional medical community.

Personal Advice Among Physicians

The classic study within this area was the diffusion of a new drug project, conducted to determine the sources of information and influence among doctors.[1] This study's procedure, findings, and conclusions are detailed in chapter 2 (The Drug Study) but let us review the major findings. The study found that colleagues were more important sources of information and influence than were media sources. Moreover, the factor most strongly associated with the timing of adoption of the new drug was the extent of the doctor's integration in the medical community. That is, the more frequently the doctor appeared on other doctors' maps of personal networks, the more likely he or she was to be an innovative early adopter of the new drug. The doctor's social integration and network position proved more important than the doctor's age, medical school, income of patients, readership of medical journals or any other factors examined. Thus, the researchers attributed medical innovativeness to the extent to which the doctors were integrated in their respective medical communities.

Many studies on the diffusion of medicines among physicians revealed the importance of personal influence.[2] In one of the more complex studies, conducted by Avorn and Soumerai,[3] personal influence was compared to other sources by means of a four-state experimental design. The study population consisted of 435 physicians, randomly assigned to one of three groups: 1. a group that received face-to-face educational visits by a trained pharmacist in addition to printed material; 2. a group that received only printed material; and 3. a control group. The dependent measure was the reduction of prescribing targeted drugs. Analysis of the results in terms of the desired reduction in prescriptions revealed that the group exposed to personal contact (and printed material) reduced prescriptions by 14 percent while the print-only group and the control group did not change significantly. These findings are consistent with those from other research areas ranging from smoking[4] to patient compliance.[5]

In another study utilizing a large group of physicians, Schaffner and his colleagues reported that inappropriate prescribing of target drugs declined when practitioners were visited by "physician counselors."[6] The average number of prescriptions written per doctor was reduced by 54 percent of the group, with a reduction of 18 percent in the number of doctors prescribing the targeted drugs, and a 44 percent reduction in the number of patients per physician receiving these drugs. All of these measures were significant and higher than those recorded in control groups. The persistence of the change was examined by a follow-up study:[7] results indicated that doctors visited by counselors persisted in their improved prescribing behaviors for all study drugs. The same pattern was also revealed by both a study on the effect of personal influence on the rate of prescribing Diazepam (e.g., Valium),[8] and a study undertaken to change the prescribing patterns of physicians in the New Mexico Medicaid program.[9] Thus, personal influence was found to be a powerful change agent when attempting to shape physicians' decision-making.

Personal Influence Among "Clients"

The second form of medical communication flows between the "clients," or the individuals who are not medical professionals. Such flow was documented by several studies,[10] and summarized by Booth and Babchuk:

> When faced with an impending decision, all but the most isolated individuals have occasion to contact a friend, kinsman, or acquaintance who can provide pertinent information, counsel or support...Such a decision confronts the middle-aged or older individual who finds, for one reason or another, that the physician or other health service he has been accustomed to using is no longer adequate or available.[11]

The reliance on personal, non-professional advice in the health care domain should not be confined to primitive or traditional societies. Modern individuals—even when accustomed to using the professional services of a clinic, physician, or other health care agencies—may turn for a "second opinion" from a personal source. Moreover, the availability of personal sources may be the motive: the professional agencies may be closed, unavailable or requiring reservations and waiting. Many of us, when selecting these professionals, turn to personal guidance and advice: "Which doctor would you recommend?" or "What do you think of this medical insurance plan?" may serve as good examples of such advice-seeking.

Booth and Babchuk were also responsible for one of the earliest attempts to relate the opinion leadership concept to the area of medical decisions. They identified the "medical opinion leaders" in a probability sample of 800 adults (all 45 years of age and older), residing in two American midwestern urban areas. To screen the influentials, all respondents were asked if they have given advice to others regarding seeing a new doctor or using a medical service. Apart from physicians and para-medical personnel, 19 percent (148 persons) identified themselves as opinion leaders, reporting 523 others as being advised by them. Among these leaders, the researchers distinguished between "occasional opinion leaders" (those who advised only one person during the last year), and "active opinion leaders" (reported influence on several different occasions).

To test the effectiveness of the leaders, Booth and Babchuk applied a somewhat questionable method, asking the influentials themselves whether their followers eventually used the service suggested by the opinion leader. Apart from its unsatisfactory validity, this method does not reveal all the types of potential influence and advice-giving. Yet, a remarkably high proportion (88 out of 95) of the leaders reported that their counsel had been followed. A case-by-case examination of each of the clients who did not follow the influential's medical advice found them to be aged blue-collar individuals who were not related to the influential: "advisers failed when they had limited social leverage, only nominal interest in the client, and when their opinion leadership role was unlikely to be threatened if the client rejected the advice."[12]

Who Are the Non-Professional Medical Leaders?

Booth and Babchuk distinguished between active leaders, occasional leaders and non-leaders, and argued that such distinction is required to characterize the medical opinion leadership. When comparing the three groups, they found that occasional leaders did not differ significantly from the non-leaders (the rest of the sample). On the other hand, active medical opinion leaders were different in a number of respects from both the occasional leaders and the non-leaders.

The first comparison revealed that active leaders were better-informed individuals and had first-hand knowledge of the health facilities or personnel about which they offered advice. Second, a disproportionate number of the active leaders were women, which, according to Booth and Babchuk "is consistent with the care-of-the-sick-role often assigned to females."[13] And third, their self-image as leader was coordinated with their advisory role. Furthermore, the social profile of the active leaders in health care issues was unique: unlike other areas where opinion leaders were found to be equally distributed in all social strata (see chapter 5), a different pattern emerged when comparing the occasional and active leaders. The occasional leaders were equally distributed in all social strata but active leaders were under-represented in the lower strata. More active opinion leaders were found in the middle class than in the two lower classes while the frequency of occasional leaders was almost the same in all classes. Why should the distribution of active opinion leadership be positively correlated with social class while occasional leadership is not? The researchers' answer suggests that in the area of personal health care "social-class distinctions signify qualities that legitimate the adviser's position as an influential, link him with sources of information relevant to his area of leadership, and in other ways enhance his performance as an influential."[14] Though no empirical support was provided for such an explanation, the lower-class respondents in the study rated lower on these qualities and had fewer active influentials among them.

Another characteristic of the active opinion leaders in this domain was social gregariousness. These leaders were found to have more social ties, more friends, and more social contacts than the occasional leaders and the non-leaders. They were also more involved in formal voluntary associations and in every measure of social gregariousness. This may explain why occasional opinion leaders were found to restrict their influence to a spouse or close relatives while active leaders, on the other hand, were likely to influence a wider range of followers including acquaintances, co-workers, relatives, and friends. The active influential combines more activity in the flow of medical guidance, more social integration, and more activation of his or her social ties for information and influence.

The importance of the active-occasional distinction suggested the possibility of multi-step flow when information flows from prominent leaders to less active ones and from them to others. Yet, little evidence was found for such multi-step flow: most of the exchanges of information and influence did not involve a third party. In the case of a third actor, it was mainly for reassurance and not an additional step of flow: "In the case of medical decisions, the function of multi-step patterns was not to inject more information into the decision-making process, but to provide emotional support for the opinion leader."[15]

The Practical Use of Non-Professional Medical Opinion Leaders

The concept of opinion leadership and its potential for the diffusion of information appeared to attract more commercially minded researchers, mainly in the area of marketing and consumer behavior in the area of health care several projects also involved the use of opinion leaders, both among the professional community (like doctors or dentists) and among the potential clients. This section will examine the practical activation of the non-professional leaders in the area of health care.

The "public" opinion leaders in this domain may serve to identify a community's needs, expectations, and attitudes, to act as change agents and to support such a change program with their personal authority. Such an attempt was applied to develop a community-oriented mental health program in Nigeria.[16] Modern psychiatric therapeutic approaches have only recently and very slowly been introduced to Nigeria and other parts of Africa, and modern health care personnel and facilities are rather scarce and relatively inaccessible to most of the population. Moreover, Nigeria, like many other Third World countries, lacks the financial, organizational, and human resources needed for the development of a modern mental health care program. Therefore, the mental health program was geared toward the prevention of mental illness based on the maximum utilization of the very limited health workers and facilities.

An experiment in preventive psychiatry was started at Igbo-Ora in Western Nigeria. The objectives of the experiment were: (a) to promote mental health education; (b) to encourage the use of a newly established psychiatric facility; and (c) to develop community-oriented care for the mentally ill. The first stage of the experiment involved mental health care education for the local opinion leaders. However, no details are reported regarding the identification of these community influentials. Once identified, they were exposed to organized discussions and lectures that introduced them to psychiatric symptomatology. The rationale behind this training was that these people are likely to serve as the referral agents for those who may need psychiatric care and: "More important, such individuals are in a position to disseminate information about the scope of the new program in the community."[17]

At the second stage, a survey of the knowledge and attitudes of the exposed individuals was conducted in order to assess the effectiveness of the health education program. Once the researchers were convinced that the level of awareness, openness, and information regarding mental health care reached a satisfactory level (among the exposed leaders), they continued to the third stage: the formal opening of a psychiatric clinic. Lacking any control group or control measures, the validity of the procedure is rather limited. Yet, the reports on a fifteen-month intake at the clinic, and especially some individual cases (reported in the paper) may indicate the success of the program, such as an interesting finding relating to the role of the "spiritual healers." The importance of traditional healers was acknowledged by the researchers and they tried to establish cooperation with them by including them among the selected medical influentials and subjecting them to the training and information. This step proved to be efficient as the spiritual healers brought their clients to the clinic and used their influential status to promote the clinic and its services. Once again, the importance of avoiding a conflict with traditional values and institutions was highlighted in the project's conclusions: "mental health education conducted in an atmosphere of equality and respect for the belief system of others helps in removing resistance and in developing enough trust for cooperation between the western therapeutic approaches and traditional healing practices."[18]

Lay opinion leaders were also used in a special project to promote reduction of heart disease risk factors in North Karelia, Finland.[19] Over 800 lay opinion leaders were identified in numerous villages in this relatively traditional, rural farming area. First, local informants from each village were selected, with the help of the heart association staff together with the local representatives of the association. These informants, in turn, were interviewed in order to identify two opinion leaders in each of the villages. These leaders were usually found to be active members of local organizations (e.g., farmers' union, homemakers' club, village committee, and others).

The 800 opinion leaders identified by the informants were then asked to participate in a training program that introduced them to the nature and background of cardiovascular ailments, the risk factors involved, and the measures required to reduce these risks. Of the original 800 leaders, 399 remained active in the project six years after the initial training. The analysis of data regarding these lay opinion leaders revealed that most of them were women (267 out of 399); their median age was 52 years; 86 percent were married and the majority lived in large villages. The median number of years of education was seven (this was a poorly educated population), and on the average they were members of four different associations or organizations.

The training program's first success was in initiating communication from the lay opinion leaders to others: most of them reported that after the training they frequently discussed with others issues related to heart problems and disease (about 59 percent of them did so with people outside their household during the week preceding the interview). According to their impressions, 15 percent of the people responded "very positively" and 60 percent "positively." Only 1 percent were reported as "negative" responses. Discussions about physical activity were reported to be the easiest (80 percent of the leaders rated them as easy or very easy to discuss and 42 percent rated them as easy or very easy to influence towards a change), while the issues of smoking, blood pressure, and diet were rated as more difficult to discuss and to influence. Did they really influence? A partial answer is given by their effectiveness in persuading people to stop smoking, to have blood pressure measured, and to use properly drugs and other measures. Altogether 40 percent of the influentials reported that they influenced at least one person to stop smoking. Thirty-six percent reported that at least one person was convinced by them to stop smoking, and 3 percent reported that as many as six or more persons had stopped smoking as a result of their influence. The data also point to the self-reported success of the trained leaders in promoting behaviors related to hypertension and heart disease problems. sixty percent of the influentials reported convincing at least one person to have his or her blood pressure measured. Twenty-eight percent were effective in convincing at least one person to resume interrupted follow-up treatment. Thirty-four percent of the leaders were successful in promoting the proper use of antihypertensive drugs, and 46 percent in directing people to consultation with a doctor because of alarming symptoms. Twenty-nine percent convinced at least one person to join a prevention group.

One may question the validity of such self-reported measures of success. For instance, the lay opinion leaders may under- or overestimate their impact or be unaware of the hidden effects of their communicative activity. Yet, some validation was provided by "external" measures, such as the reports of the project's team and the workers of the health center, which all pointed to the positive impact of the program. Moreover, the concluding part of the report provides even a stronger evidence:

> We believe that the contribution of the lay workers [i.e., the influentials] to the overall achievements of the project is greater than the reported direct impacts because in many ways they supported other project activities in their neighborhoods, and through their own examples promoted the general project objectives...The overall evaluation of the project interventions in North Karelia from 1972 to 1982 showed a major impact on behaviors and risk factors related to cardiovascular disease, i.e., a 28 percent reduction in smoking when adjusted for simultaneous changes in a matched reference area, and the coronary mortality rates here were reduced significantly more than in the rest of the country. We feel, therefore, that the reported lay leader activity was a useful part of the project intervention.[20]

During the late 1980s and especially during the 1990s the world was threatened by the discovery of the human immunodeficiency virus (HIV), which leads to the mortal disease of acquired immunodeficiency syndrome (AIDS). The fact that people frequently seek personal advice on medical issues in general and on AIDS in particular,[21] led researchers to consider the opinion leadership concept. The motive was to reduce those high-risk sexual behaviors that increase the likelihood of infection by the HIV virus, as reductions in high-risk sexual behavior among homosexual men in urban centers appeared to limit the spread of the virus in these communities. Such findings led a team from the University of Mississippi Medical Center to conduct an experiment on reducing HIV risk behavior by using opinion leaders in gay communities.[22]

Higher HIV risk behavior levels were found among homosexual men in small cities,[23] thus guiding the project to target the male homosexual communities in small cities (in Biloxi and Hattiesburg, Mississippi, and in Monroe, Louisiana). One community (Biloxi) was randomly selected to receive intervention while the other two communities served as comparison control cities. In the intervention city, a three-stage process identified and trained opinion leaders among gay men to endorse behavior changes among their peers. To identify the leaders in this specific gay community, four club bartenders familiar with the community were trained to observe social interaction patterns in their gay clubs. Each made unobtrusive observations for one week, recording first names and a physical identifier for thirty men observed to socialize and be greeted positively most often by men in the clubs. Recording sheets were cross-matched for repeated mention; 36 of a total of 82 names received multiple nominations and were considered key popular people. Twenty-two were located, entered in the program, and asked to suggest another influential person in this community. The total group of influentials consisted of 39 men and 4 women (average education level of 13.8 years, average age of 30 years, and 91 percent were white).

The next step was "training the opinion leaders," which consisted of four weekly, 90-minute group sessions. In these sessions, the influentials were introduced to basic epidemiology on HIV infection, high-risk behavior, and precautionary changes needed to reduce risk.[24] They were taught strategies for persuasive discussions (including role playing with the participants, teaching how to present oneself as an example) and experimented with gay male friends. The outcomes of the real-life conversations were reported to the group and discussed by the group members. Of the 43 opinion leaders who began the intervention, 35 attended all the sessions. Following the training, the review of the leaders self-monitoring forms indicated that 371 peer conversations were monitored during the first two weeks. The amount of the contacts was probably larger as the leaders' activity continued beyond the first two-week period.

What was the impact of using opinion leaders to change the behavior of gay people regarding risky sexual practices? To assess the impact of the intervention, 659 individuals were surveyed in the intervention city (n=328) and the two comparison cities (n=331) before the intervention program. Then 608 were surveyed again 3 months after the intervention program (278 in the intervention city, 330 in the comparison cities). The overlap between the two samples (pre- and post-intervention) was not intended but because the researchers sampled 81 percent of all men patronizing the gay clubs in the study cities, a considerable overlap of the samples was found (ranging from 24 to 47 percent in each city). The surveys, conducted in the clubs included demographic information and measures of knowledge about HIV risk behaviors, risk reduction steps, and personal sexual behavior, including the use of low-risk practices.

A comparison of the behavioral changes caused by the intervention (causality is suggested because of the experimental design applying matched communities) revealed significant changes: the experimental community, exposed to the trained opinion leaders, changed its

HIV-risk behavior far more than the control communities. There was a decreasing engagement in unprotected anal intercourse among the gay individuals of the experimental city while the control cities revealed a lower decrease or no decrease at all. Similarly, there was an impressive increase registered in the experimental group in the use of condoms, while the control groups reported a troubling decrease in the use of this protective measure. Finally, the intervention produced a decrease in the proportion of individuals who reported multiple sexual partners in the preceding two months, an effect not found in the comparison cities.[25]

The results provide convincing evidence to the impact of this intervention program: "This study found that engaging key opinion leaders popular with gay men in small cities to serve as behavior change endorsers to their peers, produced reductions in the proportion of men in the population who engaged in high-risk activities and produced concomitant, population-wide increases in precaution-taking."[26] As the researchers noted, their findings combined with other studies on the activation of opinion leaders as change agents suggest an efficient and cost-effective prevention model for various health care issues, including drugs, smoking, physical awareness, birth control, and risky sexual behaviors.

The Practical Use of Professional Opinion Leaders

The first study of opinion leadership in the health care domain, namely the Drug Study, focused on the professional community of dentists. Subsequent studies further examined the role of influentials among physicians, medical staff, and dentists in terms of a practical activation of these leaders. For example, Soumerai and Avorn, after reviewing the literature and conducting their own experiment, suggested a method of "educational reach" (or "academic detailing") based on the identification of opinion leaders among physicians, stimulating these influential physicians' participation in educational interactions and activating them as change agents.[27] Stross and Bole observed that in surveys of community physicians, the physicians could easily identify the influentials among them. These opinion leaders were subsequently enlisted in a program to upgrade their colleagues' arthritis treatment decisions.

The Stross and Bole study examined the impact of an educational program about rheumatoid arthritis (RA) that utilizes influential physicians.[28] The influentials were identified by using a procedure suggested and described by Hiss, MacDonald, and Davis.[29] The physicians were selected from six communities and were matched for size, number of physicians, hospital resources, etc., and were randomly assigned to intervention and control groups. All the practitioners in the study were asked to keep a log regarding their patients diagnosed with rheumatoid arthritis, during a two-month period before the intervention and one year after. The influentials in the intervention groups were then exposed to the program, designed to educate them on the need to reduce use of salicylate, and increase physical therapy for RA patients.

After completion of this program, the influential physicians returned to their home communities to disseminate what they had learned. After one year, the comparison of the experimental and control hospitals revealed the success of the program. While no changes were recorded in the control group, statistically significant changes were monitored in the experimental group in which the opinion leaders were operating. Both of the measures recommended for the RA treatment (i.e., reduction of corticosteroid usage and increased use of physical therapy) changed in the experimental hospitals.[30] The results led the researchers to conclude: "Based upon the data available now, we conclude that continuing medical education delivered by community-based educationally influential physicians is an effective way of changing physician behavior."[31]

One of the more recent research projects attempted to activate opinion leaders to encourage physicians to implement practice guidelines.[32] Using a comparative research design, two strategies for encouraging local implementation of a surgical practice guideline were compared. The two strategies were (a) audit with feedback; and (b) using opinion leaders identified by their colleagues. The clinical issue was the practice of administrating Cesarean sections for women who had previously had a Cesarean section, a practice that was consistently inappropriate relative to the research evidence. The objective was to evaluate whether these strategies would, under usual clinical circumstances with non-volunteer community physicians, lead to change in terms of compliance with the guideline recommending the trial of labor and vaginal birth.

The study was conducted in Ontario, Canada, during a two-year period (1988–1989), providing enough time for monitoring the changes. Sixteen counties were randomly selected and randomly assigned to one of the two intervention or control groups. One hospital from each county was randomly selected and invited to participate in the assigned study group. All hospitals agreed to participate thus giving a random and full representation of the population. The intervention in the experimental groups were either of audit and feedback method (A/F) or the opinion leaders' education method (OLE). The control groups (i.e., control hospitals) were not exposed to either method. The A/F method involved the use of medical audit charts of the use of Cesarean sections in cases of women with a previous Cesarean section, and the discussion of the audit results (in meetings of the medical staff) to provide feedback. The OLE method required, first, to identify the opinion leaders among the physicians by mailing a questionnaire to all physicians engaged in obstetrical care in the four hospitals of the experimental group. This questionnaire, designed to identify opinion leaders, was validated in a previous study of 300 physicians.[33] The opinion leaders identified in each hospital were then asked to attend a special workshop on evidence for the practice guideline's recommendations.

Following the workshop, the influentials were asked to use their positions to influence others by: 1. mailing personal letters to each colleague in their hospital with material regarding the recommendations; 2. mailing a second wave of information, signed by the influential, addressing topics that the influentials agreed were of concern to colleagues who might wish to consider implementing the practice guidelines; 3. hosting a meeting with a an expert speaker on vaginal birth after Cesarean section; and 4. using their regular formal and informal contacts with colleagues. These forms of intervention were based on previous studies using opinion leaders in medical professional communities.[34]

The primary outcome measures were the physicians' rates for trial of labor and for vaginal birth over the 24-month study period. The rates were calculated for each group (audit and feedback method, opinion leaders method, and control group), expecting the intervention to increase the implementation of the practice guideline (i.e., trial of labor or vaginal birth). Table 13.1 presents the post-intervention measures compared for the three groups in terms of percentages of birth practices following a certain procedure out of the eligible cases (births with previous Cesarean section).

The comparison of the post-intervention practices revealed the impact of using the influentials as change agents. While the audit and feedback method did result in the expected change (there is no significant difference between the audit/feedback and the control groups), the opinion leaders' group did change, and in the desired direction. Physicians in the leaders' intervention group were much more likely to offer a trial of labor (74.2 percent of them did so, compared to 51.3 and 56.3 in the other groups), more likely to perform a trial of labor (38.2 percent compared to 28.3 and 21.4), more vaginal births (25.3 percent compared to 14.5 and 11.8) and less Cesarean sections (53.7 percent compared to 66.8 and 69.7). Even in the opinion leaders' group, about half the women eligible for a trial of labor still underwent an elective Cesarean section but the rate was 21 percent lower than in the other groups.

Table 13.1

Birth Practices Compared for the Three Study Groups

	% of Cases by Group			Differences*		
Practice	Control Group	Audit and Feedback	Opinion Leaders	%	F	P<
Offered a trial of labor	51.3	56.3	74.2	+40	10.1	.002
Underwent a trial of labor	28.3	21.4	38.2	+46	7.9	.007
Underwent a vaginal birth	14.5	11.8	25.3	+85	9.7	.003
Elective Cesarean section	66.8	69.7	53.7	−21	11.3	.001
Unscheduled Cesarean section	18.7	18.6	21.4	+14	1.9	n.s.

* Differences are between the opinion leaders group and the two other groups (control and audit/feedback) combined.

From "Opinion Leaders vs. Audit and Feedback to Implement Practice Guidelines," by J. Lomas et al., *JAMA* 265 (17), 1991, p. 2206, table 2. Copyright © 1991, American Medical Association.

Other important differences were revealed in the duration of stay in the hospital (shorter in the opinion leadership group), and various clinical measures, including Apgar scores, which were significantly better in the leaders' group.[35] An analysis of Cesarean section rates in 1987 (a year before the experiment) and the 1988–1989 intervention period revealed a strong impact of the leaders' activation toward the end of the two-year period. The mean rate for the leaders' group dropped by 11.9 over this period, whereas in both the control and the audit/feedback groups the mean rate increased, by 4.7 percent and 6.7 percent, respectively. Surveys conducted among the physicians revealed a widespread effect of the leaders' intervention program compared with both the other method and the control group. A higher percentage of doctors in the leaders' group were aware of the practice guidelines (60.3

percent compared to 43.5 and 46.2 in the audit/feedback and the control group, respectively), agreed with the recommendations (54.4 percent, compared to 45.6 and 39.7), and reported consequent changes in practice (30.9 percent compared to 23.9 and 23.1). Finally, 70 percent of the obstetricians in the leaders' communities reported changes in practice to comply with the guideline, whereas fewer than 30 percent reported such changes in the control and the audit/feedback communities. All the measures utilized resulted in the same conclusion: "When applied to physicians in community hospitals, the educational strategy of opinion leadership doing 'detailing' based on the guideline produced a significant impact on practice patterns."[36]

The influentials among the professionals in health care may not only promote innovations, practices, and techniques. They may also block them. In chapter 4, when we examined typologies of opinion leaders, we found the use of "negative" and "positive" leaders. The negative leaders are the anti-innovation leaders or innovation rejecters. The notion of negative opinion leaders was applied to the study of the diffusion of technological innovations among dentists.[37] The study focused on the use of non-precious alloys fused to porcelain as a gold substitute in the construction of crowns and bridges among dentists and prosthodontics. Data came from dentists in the Boston area (63 interviewed at home or at the office) and a national probability sample of the members of the two largest organizations in this field,[38] using a mailed questionnaire yielding 182 responses. Opinion leadership was measured by asking the dentists to identify those individuals they regard as the most technically competent and to whom they would refer, given the opportunity. Both samples (national and Boston area) were asked the same question. Considering that no constraints were put on the choice and the geographical spread, the analysis revealed a surprising amount of convergence nationwide: most of the dentists' choices identified the same four influentials. In the Boston area sample, as expected, the convergence was even more evident with one influential receiving over 54 percent of the choices. The chosen leaders were identified also as "negative" or "positive" leaders, according to their attitudes toward the innovation (i.e., the use of non-precious metals as gold substitute in dental restorations). The impact of the leaders' attitudes was revealed by comparing the groups who chose a positive or a negative influential.

Clear discrepancies were found between the dentists who cited a pro-innovation or an anti-innovation leader. The "followers" of a positive leader expressed more positive attitudes than those "following" a negative leader. Furthermore, the groups differed in actual practice as well. Non-users of the innovative practice, or those who tried it but discontinued use, were more likely to cite a negative opinion leader. Positive leaders were chosen more often by dentists who adopted the new practice and continued to use it.

Despite the significant correlation between the leaders' attitudes and their followers' behavior and attitudes, it is not clear from this study's data and analysis whether the influentials actively shaped the choices of their followers or whether they served instead as rallying points around which pro and con opinion would cluster: "Perhaps the professionals make up their minds about the innovations and simultaneously—or even after the fact—cite expert opinion to legitimize their personal decisions in a kind of post-purchase rationalization."[39] As the evidence in this study was merely correlational with no controls for establishing causality, the true impact of negative or positive leadership was not assessed. But even if anti-innovation influentials were assumed to reinforce and legitimize rather than to sway innovation adoption decisions, they would still serve an important function in the diffusion process and the professional's decision-making: the anti-innovation influentials may affect the diffusion process regardless of whether they are passive legitimizers for existing negative information about a controversial innovation, or active disseminators of anti-innovation information and influence.

Implications for Medical Programs

The cumulative empirical evidence of the important role played by key influentials in the health care domain led to several practical implications. These could be divided according to their target audiences: (a) the non-professional influentials, used to reach the patients or potential patients of health care services; and (b) the professional influentials, used to reach the medical community. Referring to the first, Booth and Babchuk conclude:

What implications do these findings have for the widespread dissemination of information about medical services? How can a health care agency take advantage of existing interpersonal networks to get such information where it is most needed? One approach is a program of 'grass-roots' personal contact supplemented by mass-communicated information complementing and legitimizing agency efforts. This mode of delivering important messages has been utilized...and has been proved to be quite effective.[40]

When doctors and medical professionals are targeted, the use of opinion leaders may have powerful impact, if activated properly. Soumerai and Avorn outlined the principles of such programs, entitled as "academic detailing":

> A key pharmaceutical marketing strategy is to identify and involve local physician opinion leaders: those individuals who tend to be early adopters of pharmaceutical innovations and important and respected sources of influence for other physicians in their communities...Through these informal social networks, a 'contagion' response is seen after adoption by the opinion leader, aided by the pharmaceutical representatives who may refer to these respected peers in their own detailing of other practitioners. The involvement of such opinion leaders in the design and implementation of quality of care or cost-containment educational interventions can also increase their effectiveness.[41]

It should be noted that the adoption of the opinion leadership concept for practical implementation in health care programs called for supportive modes of operation that included (a) the involvement of the influentials in the design and implementation of an innovation or practice; and (b) a mass-mediated campaign to back up and support the influentials' personal promotion. These two elements may involve more complex (and expensive) intervention programs but also more promising interventions. Such interventions may have medical as well as economic consequences. In a formal economic and policy analysis of an intervention program aiming to educate physicians in reducing the use of prescription drugs, Soumerai and Avorn found that implementation of this intervention for 10,000 physicians would lead to Medicaid savings of over $2 million while costing only $1 million.[42] They also estimated that targeting of higher-volume prescribers would even be more productive and result in a benefit-to-cost ratio of 3.0 or more. Ray, Schaffner, and Federspiel who activated physician-counselors to reduce the use of antibiotics, found that their intervention program resulted in a significant decreases in inappropriate prescribing of oral cephalosporines, associated with reductions in Medicaid expenditures of $43,474, or $950 per physician within the first two years.[43]

While this book is being written, increasing attention is given to the spread of the HIV virus and the resulting AIDS. The alarming statistics on the spread of the virus, the shocking predictions on the increase in future infections and victims, and the diffusion of the virus to groups that were perceived as safe from it—all led to growing interest in the contribution of social sciences to modern medicine. As the Dean of the School of Public Health at the University of Michigan, June Osborn has pointed out, we are paying the price in this crisis for allowing the natural sciences to get so far ahead of the social and behavioral sciences.[44] When the AIDS scare created the need to educate, to create awareness and change attitudes, the opinion leaders concept re-emerged.

Public education to prevent the spread of the HIV infection was the subject of a special program focusing on: (a) who should be educated? (b) what messages should be communicated? and (c) who should do the educating?[45] Drawing on the knowledge and insights from previous health care experiences and studies, Siegel argues that it is essential to recognize the need to transcend merely transmitting knowledge to the public: "In the past, health promotion campaigns have often been characterized by the naive belief that if you just give people information, they will behave in ways that the facts indicate will promote their health. Available data, however, clearly demonstrate that while the relationship between knowledge and behavior is positive, it is weak."[46] If we are to induce and maintain behavior change by creating awareness, changing attitudes and motivation for a change—the conventional campaigns—will not suffice. As a result, a growing attention is given to social agents of change: when discussing who should do the educating, Siegel points to the opinion leaders. "Greater attention should be made of opinion leaders. . . Because these people are respected and trusted, much of the public will seek to emulate their values and attitudes."[47]

Like in the case of many other crises, the AIDS crisis resulted in a public quake and the consequent after-shocks hit the scientific community. The revealed impotence of conventional methods of education and behavioral changes combined with the medical and natural sciences acknowledgement that the answer is at least partly to be found in education and influence have led to the recognition of the practical value of the opinion leadership concept. It appears that the opinion leaders have re-emerged and bloomed through the cracks created by the sediments remaining from the tidal wave of a social crisis.

Conclusions

• Personal advice and guidance plays an important role in two dimensions of health care: exchange of information and influence among medical professionals and among the "clients," the non-professionals. Both types were documented by studies, highlighting the role of personal influence among physicians and medical staff as well as among the patients.

• In the medical domain the flow of influence, unlike other domains, appears to involve tension and even anxiety. The need to rely on personal authority, prestige, and experience is heightened by the nature of problems that often involve sickness, pains, fears, and personal worries and anxieties.

• Among the health care professionals (doctors, dentists, nurses, and others) as well as the patients (or potential patients) there are certain influentials, the health care opinion leadership. Their guidance, advice, and information affect the decisions and attitudes of both the professionals and the non-professionals.

• Several projects involved the activation of opinion leaders, both among the professional community (like doctors or dentists) and among the potential clients. Those studies revealed the practical value of the medical opinion leaders who may act as "positive" promoters of innovations, practices, and knowledge, as well as "negative" leaders who block innovations, new technologies, or practices.

• Practical implications of the opinion leadership concept and research in the health care domain include programs designed for the activation of professional and non-professional influentials to disseminate information and legitimize health care practices, in terms of awareness, knowledge, and acceptance.

• The implementation of programs based on influentials as change agents may not only be helpful in terms of personal health care but also in economic measures, such as reducing Medicaid expenditures, minimizing the inappropriate use of prescriptions and overpromotion of drugs by pharmaceutical marketing, and preventing the use of addictive drugs.

Part 4

The Fight for Survival

The "golden age" of the opinion leadership concept yielded hundreds of studies and reports, applications, and developments. The concept's theoretical and practical appeal crossed the boundaries between disciplines, societies, and cultures. It attracted researchers from medicine to politics, marketing to family planning, AIDS prevention to clothing fashion, and agriculture to birth control. However, the concept has been a subject of growing criticism. The weaknesses and shortcomings of the original conceptualization of opinion leadership, and especially that of the two-step flow model, were exposed by several studies, which resulted in a critical perspective combining theoretical, ideological, and methodological aspects.[1]

In the following chapters, we will examine the criticisms of the original opinion leadership concept. The wave of criticism, though concentrating on real weaknesses, caused a decline in the popularity and attraction of the original concept. In fact, it caused an "over-kill" by avoiding to preserve those elements that were not questioned or, following certain modifications, proved to be valid. This was a "fight for survival" of a paradigm, with dynamic exchanges of criticism, answers, modifications, and lingering debates. Yet, a new conceptualization of the influentials emerged from amidst the turmoil. The concluding chapters will present the new measure of influenceability, its relevance to the original opinion leaders idea, and its applicability to media effects and especially the process of agenda-setting. As we will demonstrate, the new scale and measures used to study the influentials, led to a substantial breakthrough. It highlighted the influential's functions in the process of shaping the public agenda or forming and molding the climate of opinion thus reviving and preserving the notions of personal influence, limited and "mediated" mass communication effects, and the existence of "people who influence people."

14

Criticism and Modifications

Numerous criticisms have been directed at the two-step flow model and the related concept of opinion leadership. This chapter reviews the criticism of the original concept, according to the following categories: theoretical-ideological criticism and empirical-methodological criticism. Some of the critics suggested modifications and amendments to the original model and these will be detailed in the concluding section of this chapter.

Theoretical-ideological Criticism

The studies conducted by Lazarsfeld and his colleagues between 1940 and 1960 did not only discover the opinion leaders and their mediating role between the mass media and the public attitudes and choices; they also established the so-called "limited effects" paradigm. The media, according to the Columbia research tradition, were not as powerful as was assumed. The public was found to be more active, less lonely, and less vulnerable. Defended by their selective consumption of the media and by the selective mediating function of the opinion leaders, people could fend off media influences and protect their attitudes, preferences, and values. The limited-effects of the media as a central element in the opinion leadership and two-step flow became the main source for the theoretical-ideological criticism directed at this paradigm.

In 1978, Todd Gitlin published *Media Sociology: The Dominant Paradigm*, charging that the limited-effects paradigm was masking the true power of the media.[1] According to Gitlin,

The dominant paradigm in media sociology. . . has drained attention from the power of the media to define normal and abnormal social and political activity, to say what is politically real and legitimate and what is not. . . By its methodology,

239

media sociology has highlighted the recalcitrance of audiences, their resistance to media-generated messages, and not their dependency, their acquiescence, their gullibility.[2]

Gitlin argued that the most single influential theory in media sociology has been the two-step flow concept with its emphasis on the opinion leaders as playing a crucial role in the flow of mass communication. Gitlin, who attributed to the media powerful effects, rejected the two-step flow model and the functions related to the opinion leaders. The opinion leader is celebrated, he argued, because administrative researchers study proximate causes that are accessible to their patrons, the media organizations themselves, and the dominant values of the capitalist society:

> If we step back from the Decatur study and its successors to the general style of thought they embody, to their sociological tenor, we find a whole and interwoven fabric of ideological predispositions and orientations. We find, in particular, an *administrative point of view* rooted in academic sociology's ideological assimilation into modern capitalism and its institutional rapprochement with major foundations and corporations...The crucial point is that the administrative mentality of Lazarsfeld and Stanton harmonized with the corporate interest of CBS [television network] and with the practical program of the Rockefeller Foundation and with the swelling positivist mode of American social science.[3]

The ideological-theoretical bias of Lazarsfeld, according to Gitlin, is manifested in *Personal Influence*. These theoretical assumptions, rooted in the behaviorist orientation of the researchers, should be regarded as *limiting* and *weakening* the findings and the subsequent interpretations. These assumptions were:

1. *Commensurability of modes of influence.* The impact of the mass media was presumed to be comparable to personal influence, with the two "forms of influence" regarded as functional equivalents.
2. *Power as distinct occasions.* The measurement of influence by studying discrete incidents in a "behaviorization of power" was typical to the Columbia studies.
3. *Commensurability of buying and politics.* The areas of marketing, politics, fashion, and movie-going were perceived as comparable within a single theory and measurable by a single method.

4. *"Change" as the sole dependent variable.* Influence was identified by the occurrence of "attitude change," disregarding the case of reinforcement as an effect or the prevention of a change as an effect.
5. *Opinion leaders as followers.* The opinion leaders, defined as experts by their acquaintances, were perceived as influentials while they are actually mere conduits for the media.[4]

The strongest point in the ideological-theoretical criticism, even according to Katz himself,[5] is in the issue of change vs. maintaining status quo. The Columbia scholars and their followers emphasized the role of the media in "reinforcement," in preventing changes[6] while measuring influence in terms of attitude *change*. The criticism, thus, focuses on the latent power of the media to prevent changes and maintain the status quo, which should not be regarded as a residual category but as a major function. Katz summarizes this claim directed at his own work, some thirty years later:

> The hegemonic mission of the media, in other words, is not to tell us what to think or what to think about, but what *not* to think, what *not* to think about...Gitlin accuses the administrative researcher of giving legitimacy to the elites who set agendas, specify choices, or, worse, deliberately offer false choices between things that are the same or about which the establishment is indifferent.[7]

This "illusion of choice" is guiding the researchers who measure impact only by change of attitude when comparing products and candidates while excluding those issues not to be considered or thought of. Horkheimer and Adorno,[8] and Hall,[9] each in a different way, warned that the media produce the illusion of classness and consensus by ruling certain position and certain genres in and out of order.

In addition to being guided by an "administrative mentality," the Columbia studies and especially the work of Lazarsfeld, were criticized for being "marketing oriented": "Although he became known in the U.S. as a member of the sociology faculty at Columbia, Lazarsfeld's basic academic orientation was to the psychology of marketing," noted Chaffee and Hochheimer.[10] Gitlin argued that Lazarsfeld brought to the American academy a particular variant of administrative thought—the marketing orientation. Gitlin examined the personal biography of Lazarsfeld, his education, early publications, and funding sources, to expose the ideological and institutional commitments that guided

Lazarsfeld to the marketing oriented perspective. The fact that Lazarsfeld's projects were supported and funded by the Rockefeller Foundation, Columbia University's Office of Radio Research, *Life* magazine, CBS television network, and others was perceived as a source of bias, especially with regard to minimizing media effects. Gitlin, for example, was quite frank about it:

> The Rockefeller program insisted on underwriting only studies that were consonant with the empiricist program, and at least one instance Lazarsfeld described, the hand that paid the piper did actually and directly, and apparently despite Lazarsfeld's hesitation, call the proverbial tune.[11]

When Lazarsfeld invited Adorno to the United States in 1938, he wanted to link Adorno's ideas to his empirical research at Columbia. Yet, Adorno found the funding sources somewhat limited the scope of research and indirectly criticized Lazarsfeld by writing:

> Naturally there appeared to be little room for critical social research in the framework of the Princeton Project. Its charter, which came from the Rockefeller Foundation, expressly stipulated that the investigations must be performed within the limits of the commercial radio system prevailing in the United States. It was thereby implied that the system itself, its cultural and sociological consequences and its social and economic presuppositions were not to be analyzed.[12]

The theoretical-ideological criticism founded its arguments upon the link between ideology and theory, between the desire for harmonious relations among social institutions and the functional, harmonizing role of opinion leaders. Most of the criticism at this theoretical level was within the lingering debate on the power of mass media. Both sides were guided by their basic views on the nature of society and social stability. The emergence of the opinion leaders concept seemed to the critical school as an attempt to conceal the real power of the media by proposing "human mediators," "longer chain of influence," and an emphasis to the "part played by people." And the debate on this level is far from ending. As Katz noted, "much of the history of this enterprise [communication research], discipline or not, can be written as a set of continuing arguments with Paul Lazarsfeld. Far from subsiding, these arguments have become more pointed in the last decade."[13]

Empirical-methodological Criticism

The empirical-methodological weaknesses of the two-step flow model and the opinion leadership concept, as they were studied and measured by the early studies, included the following aspects:

Ignoring the Evidence of Direct Flow

Many studies indicate that major news stories are spread directly by the mass media to a far greater extent than by personal sources. Westley cited several studies supporting the direct flow.[14] One of these was Deutschmann and Danielson's report on several studies of the diffusion of knowledge of major news stories.[15] Their summary listed several key findings:

1. Initial mass media information on important events goes directly to people on the whole and is not relayed to any great extent.
2. People talk about important news they have learned from the mass media.
3. Opinion leaders, who have more information, may do supplementary relaying (concurrent with the reinforcement function) when the topic arises.

Deutschmann and Danielson found little confirmation for a two-step flow and activation of the opinion leaders in the case of major news events. Interpersonal communication regarding the news was present, but unimportant as far as *diffusion* was concerned. We should note, however, that their studies dealt only with important events, characterized by high interest and rapid diffusion. Moreover, they studied only diffusion of information and not forming, reinforcing of, or changing attitudes. Later, Greenberg verified the one-step flow by his finding that major news through mass media goes directly to a majority of the public.[16] But Greenberg argued that interpersonal flow as the primary source is more evident in the diffusion of events that receive *maximum* or *minimum* attention from the population. For example, interpersonal communication accounted for 57 percent of initial learning of John F. Kennedy's assassination.[17] Thus, Greenberg suggested that personal channels are more active in the case of events that come to the attention of nearly everyone or practically no one. He also highlighted the distinction between "importance" of a news event and the "attention" given to it, a distinction that serves as additional criticism (see "Ignoring the More-than-two-step Flow," which follows).

In a study of the diffusion of the news about President Johnson's decision not to run again for presidency (March 31, 1968), Allen and Colfax found support for a direct, one-step flow.[18] Only 5 percent of the respondents heard the news by word-of-mouth. Similarly, the study of the diffusion of the announcement of Pope Paul regarding the Catholic Church position on birth control, found that of those who heard the story, virtually all (97.8 percent) heard it from the mass media.[19] Indeed, few respondents in American national surveys identify "other people" as an important source of news.[20] Robinson found that on a typical day respondents reported fewer than 10 percent of their most interesting conversations concerned things in the news media,[21] while in another study he found the press as the "political kingmaker," when their endorsement directly affected voters' choices.[22] It appears that at certain instances of news events, and especially with regard to diffusion of knowledge (as opposed to attitudes), the two-step flow model "does not square well with recent empirical findings."[23]

Ignoring Horizontal Flow

The assumption of vertical flow underlies the original opinion leadership concept. It assumes that opinion leaders get their information from the mass media and pass it on to their followers. However, such perception ignores the possibility that opinion leaders rely on other sources (interpersonal too), or that some of the flow is horizontal, among leaders or among followers, in the form of "opinion sharing." Troldahl and Van Dam reported a study of face-to-face communication about major topics in the news.[24] They measured opinion leadership by questioning whether anyone had asked the person for his or her opinions on a topic and whether the person had asked anyone about the topic. Thus they identified "opinion givers" and "opinion askers." However, they found that three-fourths of the conversations involved *both* giving and asking, or in other words a substantial amount of "opinion sharing."

Moreover, Troldahl and Van Dam found that frequent conversations are more prevalent among opinion leaders than between opinion leaders and the followers, a horizontal flow that had been advanced by Wright and Cantor.[25] In a study of the American electorate during election campaign, Robinson studied the consumption of mass media and interpersonal communication.[26] The analysis concentrated on political opinion giving and opinion receiving during the 1968 campaign. It revealed a strong correlation (.40) between the two, indicating that "instead of the population being divided into opinion leaders and opinion receivers, to a large extent the two terms refer to the same people"[27] and offering a strong confirmation for the "opinion sharing" notion. In chapter 6 (Who Leads the Leaders?) we reviewed the studies on the sources of the influentials. They were found to rely heavily on a multitude of sources, including interpersonal communication with their peers. This led Robinson to suggest that, "The considerable conventional activity *within* the ranks of the opinion leaders deserves far more recognition, and perhaps primary attention, in the model."[28]

Ignoring the More-than-two-step Flow

The limitation of the original model to two steps was criticized even by the Columbia scholars themselves, suggesting "longer chains of influence." This idea was later developed into multi-step models, discussed later in this chapter. The additional steps included the leader-to-leader flow, the follower-to-follower flow, the upward flow from follower to leader,[29] the more active leader to a less active leader, from the media directly to the public, and other options. The original two-step terminology can be used to describe only one case of many forms of flow, affected by the nature of the item, time frame, form of exchange (influence or information), cultural and social setting, and other variables. Nevertheless, though this pattern is a frequent mode of flow, it should not exclude the existence of longer or shorter chains of flow.

The Use of Crude Dichotomy Between Leaders and Non-leaders

The classification of individuals into two broad categories of leaders and non-leaders was a source of consistent criticism. Lin concluded that "the definition of the opinion leader versus non-opinion leader dichotomy is also unclear and the problem is further confounded by varying operationalizing methods."[30] Troldahl and Van Dam compared the two categories (opinion givers and opinion askers) and were surprised to find *no* significant differences in mass media use, nor in gregariousness, nor in self-perceived opinion leadership.[31] But they soon realized that a solution may be found by further dividing the population. They added a third category (the "inactives" who had not talked to anyone about the topic) and compared the three groups. Using the new classification they found clear differences between the opinion givers, askers, and inactives. Many of the more recent studies of the influentials applied a rank-order categorization and even continuous measurement. As reviewed in chapter 3, the methods of identifying opinion leaders have become more sophisticated and that included the use of *continuum* of opinion leadership rather than the use of crude dichotomy.

Additional support to the continuous measures of leadership came from the use of "network analysis." The use of sociometric measures in large communities, made possible by modern technology and sophisticated programs, allowed the researchers to study the network centrality of the influentials, their communicative activity and their connectivity and translate these into a more sensitive measure of leadership.

Standardization of Measurement for Information and Influence

The term "flow of ideas," frequently used by the Columbia researchers, should be replaced by two terms—the flow information and the flow of influence. In fact, such distinction would have saved a considerable amount of criticism: most of the instances of direct flow were related to flow of news (i.e., information) while the opinion leaders were related more to choices (i.e., influence). The confusion of the two types of communications had serious empirical implications: the methodological design involved decision-making (such as public affairs issues), awareness and knowledge, leading Chaffee and Hochheimer to argue: "The Columbia research design *was largely inappropriate* to understanding the dynamics of political behavior, communication flow, and information-seeking."[32]

The decision-making process involves different stages that were often perceived as comprising the stages of awareness, interest, evaluation, trial, and adoption. In each of these stages, different sources may be used thus requiring a methodological differentiation between information (more evident in the early stages) and influence (more evident in the later stages). Van Den Ban's study showed that opinion leaders as well as their followers are influenced by mass media and by other people; but the reliance on these sources varies during different stages of the adoption process.[33] Weimann compared the role of opinion leaders in the dissemination of various information items (gossip, general news, and consumer information) and decision-making items involving influence, and found that their functions vary in the flow of information when compared to influence.[34] Individuals who are active disseminators of information may not be the opinion shapers in decision-making items and moreover, the followers rely on different sources according to their position on the awareness-to-adoption process.

Standardization of Measurement Across Domains

At this stage, after reviewing the studies in such various domains as marketing, politics, fashion, science, and agriculture, we are aware of the variance across domains. The differences are significant in many aspects of opinion leadership, from their characteristics to their impact. Yet, the original concept of opinion leadership applied a "standard" measurement to diverse domains. Gitlin argues that such standardization reflects the administrative approach, the political values of capitalist ideology, and the marketing orientation of Lazarsfeld and his followers. Even if we do not accept this ideological reasoning, it is clear that the same measurement was applied to political issues as well as to movie-going, fashion, and daily shopping. While Gitlin stresses the "commensurability of buying and politics," the criticism is directed even to the standardization of the "buying domain" itself. As described in chapter 7, even within the marketing area there are significant differences across product categories; thus the validity of any generalization is questionable. It is evident, today, that the influentials' identity and functioning should be studied in specific methods and measures developed for each domain.

Standardization of Measurement Across Cultures and Societies

The opinion leaders concept appealed to scholars from various disciplines and areas. It also attracted a wide range of researchers and followers from many countries and cultures. However, their studies only exposed the problems arising when implementing the concept in different cultural and social settings. For instance, in developing societies where the mass media are scarce, the applicability of the opinion leadership idea is quite unique. In his review of cross-cultural studies on the two-step flow model, Bostian argued that opinion leaders differ across societies.[35] Based on the studies conducted in modern (mainly industrial) and developing (non-industrialized, rural) societies, Bostian compiled a list of specific attributes of the two-step flow model. When applied to developing societies these attributes are:

1. Mass media messages are less influential and instrumental.
2. The opinion leaders rarely rely on the media as their sources of information.
3. When the media is instrumental and relevant (that is, in more advanced societies), the two-step model operates at a higher level than in developing countries.

4. Interpersonal channels and thus the two-step flow are more important than in developing societies.

5. Influence is an important relay of information: most information is relayed because of persuasive element and not as a result of information-seeking.

6. Opinion leaders and their followers share fewer characteristics than do their counterparts in developed societies.

7. The relation between innovativeness and opinion leadership is stronger in progressive than in traditional societies.

This comparison illustrates how the identity, functions, features, and traits of opinion leaders vary across societies. Needless to say, adding other cross-cultural differences (e.g., modernization, political systems, technology, or religiosity) would expose more cultural-bound differences in opinion leadership.

The Use of Short Time Frames

The Columbia studies had limited samples of time and "their implicit ahistorical assumption of the homogeneity of times was unavoidable," argued Chaffee and Hochheimer.[36] Katz and Lazarsfeld reminded the reader of *Personal Influence* in one footnote that "the study was completed before the general introduction of television,"[37] yet their conclusions generalized about the flow of mass communication. The problem is not merely the predating of television or other social changes, but the larger question of employing short time framework when studying long-term, historical processes. Gitlin noted:

> As their rhetoric makes clear, Katz and Lazarsfeld did not intend simply to make assertions about the relations between more and less media-exposed women in Decatur, Illinois, in the summer of 1945; *they intended general statements, valid across the boundaries of time.* Because of the methodological difficulties that would be entailed in studying long-run effects in a positive fashion, they and their followers constructed a paradigm, which would then be taken as valid over the historical long haul.[38]

The study of media effects by tracing short-term changes of opinion or choice is far from reflecting the long-term, accumulative impact of media messages. It is also far from reflecting the actual functioning of personal influence and the more influential individuals. Thus, in terms of time framework, the original studies attempted to present a general pattern while both predating significant changes (e.g, the power of television) and applying short-term measures.

Empirical Discrepancies

The identification of opinion leadership has become a developing area of research. As our review in chapter 3 explains, more sophisticated and sensitive methods were developed, tested, and validated. Yet, most of the opinion leadership conceptualization is based on the early studies, which applied questionable tactics and measures. For instance, Katz and Lazarsfeld used only two questions to identify the influentials.[39] The distribution of scores on these two questions was categorized into "leaders" and "followers." Later research suggested that such measurement is over-simplified, creating the limited leader/non-leader dichotomy, and low in its reliability and validity.

Moreover, even in the vintage *Personal Influence*, numerous discrepancies were included. Some of these were discrediting the idea of two-step flow or that of opinion leadership. For example, Katz and Lazarsfeld reported that fifty-eight percent (of the *changes*, not the *changers*) were apparently made without involving any remembered personal contact, and were, very often dependent upon the mass media.[40] This finding is in fact very consistent with the old "hypodermic" notion of powerful media. Gitlin argued that this, as well as other discrepancies, were "pushed off to one side" while the findings supporting the general theory were highlighted.[41] Indeed, the data reported by Katz and Lazarsfeld often reveals their methodological problems. As an illustrative example, one can look at the method of "validation": people named as influentials were asked to confirm that status. It appears that the rates of confirmation were rather low in the public affairs domain. Only 37 percent of the designated leaders confirmed their status (compared to 71 percent for marketing influentials and 61 percent for fashions). This may stem from the low validity of the leadership scale or at least when applied to certain domains, the existence of direct flow in the case of public affairs or a more complex form of flow of influence less known to the influential than to the influencee. At the beginning of chapter 4 we discussed a potential typology of influence including those types that are not traced by the conventional survey design. The commonly phrased "who influenced you?" or "did you influence others?" scales are not designed to identify and measure all forms of influence.

Modifications and Amendments

The criticism of the early conceptualization and measures resulted in several modifications of the original model. As early as 1955 Menzel and Katz noted: "We found it necessary to propose amendments to the two-step flow of communication by considering the possibility of multi-step rather than two-step flow."[42] Yet, many more amendments and re-formulations followed, leading to new and modified versions of the concept and its implications. Let us examine the main modifications with regard to the role of the opinion leaders. Some of these are already established and validated changes while some are still at the suggestion stage:

Multi-step Flow

The basic two-step model was replaced by a more complex model, which includes the following optional directions of flow:

- *Horizontal* (among leaders, among followers) and *vertical* (leaders to followers, active to inactive)
- *Direct* (linking two actors directly) and *indirect* (linking actors through a third party or a chain of intermediaries)
- *Downward* (leaders to followers, media to public) and *upward* (from opinion leaders to media, followers to influentials, marginals to centrals)

In Robinson's suggested modification of the two-step model,[43] there are six possible "linkages" or directions of flow: 1. media to opinion leaders; 2. media to less attentive; 3. opinion leaders to less attentive; 4. opinion leaders to opinion leaders; 5. less attentive to opinion leaders; and 6. less attentive to less attentive. These options illustrate the varieties included in a multi-step model. They include direct flow (e.g., media to less attentive), indirect (media to less attentive through opinion leaders), vertical (e.g., media to opinion leaders), horizontal (leaders to leaders or less attentive to less attentive), downward (leaders to less attentive), and upward (less attentive to opinion leaders).

Adding to the complexity, and to the accuracy of the model, is the needed distinction between the flow of "information" and of "influence." This may explain why often the media are used as main sources of direct information while in terms of decision making or the flow of influence, less direct and more personal communications are involved. Moreover, it may involve the first step of media-to-leaders as a flow of information followed by a second step of influence from leaders to their followers:

"information characterizing the link between the mass media and opinion leaders, and influence the link by which opinion leaders structure this information to influence those less active."[44]

Continuous Measures of Leadership

Since the early measure based on a two-item scale, various measures have been developed. As reviewed in chapter 3, four main methods of identifying opinion leaders have emerged in the expanding research in this area. These are: 1. the sociometric method; 2. the informants' ratings method; 3. the self-designation method; and 4. the observation method. The various methods were compared and found to have varying validity and efficiency according to the population studied, the subject area, and other factors. Nevertheless, within the various methods opinion leadership has been perceived as a continuous variable rather than a simple dichotomy,[45] thus requiring a much more sophisticated measurement and scaling. Many of the attempts reported earlier in this book resulted in improving the measures, their validation, and their accuracy. For example, one of the main limitations of the validation procedures of the opinion leadership scales concerns the level of measuring leadership and the other constructs: both should be studied at the same level of specificity. Measures of self-esteem, innovativeness, or information seeking should be applied at the same level of the opinion leadership measurement: if the leadership is identified and measured within a specific domain (cars, for example), then the construct measures of innovativeness or information seeking or any other measure, should be studied in the same domain (information seeking about cars, innovativeness about cars, etc.).

The Mergence with Network Analysis

The developing theory and methodology of network analysis, combined with technological innovations that facilitated the sociometric study of large communities contributed to "modernizing" the concept of personal influence. As Sheingold, who called for the use of social networks data as a "resurrection" of the Columbia research agenda,[46] argued:

The analytical focus of most of the Columbia work is on individual decision making. . . An alternative focus is the social networks through which information and influence flow. This raises the question of how information gets to the individual, in contrast to what information finally arrives. Social networks constitute social structures, which exist independent of the perceptions of discrete individuals. The information an individual receives may enamate from others with whom he is not in direct contact and of whom he may be unaware. Thus, network structures cannot be directly studied within the confines of self-report data. Direct network data are required.[47]

Much research on social networks has been done in the recent decades and some of it has focused upon the role of influentials or "centrals," applying various structural measures taken from network analysis procedure.[48] Modern network analysis may owe some of its prosperity to modern technologies of data processing, namely high-speed computers, special programs for sociometric data analysis, and sophisticated mathematical procedures, such as matrix algebra and sociometric topology. Yet, it was not merely technology but, moreover, the potential. Network analysis provided a promising bridge between small groups and individuals at the micro level and large-scale social process at the macro level. Granovetter argued that "the analysis of processes in interpersonal networks provides the most fruitful micro-macro bridge. In one way or another, it is through these networks that small-scale interaction becomes translated into large-scale patterns, and that these, in turn, feed back into small groups."[49]

The feasibility of network analysis to study opinion leadership was demonstrated by several empirical studies.[50] These studies soon revealed the centrality of opinion leaders in their social networks. A study of the communication networks in a Israeli Kibbutz, found that opinion leaders are the "sociometric stars" in highly dense network. (This project will be presented in the next chapter.) In flow of information and influence, the "centrals" or the opinion leaders were more active. They were the most frequent disseminators of information items (except for gossip), the most active influentials, and their activity rated higher on each of the efficiency scales. (That is, messages originating from them were regarded as more accurate and more credible, and were diffused faster.)[51] Though this study highlighted the role of "marginals" as the individuals who bridge different groups or cliques by their frequent inter-group communication, the intra-group flow was carried out mainly by the opinion leaders, enjoying their centrality within their cliques or social groups.

Similar findings were revealed in studies of scientific opinion leaders. Chapter 11 detailed the various studies relating the network positions to the status of scientific influentials. The accumulating findings from numerous studies in various scientific areas indicated clearly the presence of an "invisible college," a term coined by Crane in her research on networks of scholars linked to central, influential scientists.[52] As recalled earlier, innovations adopted by these central figures were more widely accepted by other members of the field than innovations they did not adopt. A similar pattern was reported by Zaltman and Blau who studied 977 high-energy physicists from thirty-six countries.[53] In the political domain, Schenk and Pfenning related measure of network characteristics to political leadership in German samples and found a strong correlation between leadership and the networks size and multiplexity.[54] Multiplexity refers to the multidimensionality of the relationships in the network thus indicating that opinion leaders are involved in networks that combine various dimensions of social ties. The social accessibility of the influentials is facilitated and activated by their network characteristics: central positions, involvement in multiplex and large networks, and links to interlocking and radial networks.

In fact, the Columbia researchers noted the potential of network analysis. The major finding reported in *The People's Choice* was the correlation between opinion leadership and exposure to the mass media. From this, originated the two-step model. But in the next project, reported in *Voting*, opinion leaders, in addition to being heavily exposed to the media, were also prone to seek the advice of others, leading the authors to suggest that ". . .unending circuits of leadership [run] through the community like a nerve system through the body."[55] Several decades later this "nerve system" was studied by the advanced methods of network analysis.

The Uses of Media: Form vs. Amount of Exposure

One of the main weaknesses of the original conceptualization of opinion leadership was the somewhat over-simplified role of the mass media. The opinion leaders were perceived as more exposed to the media and consequently better informed than the others. However, several studies determined that (a) opinion leaders are not always more exposed to the media than non-leaders[56] and (b) opinion leaders often rely on non-media sources. Consequently, more attention was paid to the form of media consumption (as opposed to the simple measure of amount of exposure).

Regrettably, only few studies set out to examine this aspect of opinion leadership. Nevertheless, those that did, provided support for this suggested trait of the influentials (see detailed review in chapter 6). For example, Richmond tested the information acquisition skills of opinion leaders.[57] She reported that "it was found that under either voluntary or forced exposure conditions, individuals reporting high opinion leadership acquire more information than people reporting either moderate or low opinion leadership."[58] The findings of a study conducted by Levy on opinion leadership and the uses of television news highlighted another dimension of the form of media exposure related to leadership.[59] Levy found that public affairs leaders do not differ from non-leaders in their amount of television news consumption but rather in the *uses* of their exposure. He reported very weak correlations between amount of television news viewing and opinion leadership but a direct and strong relationship between opinion leadership and endorsement of cognitive orientation. As opinion leadership increased, the viewing of television news was explained by cognitive needs and mainly the need of information acquisition and cognitive orientation. As Levy suggested, these findings make it more important to examine possible *qualitative* differences between opinion leaders and non-leaders in terms of their forms of consumption and not mere amount of exposure.

The various modification and amendments revived the interest in the opinion leaders and their functioning within a multi-step model. One of the recent attempts was initiated in Germany and followed up by studies in Israel and the United States—the study of the "influentials." The next chapters will present this new measure and its different conception of the opinion leaders.

The Influentials:
Reemergence of Opinion Leaders?

The concept of opinion leadership has been related to a lingering theoretical and methodological debate. This chapter examines a new measure to identify opinion leaders (the Strength of Personality Scale) developed by the Allensbach Survey Center in West Germany. The results of applying this measure in Germany, the United States, and Israel were confirming of its validity and efficiency. The findings, however, do not suggest that the influentials identified by this scale are the opinion leaders according to the original conceptualization but fit better the more sophisticated characterization of opinion leadership that stemmed from remodifications of the original concept of opinion leaders.

PS: The Emergence of a New Scale

The measurement of opinion leadership was subjected to theoretical and empirical criticism. This criticism, combined with the need for more sophisticated and validated measurement of opinion leadership, has led to the development of new measurement procedures. One of the recent attempts was initiated by the German public opinion scholar Noelle-Neumann, and the German survey research center, the *Allensbach Institut für Demoskopie.* It was the German news magazine *Der Spiegel* that initiated the process: interested in what they referred to as "the active consumers who set standards in their community," managers of *Der Spiegel* challenged the Allensbach Institute with the task of developing an instrument that would identify the influentials.[$] The researchers, directed by Noelle-Neumann, tested numerous questionnaire items related to self perceived personal influence.[1] These early scales were tested and refined after years of pretest with national samples in Germany. The resulting scale was entitled the Strength of

Personality Scale (*Personlichkeitsstärke*). It was established after a factorial reduction of a 34-item questionnaire administered to a representative sample of 3,542 residents of then West Germany. The final version of the scale includes 10 items that were later weighted according to their part-whole correlations with the total scale, with the scores on this scale range from 75 to 149. Table 15.1 presents the items and their weights.

Table 15.1

The Personality Strength (PS) Scale and Weighting

| | Weight | |
Item	yes	no
1. I usually count on being successful in everything I do	13	7
2. I am rarely unsure about how I should behave	14	7
3. I like to assume responsibility	15	7
4. I like to take the lead when a group does things together	17	8
5. I enjoy convincing others of my opinions	15	7
6. I often notice that I serve as a model for others	16	8
7. I am good at getting what I want	14	7
8. I am often a step ahead of others	18	9
9. I own many things others envy me for	15	9
10. I often give others advice and suggestions	12	6

Maximum score: 149
Minimum score: 75

Note: The procedure of weighting is detailed by Noelle-Neumann.[2]

The respondents were divided into four approximate quartiles, thus yielding four levels of personal strength (strong, above average, moderate, and weak). To test the scale's reliability, a test-retest procedure was applied. A panel of 716 Germans from the North Rhine-Westphalia region were measured twice (with approximately six months between the two measurements). The correlations of the test-retest were all strong and statistically significant and did not vary considerably across subpopulations. (They range from the lowest Gamma coefficient of .61 to the highest coefficient of .68.) Moreover, another testing procedure was employed: using a sample of 8,000 Germans interviewed in Germany, 1984, a split-half method tested the scale internal consistency. The coefficient found between the two parts of the scale was .80, indicating a significant consistency.

The Validation of the Personality Strength Scale

The procedure used by the Allensbach Institute to validate the scale involved the comparison of the scale ratings with the interviewer's impression (whether the respondent "radiates strength and energy" as opposed to "being boring," whether the respondent gave the impression of "being a model for others" and whether he or she appeared "self-assured" during the interview). The relationship between the scale and the interviewers' ratings was studied in numerous surveys using national samples in Germany.[3] A comparison of the PS scale ratings and the interviewers' ratings reveals strong correlations. The respondents with higher personality strength (PS) levels appeared to be more impressive in terms of personal energy or charisma, and the ability to serve as model for others. However, this test is weakened by the possibility that the interviewers were influenced by the respondent's self-assessment. The need to validate the scale by an "external" criterion led to an additional study, conducted in a different society and cultural setting.[4]

The scale was administrated to Israeli samples. The first (n=650) was randomly drawn from the adult, Jewish population of Israel. The respondents were interviewed at home with a pre-structured questionnaire that included thirty-four statements among which were the final ten PS scale items. (The respondent had to choose those cards that carry statements suited to his self-assessment, thus dichotomizing the answers.) Additional questions included socio-demographic characteristics, measures of community participation, media exposure and use, functioning as advice-givers in various areas, patterns of sociability, and social involvement. This first sample was used to examine the applicability of the PS scale to another society and to study cross-cultural differences.

The first step involved cross-cultural comparison of the scale's results by applying several statistical procedures to the data collected in the German sample (n=3542) and the first Israeli sample (n=650). A factor analysis of the responses to the thirty-four-item questionnaire was performed for both samples (using a principal components solution with varimax rotation). It revealed that in both samples the same ten items used for the PS scale emerged as strongly loaded on one factor, accounting for approximately 41 percent of the variance in each sample. This suggests stability across social and cultural settings. A split-half reliability test for both samples yielded coefficients of .78 and .76 for the German and Israeli samples, respectively. When the ten-item scale itself is factor analyzed, two distinct factors emerge: a principle one accounting for 75 percent of the variance (72 percent in the Israeli sample) that includes seven items (1, 2, 3, 4, 5, 7, and 10) and a second factor that includes three items (6, 8, and 9). The first factor was suggested to measure *internal* sources of influenceability, whereas the second describes *external* origins, derived from comparison with other people.[5]

Following the procedure of the Allensbach studies, the relationships between the PS and socio-demographic characteristics were examined. The breakdowns of the German and the Israeli national samples, obtained by cross-classifying PS groupings with various socio-demographic factors, indicate that PS is related to various social characteristics,and these relationships are very similar for both populations. In terms of gender, there is a sharp difference between males and females: males score higher on PS. For instance, male-to-female ratio in the "strong" PS level is 1.47 in the German sample and 1.88 in the Israeli one. In the "weak" PS category, females outnumber males by a ratio of 1.42 in Germany and 2.18 in Israel. PS was also unevenly distributed by age groups. The highest PS scores are more frequent in the 30–39 age group (in both samples) while the "weak" level is more frequent in the 60 plus age group: 23 percent of this age group are rated as "weak" in the German sample and 48 percent in the Israeli one. The strongest distinction is revealed by social economic status (SES) classification. A person in the higher SES levels has more than three times as much chance to be ranked as "strong" PS as a person in the lower SES levels. The weaker PS persons are much more frequent among the lower SES. Again, this pattern is almost identical for both populations. However, this relationship does not indicate direction of causality. Opinion leaders may achieve their leadership through social acknowledgment of their education, income, occupation, and popularity; they may also achieve higher social positions because of their stronger personality. The Israeli study included a question about military service (obligatory for all Israeli men and women), and the analysis revealed that the military ranking is highly correlated with the PS grouping (gamma=.75). Thus, 54 percent of the officers were rated in the "strong" PS, while 61 percent of the non-officers were rated in the "weak" PS.

Although the PS scale yields similar results in two different societies, this does not indicate its validity. Is it really a measure of influenceability? The application of the PS scale to a social network that was mapped by its communication links, personal positions and flow of information and influence may provide the "external" criteria for testing the scale's validity. For this purpose a second population was used. It was the entire Israeli kibbutz community (270 members) that underwent a sociometric mapping of its personal communication network and of the flow of information and influence in this network.[6] A sociometric mapping of the personal communication network was obtained by interviewing every member of the community. Each respondent was asked to list his or her conversational ties with other members (unlimited number of choices) and was instructed to rate the strength of each tie by three scales (importance, frequency of contacts, and tenure of the tie), thus operationalizing Granovetter's definition of ties' strength. Every tie was rated by the two connected persons and the scores given by each member of the dyad to the same tie were summed, thus adding the element of mutuality. The sociometric data was arranged in a who-to-whom matrix with each entry (n=2,511 ties) representing a communication tie, characterized by its strength.

To study the actual flow of use of a tie for communicating information, six different items were used, two from each category: "general news," "consumer information," and "gossip."[7] None of these items were publicized formally, but were disseminated, a month prior to the study, by means of interpersonal communication. To trace the flow, each member was asked whether he or she was aware of each of the items and to report on the source of his/her knowledge (who told him/her). Regarding flow of influence, two decision-making items were used. These were two issues later put to vote in the *assefa*, the general assembly: a decision to allow young members, after their military service, to spend a year outside the kibbutz, and a decision to accept or reject the application of a candidate for full membership. Each individual was asked about consulting, seeking advice or being influenced when making up his or her mind regarding these issues. The entries about flow of information and influence were added to the sociomatrices, in order to identify network positions and their activity in the flow of information and influence. Finally, we applied the PS scale and cross-classified this measure with the communication network attributes (position and activity) for each subject.

The communication matrix included 2,511 entries connecting the 270 members of the kibbutz. The analysis of the 270×270 matrix structure according to Richard's procedure[8] revealed sixteen cliques. Using the clique identification, the network position of each individual in his or her clique was computed, using the number of links with members of the clique. The division into four quartiles (of number of ties) resulted in four levels of network positions, from "marginals" to "centrals." This measure, originally gathered for a network analysis, was compared with the results of applying the PS scale to the same respondents. The two measures were highly correlated: a correlation coefficient of .54 was found between amount of communication links (in the entire network) and the PS measure. This correlation was somewhat higher (.59) when relating PS score to amount of communication links within the clique. (The difference between the coefficients is not statistically significant.) Individuals with a high PS score are better linked to other individuals in their community and especially to others in their social group. This relationship is clearer when the groupings according to the two scales are cross-classified, as presented in table 15.2.

Table 15.2

Network Position and PS Score

Network Position	Strength of Personality				
	Strong	Above average	Moderate	Weak	Total
Central	58	17	14	11	100% (65)
High medium	31	28	25	16	100% (68)
Low medium	15	28	31	26	100% (68)
Marginal	3	13	23	61	100% (69)

Chi square = 85.23, d.f. = 9, p < .0001
Gamma = 0.686, p < .0001

From "The Influentials: Back to the Concept of Opinion Leaders?" by Gabriel Weimann, *Public Opinion Quarterly*, 55, 1991, p. 273, table 2. Reprinted by permission of the University of Chicago Press.

Individuals with central positions in their groups are clearly those with higher levels of PS: 58 percent of those who are centrally positioned in the communication network rated as "strong" PS, while only 3 percent of the "marginals" rated as "strong" PS individuals. The same applies to other network positions, with decreasing PS score according to lower network position (61 percent of the "marginals" in their groups are rated as "weak" on the PS scale while only 11 percent of the "centrals" belong to this category of PS). The strong gamma coefficient of .68 indicates that these two indicators are inter-related. The early studies of the Allensbach Institute found the same pattern though not by sociometric measures. For example, the German surveys revealed that high PS respondents report having more friends and acquaintances: 67 percent of the "strong" PS group reported having many friends and acquaintances, compared to only 49 percent of the "above average," 37 percent of the "moderate," and 20 percent of the "weak."[9] While one may question the validity of such self-assessments, the data from the sociomatrix obtained by a mapping of actual communication links in the Israeli kibbutz community, reveal the same relationship.

The final and crucial validity test of the PS scale is its ability to predict communicative and influential behavior. To do so, measures of the actual flow of various information and decision-making items in the kibbutz community were compared with the PS scores. As the mapping of the communication activity was based on dyadic measurement ("who-to-whom"), the comparison of communicative activity of individuals according to their PS level was possible. This involved a cross-classification of each tie activated for the flow of a specific item with the communicator's PS level. Table 15.3 presents the communicative activity of the four PS groups in terms of their relative share in the flow. The activity rates are the percentages of the ties activated by each level of PS in the flow of six information items and two decision-making items. The higher the percentage, the more active the individuals from the specific PS group were. In other words, a bigger share of the communication flow originated from communicators from a specific PS level.

Table 15.3

Communicative Activity by PS Level

| | Percent of Ties Activated* | | | | | | |
| | Strong | | | Weak | | | |
Item	1	2	3	4	total	x^2	p<
Gossip							
item 1	22	31	32	15	100% (425)	7.7	n.s.
item 2	24	26	28	22	100% (382)	5.6	n.s.
General News							
item 1	34	26	24	16	100% (501)	6.5	n.s.
item 2	38	22	22	18	100% (474)	9.4	.05
Consumer information							
item 1	41	28	19	12	100% (375)	18.8	.001
item 2	39	31	17	13	100% (381)	17.6	.01
Decision-making							
item 1	48	31	19	2	100% (346)	45.2	.001
item 2	46	29	18	7	100% (366)	33.2	.001

*Note: Percentage of ties activated by a communicator whose PS level is 1, 2, 3, or 4. For example, 22 percent of the ties activated for Gossip item 1 originated from a communicator with a "strong" PS level.

From "The Influentials: Back to the Concept of Opinion Leaders?" by Gabriel Weimann, *Public Opinion Quarterly*, 55, 1991, p. 274, table 3. Reprinted by permission of the University of Chicago Press.

The proportions of ties activated by various levels of PS vary across items. However, except for the flow of gossip, the most active communicators are those with higher levels of PS. The majority of ties activated for the flow of news, consumer information and influence originated from individuals with stronger PS. The rates of activation decreased for lower levels of PS, indicating the strong relation between communicative activity and strength of personality (except for gossip). This relation is evidently more significant for decision-making items than for information items. In the case of influence flow (the last two items), almost half of the flow originated from individuals with "strong" PS while only 2 to 7 percent of this flow originated from the "weak" PS group. Another way to look at the relationship between communicative activity and PS is by comparing the communicators and non-communicators in terms of their PS scores. For each of the items studied, we computed the average PS for the "communicators" (those who were listed by the respondents as the source of information or influence) and the "receivers" (those that were not listed as sources). Table 15.4 presents the results of these comparisons.

Table 15.4

PS Averages of Communicators and Noncommunicators

| Item | Average PS of: | | t^* | $p<$ |
	Communicator	Noncommunicator		
Gossip				
item 1	116.8	114.5	1.08	n.s.
item 2	117.1	115.7	0.65	n.s.
General News				
item 1	120.2	109.8	4.19	.001
item 2	116.2	109.1	2.81	.01
Consumer information				
item 1	133.4	102.8	12.24	.001
item 2	130.9	104.6	10.52	.001
Decision Making				
item 1	137.9	101.5	14.57	.001
item 2	138.3	100.6	15.09	.001

*Note: A t-test was conducted for the differences between the averages under the null hypothesis of no significant difference.

The pattern revealed by the averages in table 15.4 confirms our previous finding: the PS averages are significantly higher for the communicators for most of the information items and for both decision-making items. This difference is largest for the flow of influence and smallest (and actually not significant) for the flow of gossip. Thus, individuals with stronger PS are more active as communicators of news and consumer information and are clearly the influentials for decision-making items.

The Influentials as Opinion Leaders?

From a theoretical perspective, the identification of the "influentials" should be related to the concept of opinion leaders. The criticism of the concept of opinion leaders has highlighted its methodological deficiencies and its emphasis on the two-step-flow model. However, a better measurement procedure and a more realistic presentation of the influentials, regardless of the media effects controversy, should cause a revision of this concept. The successful identification of the influentials by means of the PS scale, validating the identification by "external" criteria, and pointing to the role of these influentials in the flow of interpersonal communication and influence may suggest a "return to the opinion leadership concept." However, a closer examination of the German and Israeli studies reveals that despite the many similarities between the PS scale's influentials and the opinion leaders, these terms are not fully interchangeable (at least not with the original conceptualization of opinion leaders). Four differences emerge from such comparison:

Continuum vs. Dichotomy

While the original opinion leadership concept was based on the leader-follower dichotomy, PS scaling reveals that influenceability is, rather, a continuous variable. The possibility of continuum was suggested by later studies of opinion leaders[10] but most studies in this area applied a two-category distinction.

Mass Media Use

Opinion leadership was related to increased exposure to mass media sources. However, this relationship did not apply to the PS scale influentials. It appeared, in both the German and Israeli studies, that the influentials rely heavily on personal sources not only for the dissemination of information but also as personal sources. Moreover, the significant differences across PS levels in terms of media use were found in patterns of media consumption (i.e., preferred contents or channels) but not merely in simple measures of amount of exposure.[11]

It is the quality of media consumption rather than its quantity that differentiates levels of influenceability. Some later studies of opinion leaders' media use did suggest several modifications of the leaders' reliance on media and personal sources.[12]

Heterogeneity vs. Homogeneity

While opinion leaders were found by Katz and Lazarsfeld to be fairly evenly distributed among the different social strata, the influentials (as measured by the PS scale) were concentrated in higher SES levels. Again, later studies of opinion leadership also revealed this unequal distribution.

Overlap of Leadership Domains

The opinion leaders were found to differ from one subject area to another with very little overlap, while the influentials were found to be active in several domains with considerable overlap.[14] Again, later studies of opinion leadership areas found such overlap, even in the data used by Katz and Lazarsfeld.[15] Such overlap was revealed frequently across "closely related" areas or "interests' clusters."[16]

Thus, it appears that the influentials are not the opinion leaders according to the original definition but better fit the more sophisticated characterization that stemmed from the growing criticism of early studies on opinion leadership. The PS scale appears to provide us with a more sensitive, better validated, and more sophisticated measure of personal influenceability. Yet, it should not be conceptualized as a personal or psychological trait but, rather, as a combination of social and personal characteristics. As Katz noted, being an influential requires three attributes: 1. *who one is*—the personification of certain values; 2. *what one knows*—competence in certain areas; and 3. *whom one knows*—strategic social location. The PS scale was found to relate to all these measures: individuals rated as influentials on this scale combined personal traits, competence, and social networks positions, thus revealing the multidimensional nature of this phenomenon.

The Influentials as Leaders and Agenda-setters

The identification procedure of the influentials through the PS scale and its validation by means of "external" criteria and cross-national application as described in the previous chapter, led to several questions of empirical significance: (a) what are the social and personal characteristics of the influentials? (b) what are their sources of information and influence? and (c) what are their functions in the flow of information and influence?

This chapter provides the answer to these questions, based on several studies conducted in Germany, the United States, and Israel. The German database comprises two major surveys conducted in Germany during the 1980s by the Allensbach Institute, under the supervision of Elisabeth Noelle-Neumann. The first survey (Allensbach Survey 4693) involved 3,843 respondents and the second, a multi-media market analysis, questioned 8,000 respondents. Both groups were stratified samples of citizens of the then German Federal Republic (i.e., West Germany and Berlin), were 14 years old or older, and were interviewed at home by the field staff of Allensbach. The samples were representative of the West German adult population in terms of geographic location, population density, gender, age, and occupation.[1] The Israeli sample, described in the previous chapter, involved 650 respondents, randomly drawn from the adult Jewish population of Israel also interviewed at home, by a research team from Haifa University, Israel.[2] The third database comes from an America study of adolescents conducted by a team the University of Chicago, headed by Mihaly Csikszentmihalyi.[3]

Who Are the influentials?

As we learned earlier, the Strength of Personality scale was found to correlate with certain socio-demographic variables. Cross-classifying

PS groupings with such characteristics indicated that PS is related to gender, age, and social economic status (SES). Moreover, the results of the German and the Israeli studies are very similar. In terms of gender, males score higher on PS. PS was also unevenly distributed by age groups: the highest PS scores are more frequent in the 30 to 39 age group (in both samples) while the "weak" level is more frequent in the 60 plus age group. The most obvious relationship of PS is with the SES measure. Most of the influentials in both the German and the Israeli populations came from higher SES levels: the lower the SES level, the higher the frequency of low PS individuals.

Another predictor of PS level was *social connectivity*. Various measures were applied to examine the respondents' social gregariousness, participation in community affairs, and amount of social ties. The two samples reveal similar patterns of social activities as related to PS. Individuals with higher PS levels in both countries reported having many friends and the tendency to give this answer declines with the decline in PS level. The influentials are clearly those who have more friends, are more socially active members and hold offices in social groups, clubs, parties, or action groups and unions. The patterns of the positive correlations between measures of social connectivity/activity and PS level are identical for both studies. The dissimilarities are found in the frequencies of certain replies,[4] yet the patterns of relationship with the PS scale are identical.

The most powerful predictor of the influenceability level was *life style*. When we looked at the various reports and analyses provided by the Allensbach Institute and the databases of the Israeli and German samples a consistent pattern emerged. Noelle-Neumann and her colleagues used terms, such as "life goals," "personal life values," "leisure pursuits," and "personal activities" to characterize the influentials. In all of the various measures and indices, the influentials differed from others (lower PS levels) in a combination of life style values (VALS, as described in chapter 7). They seek specific gratifications, are engaged in certain activities, and allocate their leisure time in a unique way. Let us review some of the data and analyses that led us to the life-style concept.

The German surveys applied various measures and variables: a first attempt included a list of eighteen items referring to personal life goals, and asked the respondents to indicate which were more important for them to achieve in their own lives. When the answers were compared across PS levels, significant differences emerged, especially with certain goals.[5] Similar differences were found in the German study when leisure activities were compared across PS levels and, similarly, when profession-related values were used for the comparison. In all three sets of measures, each applying multi-variable measures, PS was found to be a significant predictor. As expected, there are cultural differences between the two societies (e.g., the Israelis are more outdoor-oriented than the Germans). However, the relationship between leisure-time activities and PS levels are very similar. There are certain activities with preferences that do not differ over PS groups, while others are clearly related to PS level. Let us summarize these relationships:

1. Higher PS levels rate higher on:
   • reading books
   • reading newspapers
   • participating in sports
   • being with friends
   • hosting friends
   • going for trips
   • going to the movies, theater, or concerts

2. Higher PS levels do not rate higher on:
   • watching television
   • listening to the radio
   • staying at home
   • doing nothing

These patterns were identical for both societies despite the general cultural differences in leisure activities. The revealed differences may indicate that the various PS levels represent different orientation towards life in general. If PS reflects a generalized attitude toward life, members of each PS group should endorse a different pattern of personal goals. However, as the life values may be affected by the individual's background (education, class, income, etc.) one must control for the effects of these variables. To do so, we subdivided the respondents in the German and the Israeli databases according to socio-economic class, in addition to their PS level and their answers regarding a list of eighteen values.

Three patterns emerged. First, higher PS individuals more frequently endorse more frequently certain goals. Second, this pattern is found in both SES levels, indicating that the perception of life goals is related to PS independent of social class. Third, though there are differences between the levels of SES, in most cases PS makes a greater difference in endorsement of life goals. There is, however, interesting variance across the goals. Let us first review these patterns in the German sample.

The strong PS, the influentials, contrast lower levels of PS in certain values or goals they regard as more important. They rate more frequently goals relevant to their influential status, such as "to keep learning new things," or "to be there for others," and "to have many good friends." For both SES levels, the most frequent endorsers of these values come from the strong PS group. When the ratios between the strong to weak PS groups in the endorsement of these values are compared, the strong PS endorse all values except one, from twice to four times as often as the weak PS. Other values, such as "to succeed professionally," "to discover my abilities," "to be happy with my work/job," and, to a lesser extent, "to have my freedom," were all strongly associated with the influentials. When we applied the same list of values to the Israeli sample, a somewhat distinctive pattern emerged. The PS scale was here too associated with certain life goals, but not entirely the same as in the German population.

The Israeli sample's general endorsement of life goals differed, as expected, from the German pattern. For example, we found among the Israeli sample greater support for values related to their country and national independence and security. (Values, such as "to live in a free country," or "to live a secure life" were generally more frequently endorsed by Israeli respondents.) But when we cross-classified the life goals' endorsement with PS and SES levels, the general pattern was revealed: as in Germany, PS level were strongly associated with certain life goals. Again, the effect of PS is found in both SES levels and is stronger than the effect of SES. As in Germany, some of the values endorsed more frequently by the Israeli influentials are associated with their status. They too, like their German counterparts, more frequently rated goals such as "to keep learning new things," or "to be there for others," and "to have many good friends." For both SES levels, the most frequent endorsers of these values come from the strong PS group.

It is noteworthy that there are some values with endorsement that does not vary across PS levels. For example, in both societies, "to have firm religious belief" was strongly related to social class but not to PS. Yet, those values related to the functioning of an influential (e.g., having many friends, being there for others, learning new things, and being independent) were related to higher PS in both societies. In his study of America, adolescents, Csikszentmihalyi used the final ten-item PS scale and various measures of self-image, personality traits, teacher's ratings, and other variables.[6] One of the strongest predictors of opinion leadership (in terms of PS score) among the adolescents was their self-perceived life goals: it correlated with PS ($r=.40$, $n=173$) and did not change for boys ($r=.40$, $n=78$) or girls ($r=.42$, $n=95$).

Finally, the PS scale was found to be associated with specific expectations from work and professional career and with work-related values. The Allensbach studies provided the evidence by cross-classifying the respondents' answers to a set of ten items focusing upon work and career. They included questions about work values and preferences. (For example, is it important that the work/job involves contact with other people, contributes to the well-being of the community, involves the use of modern technology, and provides career opportunity and promotion?) Most of these measures differed sharply across PS levels.[7] If we review the accumulating findings regarding life goals, personal values, leisure pursuits, and work-related priorities an overall model of life style appears. On all of the various dimensions of work, leisure, and life goals, the influentials differed from others. They seek specific gratifications, are engaged in certain activities, and allocate their leisure time in a unique way.

The Influentials' Use of Mass Media

As noted in chapter 15, the influentials' exposure to mass media and their use of the media differed from those attributed to the opinion leaders. The opinion leadership conceptualization highlighted the leaders' higher exposure to mass media and especially to those related to their field of expertise. However, the simple exposure-leadership relationship cannot be applied to the influentials: it is the *form* and *quality* of media consumption, rather than its quantity, that characterizes levels of influenceability. Let us examine the patterns of media use, which correlated with influenceability, according to medium:

Newspaper and Magazine Readership

The influentials were found to read more newspapers and magazines and to spend more time reading the papers (in both the German and Israeli studies). However, stronger correlations emerge when the *form* of readership is examined. The studies were not only measuring general readership but investigated the type of paper or magazine the respondents read, the preferred contents, and the amount of time spent reading. In all of these measures, significant differences between the PS levels were found. Let us illustrate some of the evidence by focusing upon some measures of readership. Table 16.1 presents the results found in the German and Israeli national samples, compared for the strong and weak PS groups.

Table 16.1

Readership and PS Scale

Activity	Sample	Strength of Personality		Overall
		Strong	**Weak**	**Overall**
Read newspapers	Israeli	87	53	71
	German	75	50	63
Read magazines	Israeli	31	17	24
	German	60	38	51
Read books	Israeli	45	17	34
	German	54	26	42
Read books:				
• daily	Israeli	13	8	9
	German	12	6	9
• several times	Israeli	21	13	16
a week	German	22	15	17
• have not read	Israeli	19	47	33
in the last year	German	18	49	31

Note: The rates in the table are percentages. Read, for example, 62 percent of the Israelis classified as strong PS answered that they like to watch television in their leisure time. German data come from the multi-media market analysis, n = 8,000, and the Israeli national sample, n = 650.

The influentials are clearly more exposed to all types of print media: they read more books, newspapers, and magazines than the others. Despite the expected national differences. (For example, although Germans in general read more books and magazines, they read less daily newspapers than the Israelis.) The general trend in both societies is the same: higher exposure among the higher PS individuals. However, the amount of exposure conceals more significant differences: the selection of channel or content. This pattern could be exposed only by examining the selection of publications read by the various PS groups. In the study conducted for the German magazine, *Der Spiegel*, the readership of various German publications (daily papers, and weekly and monthly magazines) was compared across PS levels.[8]

A close examination of the reading habits of various PS levels shows that selection patterns are significantly related to influenceability. In certain publications, the influentials' readership is similar to that of the others: they do not read television magazines, women's magazines, most of the weeklies, and one daily (*Bild*) more than lower PS individuals.

Table 16.2

Newspapers/Magazine Readership by PS in Germany

Publication*	High	Above average	Moderate	Weak	Overall
		Strength of Personality			
Dailies					
Bild	22.2	25.2	24.4	23.6	24.0
Frankfurter Allge.	5.5	2.3	1.5	0.5	2.4
Handelsblatt	1.6	1.0	0.4	0.4	0.8
Süddeutsche Zeit.	3.1	2.1	1.5	0.3	1.8
Die Welt	2.9	1.3	0.7	0.5	1.3
General weeklies					
Bunte	10.8	11.4	9.3	9.0	10.2
Neue Revue	8.9	9.1	7.3	6.0	8.0
Quick	9.3	8.5	6.9	5.0	7.6
Stern	24.7	20.4	17.0	10.0	18.4
Bild am Sontag	18.6	19.8	18.1	16.4	18.4
Television magazines					
Bild + Funk	6.4	7.7	5.1	4.4	6.1
Fernsehwoche	10.2	10.4	10.9	9.0	10.4
Horzü	26.4	24.0	25.8	24.0	25.0
TV Hören and Sehen	14.2	15.3	14.5	11.5	14.1
News magazines					
Der Spiegel	18.1	10.8	6.9	2.4	9.7
Die Zeit	7.3	3.9	2.2	1.0	3.6
Das Beste	16.1	12.4	10.7	5.9	11.5
Business magazines					
Wirtschaftswoche	2.6	0.8	0.2	0.1	0.9
Capital	8.6	3.4	1.8	0.3	3.5
DM	7.0	4.4	2.6	0.7	3.7
Industrielmagazine	2.4	0.8	0.5	0.1	0.9
Manager magazine	3.2	0.8	0.4	0.2	1.1
Women's magazines	(Women only, n = 1,978)				
Brigitte	11.3	14.3	13.4	10.9	12.8
Freundin	8.2	9.9	9.5	6.5	8.8
Für Sie	8.9	10.1	10.3	7.4	9.4
Burda	8.9	10.9	11.0	7.1	9.8
Petra	4.6	5.9	6.1	4.2	5.3

* Selected publications only. The rates in the table are percentages. Read, for example, 22.2 percent of the strong PS read the German daily *Bild*, while the last column presents the percentage of readers from the general population. (Thus, *Bild* enjoys the readership of 24 percent of the German population.)

And yet, in certain publications there is a higher rate of influentials-as-readers: these are most of the dailies, most of the weeklies (especially *Der Spiegel, Stern, Die Zeit,* and *Capital*), and economic magazines. If we consider the content and quality of these publications, the relationship is clear: the influentials prefer the quality papers (and not the low-key *Bild*), the quality weeklies, and the economic and political publications. In these categories their readership is, on average, as high as five times more than the weak PS readership. In certain publications, the strong-to-weak PS ratio is even higher: 28.7 (*Capital*), 26 (*Wirtschaftswoche*), 11 (*Frankfurter Allgemeine Zeitung*), 10.3 (*Süddeutsche Zeitung*), 10 (*DM*), and 7.5 (*Der Spiegel*). We were interested to learn whether this selective, quality-seeking readership applies also to the Israeli influentials. The Israelis have less publications but the variance in quality and content is present thus allowing for the measurement of the readership patterns according to PS levels. Table 16.3 presents the data obtained when readership was cross-classified with PS level in the Israeli national sample.

Table 16.3

Newspapers/Magazine Readership by PS in Israel

Publication*	High	Above average	Moderate	Weak	Overall
		Strength of Personality			
Dailies					
Yediot	53.4	57.8	52.4	59.8	55.6
Ma'ariv	27.8	24.6	26.2	25.9	26.7
Ha'aretz	14.4	7.9	6.1	2.2	7.7
General weeklies/monthlies					
Monitin	14.9	11.2	6.7	4.0	9.7
Haolam Haze	9.3	7.3	3.7	1.7	5.7
Status	2.1	1.6	1.8	1.6	1.8
Politica	9.7	7.6	4.3	1.2	5.3
Women's magazines		(Women only, n = 347)			
Laisha	43.8	49.2	52.1	52.6	48.6
At	41.2	35.6	37.4	36.1	37.4

* Selected publications only. The rates in the table are percentages. Read, for example, 53.4 percent of the strong PS read the Israeli daily *Yediot*, while the last column presents the percentage of readers from the general population. (Thus, *Yediot* enjoys the readership of 55.6 percent of the Israeli population.) Readership of dailies is for weekdays only. (It is somewhat higher on weekends.)

The PS level is related to readership of selected publications: the influentials do not differ from others in reading the popular dailies (*Yediot* or *Ma'ariv*) or the women's magazines (*Laisha* and *At*). However, like their German counterparts, the Israeli influentials prefer certain publications. These are the daily *Ha'aretz*, known for its more sophisticated style and contents (especially with regard to politics and economy), magazines such as *Monitin* (devoted to social, entertainment, and cultural issues) and *Haolam Haze* (politically left-oriented at the time of the study), and *Politica* (devoted to politics and social issues). The ratios of strong-to-weak PS readership are remarkably high for these publications, averaging more than five times as many influentials among the readers as weak PS individuals.

Another way to look at selective patterns of exposure is by examining the content selection or content preference. The Israeli study included questions about readership of the editorial columns, political analysis and economic analysis sections, foreign news, sports, and entertainment. When these preferences were compared across PS levels, several findings were revealed: the high PS individuals do not read more reports on news, sports, or entertainment than the others. Differences are found only in several contents: the influentials read more political and economic analysis columns, including editorials, interpretations, and discussions of events. This may explain why we found that in both countries the influentials spend more time reading the papers even if they read the same papers. Thus, it is the form of consumption rather than the amount of exposure that typifies the influentials. Form of consumption combines selection of publication, selection of contents, and the amount of time devoted to reading.

Television Viewership

Television viewership in general was not associated with PS level. Moreover, contrary to the expected direction, it appears that in both countries the influentials tend to watch *less* than the others. Heavier viewership is found among the weaker PS in both samples. This is better reflected in a survey of hour-by-hour viewing when compared across PS groups. Noelle-Neumann presented the average percent of viewers from each PS group in one of Germany's leading TV networks (ARD and ZDF). She found that the higher the PS, the lower the average viewership for both networks.[9] This finding certainly stands in sharp contrast with the traditional concept of the opinion leaders and the two-step flow model: the influentials are less exposed than the others to this important medium. As we saw earlier, high PS spend less time watching television and prefer other leisure activities, such as reading or social functions. One potential explanation is that the influentials seek more informative sources than television, thus allocating their time to readership and various social activities, which leave them little time for television.

A more promising suggestion emerged from the analysis of content viewership instead of amount of viewership. Unlike the insignificant differences in general viewing, notable variation across the PS levels appeared in program preference. The largest discrepancies appeared in certain television contents. The influentials were more exposed to the following types of programs: news, documentaries, discussion panels, and political debates.[10] However, influentials' viewership is lower than the average regarding comedies, drama, sports, light entertainment, and soap operas. No differences were found with regard to films and television series, investigative reports, quiz shows, and contests. This pattern, again, indicates that PS is better related to form and content rather than to overall exposure. The influentials watch television less, but when they do watch, their program preferences differ from the non-influentials in a similar way to their press content preferences.

The Functions of the Influentials

The influentials are identified by the PS scale, which measures general trait of influenceability but does not specify the unique features of this influence or the functions of these high PS individuals. To do so, the Allensbach Institute questioned the German national sample (n = 3,843) with both the PS items as well as a set of questions regarding areas of expertise and advice-giving. Cross-tabulating these two sets, as presented in table 16.4,[11] may indicate the influentials' self-perceived functions.

The influentials report having been asked for advice and having been considered an expert in every domain. An analysis of variance revealed that the rates differ when comparing the PS groups (i.e., the columns; F = 28.01, p < .0001) while there is also significant effect of the domains (i.e., when comparing the rows; F = 16.23, p < .001). This indicates that in each domain the groups differ in their advice-giving with the high PS as the most active or the frequent experts. However, there is some variance across the domains: the influentials advice is most sought after in interpersonal issues ("dealing with others") and recreation (vacation, going out and dining) but in these areas other PS groups are also more active. If instead of mere frequencies we will look

Table 16.4

Self-perceived Functions by PS

Where my advice is sought; where I am considered an expert*	Strength of Personality			
	High	Average	Moderate	Weak
In dealing with others	47	35	21	12
How and where to spend vacations	46	31	19	9
Good places to go out to eat	42	31	18	9
In technical things	34	23	14	8
Regarding home decoration	32	24	16	6
Fashions, what to wear	23	23	16	7
Cars	29	20	12	8
Financial matters	29	15	6	2
Art, theater, and music	23	14	10	3
Political matters	26	10	5	2
Teach or instruct others				
On the job	33	16	6	3
In my free time	20	14	8	3

*Note: The rates in the table represent the percent of each PS group giving a positive answer. Only selected domains are presented. Read, for example, 47 percent of the strong PS are asked for advice or considered as experts in the area of "dealing with others."

at the strong-to-weak ratio, the dominance of the influentials is clearly in two areas: the financial domain (ratio of 14.5 of strong-to-weak PS) and the political domain (ratio of 13). The reliance on the influentials in these issues is more critical than in other domains where other individuals may also be active.

The lower part of table 16.4 examines the functioning of the influentials in instructing or teaching others. Both at work or in their free time, the high PS individuals are more active instructors: the differences across PS levels are statistically significant ($F=9.7$, $p < .003$) with a strong-to-weak PS ratio of 11 (on the job) and 6.7 (in free time). If we combine these answers with previous finding regarding availability ("to be there for others," see tables 16.3 and 16.4), interpersonal guidance, advice-giving and accessibility are considered by the influentials as characterizing their functions.

The high frequency of the influentials in most areas necessitates the existence of some overlap across areas of expertise. The issue of overlapping domains or "generalized leaders" was well documented by opinion leadership studies (see the review in chapter 4) but does it relate to the influentials as well? Correlating the frequencies of advice-giving in the various areas (the original list includes sixteen domains) allows for the analysis of such "generalized influentials," or overlapping domains of influence. However, there are 120 coefficients (among the sixteen domains) and 240 for the two samples studied, requiring a more sophisticated method to explore the interrelationships. This was accomplished by a Smallest Space Analysis (SSA), a procedure that maps the variables according to their inter-correlations.[12] The higher the correlation, the closer the two variables are positioned, so when a group of variables (or domains in our case) are strongly interrelated, a cluster appears on the map. The clusters themselves are arranged according to their inter-correlations, thus indicating how the clusters associate with other clusters. This procedure, applied separately to both the German and Israeli samples, resulted in two maps of domains, each with clusters of domains. Table 16.5 presents these clusters: in each cluster the first variable is the central one or the one with the strongest correlation to other variables in the same cluster.

The first finding of the SSA procedure is that there are almost no "generalized influentials": the inter-correlations among most domains are very low, indicating that influentials active in one domain are not very likely to be active in *all* the other domains and for that matter not even in *most* of the other domains. Nevertheless, there are some significant correlations among certain areas, creating clusters of specific domains. Not all domains are clustered with others, thus creating single-domain clusters; but most areas do correlate, with a striking similarity across the two societies.

The German sample's analysis produced six clusters. Their arrangement in table 16.5 reflects the inter-relationships with the first and last clusters the most remote (or lowest correlation). The first cluster produced is of related domains. It shows high correlations among influentials' advice-giving regarding raising children, cooking, health issues, household issues, and home decoration. These areas are closely related, reflecting various aspects of domestic household issues from family to health care, cooking to home decoration. As expected, these are mainly female influentials who occupy these positions. When the SSA analysis was performed separately for each gender, this cluster was even more significantly inter-correlated among females while males' "stronger" cluster was combining the areas of technical issues and cars. The second cluster, closer to the first cluster than the others, is comprised of two domains: dealing with others and religion. This combination may reflect advice-giving in matters concerning personal conduct and interpersonal relationship.

Table 16.5

The Overlap of Influentials' Domains (SSA Mapping)*

The domains:	1. Technical issues	9. Health matters
	2. Politics	10. Religion
	3. Finance	11. Art, theater, and music
	4. Dealing with others	12. Dining
	5. Fashion	13. Raising children
	6. Cooking	14. Wine
	7. Household	15. Cars
	8. Vacationing	16. Home decoration

The German Sample

Cluster 1:
  13. Raising children
  6. Cooking
  9. Health
  7. Household
  16. Home decoration

Cluster 2:
  4. Dealing with others
  10. Religion

Cluster 3:
  12. Dining
  14. Wine
  11. Art, theater, and music
  8. Vacationing
  5. Fashion

Cluster 4:
  1. Technical
  15. Cars

Cluster 5:
  2. Politics

Cluster 6:
  3. Finance

The Israeli Sample

Cluster 1:
  13. Raising children
  4. Dealing with others
  9. Health

Cluster 2:
  7. Household
  16. Home decoration
  6. Cooking

Cluster 3:
  10. Religion

Cluster 4:
  8. Vacationing
  11. Art, theater and music
  5. Fashion
  12. Dining
  14. Wine

Cluster 5:
  1. Technical
  15. Cars

Cluster 6:
  3. Finance

Cluster 7:
  2. Politics

The third cluster in the German study combines areas that all relate to recreation and entertainment: dining, wine, art, theater, music, vacationing, and, to a lesser extent, clothing fashion. These areas are indeed closely related, thus it is not surprising to find the same influentials active in most of them. The next domain, dominated mainly by male influentials, combined technical issues and cars: again a case of closely related skills and interest. Finally, at the end of the continuum, we find two single-domain clusters, one of political issues and the last of financial matters. In each domain we find specialized experts, influentials who are active only in one of these areas. Moreover, the location of these clusters indicates that they are remote from other areas, and contrast especially the domestic domains (first cluster). Though there is some overlap between these two clusters themselves, it is not significant enough to group the two areas together.

When the same procedure was applied to the Israeli sample a very similar pattern emerged: the overall overlap was insignificant, indicating that in Israel too the influentials are more specialized in domain or clusters of domains. The clusters revealed by the SSA procedure resembled those of the German influentials. Again, we have clusters of the domestic, household issues but in Israel they constitute two distinct clusters. The first included raising children, dealing with others and health care issues, reflecting the family domain. The second (and closest) cluster included household, home decoration, and cooking, all part of domestic household life. These two domains were also dominated by female influentials. (Among the female respondents these two clusters were often combined into one.) Though not entirely similar to the German pattern, the Israeli clusters are also structured according to closely related issues. Thus, the fourth cluster in Israel is the identical recreation and entertainment realm as in Germany. (There is a different ordering of domains within the cluster: wine, as expected, plays a more significant role in the German setting).

Cross-national similarity of clustering is also found with regard to the technical/cars cluster and the single-domain clusters of politics and financial matters. In these areas, in both societies, highly specialized influentials were active (i.e., influentials whose expertise is only within the political or financial domain). An interesting finding in Israel was that religious issues constitute a single-domain cluster. This may be the result of a diversified society, divided by ethnic, religious, national, and cultural splits. It may reflect the unique status of religious influentials in the traditional communities of Jewish, Muslim, and Christian Israelis. Combining the religious diversification with the traditional, less modernized religiosity, may account for the independent cluster of religious issues.

When Noelle-Neumann tested her PS scale, she noted that those high PS individuals may have several communicative functions. The first was that of "multipliers," those who use their many contacts and the status of an expert to channel information and influence to others.[13] This led Noelle-Neumann to another suggestion, that of the "trend-setters." Though she never fully tested this idea, Noelle-Neumann found some evidence to the role of the influential as trend-setters. This first evidence led us to the concept of agenda-setting and its potential relevance to the influentials' functions.

Agenda-setting: The Individual Dimension

Research on the agenda-setting process of the mass media stems directly from the notion suggested by Bernard Cohen that the mass media:

> ...may not be successful in much of the time in telling people *what to think*, but it is stunningly successful in telling its readers *what to think about*...The world will look different to different people, depending...on the map that is drawn for them by writers, editors, and publishers of the papers they read.[14]

In other words, even though the media may not be very successful in telling us what opinions to hold, they are often quite effective in telling us what to have opinions about (or what *not* to think of). This idea led to an impressive empirical effort to study media agendas, public agendas, and the relationships between them.[15] The two agendas were related in a causal relationship:

> Through their day-by-day selection of news stories and decisions about how to display those stories, the editors of our newspapers and the producers of our local and national television news programs provide us with significant cues about *what are the important issues of the day*. This agenda-setting influence of the news media results from the necessity to choose some topics for the daily news report and to reject others...In any event, issues prominent on the news agenda are perceived by the public to be important, and, over time, frequently become the priority issues on the public agenda.

The process of agenda-setting may be divided into three components: 1. *media agenda-setting*—when the priority of issues in the media is the dependent variable, thus seeking factors that influence media selection; 2. *public agenda-setting*—when the perceived importance of issues by the public is considered as the dependent variables, seeking the factors that shape these perceptions; and 3. *policy agenda-setting*—concerning the arrangement of issues regarded as more important by policy makers and the factors affecting their perceptions. Rogers and Dearing propose a model in which the three agendas, those of the media, the public, and the policy makers are interacting and influencing each other.[17] McCombs explained the appeal of the media-public agenda-setting research:

> Its initial empirical exploration was fortuitously timed. It came at that time in the history of mass communication research when disenchantment both with attitudes and opinions as dependent variables, and with the limited effects model as an adequate intellectual summary, was leading scholars to look elsewhere.[18]

The primary concept of the agenda-setting process remained theoretical until the first study conducted by McCombs and Shaw provided empirical evidence, focused upon the effects of the 1968 presidential campaign on voters' agenda.[19] Though they conceptualized agenda-setting as a *process*, McCombs and Shaw applied cross-sectional analysis within the same period of time, thereby reducing the possibility of researching the time sequence. Yet, subsequent research did focus on the process of agenda setting, adding the dimension of time and relying on longitudinal studies. The more recent studies of agenda-setting have applied more sophisticated methods and measurement, more complex conceptions of the process along with multi-variate analysis.

Several developments in agenda-setting research can be traced in the recent decades. They include: 1. *inclusion of time factor*—predominantly by gathering data on the media agenda and the public agenda at two (or more) points of time, and then utilizing cross-lagged correlational analysis; 2. *more sophisticated models of the process*—including static and dynamic models,[20] varying time lags, differentiation according to medium, issue/event distinction, duration of an issue, competition with other news stories,[21] and variance according to the attributes of the public; and 3. *growing sophistication of methods and measures*—including experimentally manipulated media agenda to study its impact on the public.[22] All of these combined into a more complex agenda-theory research, which includes differences among individuals, among agenda items, among media, and over time. No wonder a review of the agenda-setting tradition revealed that the most typical trend was toward disaggregation of the units of analysis.[23]

As noted earlier, a great number of agenda-setting scholars had focused upon the media effects on the public and policy makers. Studies centered on other directions of influence flow had not been represented fully (for example, treating the media agenda as the dependent variable).[24] Charles Whitney draws our attention to another "neglected" aspect, that of the so-called "public": "In media agenda-setting, however, we have several questions to ask about the public, most notably, what is it? Is it the anonymous, aggregate audience?...If the public is something other than the aggregate anonymous audience, then what?"[25]

The agenda-setting tradition, based on aggregated data (media coverage, public opinion surveys) neglected the individual level of analysis. What is the role played by individuals in the agenda-setting process? Is there an interpersonal flow of media agendas, diffused by certain individuals? No answer, so far, was given by the numerous studies in this area. Whitney was the first, after thirty years, to suggest that there might be an answer in the analogous two-step model, empirical evidence, however, was not provided. The following analysis is a first attempt to provide the bridge, the long-awaited link to the individual level of agenda-setting process.

Influentials as Agenda-setters

To test the influentials' function in the agenda-setting process, one must establish a relationship between media agenda, influentials agenda, and public agenda. As the hypothesis of influentials as agenda-setters followed the German studies (whose findings actually initiated our pursuit of this idea), we could test it only in the later Israeli studies. Two databases were used for this analysis: (a) *the national sample survey* (n = 650) which included the PS scale and various agenda-related questions, focusing on issue awareness or issue prominence (e.g., "According to your opinion, which of the following issues do you see as more important?") or issue communications (e.g., "Which of these issues do you discuss these days with your friends, relatives, co-workers and others?"). A list of 15 issues was presented to the respondents and they could mention as many issues as they wished; and (b) *content analysis data* to study the media agenda. For that we examined the news stories in both Israeli television and press during the two months in the year preceding the survey. (One analysis was of the last month before the survey and one of ten months earlier.) Data came from coding the issues presented in the daily evening news (*Mabat*) on Israel's only television channel, and the news stories in the

Table 16.6

Media Agenda and Public Agenda

	TV Prominence		Press Prominence		Public Prominence
Issue*	t_{-1}	$t_{-1}0$	t_{-1}	t_{-10}	t_0
1. Security and defense	22.3	24.7	16.9	21.7	87.9
2. Israeli politics	21.6	20.8	24.1	17.3	76.1
3. Occupied territories	17.6	19.2	12.3	11.6	87.6
4. Work relations, strikes	11.4	7.3	11.8	9.7	64.3
5. Unemployment	7.2	1.8	2.3	1.8	58.1
6. Inflation/prices	5.6	4.1	4.6	6.3	57.8
7. Crime	4.2	6.7	3.8	4.8	53.7
8. Taxes	2.9	2.1	3.2	1.8	69.6
9. Emigration/immigration	1.5	2.4	7.3	6.4	41.5
10. Israel-US relations	1.4	3.8	1.4	2.9	24.7
11. Events in Europe/ North America	1.2	4.2	7.9	9.1	23.5
12. Education	1.1	.4	2.2	1.2	17.4
13. Health	.9	.3	.3	.5	9.7
14. Religion	.9	1.5	.2	1.1	18.4
15. Events in Asia/Africa	.2	.5	1.7	3.8	11.3
Total	100%	100%	100%	100%	

*Note: Only most dominant issues are presented. Percentages of public prominence sum up to more than 100% as respondents could choose several categories.

country's leading dailies (namely *Yediot*, *Ma'ariv*, and *Ha'aretz*). Units of analysis were the news items, each coded according to its dominant theme, determined by the amount of time or space allocated for that issue in the story. The merging of the two databases created several measures, which all centered around issue prominence and could be correlated: media agenda (issue ranking according to prominence) in each medium separately and in two time points (one month and ten months prior to survey, denoted as t_{-1}, and t_{-10}), and the issue prominence of the individuals and their PS levels. Table 16.6 presents the prominence of the sixteen issues in the various media (at t_{-1}, and t_{-10}) and the general public.

The prominence rates in table 16.6 indicate the similarities and discrepancies between (and within) media agenda and the public agenda. It appears that both the media and the public rate security and defense, Israeli politics and the occupied territories issues as the most important (though their priorities vary across media, time, and from media to public agendas). The discrepancies are evident, for example, in the higher prominence of Israeli politics in the media than on the public agenda, or the higher importance attributed by the public to taxes, inflation, and prices than revealed in media coverage. However, we were more interested in the relationship of the PS measure to these correlations. To analyze these relationships, we divided the public by PS scores into four groups and computed correlations between the groups agendas (prominence of issues) and the various media agenda. Table 16.7 presents these correlations, including those with those of the entire population and the four PS groups.

Table 16.7

Correlating Media Agenda and Public Agenda by PS Level

	TV (t_{-1})	TV (t_{-10})	Press (t_{-1})	Press (t_{-10})	General Public	PS* 1	2	3	4
1. TV (t_{-1})	-	.95	.89	.88	.84	.93	.87	.82	.76
2. TV (t_{-10})		-	.88	.92	.77	.73	.76	.81	.82
3. Press (t_{-1})			-	.92	.70	.83	.75	.65	.61
4. Press (t_{-10})				-	.68	.59	.64	.71	.74

*PS level range from 1 (strong) to 4 (weak). All coefficients are statistically significant, $p < .01$.

The correlations among the media's agendas (left part of table 16.7) are hardly surprising. Many studies have indicated the cross-media similarity of news-making by applying identical criteria of newsworthiness, selection, and prominence of reports. The within-medium correlations (television at two time points) are somewhat higher (.92 for television, .92 for press) than between-media (average correlation of TV-press is .89). The correlations with the public agenda (see "general public" column) are not that high but are very significant. They range from a coefficient of .68 (press ten months before and public agenda) to .84 (television in recent months and public agenda). It is clear that television agenda is more significant than the press agenda and that recent month's coverage is more effective than the coverage ten months ago. Thus, consistent with the findings of many agenda-setting studies, both medium and time play a role in relating media agenda to public agenda.

The more "innovative" findings emerge when PS is introduced (see right side of table 16.7). The correlations vary considerably across the PS levels in a consistent an interesting pattern: for the short-term effect (effect of coverage in recent month), for both TV and press, the higher the PS—the higher are the correlations. But an entirely *reverse* pattern emerges in the long-term effect: the higher the PS, the lower the correlations. The interpretation of this finding is not easy, at this stage. It appears that the influentials' agenda of public issues is well correlated with that of recent coverage in the media (more with that of television than that of the press) but this association fades away with time. This may indicate that the influentials are *faster* in picking up the trends and the issues from the media or that they are also *communicating to others* these issues and thus stronger correlations appear for the lower PS individuals only later. *Is there a two-step flow in the agenda-setting process?*

The influentials, as we found out earlier, are more exposed to certain media contents, and especially to informative and interpretative contents. Their pattern of media consumption may explain the fact that their agendas correlate so well with those of the media. After all, they are heavier consumers of those media formats, which are agenda-setters. The question remains, are they playing an active role in diffusing media agendas to their followers? Some support for this function is found in several analyses performed on the Israeli sample. One of the questions used was "Which of these issues you discuss these days with your friends, relatives, co-workers, and others?" (followed by the list of 15 issues). For each of the issues, we computed the amount of discussants (individuals who discussed the specific issue recently) according to PS level. We found that in *every issue* the highest rate of personal communication originated from high PS individuals. The rates of communications declined with lower PS level, in each issue. The highest communicative activity of the influentials were found in the "domestic" domains of politics and economy (taxes, prices, inflation), while the lowest activation of the influentials were found in "external issues" (event in other countries, relationships with the United States). Thus, as expected, the influentials are more active than others in discussing public issues, but is this communicative activity related to the media? The final link is between media agenda and personal communication. Is there a relationship and is this relationship affected by PS?

To establish the relationship between media agenda and the influentials' relaying this agenda to others, we computed the correlations between the various media agendas (prominence in each medium and at the two points of time) and discussing the issue with others, for each PS level separately. The results are presented in table 16.8.

Table 16.8

Correlating Media Agenda and Personal Communication by PS Level

	PS level			
	1	**2**	**3**	**4**
1. TV (t_{-1})	.87**	.76**	.34*	.21
2. TV (t_{-10})	.36*	.19	.17	.18
3. Press (t_{-1})	.89**	.67**	.11	.14
4. Press (t_{-10})	.27*	.23	.16	.17

Note: PS levels range from 1 (strong) to 4 (weak).
* $p < .01$
** $p < .001$

There are clearly strong correlations between media prominence and personal communications; but they are evident and significant only for the high PS individuals, and they vary over time. Only the influentials' personal communication correlate significantly with media prominence, across both media and time. (See the first column in table 16.8.) The correlations are much stronger for the short-term effect, that is, with the coverage in the recent month. The lower PS individuals have weak relationships between their willingness to engage in personal communication and media coverage of issues, even after ten months. Yet, we found that their agendas correlate strongly with media agendas after longer periods of time. They are passive, slower receivers of media agenda while the influentials are active receivers and transmitters of media agenda, following it closely, diffusing it to others through their personal communications, and move with the media's changing agenda in faster pace.

Let us review the main conclusions regarding the influentials' role in the agenda-setting process: (a) they are more exposed to media contents that focus on public issues; (b) their personal agendas correlate strongly with media agendas, moving in accordance with media's changing agenda thus affected by recent changes in issues' prominence; (c) they are more active in discussing these issues with others; and (d) their willingness to discuss issues is affected by the issues' prominence in the media thus declines with media's decreasing attention and coverage. The non-influentials need a longer time period to match their agenda with that presented in the media but are not active in diffusing this agenda to others. This may suggest a *multi-step agenda-setting process* in which the media agenda influence some people directly, some via personal communication and some through the combined flow from interpersonal and media sources. The influentials appear to play an important role in this process, as active intermediaries between media and public agendas. However, to establish it empirically a more sophisticated research design is required. Our cross-sectional analysis and its findings should encourage future attempts, which will need longitudinal studies, monitoring over time the changes in both media and public agendas. When individual attributes, such as PS will be applied, the role of certain influential persons in the agenda-setting process will be fully explored.

The opinion leaders concept, changed, modified, and remodified, is still a living, developing, and promising idea. Its recent re-emergence in the form of a more sophisticated measure, the PS scale, highlighted the roles of certain individuals, the influentials. They are the "multipliers," the trend-setters, the source for guidance and advice, the human transmitters of mass-mediated climate of opinion, issues, and agendas. The concept of the opinion leaders, born a half century ago, had its golden days, its challenges, and decline. It survived, mainly through growing sophistication and constant modifications. Future research should involve the promise of integration between micro-level units and macro-level processes, such as the climate of opinion, the formation of public opinion, and the agenda-setting process. The human bonds, the active bridges, which link small groups to large social entities, individuals to collectives, personal attitudes to public opinion, and the flow of media contents to social processing mechanisms are the influentials among us.

Notes

Part1

Chapter 1

1. Robert L. Cohn, *The Shape of Sacred Space: Four Biblical Studies*, Chico, California: Scholars Press, 1981, pp. 7–23.

2. W. Gunther Plaut, ed. *The Torah: A Modern Commentary*, New York: Union of American Hebrew Congregations, 1981, p. 465.

3. John Carmody, Denise Lardner Carmody, and Robert L. Cohn, *Exploring the Bible*, Englewood Cliffs, New Jersey: Prentice Hall, 1988, Chapter 4.

4. Paul F. Lazarsfeld, Bernard Berelson, and Hazel Gaudet, *The People's Choice*, New York: Duell, Sloan, and Pearce, 1944.

5. The first use of the term appears in *The People's Choice*: "ideas often flow from radio and print to the opinion leaders and from them to less active sections of the population," Lazarsfeld, Berelson, and Gaudet, ibid., p. 151.

Chapter 2

1. Leonard Broom and Philip Selznick, *Sociology*, 2nd edition, Evanston, Illinois: Row and Peterson, 1959, p. 38.

2. For a review of this theory, see Jeffrey L. Bineham, "A Historical Account of the Hypodermic Model in Mass Communication," *Communication Monographs*, 55 (3), 1988, pp. 230–246.

3. For a review of these factors, see Nan Lin, *The Study of Human Communication*, Indianapolis: Bobbs-Merrill, 1971, pp. 149–150.

4. Wilbur Schramm, *Mass Communication*, Urbana, Illinois: University of Illinois Press, 1960, p. 292.

5. Lin, op. cit., p. 150.

6. On the Payne Fund studies, see Herbert Blumer, *The Movies and Conduct*, New York: Macmillan, 1933; and Ruth C. Peterson and L. L. Thurstone, *Motion Pictures and the Social Attitudes of Children*, New York: Macmillan, 1933.

7. Harold L. Lasswell, *Propaganda Technique in the World War*, New York: Alfred A. Knopf, 1927, pp. 220–221.

8. Paul Lazarsfeld and H. Menzel, Mass Media and Personal Influence, in W. Schramm (ed.), *The Science of Human Communication*, New York: Columbia University Press, 1963, p. 96.

9. Following citations are from this version: Paul F. Lazarsfeld, Bernard Berelson and Hazel Gaudet, *The People's Choice*, New York: Columbia University Press, 1948.

10. Katz, Elihu. "The Two-Step Flow of Communication: An Up-to-date Report on an Hypothesis," *Public Opinion Quarterly*, 21, 1957, pp. 61–78.

11. Lazarsfeld, Berelson, and Gaudet, op. cit., pp. 135–152.

12. Ibid., pp. 50–51.

13. Ibid, p. 51.

14. "Overall, *The People's Choice* remains one of the most sophisticated survey research studies in the history of social science. Its place in the development of mass communication theory is undisputed. It forced communication theorists to reconsider the mass society concept, the powerful influences idea, the role of social category membership, and the significance of interpersonal ties. Few studies in the history of mass communication research have had such an impact." Shearon A. Lowery and Melvin L. DeFleur, *Milestones in Mass Communication Research*, New York: Longman, 1988 (second edition), p. 102.

15. The results of this study were reported by Robert K. Merton, "Patterns of Influence," in Paul F. Lazarsfeld and Frank N. Stanton (eds.), *Communications Research*, New York: Harper and Brothers, 1949, pp. 180–219.

16. Ibid., p. 180.

17. Ibid., p. 182.

18. Ibid., p. 186.

19. Ibid., p. 197.

20. Ibid, p. 201.

21. Elihu Katz and Paul F. Lazarsfeld, *Personal Influence*, New York: The Free Press, 1955.

22. It is interesting to note that four decades later, when a new wave of studies on opinion leaders emerged in Germany (by Elisabeth Noelle-Neumann and the German Survey Research Center, the Allensbach Institut für Demoskopie), it was initiated by a German news magazine, *Der Spiegel*, interested in locating influentials among the magazine's readers (again, for commercial purposes).

23. The size of the sample was dictated by the financial resources (Katz and Lazarsfeld, op. cit., p. 335).

24. Ibid., p. 236.

25. On the use of personal networks as opinion leaders' sources of information, see G. Weimann, "On the Importance of Marginality: One More Step into the Two-step Flow of Communication," *American Sociological Review* 47 (6), 1982, pp. 764–773.

26. There are several reports on this study. See for example: Herbert Menzel and Elihu Katz, "Social Relations and Innovation in the Medical Profession," *Public Opinion Quarterly*, 19, 1955, pp. 337–352; Elihu Katz, "The Two-step Flow of Communication: An Up-to-date Report on an Hypothesis," *Public Opinion Quarterly*, 21, 1957, pp. 61–78; Elihu Katz, et al., "Traditions of Research on the

Diffusion of Innovations," *American Sociological Review*, 28, 1963, pp. 237–253; James Coleman et al., "The Diffusion of Innovation Among Physicians," *Sociometry*, 20, 1957, pp. 253–270; and James Coleman, Elihu Katz, and Herbert Menzel, *Medical Innovation: A Diffusion Study*, 1966, Indianapolis: Bobbs-Merrill.

27. Katz, op. cit., pp. 73–75.

28. For a review of these "powerful media" and "mass society" theories, see Melvin DeFleur, *Theories of Mass Communication*, New York: David McKay, 1970, or William Kornhauser, *The Politics of Mass Society*, Glencoe, Illinois: Free Press, 1953.

29. Katz, op. cit., p. 62.

30. For example, John P. Robinson, "Interpersonal Influence in Election Campaigns: Two-step Flow Hypotheses," *Public Opinion Quarterly*, 40, 1976, pp. 304–319.

31. For a review see Walter Weiss, "Effects of the Mass Media of Communication," in Gardner Lindzey and Elliot Aronson (eds.), *Handbook of Social Psychology*, Vol. 5, 1969, Boston: Addison-Wesley, pp. 77–195.

32. Stycos, J. M., "The Potential Role of Turkish Village Opinion Leaders in a Program of Family Planning," *Public Opinion Quarterly*, 29, 1965, pp. 120–130.

33. Katz, op. cit., p. 76.

Part 2

Chapter 3

1. Several hundreds of these opinion leaders studies are summarized by Everett Rogers and Floyd F. Shoemaker, *Communication of Innovations: A Cross-Cultural Approach*, New York: The Free Press, 1971.

2. Jacob L. Moreno, *Who Shall Survive?*, Beacon, New York: Beacon House, 1953.

3. Everett Rogers, *Diffusion of Innovations*, New York: The Free Press, 3rd edition, 1983, p. 279.

4. On this procedure, see Everett Rogers and Lawrence D. Kincaid, *Communication Networks: Toward a New Paradigm for Research*, New York: The Free Press, 1981, pp. 109–110.

5. Sethu M. K. Rao and C. Bhaskaran, "Application of Sociometric Techniques in Identifying Opinion Leaders in Two South Indian Villages," *Group Psychotherapy, Psychodrama, and Sociometry*, 31, 1978, pp. 46–50.

6. On the notion of the strength of weak ties, see Mark S. Granovetter, "The Strength of Weak Ties," *American Journal of Sociology*, 73, 1973, pp. 1360–1380; and "The Strength of Weak Ties: A Network Theory Revisited," in R. Collins (ed.), *Sociological Theory*, San Francisco: Jossey-Bass, 1983, pp. 201–233.

7. Gabriel Weimann, "On the Importance of Marginality: One More Step into the Two-step Flow of Communication," *American Sociological Review*, 47, 1982, pp. 764–773; and "The Strength of Weak Conversational Ties in the Flow of Information and Influence," *Social Networks*, 5, 1983, pp. 245–267.

8. On the NEGOPY procedure, see William D. Richards, *A Manual for Network Analysis*, Mimeo, Stanford: Stanford University, Institute for Communications Research, 1975; and "Network Analysis Methods: Conceptual and Operational Approaches," paper presented at the Fourth Annual Colloquium on Social Networks, Honolulu, University of Hawaii. A detailed illustration is provided by Rogers and Kincaid, op. cit., pp. 163–182.

9. Rogers, op. cit., p. 279.

10. A. W. Van Den Ban, "A Revision of the Two-Step Flow of Communication Hypothesis," *Gazette*, 10, 1964, pp. 237–249.

11. P. Puska et al., "Use of Lay Opinion Leaders to Promote Diffusion of Health Innovations in a Community Program: Lessons from the North Karelia Project," *Bulletin of the World Health Organization*, 64 (3), 1986, pp. 437–446.

12. Ibid., p. 445.

13. For a review of studies using this method, see Everett Rogers and David G. Cartano, "Methods of Measuring Opinion Leadership," *Public Opinion Quarterly*, 26, 1962, pp. 435–441.

14. Paul Lazarsfeld, Bernard Berelson, and Hazel Gaudet, *The People's Choice*, New York: Columbia University Press, 1948; Elihu Katz and Paul Lazarsfeld, *Personal Influence*, New York: The Free Press, 1955.

15. Lin, Nan, *The Study of Human Communications*, Indianapolis: Bobbs-Merrill, 1971; Weimann, G., 1982, op. cit., p. 764–773.

16. Bruce Gunn, Kenneth L. Koonce, and David M. Robinson, "A Survey Design for Isolating Opinion Leaders in the Open Marketplace," *Economic and Business Bulletin*, 24, 1972, pp. 27–34.

17. The wording of the questions are in table 1, ibid., p. 30.

18. Ibid., p. 33.

19. The methodology of this study is detailed in Everett Rogers, "Characteristics of Innovators and Other Adopter Categories," *Ohio Agricultural Experiment Station Research Bulletin*, 882, 1961.

20. This scale has two components of opinion leadership: 1. The respondent's self image as an opinion leader (questions 2, 3, and 6), and 2. the respondent's perception of past interaction with others (questions 1, 4, and 5). Nevertheless, a Guttman scaling analysis yielded a coefficient of reproducibility of 91.4, indicating that these six items appear to measure a single dimension. See Rogers and Cartano, op. cit., pp. 439–440.

21. For review, see Rogers and Cartano, ibid., pp. 440–441.

22. Eugene A. Havens, "Social Psychological Conditions Affecting the Adoption of Farm Innovations," Unpublished Ph.D. dissertation, Columbus, Ohio State University, 1962.

23. James S. Fenton and Thomas R. Leggett, "A New Way to Find Opinion Leaders," *Journal of Advertising Research*, 11, 1971, pp. 21–25.

24. Ibid., p. 25.

25. Lawrence G. Corey, "People Who Claim To Be Opinion Leaders: Identifying Their Characteristics by Self-Report," *Journal of Marketing*, 35, 1971, pp. 48–53.

26. For example, the automobile opinion leadership study used the following question: "When it comes to knowing about automobiles, which of the following statements comes closer to describing you? 1. Friends and relatives usually come to me for advice and information; 2. I usually go to friends or relatives for advice and information."

27. Op. cit., p. 52.

28. Danny N. Bellenger and Elizabeth C. Hirschman, "Identifying Opinion Leaders by Self-Report," in B. A. Greenberg and D. N. Bellenger (eds.), *Contemporary Marketing Thought*, Chicago: American Marketing Association, 1977, pp. 341–344.

29. Ibid., p. 343.

30. Verling C. Troldahl and Robert Van Dam, "A New Scale for Identifying Public-affairs Opinion Leaders," *Journalism Quarterly*, 42, 1965, pp. 655–657.

31. Charles W. King and John O. Summers, "Overlap of Opinion Leadership Across Consumer Product Categories," *Journal of Marketing Research*, 7, 1970, pp. 43–50.

32. Ibid., p. 49.

33. Ugur Yavas and Glen Rieken, "Extensions of King and Summers' Opinion Leadership Scale: A Reliability Study," *Journal of Marketing Research*, 19, 1982, pp. 154–155.

34. Glen Rieken and Ugur Yavas, "Internal Consistency Reliability of King and Summers' Opinion Leadership Scale: Further Evidence," *Journal of Marketing Research*, 20, 1983, pp. 325–326.

35. Ibid., p. 325.

36. For example, Steven A. Baumgarten, "The Innovative Communicator in the Diffusion Process," *Journal of Marketing Research*, 12, 1975, pp. 12–18; Oded Gur-Arie, Richard M. Durand, and Subhash Sharma, "Identifying Moderating Variables Using Moderated Regression Analysis," in R. S. Franz, R. M. Hopkins, and A. G. Toma (eds.), *Proceedings: Southern Marketing Association*, Lafayette: Southern Marketing Association, 1979, pp. 189–192.

37. Terry L. Childers, "Assessment of the Psychometric Properties of an Opinion Leadership Scale," *Journal of Marketing Research*, 23, 1986, pp. 184–188.

38. On this scale, see Linda L. Price and Nancy M. Ridgway, "Development of a Scale to Measure Use Innovativeness," *Advances in Consumer Research*, 10, 1983, pp. 679–684.

39. Kenny K. Chan and Shekhar Misra, "Characteristics of the Opinion Leader: A New Dimension," *Journal of Advertising*, 19 (3), 1990, pp. 53–60.

40. Ronald E. Goldsmith and Rene Desborde, "A Validity Study of a Measure of Opinion Leadership," *Journal of Business Research*, 22, 1991, pp. 11–19.

41. This twenty-item scale measures global innovativeness. See Thomas H. Hurt, Katherine Joseph, and Chester D. Cook, "Scales for the Measurement of Innovativeness," *Human Communication Research*, 4, 1977, pp. 58–65.

42. This ten-item scale measures "attitude toward self." See Morris Rosenberg, *Society and the Adolescent Self-image*, Princeton, New Jersey, 1965, Princeton University Press.

43. This five-item scale measures consumers' assertiveness. See Marsha L. Richins, "An Analysis of Consumer Interaction Styles in the Marketplace," *Journal of Consumer Research*, 10, 1983, pp. 73–82.

44. Goldsmith and Desborde, op. cit., p. 18.

45. Herbert I. Abelson and Donald W. Rugg, "Self-designated Influentiality and Activity," *Public Opinion Quarterly*, 22, 1959, pp. 566–567. Quote from p. 567.

46. Bruce H. Bylund and David L. Sanders, "Validity of High Scores on Certain Self-evaluation Questions," *Rural Sociology*, 32, 1967, pp. 346–351.

47. Alvin J. Silk, "Response Set and the Measurement of Self-designated Opinion Leadership," *Public Opinion Quarterly*, 35, 1971, pp. 382–397.

48. The "within-scale" Yule's Q values for the furniture opinion leadership ranged from .349 to .963 with a median of .729, and for the cooking leadership ranged from .179 to .893 with a median of .573.

49. Alan S. Marcus and Raymond A. Bauer, "Yes, There Are Generalized Opinion Leaders," *Public Opinion Quarterly*, 28, 1964, pp. 628–632.

50. For a review of the research on overlap in opinion leadership, see Rogers, op. cit. pp. 288–293, as well as chapter 4 in this book.

51. In a later study (in the rock music album domain), the correlation between the opinion leadership scale with the yes-saying scale was also revealed to be significant (r=.14, p<.03) but not powerful (accounting for less than 2 percent of the leadership scores). See Goldsmith and Desborde, op. cit., pp. 16–17.

52. Herbert Hamilton, "Dimensions of Self-designated Opinion Leadership and Their Correlates," *Public Opinion Quarterly*, 35, 1971, pp. 266–274.

53. Ibid., p. 273.

54. Ibid., p. 273.

55. Rogers., op. cit., p. 280.

56. Jeffrey A. Kelly et al., "HIV-risk Behavior Reduction Following Intervention with Key Opinion Leaders of Population: An Experimental Analysis," *American Journal of Public Health*, 81, 1991, pp. 168–171.

57. Based on Everett Rogers, *Diffusion of Innovations*, New York: The Free Press, 3rd edition, 1983, p. 278.

58. Such attempts were reported by Herbert I. Abelson and Donald W. Rugg, "Self-designated Influentiality and Activity," *Public Opinion Quarterly*, 22, 1958, pp. 566–567; Carlton R. Sollie, "A Comparison of Reputational Techniques for Identifying Community Leaders," *Rural Sociology*, 31, 1966, pp. 31–309; Everett M. Rogers and Lynne Svenning, *Modernization Among Peasants: The Impact of Communication*, New York: Holt, Rinehart, and Winston, 1969.

59. Jacob Jacoby, "The Construct Validity of Opinion Leadership," *Public Opinion Quarterly*, 38, 1974, pp. 81–89.

60. Ibid., p. 87.

Chapter 4

1. Herbert Hamilton, "Dimensions of Self-designated Opinion Leadership and Their Correlates," *Public Opinion Quarterly*, 35, 1971, pp. 266–274.

2. This procedure was first applied by Katz and Lazarsfeld in the Decatur study. See Elihu Katz and Paul F. Lazarsfeld, *Personal Influence*, New York: The Free Press, 1955.

3. Hamilton, op. cit., p. 274.

4. John Saunders, J. Michael Davis and David M. Monsees, "Opinion Leadership in Family Planning," *Journal of Health and Social Behavior*, 15(3), 1974, pp. 217–227.

5. John W. Kingdon, "Opinion Leadership in the Electorate," *Public Opinion Quarterly*, 34, 1970, pp. 256–261.

6. Ibid., p. 259.

7. Alan Booth and Nicholas Babchuk, "Informal Medical Opinion Leadership Among the Middle Aged and Elderly," *Public Opinion Quarterly*, 36, 1972, pp. 87–94.

8. Ibid., p. 89. However, the researchers noted one exception: in the case of husband-wife exchanges, the husband was as likely as the wife to act as an opinion leader.

9. Veronica G. Thomas and Lawrence W. Littig, "A Typology of Leadership Style: Examining Gender and Race Effects," *Bulletin of The Psychonomic Society*, 23(2), 1985, pp. 132–134.

10. E.A. Fleishman, *Manual for Leadership Opinion Questionnaire*, Chicago, Illinois: Science Research Associates, 1969.

11. Thomas and Littig, op. cit., p. 133.

12. Erica Bates, "Opinion Leaders in a Psychiatric Hospital Community," *Social Science and Medicine*, 5, 1971, pp. 615–620.

13. Everett M. Rogers and Lynne Svening, *Modernization Among Peasants: The Impact of Communication*, New York: Holt, Rinehart, and Winston, 1969.

14. Appa G. Rao and Everett M. Rogers, "Caste and Formal Education in Interpersonal Diffusion of an Innovation in Two Indian Villages," *Indian Journal of Extension Education*, 16, 1980, pp. 1–9.

15. Dorothy Leonard-Barton, "Experts as Negative Opinion Leaders in the Diffusion of a Technological Innovation," *Journal of Consumer Research*, 11, 1985, pp. 914–926.

16. The American College of Prosthodontics and The American Society of Prosthodontics.

17. Leonard-Barton, op. cit., p. 925.

18. Robert Merton, *Social Theory and Social Structure*, Glencoe, Illinois: The Free Press, 1957, p. 413.

19. Katz and Lazarsfeld, op. cit., p. 334.

20. Alan S. Marcus and Raymond Bauer, "Yes: There Are Generalized Opinion Leaders," *Public Opinion Quarterly*, 38, 1964, pp. 628–632.

21. Thus, the formula for the expected value of leadership only in marketing and public affairs is: Pm x Ppa x (1-Pf) where Pm is the probability of being a marketing leader; Ppa is the probability of being a public affair leader, and 1-Pf is the probability of *not* being a fashion leader.

22. Frederick Emery and Oscar Oeser, *Information, Decision, and Action: A Study of the Psychological Determinants of Changes in Farming Techniques*, New York: Cambridge University Press, 1958.

23. Eugene Wilkening, Joan Tully and Hartley Presser, "Communication and Acceptance of Recommended Farm Practices Among Dairy Farmers of Northern Victoria," *Rural Sociology*, 27, 1962, pp. 116–119.

24. Alvin Silk, "Overlap Among Self-Designated Opinion Leaders: A Study of Selected Dental Products and Services," *Journal of Marketing Research*, 3, 1966, pp. 255–259.

25. Ibid., p. 259.

26. Charles W. King and John O. Summers, "Overlap of Opinion Leadership Across Consumer Product Categories," *Journal of Marketing Research*, 7, 1970, pp. 43–50.

27. Ibid., p. 49.

28. Melvin L. DeFleur, "The Emergence and Functioning of Opinion Leadership: Some Conditions of Informal Transmission," pp. 257–278 in Norman F. Washburne (ed.), *Decisions, Values, and Groups*, Vol. 2, 1962, New York: Macmillan, p. 268.

29. Jacob Jacoby, "The Construct Validity of Opinion Leadership," *Public Opinion Quarterly*, 38, 1974, pp. 81–89.

30. Ibid., p. 88.

31. David B. Montgomery and Alvin J. Silk, "Clusters of Consumer Interests and Opinion Leaders' Spheres of Influence," *Journal of Marketing Research*, 8, 1971, pp. 317–321.

32. James H. Myers and Thomas S. Robertson, "Dimensions of Opinion Leadership," *Journal of Marketing Research*, 9, 1972, pp. 41–46.

33. Ibid., p. 45.

34. Virginia Peck Richmond, "Monomorphic and Polymorphic Opinion Leadership within a Relatively Closed Communication System," *Human Communication Research*, 6(2), 1980, pp. 111–115.

35. D. P. Yadav, Communication Structure and Innovation Diffusion in Two Indian Villages, Ph.D. dissertation, 1967, East Lansing: Michigan State University.

36. T. Sengupta, "Opinion Leaders in Rural Communities," *Man in India*, 48, 1968, pp. 156–166.

37. E. B. Attah, An Analysis of Polymorphic Opinion Leadership in Eastern Nigerian Communities, Master's thesis, 1968, East Lansing: Michigan State University.

38. L.K. Sen, Opinion Leadership in India: Diffusion of Innovations. Research Report 22, Department of Communication, 1969, East Lansing: Michigan State University.

39. Everett Rogers and Floyd F. Shoemaker, *Communication of Innovation: A Cross-cultural Approach*, 1971, New York: The Free Press, p. 224.

40. C. H. Dodd, Homophily and Heterophily in Diffusion of Innovations: A Cross-cultural Analysis in an African Setting, paper presented at the Speech Communication Association Convention, New York, November 1973.

41. Y. C. Ho, Homophily in the Diffusion of Innovations in Brazilian Villages, Master's thesis, 1969, East Lansing: Michigan State University.

42. Richmond, op. cit., p. 113.

43. H. R. Witteman and P. A. Andersen, The Polymorphic Opinion Leadership Test: Development and Validation, paper presented to the Western Speech Communication Association Convention, 1976, San Francisco.

44. Virginia Peck Richmond, "The Relationship Between Opinion Leadership and Information Acquisition," *Human Communication Research*, 4, 1977, pp. 38–43.

45. J. C. McCroskey, "Validity of the PRCA as an Index of Oral Communication Apprehension," *Communication Monographs*, 45, 1978, pp. 192–203.

46. H. T. Hurt, K. Joseph, and C. D. Cook, "Scales for the Measurement of Innovativeness," *Human Communication Research*, 4, 1977, pp. 58–65.

47. Richmond, op. cit., p. 115.

48. Booth and Babchuk, op. cit, pp. 87–94.

49. Ibid., p. 91.

Chapter 5

1. Elihu Katz and Paul F. Lazarsfeld, *Personal Influence*, Glencoe, Illinois: The Free Press, 1955, p. 138.

2. Elihu Katz, "The Two-step Flow of Communication: An Up-to-date Report on an Hypothesis," *Public Opinion Quarterly*, 21, 1957, pp. 61–78.

3. R. D. Mann, "A Review of the Relationships Between Personality and Performance in Small Groups," *Psychological Bulletin*, 56, 1959, pp. 241–270.

4. For example, B. M. Bass, *Stogdill's Handbook of Leadership*, New York: The Free Press, 1981.

5. Dean Keith Simonton, "Intelligence and Personal Influence in Groups: Four Nonlinear Models," *Psychological Review*, 92, 1985, pp. 532–547.

6. Ibid., p. 546.

7. C. A. Gibb, "Leadership," in G. Lindzey and E. Aronson (eds.), *Handbook of Social Psychology*, Vol. 4, Reading, Massachusetts: Addison-Wesley, 1969, pp. 205–282.

8. James H. Myers and Thomas S. Robertson, "Dimensions of Opinion Leadership," *Journal of Marketing Research*, 9, 1972, pp. 41–46.

9. Using direct questions on the frequency of talking with friends and relatives on the specific item (measure of discussion), on how much the individual knows about the topic in comparison to his or her friends and relatives (knowledge), and on how interested he or she is in each topic area (interest). Innovativeness will be discussed in the following section.

10. For example, see Everett M. Rogers and Lynne Svenning, *Urbanization Among Peasants*, New York: Holt, Rinehart, and Winston, 1969, pp. 223–231.

11. Glen Rieken and Ugur Yavas, "Seeking Donors Via Opinion Leadership," *Journal of Professional Services Marketing*, 2, 1986, pp. 109–116.

12. For example, Marsha L. Richins and Teri Root-Schaffer, "The Role of Involvement and Opinion Leadership in Consumer Word-of-Mouth: An Implicit Model Made Explicit," *Advances in Consumer Research*, 15, 1988, pp. 32–36.

13. John O. Summers, "The Identity of Women's Clothing Fashion Opinion Leadership," *Journal of Marketing Research*, 7, 1970, pp. 178–185.

14. Barbara B. Stern and Stephen J. Gould, "The Consumer as Financial Opinion Leader," *Journal of Retailing Banking*, 10, 1988, pp. 43–52.

15. For example, James A. Palmore, Paul M. Hirsch, and Ariffin Marzuki, "Interpersonal Communication and the Diffusion of Family Planning in West Malaysia," *Demography*, 8, 1971, pp. 411–425.

16. Joseph R. Mancuso, "Why not Create Opinion Leaders for New Product Introductions?" *Journal of Marketing*, 33, 1969, pp. 20–25.

17. For example, John P. Robinson, "Interpersonal Influence in Election Campaigns: Two-step Flow Hypotheses," *Public Opinion Quarterly*, 26, 1976, pp. 304–319.

18. For a review of studies on opinion leadership and cosmopoliteness, see Florangel Z. Rosario, "The Leader in Family Planning and the Two-step Flow Model," *Journalism Quarterly*, 48, 1971, p. 297.

19. For a review of the studies on the role of involvement in opinion leadership, see Richins and Root-Schaffer, op. cit., pp. 32–33.

20. For example, Peter H. Bloch and Marsha L. Richins, "A Theoretical Model for the Study of Product Importance Perceptions," *Journal of Marketing*, 47, 1983; Marsha L. Richins and Peter H. Bloch, "After the New Wears Off: The Temporal Context of Product Involvement," *Journal of Consumer Research*, 13, 1986, pp. 280–285.

21. Lawrence F. Feick and Linda L. Price, "The Market Maven: A Diffuser of Marketplace Information," *Journal of Marketing*, 51, 1987, pp. 83–97.

22. For a review of the literature on these two models, see Meera P. Venkatraman, "Opinion Leadership, Enduring Involvement and Characteristics of Opinion Leaders: A Moderating or Mediating Relationship?" *Advances in Consumer Research*, 17, 1990, pp. 60–67.

23. Ibid., pp. 64–65.

24. On this distinction, see Hubert Gatignon and Thomas S. Robertson, "A Propositional Inventory for New Diffusion Research," *Journal of Consumer Research*, 11, 1985, pp. 849–867.

25. James W. Taylor, "A Striking Characteristic of Innovators," *Journal of Marketing Research*, 14, 1977, pp. 104–107.

26. Thomas S. Robertson and James H. Myers, "Personality Correlates of Opinion Leadership and Innovative Buying Behavior," *Journal of Marketing Research*, 6, 1969, pp. 164–168.

27. Ibid., p. 167.

28. Jacob Jacoby, "Personality and Innovation Process," *Journal of Marketing Research*, 8, 1971, pp. 244–247; Elizabeth B. Goldsmith and Ronald E. Goldsmith, "Dogmatism and Confidence as Related Factors in Evaluation of New Products," *Psychological Reports*, 47, 1980, pp. 1068–1070.

29. John H. Myers and Thomas S. Robertson, "Dimension of Opinion Leadership," *Journal of Marketing Research*, 9, 1972, pp. 41–46.

30. James W. Taylor, op. cit., pp. 104–107.

31. Kenny K. Chan and Shekhar Misra, "Characteristics of the Opinion Leader: A New Dimension," *Journal of Advertising*, 19, 1990, pp. 53–60.

32. Everett M. Rogers, *Diffusion of Innovations*, 3rd edition, New York: The Free Press, 1983, p. 284.

33. Holly L. Schrank and D. Lois Gilmore, "Correlates of Fashion Opinion Leadership: Implications for Fashion Process Theory," *The Sociological Quarterly*, 14, 1973, pp. 534–543.

34. Ibid., p. 540.

35. Rogers, op. cit., p. 284.

36. On the social conformity characterizing village opinion leaders, see Rogers, ibid., pp. 229–230.

37. Ibid., p. 230.

38. Ibid., p. 231.

39. Oded Gur Arie, Richard M. Durand and William O. Bearden, "Attitudinal and Normative Dimensions of Opinion Leaders and Non-leaders," *The Journal of Psychology*, 101, 1979, pp. 305–312.

40. Kenny K. Chan and Shekhar Misra, "Characteristics of the Opinion Leader: A New Dimension," *Journal of Advertising*, 3, 1990, pp. 53–60.

41. Roy E. Carter and Peter Clarke, "Public Affairs Opinion Leadership Among Educational Television Viewers," *American Sociological Review*, 27, 1962, pp. 792–799.

42. Verling C. Troldahl and Robert Van Dam, "Face-to-face Communication about Major Topics in the News," *Public Opinion Quarterly*, 29, 1965, pp. 626–634.

43. See table 2, ibid, p. 632, and especially the large differences when comparing opinion-givers to inactives.

44. M. R. Heath and S. J. Bekker, *Identification of Opinion Leaders in Public Affairs, Educational Matters and Family Planning in the Township of Atteridgeville*, Pretoria: Human Sciences Research Council, 1986.

45. See table 1, in Rieken and Yavas, op. cit., p. 114.

46. James S. Fenton and Thomas R. Leggett, "A New Way to Find Opinion Leaders," *Journal of Advertising Research*, 11, 1971, pp. 21–25.

47. J. Sean McCleneghan, "A Longitudinal Study of High School Opinion Leaders for USAF Panel," *Journalism Quarterly*, 54, 1977, pp. 357–361.

48. Alan Booth and Nicholas Babchuk, "Informal Medical Opinion Leadership among the Middle Aged and Elderly," *Public Opinion Quarterly*, 36, 1972, pp. 87–94.

49. John O. Summers, "The Identity of Women's Clothing Fashion Opinion Leaders," *Journal of Marketing Research*, 7, 1970, pp. 178–185.

50. One of the first attempt to relate the two was by Edward O. Laumann, *Bonds of Pluralism: The Form and Substance of Urban Social Networks*, New York: Wiley, 1973. The compatibility of the two concepts is discussed and illustrated

by Everett M. Rogers and Lawrence D. Kincaid, *Communication Networks: Toward a New Paradigm of Research*, New York: The Free Press, 1981.

51. Carl A. Sheingold, "Social Networks and Voting: The Resurrection of a Research Agenda," *American Sociological Review*, 38, 1973, pp. 712–720.

52. For a review, see Michael Schenk, "Massenkommunikation und Interpersonale Kommunikation," *Kölner Zeitschrift für Soziologie und Sozialpsychologie*, 30, 1989, pp. 406–417; Michael Schenk, "Politische Meinungsfuhrer," *Publizistik*, 30, 1985, pp. 7–16; and Michael Schenk and Uwe Pfenning, "Opinion Leadership Reconsidered: A Social Network Approach," paper presented at the European Conference on Social Network Analysis, Paris, June 1991.

53. Gabriel Weimann, "On the Importance of Marginality: One More Step into the Two-step Flow of Communication," *American Sociological Review*, 47, 1982, pp. 764–773.

54. See tables 1–4, ibid., pp. 767–770.

55. Diana Crane, *Invisible Colleges*, Chicago: The University of Chicago Press, 1972.

56. G. Zaltman and J. Blau, "A note on an International Invisible College in Theoretical High Energy Physics," unpublished report, Northwestern University, 1969, quoted in Crane, ibid., p. 53.

57. S. Crawford, *Informal Communication Among Scientists in Sleep and Dream Research*, Unpublished Doctoral dissertation, University of Chicago, 1970.

58. Ibid., p. 13.

59. Rogers, op. cit., p. 282.

60. James, Coleman, Elihu Katz and Herbert Menzel, *Medical Innovation: A Diffusion Study*, 1966, Indianapolis: Bobbs-Merrill.

61. For a review see Everett M. Rogers, op. cit., pp. 288–304.

62. John Saunders, J. Michael Davis, and David M. Monsees, "Opinion Leadership in Family Planning," *Journal of Health and Social Behavior*, 15, 1974, pp. 217–227.

63. See Schenk and Pfenning, op. cit., table 1.

64. The term "leaders" is somewhat misleading: the opinion leaders are not necessarily more charismatic, leadership-type individuals. One should be careful not to confuse opinion leadership with political leadership, with the status of opinion-makers, or with the celebrities who serve as models for imitation and admiration.

65. Charles R. Wright and Muriel Cantor, "The Opinion Seeker and Avoider: Steps Beyond the Opinion Leader Concept," *Pacific Sociological Review*, 10, 1967, pp. 33–43.

66. Ibid., p. 43.

67. For a review, see Rosario, op. cit., pp. 296–297.

68. The experiments on persuasion and communicator credibility have shown that opinions change in the direction advocated occurred significantly more often when it originated from a high credibility source. Carl Hovland et

al., *Communication and Persuasion*, New Haven: Yale University Press, 1953, pp. 99–133.

69. Myers and Robertson, op. cit., p. 44.

70. See Troldahl and Van Dam, table 2, op. cit., p. 632.

71. Lawrence G. Corey, "People Who Claim to be Opinion Leaders: Identifying Their Characteristics by Self-report," *Journal of Marketing*, 35, 1971, pp. 48–53.

72. Ibid., p. 51, see also table 6, p. 52.

73. Virginia P. Richmond and James C. McCroskey, "Whose Opinion Do You Trust?" *Journal of Communication*, 25, 1975, pp. 42–50.

74. The question asked was about the "person whose opinion you most often seek concerning movies you might want to attend/changing clothing styles/voting and candidates for political office."

75. The question asked was about "the person you would prefer to get notes and other information about the class/about an elective course."

76. Ibid., pp. 49–50.

77. Ronald E. Goldsmith, Melvin T. Stith and J. Dennis White, "Race and Sex Differences in Self-identified Innovativeness and Opinion Leadership," *Journal of Retailing*, 63, 1987, pp. 411–425.

78. Ibid., p. 423.

79. M. R. Heath and S. J. Bekker, op. cit., pp. 68–74.

80. Ottar Hellevik and Tor Bjorklund, "Opinion Leadership and Political Extremism," *International Journal of Public Opinion Research*, 3, 1991, pp. 157–181.

81. For example. Fenton and Leggett, op. cit., p. 23; Carter and Clarke, op. cit., pp. 794–796.

Chapter 6

1. A. W. Van Den Ban, "A Revision of the Two-step Flow of Communication Hypothesis," *Gazette*, 10, 1964, pp. 237–249.

2. See Table 1, ibid., p. 241.

3. Stycos, J. M., "The Potential Role of Turkish Village Opinion Leaders in a Program of Family Planning," *Public Opinion Quarterly*, 29, 1965, pp. 120–130.

4. Iliya F. Harik, "Opinion Leaders and the Mass Media in Rural Egypt: A Reconsideration of the Two-step Flow of Communication Hypothesis," *American Political Science Review*, 65, 1971, pp. 731–740.

5. M. R. Heath and S. J. Bekker, *Identification of Opinion Leaders in Public Affairs, Educational Matters, and Family Planning in the Township of Atteridgeville*, Pretoria: Human Sciences Research Council, 1986, pp.41–55.

6. Ibid., p. 42.

7. Saunders, Davis, and Monsees, op. cit.

8. Peter A. Andersen and John P. Garrison, "Media Consumption and Population Characteristics of Political Opinion Leaders," *Communication Quarterly*, 26, 1976, pp. 40–50.

9. Based on a single item scale with five possible responses, as used and tested by Everett M. Rogers and Donald G. Catarano, "Methods of Operationalizing Opinion Leadership," *Public Opinion Quarterly*, 26, 1962, pp. 435–441. See also chapter 3 in this book.

10. John P. Robinson, "Interpersonal Influence in Election Campaigns: Two-step Flow Hypotheses," *Public Opinion Quarterly*, 40, 1976, pp. 304–319.

11. These were the respondents who "talked with any other person and tried to show them why they should vote for one of the parties or candidates." Thirty-two percent of the sample responded positively.

12. Verling C. Troldahl and Robert Van Dam, "A New Scale for Identifying Public-Affairs Opinion Leaders," *Journalism Quarterly*, 42, 1965, pp. 655–657.

13. Lyman E. Ostlund, "Interpersonal Communication Following McGovern's Eagleton Decision," *Public Opinion Quarterly*, 37, 1973, pp. 601–610.

14. Lawrence G. Corey, "People Who claim to be Opinion Leaders: Identifying Their Characteristics by Self-Report," *Journal of Marketing*, 35, 1971, pp. 48–53.

15. Martilla, op. cit., pp. 176–177.

16. Leon G. Schiffman and Vincent Gaccione, "Opinion Leaders in Institutional Markets," *Journal of Marketing*, 38, 1974, pp. 49–53.

17. See Tables 1, 2, and 3, ibid., p. 51.

18. Barbara B. Stern and Stephen J. Gould, "The Consumer as Financial Opinion Leader," *Journal of Retail Banking*, 10, 1988, pp. 43–52.

19. On all these measures, statistically significant differences were found when comparing leaders and non-leaders. See Tables 4 and 5, ibid., pp. 49–50.

20. Kenny K. Chan and Shekhar Misra, "Characteristics of the Opinion Leader: A New Dimension," *Journal of Advertising*, 3, 1990, pp. 53–60, p. 55.

21. Gary M. Armstrong and Laurence P. Feldman, "Exposure and Sources of Opinion Leaders," *Journal of Advertising Research*, 16, 1976, pp. 21–27.

22. John O. Summers, "The Identity of Women's Clothing Fashion Opinion Leaders," *Journal of Marketing Research*, 7, 1970, pp. 175–185.

23. Ibid., p. 182.

24. Steven A. Baumgarten, "The Innovative Communicator in the Diffusion Process," *Journal of Marketing Research*, 12, 1975, pp. 12–18.

25. Virginia P. Richmond, "The Relationship between Opinion Leadership and Information Acquisition," *Human Communication Research*, 4, 1977, pp. 38–43.

26. The voluntary condition let the students decide if they wanted to read the memo given to them with no further instructions while the forced exposure involved the requirement of reading the memo, made by their instructor.

27. Ibid., p. 42.

28. Mark R. Levy, "Opinion Leadership and Television News Uses," *Public Opinion Quarterly*, 42, 1978, pp. 402–406.

29. The "cognitive orientation" use was the opportunity to activate, test, reinforce, or modify attitudes about people and events by means of news exposure. The "surveillance-reassurance" use indicated a tendency to watch

the news in order to gain information to reflect upon or to give context to their lives or social situation.

30. For a review, see Everett M. Rogers, *Diffusion of Innovations*, 3rd edition, New York: The Free Press, 1983, pp. 271–311; Everett M. Rogers and Lawrence D. Kincaid, *Communication Networks: Toward a New Paradigm for Research*, New York: The Free Press, 1981.

31. Andersen and Garrison, op. cit., pp. 40–50.

32. Herbert Hamilton, "Dimensions of Self-designated Opinion Leadership and Their Correlates," *Public Opinion Quarterly*, 35, pp. 266–274.

33. See Table 3, ibid., p. 271.

34. Heath and Bekker, op. cit. pp. 56–60.

35. John Saunders, Michael J. Davis, and David M. Monsees, "Opinion Leadership in Family Planning," *Journal of Health and Social Behavior*, 15(3), 1974, pp. 217–227.

36. James A. Palmore, Paul M. Hirsch, and Ariffin Marzuki, "Interpersonal Communication and the Diffusion of Family Planning in West Malaysia," *Demography*, 8, 1971, pp. 411–425.

37. Robert M. March and Margaret W. Tebbutt, "Housewife Product Communication Activity Patterns," *Journal of Social Psychology*, 107, 1979, pp. 63–69.

38. John P. Robinson, "Interpersonal Influence in Election Campaigns: Two-step-flow Hypotheses," *Public Opinion Quarterly*, 40, 1976, pp. 304–319.

39. Verling Troldahl and Robert Van Dam, "Face-to-Face Communications about Major Topics in the News," *Public Opinion Quarterly*, 29, 1966, pp. 626–634.

40. Charles Wright and Muriel Cantor, "The Opinion Seeker and Avoider: Steps Beyond the Opinion Leader Concept," *Pacific Sociological Review*, 10, 1967, pp. 33–43.

41. Robinson, op. cit., p. 306.

42. Gabriel Weimann, "On The Importance of Marginality: One More Step into the Two-step Flow of Communication," *American Sociological Review*, 47, 1982, pp. 764–773.

43. Ibid., p. 770.

44. On the importance of weak ties, see Mark S. Granovetter, "The Strength of Weak Ties," *American Journal of Sociology*, 73, 1973, pp. 1360–1380; and "The Strength of Weak Ties: A Network Theory Revisited," in R. Collins (ed.), *Sociological Theory*, San Francisco: Jossey-Bass, 1983, pp. 201–233. The intergroup "bridging" advantages of weak ties were reported by Gabriel Weimann, "The Strength of Weak Conversational Ties in the Flow of Information and Influence," *Social Networks*, 5, 1983, pp. 245–267.

45. Weimann, op. cit., p. 769.

Part 3

1. Everett M. Rogers and Floyd F. Shoemaker, *Communication of Innovations: A Cross-Cultural Approach*, New York: Free Press, 1971.

Chapter 7

1. The introduction of consumer behavior research is based on Thomas S. Robertson and Scott Ward, "Consumer Behavior Research: promise and prospects," in Robertson and Ward (eds.), *Consumer Behavior: Theoretical Sources*, Englewood Cliffs, N.J.: Prentice-Hall, 1973, pp. 33–42, and Thomas S. Robertson, Joan Zielinski, and Scott Ward, *Consumer Behavior*, Glenview, Ill.: Scott, Foresman and Company, 1984.

2. Robertson and Ward list six different factors that resulted in "the burst of consumer behavior interest and research which emerged in the 1960s," see ibid., pp. 10–11.

3. Various hierarchical models were suggested. The earliest model had only four stages (awareness, interest, desire, and action), suggested by E. K. Strong, *The Psychology of Selling*, New York: McGraw-Hill, 1920, p. 9. McGuire's model involved six stages (presentation of message, attention to message, comprehension, yielding to the conclusion, retention of the belief, and behavior on the basis of the new belief). See William J. McGuire, "An Information Processing Model of Advertising Effectiveness", in H. L. Davis and A. J. Silk (eds.), *Behavior and Management Sciences in Marketing*, New York: Wiley, 1978, pp. 156–180. Robertson, Zilelinski, and Ward present a more common adoption process model, used in this chapter, op. cit., pp. 75–76.

4. Michael L. Ray, *Advertising and Communications Management*, Englewood Cliffs, NJ: Prentice-Hall, 1982, pp. 34–55.

5. Robertson, Zielinski, and Ward, op. cit., p. 90.

6. Thomas Robertson, *Innovative Behavior and Communication*, New York: Holt, Rinehart, and Winston, 1971.

7. Joe Kent Kerby, *Consumer Behavior: Conceptual Foundations*, New York: Dun-Donnellewy, 1975.

8. Several books contain Veblen's work on social aspects of consumption. For example, see *The Theories of the Leisure Class*, New York: Macmillan, 1915; *What Veblen Taught: Selected Writings of Thorstein Veblen*, New York: A. M. Kelly, 1936; and *The Portable Veblen*, edited by Max Lerner, New York: Viking Press, 1948. The following citations are based on the last book.

9. Ibid., pp. 125–126.

10. Kerby, op. cit. pp. 468–473.

11. Frank M. Bass, "A New Product Growth Model for Consumer Durables," *Management Science*, 15, 1969, pp. 215–227.

12. On the applicability of learning theories to marketing research, see Michael L. Ray, "Psychological Theories and Interpretations of Learning," in Thomas S. Robertson and Scott Ward (eds.), *Consumer Behavior: Theoretical Sources*, Englewood Cliffs, NJ: Prentice-Hall, 1973, pp. 45–117.

13. Arnold Mitchell, *The Nine American Lifestyles*, New York: Macmillan, 1983.

14. For a detailed description of these groups and the application of VALS program to design new products and marketing campaigns, see Stan Le Roy Wilson, *Mass Media/Mass Culture*, 2nd edition, New York: McGraw-Hill, 1992,

pp. 321–324. Additional categories and classifications were reported in The European Society for Opinion and Marketing Research (ESOMAR) seminar (Helsinki, Finland, June 1991), published as *The Growing Individualization of Consumer Lifestyles and Demand*, Amsterdam: ESOMAR Publications, 1991.

15. Herbert H. Hyman, "The Psychology of Status," *Archives of Psychology*, 38, 1942, No. 269.

16. William O. Bearden and Michael J. Etzel, "Reference Group Influence on Product and Brand Purchase Decisions," *Journal of Consumer Research*, 9, 1982, pp. 183–194.

17. Whan C. Park and V. Parker Lessig, "Students and Housewives: Differences in Susceptibility to Reference Group Influences," *Journal of Consumer Research*, 4, 1977, pp. 102–110.

18. David O. Arnold, *The Sociology of Subcultures*, Berkeley, California: Glendasary Press, 1970.

19. Reported by Robertson, Zielinski, and Ward, op. cit., p. 529.

20. Elizabeth C. Hirschman, "American Jewish Ethnicity: Its Relationship to Some Selected Aspects of Consumer Behavior," *Journal of Marketing*, 45, 1981, pp. 102–110.

21. In fact, hundreds of studies revealed the impact of personal influence on consumer decision-making. See James F. Engel, David T. Kollat and Roger D. Blackwell, *Consumer Behavior*, 2nd edition, New York: Holt, Rinehart, and Winston, 1973, pp. 393–409.

22. John Arndt, "Role of Product-related Conversations in the Diffusion of a New Product," *Journal of Marketing Research*, 4, 1967, p. 292.

23. John R. Kerr and Bruce Weale, "Collegiate Clothing Purchasing Patterns and Fashion Adoption Behavior," *Southern Journal of Business*, 5, 1970, pp. 126–133.

24. Arndt, op. cit., pp. 291–295. See also Marsha L. Richins, "Negative Word-of-mouth by Dissatisfied Consumers: A Pilot Study," *Journal of Marketing*, 47, 1983, pp. 68–78; and Vijay Mahajan, Eitan Muller, and Roger A. Kerin, "Introduction Strategies for New Products with Positive and Negative Word-of-mouth," *Management Science*, 30, 1984, pp. 68–79.

25. Charles W. King and John O. Summers, "Technology, Innovation, and Consumer Decision-making," in Reed Moyer (ed.), *Consumer, Corporate, and Government Interfaces*, Chicago: American Marketing Association, 1967, pp. 63–68.

26. George Katona and Eva Mueller, "A Study of Purchasing Decisions," in Lincoln H. Clark (ed.), *Consumer Behavior: The Dynamics of Consumer Reaction*, New York: New York University Press, 1955, pp. 30–87.

27. Elihu Katz and Paul F. Lazarsfeld, *Personal Influence*, New York: the Free Press, 1955.

28. Charles W. King, "Fashion Adoption: A Rebuttal to the Trickle Down Theory," in Stephen A. Greyser (ed.), *Toward Scientific Marketing*, Chicago: American Marketing Association, 1963, pp. 108–125.

29. Algin J. Silk, "Overlap Among Self-designated Opinion Leaders: A Study of Selected Dental Products and Services," *Journal of Marketing Research*, 3, 1966, pp. 255–259.

30. George M. Beal and Everett M. Rogers, "Informational Sources in the Adoption Process of New Fabrics," *Journal of Home Economics*, 49, 1957, pp. 630–634.

31. Mary Dee Dickerson and James W. Gentry, "Characteristics of Adopters and Non-Adopters of Home Computers," *Journal of Consumer Research*, 10, 1983, pp. 225–235.

32. Duncan G. Labay and Thomas C. Kinnear, "Exploring the Consumer Decision Process in the Adoption of Solar Energy Systems," *Journal of Consumer Research*, 8, 1981, pp. 271–278.

33. Robert A. Westbrook and Claes Fornell, "Patterns of Information Source Usage Among Durable Goods Buyers," *Journal of Marketing Research*, 16, 1979, pp. 303–312.

34. Hubert Gatingon and Thomas S. Robertson, "A Propositional Inventory for New Diffusion Research," *Journal of Consumer Research*, 11, 1985, pp. 849–867.

35. Engel, Kollat and Blackwell, op. cit., p. 395.

36. Charles W. King and John O. Summers, "Dynamics of Interpersonal Communication: The Interaction Dyad," in Donald F. Cox (ed.), *Risk Taking and Information Handling in Consumer Behavior*, Boston: Graduate School of Business Administration, Harvard University, 1967, pp. 240–264.

37. John A. Martilla, "Word-of-mouth Communication in the Industrial Adoption Process," *Journal of Marketing Research*, 8, 1971, pp. 173–178.

38. The predictors are based on the review provided by Robertson, Zielinski, and Ward, op. cit., pp. 397–399.

39. The social aspects of purchasing air conditioners and the relationship to personal influence were documented by William H. Whyte, "The Web of Word-of-mouth," *Fortune*, 50, 1954, p. 104; and Sanford L. Grossbart, Robert A. Mittelstaedt and Gene W. Murdock, "Nearest Neighbor Analysis," *Advances in Consumer Research*, 5, 1977, pp. 1140–1148.

40. William J. McGuire, "Personality and Susceptibility to Social Influence," in E. F. Borgatta and W. W. Lambert (eds.), *Handbook of Personality Theory and Research*, New York: Rand McNally, 1968, pp. 1130–1187.

41. A detailed review of these studies is provided by William O. Bearden, Richard G. Netemeyer and Jesse E. Teel, "Measurement of Individual Susceptibility to Interpersonal Influence," *Journal of Consumer Research*, 15, 1989, pp. 473–481.

42. For example, Park and Lessig, op. cit., pp. 102–110; William O. Bearden and Michael J. Etzel, "Reference Group Influence on Product and Brand Purchase Decisions," *Journal of Consumer Research*, 9, 1982, pp. 183–194; and David Brinberg and Linda Plimpton, "Self-monitoring and Product Conspicuousness on Reference Group Influence," *Advances in Consumer Research*, 13, 1986, pp. 297–300.

43. Bearden, Netemeyer, and Teel, op. cit., pp. 473–481; A later validation of SUSCEP was reported by William O. Bearden and Michael J. Etzel, "Further Validation of the Consumer Susceptibility to Interpersonal Influence Scale," *Advances in Consumer Research*, 17, 1990, pp. 770–776.

44. Julia M. Bristor, "Enhanced Explanations of Word of Mouth Communications: The Power of Relationships," *Research in Consumer Behavior*, 4, 1990, pp. 51–83.

45. Ibid., pp. 60–61.

46. Especially in Raymond A. Bauer, "Source Effect and Persuability: A New Look," in Donald F. Cox (ed.), *Risk Taking and Information Handling in Consumer Behavior*, Boston: Harvard Business School, 1967, pp. 559–578.

47. Leon Festinger, "A Theory of Social Comparison Processes," *Human Relations*, 7, 1954, pp. 117–140.

48. Veblen, op. cit.

49. Georg Simmel, "Fashion," *International Quarterly*, 10, 1904, pp. 130–155.

50. The criticism is summarized by Kerby, op. cit. pp. 473–479. The main arguments are based on the study of Charles W. King reported in his "Rebuttal to the Trickle-Down Theory," op. cit., pp. 108–125.

51. Gabriel Weimann, "On the Importance of Marginality: One More Step into the Two-step Flow of Communication," *American Sociological Review*, 47, 1982, pp. 764–773.

52. Mark S. Granovetter, "The Strength of Weak Ties," *American Journal of Sociology*, 78, 1973, pp. 1360–1380.

53. Charles Y. Glock and Francesco M. Nicosia, "Sociology and the Study of Consumers," *Journal of Advertising Research*, 3, 1963, pp. 21–27, at p. 24.

54. John B. Stewart, *Repetitive Advertising in Newspapers: A Study of New Products*, Boston: Harvard University Division of Research, Graduate School of Business Administration, 1964.

55. Lawrence G. Corey, "People Who Claim to Be Opinion Leaders: Identifying Their Characteristics by Self-report," *Journal of Marketing*, 35, 1971, pp. 48–53.

56. Martilla, op. cit., pp. 176–177.

57. See table 7, ibid., p. 177.

58. Leon G. Schiffman and Vincent Gaccione, "Opinion Leaders in Institutional Markets," *Journal of Marketing*, 38, 1974, pp. 49–53.

59. See Tables 1, 2, and 3, ibid., p. 51.

60. E. Langeard, M. Crousillat, and R. Weiss, "Exposure to Cultural Activities and Opinion Leadership," *Advances in Consumer Research*, 5, 1977, pp. 606–610.

61. Ibid., p. 607.

62. Barbara B. Stern and Stephen J. Gould, "The Consumer as Financial Opinion Leader," *Journal of Retail Banking*, 10, 1988, pp. 43–52.

63. On all these measures, statistically significant differences were found when comparing leaders and non-leaders, see tables 4 and 5, ibid., pp. 49–50.

64. Ibid., pp. 44–45.

65. Lawrence F. Feick, Linda L. Price and Robin A. Higie, "People Who Use People: The Other Side of Opinion Leadership," *Advances in Consumer Research*, 13, 1986, pp. 301–305.

66. The first attention to this important element of the two-step flow model was paid by Charles C. Wright and Muriel Cantor, "The Opinion Seeker and Avoider: Steps Beyond the Opinion Leader Concept," *Pacific Sociological Review*, 10, 1967, pp. 33–43.

67. For example, King and Summers, op. cit. pp. 253–254; Donald F. Fox, "The Audience as Communicators," in Cox, op. cit., pp. 172–187.

68. A study of the diffusion of stainless steel blades indicated that there may exist a three-or-more-step flow of communication; Jagdish N. Sheth, "Word-of-mouth in Low-risk Innovations," *Journal of Advertising Research*, 11, 1971, pp. 15–18.

69. For example, Alvin J. Silk, "Overlap Among Self-designated Opinion Leaders: A Study of Selected Dental Products and Services," *Journal of Marketing Research*, 3, 1966, pp. 255–259.

70. Charles W. King and John O. Summers, "Overlap of Opinion Leadership Across Consumer Product Categories," *Journal of Marketing Research*, 7, 1970, pp. 43–50.

71. David B. Montgomery and Alvin J. Silk, "Patterns of Overlap in Opinion Leadership and Interest for Selected Categories of Purchasing Activity," in Philip R. McDonald (ed.), *Marketing Involvement in Society and Economy*, Chicago: American Marketing Association, 1969, pp. 377–386. Supportive evidence is also reported by Herbert F. Lionberger, *Adoption of New Ideas and Practices*, Ames, Iowa: Iowa State University Press, 1960, pp. 65–66.

72. David B. Montgomery and Alvin J. Silk, "Clusters of Consumer Interests and Opinion Leaders' Spheres of Influence," *Journal of Marketing Research*, 8, 1971, pp. 317–321.

73. Martilla, op. cit, p. 177.

74. Ronald E. Goldsmith, Melvin Stith, and Dennis White, "Race and Sex Differences in Self-identified Innovativeness and Opinion Leadership," *Journal of Retailing*, 63, 1987, pp. 411–425.

75. Hubert Gatingon and Thomas S. Robertson, "A Propositional Inventory for New Diffusion Research," *Journal of Consumer Research*, 11, 1985, pp. 849–867; David F. Midgley and Graham R. Dowling, "Innovativeness: The Concept and Its Measurement," *Journal of Consumer Research*, 4, 1978, pp. 229–242.

76. Glen Rieken and Ugur Yavas, "Seeking Donors Via Opinion Leadership," *Journal of Professional Services and Marketing*, 2, 1986, pp. 109–116.

77. Thomas S. Robertson and James H. Myers, "Personality Correlates of Opinion Leadership and Innovative Buying Behavior," *Journal of Marketing Research*, 6, 1969, pp. 164–168.

78. John O. Summers, "The Identity of Women's Clothing Fashion Opinion Leaders," *Journal of Marketing Research*, 7, 1970, pp. 175–185.

79. Jacob Jacoby, "Personality and Innovation Process," *Journal of Marketing Research*, 8, 1971, pp. 244–247; Elizabeth B. Goldsmith and Ronald E. Goldsmith, "Dogmatism and Confidence as Related Factors in Evaluation of New Products," *Psychological Reports*, 47, 1980, pp. 1068–1070.

80. John H. Myers and Thomas S. Robertson, "Dimensions of Opinion Leadership," *Journal of Marketing Research*, 9, 1972, pp. 41–46.

81. James W. Taylor, "A Striking Characteristic of Innovators," *Journal of Marketing Research*, 14, 1977, pp. 104–107.

82. Summers, 1970, op. cit., pp. 178–185.

83. Kenny K. Chan and Shekhar Misra, "Characteristics of the Opinion Leader: A New Dimension," *Journal of Advertising*, 19, 1990, pp. 53–60.

84. For example, Fred D. Reynolds and William R. Darden, "Mutually Adaptive Effects of Interpersonal Communication," *Journal of Marketing Research*, 8, 1971, pp. 449–454.

85. Chan and Misra, ibid., p. 55.

86. Douglas J. Tigert and Stephen J. Arnold, *Profiling Self-designated Opinion Leaders and Self-designated Innovators Through Life Style Research*, Toronto: School of Business, University of Toronto, 1971.

87. Marsha L. Richins and Peter H. Bloch, "After the New Wears Off: The Temporal Context of Product Involvement," *Journal of Consumer Research*, 13, 1986, pp. 280–285; Marsha L. Richins and Teri Root-Shaffer, "The Role of Involvement and Opinion Leadership in Consumer Word-of-mouth: An Implicit Model Made Explicit," *Advances in Consumer Research*, 15, 1988, pp. 32–36; Meera P. Venkatraman, "Opinion Leadership, Enduring Involvement and Characteristics of Opinion Leaders: A Moderating or Mediating Relationship?" *Advances in Consumer Research*, 17, 1990, pp. 60–67.

88. Richins and Root-Shaffer, ibid., p. 34.

89. Chan and Misra, op. cit., p. 55.

90. Reported in *Newsweek*, June 1992, p. 41.

91. Lawrence G. Corey, op. cit., p. 53.

92. Robertson, Zielinski, and Ward, op. cit., p. 412.

93. Glen Rieken and Ugur Yavas, op. cit., pp. 109–116.

94. Robertson, Zielinski, and Ward, op. cit., p. 412.

95. Joseph R. Mancuso, "Why Not Create Opinion Leaders for New Product Introduction?" *Journal of Marketing*, 33, 1969, pp. 20–25.

96. Ibid., p. 25.

97. Ibid., p. 25.

98. Rieken and Yavas, op. cit., p. 115.

99. Stern and Gould, op. cit., pp. 49–52.

100. Ibid., p. 49.

101. Ibid., p. 51.

102. Ibid., p. 52.

103. Rieken and Yavas, op. cit., pp 114–115.

104. J. Michael Munson and W. Austin Spivey, "Product and Brand-user Stereotypes Among Social Classes: Implications for Advertising Strategy," *Journal of Advertising Research*, 21, 1981, pp. 37–46.

105. Robertson, Zielinski, and Ward, op. cit., p. 413.

106. Ibid., p. 413.

107. Stern and Gould, op. cit., p. 51.

108. Lawrence G. Corey, op. cit., p. 53.

109. See Everett M. Rogers, *Diffusion of Innovations*, 3rd edition, New York: Free Press, 1983, pp. 241–270.

Chapter 8

1. Herbert Blumer, "Fashion: From Class Differentiation to Collective Selection," *Sociological Quarterly*, 10, 1969, pp. 275–291.

2. Ibid., p. 290.

3. Quentin Bell, *On Human Finery*, New York: A. A. Wyn Inc., 1949, p. 12.

4. Georg Simmel, "Fashion," *International Quarterly*, 10, 1904, pp. 130–155; reprinted in *American Journal of Sociology*, 62, 1957, pp. 541–558.

5. Ibid, pp. 542–543.

6. Ibid., p. 547.

7. George B. Sproles, "Behavioral Science Theories of Fashion," in Michael R. Solomon (ed.), *The Psychology of Fashion*, Lexington, Massachusetts: Lexington Books, 1985, pp. 15–28.

8. On such revision, see Grant D. McCraken, "The Trickle-down Theory Rehabilitated," in Michael R. Solomon (ed.), *The Psychology of Fashion*, Lexington, Massachusetts: Lexington Books, 1985, pp. 39–54.

9. Gabriel Tarde, *The Laws of Imitation* (translated from French), New York: Henry Holt, 1903, p. 221.

10. Ibid., p. 193.

11. Karlyne Anspach, *The Why of Fashion*, Ames, Iowa: The Iowa State University Press, 1967.

12. Ibid., pp. 5–6.

13. Such a sequential model is presented by Sproles, op. cit., p. 56.

14. Alison Lurie, *The Language of Clothes*, New York: Random House, 1981.

15. Gregory P. Stone, "Appearances and the Self," in Arnold R. Rose, (ed.), *Human Behavior and Social Interaction*, Boston: Houghton Mifflin, 1962, pp. 86–118.

16. Terry Eagleton, *Literacy Theory: An Introduction*, Minneapolis: University of Minnesota Press, 1983, p. 97.

17. Umberto Eco, *A Theory of Semeiotics*, Bloomington: Indiana University Press, 1979, p. 37.

18. Francoise Simon-Miller, "Commentary: Signs and Cycles in the Fashion System," in Michael R. Solomon (ed.), *The Psychology of Fashion*, Lexington, Massachusetts: Lexington Books, 1985, pp. 71–81.

19. On fashion as a case of diffusion of innovation, see Margaret P. Grindereng, "Fashion Diffusion," *Journal of Home Economics*, 59, 1967, pp. 171–174; Steven A. Baumgarten, "The Innovative Communicator in the Diffusion of Innovation Process," *Journal of Marketing Research*, 12, 1975, pp. 12–18; George B. Sproles, *Fashion: Consumer Behavior Toward Dress*, Minneapolis: Burgess, 1979; George B. Sproles (ed.), *Perspectives of Fashion*, Minneapolis: Burgess, 1981.

20. D. J. Tigert, C. W. King and L. Ring, "Fashion Involvement: A Cross-cultural Comparative Analysis," *Advances in Consumer Research*, 7, 1979, pp. 17–21.

21. See table 5, ibid., p. 20.

22. For example, Baumgarten, op. cit.; Holly L. Schrank, "Correlates of Fashion Leadership: Implications for Fashion Process Theory," *The Sociological Quarterly*, 14, 1973, pp. 534–543; Rosemary Polegato and Marjorie Wall, "Information Seeking by Fashion Opinion Leaders and Followers," *Home Economics Research Journal*, 8, 1980, pp. 327–338.

23. Sproles, 1985, op. cit., p. 58.

24. Anspach, op. cit., pp. 215–216.

25. Elihu Katz and Paul F. Lazarsfeld, *Personal Influence*, New York: The Free Press, 1955, pp. 43–115.

26. Simmel, op. cit., p. 549.

27. Blumer, op. cit., p. 287.

28. Anspach, op. cit., pp. 216–218.

29. Anspach uses Jacqueline Kennedy or the Duchess of Windsor as examples for such "leaders."

30. Holly L. Schrank and D. Lois Gilmore, "Correlates of Fashion Opinion Leadership: Implications for Fashion Process Theory," *The Sociological Quarterly*, 14, 1973, pp. 534–543.

31. The scales, their items and validation are detailed by Schrank and Gilmore, ibid., pp. 236–237.

32. Elihu Katz, "The Two-step Flow of Communication: An Up-to-date Report on an Hypothesis," *Public Opinion Quarterly*, 21, 1957, pp. 61–78.

33. Tigert, King, and Ring, op. cit., p. 17. They compared (table 1) women in this category of "fashion change agent" in four cultures: English Canada, French Canada, the United States, and the Netherlands. Note that this conceptualization of "change agent" did not lead to a measurement of influence or change activity but rather to measurement of fashion involvement and innovativeness.

34. Everett M. Rogers, *Diffusion of Innovations*, New York: The Free Press, 1962.

35. T. S. Robertson and J. S. Myers, "Personality Correlates of Opinion Leadership and Innovative Buying Behavior," *Journal of Marketing Research*, 7, 1969, pp. 164–168.

36. Schrank and Gilmore, op. cit., p. 540.

37. Baumgarten, op. cit., pp. 12–18.

38. Ibid., table 4, p. 16.

39. Innovative leaders were found to be more impulsive, have lower intellectual interest, be more exhibitionistic and more narcissistic than others.

40. Ibid., p. 17.

41. John O. Summers, "The Identity of Women's Clothing Fashion Opinion Leaders," *Journal of Marketing Research*, 7, 1970, pp. 178–185.

42. Ibid., p. 181. See also table 3.

43. William R. Darden and Fred D. Reynolds, "Predicting Opinion Leadership for Men's Apparel Fashions," *Journal of Marketing Research*, 9, 1972, pp. 324–328.

44. George J. Szybillo, "A Situational Influence on the Relationship of a Consumer Attribute to New-product Attractiveness," *Journal of Applied Psychology*, 60, 1975, pp. 652–655.

45. Ibid., p. 655.

46. Joyce E. Brett and Anne Kernaleguen, "Perceptual and Personality Variables Related to Opinion Leadership in Fashion," *Perceptual and Motor Skills*, 40, 1975, pp. 775–779.

47. Locus of control describes the individual's perception of the causal relationship between events affecting him or her. A belief in external control is the expectancy that events are beyond the individual's control (e.g., related to fate, external forces, a god, luck, etc.), while a belief in internal control is the expectancy that these same events are contingent upon the individual himself. For a detailed description of the measure and the Internal-External Locus of Control Scale, see J. B. Rotter, "General Expectancies for Internal versus External Control of Reinforcement," *Psychological Monographs*, 6, 1966, pp. 91–92.

48. Field dependence measures the individual's reliance on the environmental field when field-dependent perceivers tend passively to conform to the dominant environmental field. Field independent perceivers are characterized by activity and a capacity for organization. The rod-and-frame test is used to measure this trait. For a description, see Brett and Kernaleguen, op. cit., p. 776.

49. An achievement anxiety test was used to measure two types of this anxiety: the facilitating anxiety (anxiety that aids performance in pursuit of a goal), and debilitating anxiety (anxiety that interferes with performance). On this scale see R. Alpert and R. H. Haber, "Anxiety in Academic Achievement Situations," *Journal of Abnormal and Social Psychology*, 61, 1960, pp. 207–215.

50. Bret and Kernaleguen, op. cit., p. 778.

51. Leslie L. Davis and Sharron J. Lennon, "Self-monitoring, Fashion Opinion Leadership and Attitudes Toward Clothing," in Michael R. Solomon (ed.), *The Psychology of Fashion*, Lexington, Massachusetts: Lexington Books, 1985, pp. 177–182.

52. On the notion of self-monitoring, its measurement and validation see Mark Snyder, "Self-monitoring Processes," in L. Berkowitz (ed.), *Advances in Experimental Social Psychology*, New York: Academic Press, 1979, pp. 85–128.

53. Mark Snyder and Thomas C. Monson, "Persons, Situations, and the Control of Social Behavior," *Journal of Personality and Social Psychology*, 32, 1975, pp. 637–644.

54. Sharron J. Lennon and Leslie L. Davis, "Individual Differences in Fashion Orientation and Cognitive Complexity," *Perceptual and Motor Skills*, 64, 1987, pp. 327–330.

55. Based on the finding of a previous study, S. K. Payne and M. J. Beatty, "Innovativeness and Cognitive complexity," *Psychological Reports*, 51, 1982, pp. 85–86.

56. E. C. Hirschman and W. O. Adcock, "An Examination of Innovative Communicators, Opinion Leaders and Innovators for Men's Fashion Apparel," *Advances in Consumer Research*, 5, 1978, pp. 303–314.

57. On this method measure, see D. E. Hunt, L. F. Butler, J. E. Noy, and M. E. Rosser, *Assessing Conceptual Level by a Paragraph Completion Method*, Toronto: The Toronto Institute for Studies in Education, 1978.

58. Ibid., p. 330.

Chapter 9

1. For a review, see Heinz Eulau, "The Columbia Studies of Personal Influence," *Social Science History*, 4, 1980, pp. 207–228.

2. Carl A. Sheingold, "Social Networks and Voting: The Resurrection of a Research Agenda," *American Sociological Review*, 38, 1973, pp. 712–720.

3. Paul F. Lazarsfeld, Bernard Berelson, and Hazel Gaudet, *The People's Choice*, New York: Columbia University Press, 1948; and Bernard Berelson, Paul F. Lazarsfeld, and William N. McPhee, *Voting*, Chicago: University of Chicago Press, 1954.

4. Lazarsfeld et al., op. cit., pp. 137–149; Berelson et al., op. cit., pp. 88–109.

5. Berelson et al., ibid, pp. 220–222; Lazarsfeld et al., op. cit., pp. 80–82.

6. Lazarsfeld et al., ibid., pp. 151–152; Elihu Katz and Paul Lazarsfeld, *Personal Influence*, Glencoe, Illinois: 1955; Elihu Katz, "The Two-step Flow of Communication: An Up-to-date Report of an Hypothesis," *Public Opinion Quarterly*, 21, 1957, pp. 61–78.

7. Berelson et al., op. cit., pp. 50–53, 171–177.

8. Ithiel de Sola Pool, "TV: A New Dimension in Politics," in E. Burdick and A. J. Brodbeck (eds.), *American Voting Behavior*, Glencoe, Illinois: Free Press, 1959, pp. 239–242.

9. Harold Mendelsohn and Irving Crespi, *Polls, Television, and the New Politics*, San Francisco: Chandler, 1970, pp. 297–298.

10. For a review, see Sidney Kraus and Dennis Davis, *The Effects of Mass Communication on Political Behavior*, University Park: Pennsylvania State University Press, 1976.

11. See, for example, Edward O. Laumann, "Friends of Urban Man: an Assessment of Accuracy in Reporting Their Sociometric Attributes," *Sociometry*, 32, 1969, pp. 54–59.

12. Sheingold, op. cit., p. 714.

13. V. O. Key, Jr., *Public Opinion and American Democracy*, New York: Knopf, 1961; *The Responsible Electorate*, Cambridge, Massachusetts: Harvard University Press, 1966.

14. V. O. Key, Jr., and Frank Munger, "Social Determinism and Electoral Decision: The Case of Indiana," pp. 281–299 in Eugene Burdick and Arthur J. Brodbeck (eds.), *American Voting Behavior*, Glencoe, Illinois: Free Press, p. 281.

15. Angus Campbell, Gerald Gurin and Warren E. Miller, *The Voter Decides*, Westport, Connecticut: Greenwood Press, 1971, p. 85.

16. See, for example, the return to early concepts: Warren E. Miller, "Party Identification, Realignment, and Party Voting: Back to the Basics," *American Political Science Review*, 85(2), 1991, pp. 557–568.

17. For example, Bruce A. Campbell, "Patterns of Change in the Partisan Loyalties of Native Southerners: 1952-1972," *Journal of Politics*, 39, 1977, pp. 730-761.

18. For example, Philip E. Converse and Roy Pierce, "Measuring Partisanship," *Political Methodology*, 11, 1987, pp. 143-166.

19. For a review of the criticism, see Elihu Katz, "Communication Research Since Lazarsfeld," *Public Opinion Quarterly*, 51, 1987, pp. s25-s45. Katz argues that much of the history of communication research has been a set of continuing arguments with Paul Lazarsfeld.

20. Sheingold, op. cit., p. 717.

21. Walter Dean Burnham, *Critical Elections and the Mainsprings of American Politics*, New York: Norton, 1970, p. ix.

22. Gerald M. Pomper, "From Confusion to Clarity: Issues and American Voters," *American Political Science Review*, 66, 1972, pp. 415-428.

23. Sheingold, op. cit., p. 718.

24. Stephen M. Weatherford, "Interpersonal Networks and Political Behavior," *American Journal of Political Science*, 26(1), 1982, pp. 117-142.

25. For a review of social network research, dimensions of analysis, and communication aspects, see Gabriel Weimann, "Social Networks and Communication," in M. Asante and W. B. Gudykunst (eds.), *Handbook of International and Intercultural Relations*, Los Angeles: Sage, 1989, pp. 186-203; Everett Rogers and Lawrence D. Kincaid, *Communication Networks*, New York: Free Press, 1981.

26. Edward O. Laumann, "Network Analysis in Large Social Systems: Some Theoretical and Methodological Problems," pp. 379-402 in P. Holland S. Leinhardt (eds.), *Perspectives on Social Networks Research*, New York: Academic Press, 1979, p. 391.

27. R. D Alba and C. Kadushin, "The Introduction of Social Circles: A New Measure of Social Proximity in Networks," *Sociological Methods and Research*, 5, 1976, pp. 77-102.

28. Claude S. Fischer et al., *Networks and Places: Social Relations in the Urban Setting*, New York: Free Press, 1977, p. vii.

29. Mark S. Granovetter, "The Strength of Weak Ties," *American Journal of Sociology*, 78, 1973, p. 1360.

30. The works of Holland and Leinhardt are the best examples of such structural network analysis. See P. Holland and S. Leinhardt, "A Method for Detecting Structure in Sociometric Data," *American Journal of Sociology*, 76, 1970, pp. 492-513; or the collection of papers in Samuel Leinhardt (ed.), *Social Networks*, New York: Academic Press, 1977.

31. Weatherford, op. cit., p. 118.

32. The sample consisted of 280 respondents chosen from 30 primary sampling units, and focused on the personal networks of these individuals during the 1980 campaign; Weatherford, ibid., pp. 123-124.

33. Ibid., p. 138.

34. Robert Huckfeldt and John Sprague, "Networks in Context: The Social Flow of Political Information," *American Political Science Review*, 81 (4), 1987, pp. 1197-1216.

35. Ibid., p. 1197.

36. Steven E. Finkel, Edward N. Muller and Karl-Dieter Opp, "Personal Influence, Collective Rationality, and Mass Political Action," *American Political Science Review*, 83(3), 1989, pp. 885-903.

37. Paul Allen Beck, "Voters' Intermediation Environment in the 1988 Presidential Contest," *Public Opinion Quarterly*, 55, 1991, pp. 371-394.

38. Ibid., p. 373.

39. "This tendency for women to focus their political discussions within their family seems to have withstood considerable change in the role of women and their exposure to the world outside of the family," argued Beck (ibid., p. 377). Similar findings were revealed by the early Columbia studies as well as by more recent ones, for example: Bettina Brickell, Robert Huckfeldt, and John Sprague, "Gender Effects on Political Discussion: The Political Networks of Men and Women," paper presented at the annual meeting of the American Political Science Association, Washington, D.C., 1988; Huckfeldt and Sprague, op. cit., pp. 1197-1216.

40. Beck, op. cit., p. 378.

41. Bruce C. Straits, "Bringing Strong Ties Back: Interpersonal Gateways to Political Information and Influence," *Public Opinion Quarterly*, 55, 1991, pp. 432-448.

42. Kent M. Jennings, "Gender Roles and Inequalities in Political Participation: Results from Wight-Nation Study," *Western Political Quarterly*, 36, 1983, pp. 364-385.

43. Richard G. Niemi, Roman Hedges, and M. Kent Jennings, "The Similarity of Husbands' and Wives' Political Views," *American Politics Quarterly*, 5, 1977, pp. 133-148.

44. Edward O. Laumann, *Bonds of Pluralism: The Form and Substance of Urban Social Networks*, New York: Wiley, 1973.

45. Weatherford, op. cit. pp. 117-143.

46. Huckfeldt and Sprague, op. cit., pp. 1197-1216.

47. Straits, op. cit., p. 447.

48. Laumann, op. cit.

49. Ibid., p. 98.

50. Ibid., p. 126.

51. Peter V. Marsden, "Core Discussion Networks of Americans," *American Sociological Review*, 52, 1987, pp. 122-131.

52. Elisa Jayne Bienenstock, Philip Bonacich, and Melvin Oliver, "The Effects of Network Density and Homogeneity on Attitude Polarization," *Social Networks*, 12, 1990, pp. 153-172.

53. Ibid., p. 171.

54. Edward O. Laumann and Franz U. Pappi, *Networks of Collective Action: A Perspective on Community Influence*, 1976, New York: Academic Press.

55. Francis E. Lowe and Thomas C. McCormick, "A Study of the Influence of Formal and Informal Leaders in an Election Campaign," *Public Opinion Quarterly*, 20, 1956, pp. 651–662.

56. The large sex difference was due mainly to married women who gave their husbands as their informal leaders in political matters, while such choice was not reciprocated by the husbands. It is interesting to note that even a study that revealed a growing share of female opinion leadership reported that the only area in which male opinion leaders kept their dominance was politics: see Virginia P. Richmond and James C. McCroskey, "Whose Opinion Do You Trust?," *Journal of Communication*, 25, 1975, pp. 42–50.

57. Lowe and McCormick, op. cit, p. 660.

58. Ibid., p. 660.

59. Ibid., p. 661.

60. Lazarsfeld and Katz, op. cit.

61. Bo Anderson, "Opinion Influentials and Political Opinion Formation in Four Swedish Communities," *International Social Science Journal*, 14(2), 1962, pp. 320–326.

62. Ibid., p. 328. Despite the similarities with the American studies, Anderson highlights one basic difference: the Swedish leaders in the political domain came mainly from the leadership of labor organizations. This, he argues, is explained by the Swedish political system that for several decades was dominated by a Socialist party with strong ties to the labor unions.

63. Lyman E. Ostlund, "Interpersonal Communication Following McGovern's Eagleton Decision," *Public Opinion Quarterly*, 37, 1973, pp. 601–610.

64. Ibid., p. 606.

65. Sheldon Bockman and William F. Gayk, "Political Orientation and Political Ideologies," *Pacific Sociological Review*, 20(4), 1977, pp. 536–552.

66. The question asked: "Do you know anyone in (Spectra) who keeps up with each specific issue and whom you can trust to let you know what is really going on?"

67. Campbell, Gurin, and Miller, op. cit.

68. The original analysis includes two other groups and sub-groups but for the present discussion we focus only on the leaders, decision-makers, and the others ("regular" individuals). Thus, table 9.2 is based on data derived from two tables in the Bockman and Gayk paper, op. cit., p. 545.

69. Regrettably, the report does not include the frequency of overlap between the two categories.

70. John S. Black, "Opinion Leaders: Is Anyone Following?" *Public Opinion Quarterly*, 46, 1982, pp. 169–176.

71. See table 2, ibid., p. 171.

72. Ibid., p. 175.

73. Glenn S. Omura and W. Wayne Talarzyk, "Shaping Public Opinion" Personal Sources of Information on A Major Political Issue," *Advances in Consumer Research*, 10, 1982, pp. 484–489.

74. Ibid., p. 485.

75. John P. Robinson, "The Press as Kingmaker," *Journalism Quarterly*, 51, 1974, pp. 587–594.

76. Elmo Roper, *Trends in Public Opinion Toward Television and Other Mass Media 1959–1974*, New York: Television Information Office, 1975.

77. A good example is the Norwegian referendum on membership in the European Common Market in 1972. Though 81 percent of the newspapers argued in favor of joining, the majority voted against it. A similar case was the Israeli elections of 1984 and 1988 when the press endorsed the Labor party but the voters favored the Likud party, which won both campaigns.

78. John P. Robinson, "Interpersonal Influence in Election Campaigns: Two-step Flow Hypotheses," *Public Opinion Quarterly*, 40, 1976, pp. 304–319.

79. These were the respondents who "talked with any other person and tried to show them why they should vote for one of the parties or candidates." 32 percent of the sample responded positively.

80. Ibid., p. 315. For more details on the resulting modification of the model, see chapter 15 in this book.

81. Ottar Hellevik and Tor Bjorklund, "Opinion Leadership and Political Extremism," *International Journal of Public Opinion Research*, 3, 1991, pp. 157–181.

82. The first to note this relationship, later documented in numerous studies, was Elihu Katz, "The Two-step Flow of Communication: An Up-to-date Report on an Hypothesis," *Public Opinion Quarterly*, 21, 1957, pp. 61–78.

83. On this tendency of opinion leaders, see chapters on opinion leaders in fashion, science, agriculture, family planning, and health care in this book or in Everett M. Rogers, *Diffusion of Innovations* (3rd edition), New York: Free Press, 1983.

84. The rates in table 9.4 are based on Hellevik and Bjorklund, op. cit, (table A1, p. 176.

85. There is an exception to the U-shaped curve of opinion leaders with a sharp drop in their frequency at the extreme left. Regrettably, the researchers focused their attention on the this "left dip" that represented only a small fraction of the leaders' group, while overlooking the surprising general trend of opinion leaders to be concentrated in the extremes.

86. These notions were explored by the German public opinion researcher Elisabeth Noelle-Neumann. See, for example, Elisabeth Noelle-Neumann, "The Spiral of Silence: A Theory of Public Opinion," *Journal of Communication*, 24, 1974, pp. 43–51; *The Spiral of Silence: Public Opinion—Our Social Skin*, Chicago: University of Chicago Press, 1984; "Advances in Spiral of Silence Research," *Communication Review*, 10, 1989, pp. 3–34; and "The Theory of Public Opinion: The Concept of the Spiral of Silence," *Communication Yearbook*, 14, 1991, pp. 256–287.

87. For example, Noelle-Neumann, 1989, ibid., pp. 6–9.

88. Hellevik and Bjorklund, op. cit., p. 163.

Chapter 11

1. Bernard Berelson, "On Family Planning Communication," *Demography*, 1, 1964, p. 95.

2. James A. Palmore and D.M. Monsees, "The Eastern Kentucky Private Physician-Plus-Education Program: First Evaluation and Results," in Donald J. Bogue (ed.), *The Rural South Fertility Experiments*, Chicago: Community and Family Study Center, University of Chicago, Report 1, 1966, pp. 11–26.

3. Reported in "Referral Sources for Patients Admitted to Family Planning," paper prepared by the Tennessee Department of Public Health, January 25, 1972.

4. Ronald Freedman and John Y. Takeshita, *Family Planning in Taiwan*, New Jersey: Princeton University Press, 1969.

5. D. C. Dubey and H. M. Cholden, "Communication and the Diffusion of the IUD: A Case Study of Urban India," *Demography*, 4, 1967, pp. 601–614.

6. M. Requena, "Studies of Family Planning in the Quinta Normal District of Santiago," *Milbank Memorial Fund Quarterly*, 43, October 1965, pp. 69–99.

7. R. Hill, J. Stycos, and K. Back, *The Family and Population Control*, Chapel Hill: University of North Carolina Press, 1959.

8. J. T. Fawcett et al., "Thailand: An Analysis of Time and Distance Factors at an IUD Clinic in Bangkok," *Studies in Family Planning*, 1 (19), 1967, pp. 3–12.

9. M. Noda, "Contraception in Japan: Problems of Motivation and Communication," in C. V. Kiser (ed.), *Research in Family Planning*, New Jersey: Princeton University Press, 1962, pp. 551–569.

10. J. C. Cobb et al., "Pakistan: The Medical Social Research Project at Luiliani," *Studies in Family Planning*, 1 (8), 1965, pp. 11–16.

11. Mayone, J. Stychos, "The Potential Role of Turkish Village Opinion Leaders in a Program of Family Planning," *Public Opinion Quarterly*, 29, 1965, pp. 120–130.

12. Ibid., pp. 129–130.

13. Unpublished report of the Turkish Rural Development Research Project, cited by Stycos, ibid., p. 130.

14. Donald J. Bogue, "Hypotheses for Family Planning Derived from Recent and Current Experience in Asia," *Studies in Family Planning*, 3, 1964, pp. 6–8.

15. James A. Palmore, "The Chicago Snowball: A Study of the Flow and Diffusion of Family Planning Information," in Donald J. Bogue (ed.), *Sociological Contributions to Family Planning Research*, Chicago: University of Chicago Press, 1967, pp. 272–363.

16. Ibid., p. 286.

17. James A. Palmore, "Awareness Sources and Stages in the Adoption of Specific Contraceptives," *Demography*, 5, 1968, pp. 960–972.

18. James A. Palmore, Paul M. Hirsch, and Ariffin Marzuki, "Interpersonal Communication and the Diffusion of Family Planning in West Malaysia," *Demography*, 8, 1971, pp. 411–425.

19. Florangel Z. Rosario, "The Leader in Family Planning and the Two-step Flow Model," *Journalism Quarterly*, 48, 1971, pp. 288–297.

20. Paul J. Placek, "Direct Mail and Information Diffusion: Family Planning," *Public Opinion Quarterly*, 38, 1975, pp. 548–561.

21. Ibid., p. 559.

22. Palmore, 1967, op. cit., and Palmore, 1971, op. cit. pp. 413–414.

23. Rosario, op. cit., pp. 294–297.

24. Palmore, op. cit., p. 418.

25. John Saunders, Michael J. Davis, and David M. Monsees, "Opinion Leadership in Family Planning," *Journal of Health and Social Behavior*, 15(3), 1974, pp. 217–227.

26. For a detailed comparison see Rosario, op. cit., pp. 296–297.

27. Saunders, Davis and Monsees, op. cit.

28. Ibid., p. 221.

29. Ibid., p. 227.

Chapter 11

1. According to Diana Crane, *Invisible Colleges*, Chicago: The University of Chicago Press, 1972, pp. 3–5.

2. Robert K. Merton, *Social Theory and Social Structure*, Glencoe, Illinois: The Free Press, 1957.

3. T. Kuhn, *The Structure of Scientific Revolutions*, Chicago: University of Chicago Press, 1962.

4. N. Scorer, *The Social System of Science*, New York: Halt, Rinehart, and Winston, 1966, p. 3.

5. Irwin Sperber, *Fashions in Science: Opinion Leaders and Collective Behavior in the Social Sciences*, Minneapolis: University of Minnesota Press, 1990.

6. Ibid, p. 13.

7. Georg Simmel, "Fashion," *International Quarterly*, 10, October 1904, pp. 130–155; reprinted in *American Journal of Sociology*, 62, 1957, pp. 541–558. Citations refer to the latter reprinted article.

8. Ibid, p. 544.

9. Ibid., p. 544.

10. Ibid., p. 544.

11. D. J. Price, *Little Science, Big Science*, New York: Columbia University Press, 1963.

12. Leah A. Lievrouw, Everett M. Rogers, Charles U. Lowe, and Edward Nadel, "Triangulation as a Research Strategy for Identifying Invisible Colleges Among Biomedical Scientists," *Social Networks*, 9, 1987, pp. 217–248.

13. Ibid., p. 242.

14. Thomas Schott, "Interpersonal Influence in Science: Mathematicians in Denmark and Israel," *Social Networks*, 9, 1987, pp. 351–374.

15. Ibid., p. 372.

16. Simmel, 1957, op. cit., p. 549.

17. Sperber, op. cit., p. 25.

18. Crane, op. cit. p. 22.

19. Everett M. Rogers, *Diffusion of Innovations*, New York: Free Press, 1962.

20. Crane, op. cit., p. 23.

21. On the notion of "social circles," see Charles C. Kadushin, "The Friends and Supporters of Psychotherapy; On Social Circles in Urban Life," *American*

Sociological Review, 31, 1966, pp. 786–802, and "Power, Influence, and Social Circles: A New Methodology for Studying Opinion Makers," *American Sociological Review*, 33, 1968, pp. 685–699.

22. Crane, op. cit., p. 45.

23. S. Crawford, *Informal Communication Among Scientists in Sleep and Dream Research*, Unpublished Doctoral Dissertation, University of Chicago, 1970.

24. J. Gaston, *Big Science in Britain: A Sociological Study of the High Energy Physics Community*, Unpublished Doctoral Dissertation, Yale University, 1969.

25. D. Lingwood, "Interpersonal Communication, Scientific Productivity, and Invisible Colleges: Studies of Two Behavioral Science Research Areas," paper presented to the Colloquium on Improving the Social and Communication Mechanisms of Educational Research, The American Educational Research Association, Washington, D.C., November 1968.

26. B. C. Griffith and A. J. Miller, "Networks of Informal Communication Among Scientifically Productive Scientists." In C. Nelson and D. Pollock (eds.), *Communication Among Scientists and Engineers*, Lexington, Massachusetts: D.C. Heath, pp. 125–154.

27. The following types of choices were examined: informal discussion of research, influence upon the selection of problems and techniques, relationships with teachers, and collaborative work in progress.

28. G. Zaltman and J. Blau, "A Note on an International Invisible College in Theoretical High Energy Physics," unpublished report, Northwestern University, 1969, quoted in Crane, ibid., p. 53.

29. Crawford, op. cit., p. 13.

30. Crane, op. cit., p. 73.

31. Ibid., p. 74.

32. Ibid., p. 76.

Chapter 12

1. Bryce Ryan and Neal C. Gross, "The Diffusion of Hybrid Seed Corn in Two Iowa Communities," *Rural Sociology*, 8, 1943, pp. 15–24.

2. Everett M. Rogers, *Diffusion of Innovations*, New York: The Free Press, 3rd edition, 1983, p. 32.

3. After the first five years, by 1933, only 10 percent of the Iowa farmers adopted the new corn seed. Then, in the next three years, the rate of adoption increased sharply to 40 percent. Afterwards, the rate of adoption began to level off.

4. Ibid., p. 22.

5. On the early introduction of this trickle-down process and its compatibility with the more general model of opinion leadership, see Everett M. Rogers, *Social Change in Rural Sociology*, New York: Appelton-Century-Crofts, 1960, pp. 328–334.

6. Ibid., p. 328.

7. As Rogers suggested in his "Principles of Introducing Technical Assistance": "The change agent should attempt to work through respected innovators and opinion leaders. When the right person is the first to adopt a new technological idea, its later diffusion will be speeded," ibid.

8. Herbert F. Lionberger, *Adoption of New Ideas and Practices*, Ames, Iowa: Iowa University Press, 1960.

9. Ibid., p. 61.

10. Ibid., p. 63.

11. Satadal Dasgupta, "Innovation and Innovators in Indian Villages," *Man In India*, 43 (1), 1963, pp. 29–34.

12. Ibid., p. 34.

13. A. B. Bose and P. C. Saxena, "Opinion Leaders in a Village in Western Rajasthan," *Man In India*, 46 (2), 1966, pp. 121–129.

14. Cosmopoliteness was measured by frequencies of visit to the city, camps, fairs, exhibitions, etc., outside the village.

15. T. Sengupta, "Opinion Leaders in Rural Communities," *Man in India*, 48 (2), 1968, pp. 161–166.

16. L. K. Sen, *Opinion Leadership in India: A Study of Interpersonal Communication in Eight Villages*, Hyderbad: National Institute of Communication Development, 1969, p. 26.

17. V. R. Gaikwad, B. L. Tripathi, and G. S. Bhatnagar, *Opinion Leaders and Communication in Indian Villages*, Ahmedabad: Indian Institute of Management, 1972.

18. Ibid., p. 140.

19. E. A. Wilkening, Joan Tully, and Hartley Presser, "Communication and Acceptance of Recommended Farm Practices Among Dairy Farmers of Northern Victoria," *Rural Sociology*, 27, 1962, pp. 116–197.

20. Ibid., pp. 127–128.

21. A. W. Van Den Ban, "A Revision of the Two-step Flow of Communication Hypothesis," *Gazette*, 10, 1964, pp. 237–249.

22. Ibid., p. 243.

23. Everett M. Rogers and Lynne Svenning, *Modernization Among Peasants: The Impact of Communication*, New York: Holt, Rinehart, and Winston, 1969, pp. 224–241.

24. Daniel Lerner, *The Passing of Traditional Society: Modernizing the Middle East*, New York: Free Press, 1958, p. 26.

25. Hossain Sma and B. R. Crouch, "Patterns and Determinants of Adoption of Farm Practices: Some Evidence from Bangladesh," *Agricultural Systems*, 38, 1992, pp. 1–15.

26. See for example, K. L. Bhowmik and Atrayee Bhowmik, "Orientation of Opinion Leaders and Followers in Rural West Bengal," *Society and Culture*, 7, 1976, pp. 49–61.

27. Rogers, op. cit., p. 227.

28. Lerner, op. cit., p. 399.

29. As Homans explained it, the importation of innovations from external sources is not that valuable and important for the traditional villagers and does not encourage the influential to seek external sources for innovative ideas. See George C. Homans, *Social Behavior: Its Elementary Forms*, London, Routledge, 1961.

30. On the social conformity characterizing village opinion leaders, see Rogers, op. cit., pp. 229–230.

31. Ibid., p. 230.

32. Ibid., p. 231.

33. Ibid., p. 238.

34. Steven K. Pontius, "The Communication Process of Adoption: Agriculture in Thailand," *The Journal of Developing Areas*, 18, 1983, pp. 93–118.

35. John S. Thomas, "Leadership, Innovativeness, and Centrality in a Mexican Ejido," *Human Organization*, 40 (4), 1981, pp. 349–352.

36. Ibid., p. 350.

37. Ibid., p. 351.

38. Solomon Fiah, "Training for Rural Development," *Community Development Journal*, 22, 1987, pp. 322–332.

39. D. N. Trivedi, "Modernization, Opinion Leaders and their Instrumental Information Seeking Behavior," *Indian Journal of Sociology*, 3, 1972, pp. 69–78.

40. Ibid., p. 76.

Chapter 13

1. There are several reports on this study. See for example: Herbert Menzel and Elihu Katz, "Social Relations and Innovation in the Medical Profession," *Public Opinion Quarterly*, 19, 1955, pp. 337–352; Elihu Katz, "The Two-step Flow of Communication: An Up-to-date Report on an Hypothesis," *Public Opinion Quarterly*, 21, 1957, pp. 61–78; Elihu Katz et al., "Traditions of Research on the Diffusion of Innovations," *American Sociological Review*, 28, 1963, pp. 237–253; James Coleman et al., "The Diffusion of Innovation Among Physicians," *Sociometry*, 20, 1957, pp. 253–270; and James Coleman, Elihu Katz and Herbert Menzel, *Medical Innovation: A Diffusion Study*, 1966, Indianapolis: Bobbs-Merrill.

2. For a review of these studies, see Stephen B. Soumerai, Thomas J. McLauglin, and Jerry Avorn, "Improving Drug Prescribing in Primary Care: A Critical Analysis of the Experimental Literature," *The Milbank Quarterly*, 67, 1990, pp. 268–317.

3. Jerry Avorn and Stephen B. Soumerai, "Improving Drug-therapy Decisions Through Educational Outreach," *The New England Journal of Medicine*, 308(24), 1983, pp. 1457–1463.

4. For a review, see H. Leventhal and P. D. Cleary, "The Smoking Problem: A Review of the Research and Theory in Behavioral Risk Modification," *Psychological Bulletin*, 88, 1980, pp. 370–405.

5. For a review, see D. L. Sackett and R.B. Hynes (eds.), *Compliance with Therapeutic Regimens*, Baltimore: Johns Hopkins University Press, 1976.

6. W. Schaffner, W. A. Ray, C. F. Federspiel, and W. O. Miller, "Improving Antibiotic Prescribing in Office Practice: A Controlled Trial of Three Educational Methods, *Journal of the American Medical Association*, 250, 1983, pp. 1728–1732.

7. W. A. Ray, R. Fink, W. Schaffner, and C. F. Federspiel, "Improving Antibiotic Prescription in Outpatient Practice," *Medical Care*, 23, 1985, p. 1307.

8. W. A. Ray, D. G. Blazer, W. Schaffner, C. F. Federspiel, and R. Fink, "Reducing Long-term Diazepam Prescribing in Office Practice: A Controlled Trial of Educational Visits," *Journal of the American Medical Association*, 256, 1986, pp. 2536–2539.

9. T. S. McConnel, A. H. Cushing, A. D. Bankhurst, J. A. Healy, P. A. McIlvenna, and B. J. Skipper, "Physician Behavior Modification Using Claims Data," *Western Journal of Medicine*, 137, 1982, pp. 448–450.

10. For example, see Alan Booth and Nicholas Babchuk, "Informal Medical Opinion Leadership Among the Middle Aged and Elderly," *Public Opinion Quarterly*, 36, 1972, pp. 87–94.

11. Ibid., p. 87.

12. Ibid., p. 93.

13. Ibid., p. 89. However, the researchers noted one exception: in the case of husband-wife exchanges, the husband was as likely as the wife to act as an opinion leader.

14. Ibid., pp. 89–90.

15. Ibid., p. 92.

16. Akolawole Ayonrinde and Alayiwola A. Erinosho, "The Development of a Community Psychiatric Program at Igbo-Ora, Nigeria," *International Journal of Social Psychiatry*, 26 (3), 1980, pp. 190–195.

17. Ibid., p. 191.

18. Ibid., p. 195.

19. P. Puska et al., "Use of Lay Opinion Leaders to Promote Diffusion of Health Innovations in a Community Program: Lessons from the North Karelia Project," *Bulletin of the World Health Organization*, 64 (3), 1986, pp. 437–446.

20. Ibid., p. 445.

21. M. W. Ross and J. A. Carson, "Effectiveness of Distribution of Information on AIDS: A National Study of Six Media in Australia," *New York State Journal of Medicine*, 88, 1988, pp. 239–241.

22. Jeffrey A. Kelly et al., "HIV Risk Behavior Reduction Following Intervention with Key Opinion Leaders of Population: An Experimental Analysis," *American Journal of Public Health*, 81, 1991, pp. 168–171.

23. Jeffrey A. Kelly, et al., "AIDS Risk Behavior Patterns Among Men in Small Cities," *American Journal of Public Health*, 80, 1990, pp. 416–418.

24. The HIV risk reduction behaviors included the use of condoms, avoiding excessive intoxicant use before sex, discussing precautions in advance with sexual partners, resisting coercions to engage in high-risk practices, and self-reinforcement for behavior-change efforts.

25. The analysis reported included the numbers of sexual partners (table 2, Kelly et al., 1991, op. cit., p. 170), revealing an increased number of

intervention community individuals reporting two or more sexual partners (within two months) with an increasing number of those reporting one or no sexual partners in that time period.

26. Ibid., p. 171. On the applicability of the opinion leaders concept to fighting AIDS in developing societies, see M. Debruyn, "Women and AIDS in Developing Societies," *Social Science and Medicine*, 34, 1992, pp. 249–262.

27. Stephen B. Soumerai and Jerry Avorn, "Principles of Educational Outreach ('Academic Detailing') to Improve Clinical Decision Making," *Journal of the American Medical Association*, 263, 1990, pp. 549–556.

28. J. K. Stross and G. G. Bole, "Continuing Education in Rheumatoid Arthritis for the Primary Care Physician," *Arthritis Rheum*, 22, 1979, pp. 787–791; and J. K. Stross and G. G. Bole, "Evaluation of a Continuing Education Program in Rheumatoid Arthritis," *Arthritis Rheum*, 23, 1980, pp. 846–849.

29. R. G. Hiss, R. MacDonald, and W. R. Davis, "Identification of Physician Educational Influentials in Small Community Hospitals," *Research in Medical Education*, 17, 1978, pp. 283–288.

30. For example, the use of physical therapy increased from 11 percent before the intervention to 54 percent one year after the program but only in the experimental group; the control group did not change practices. For more comparisons, see table 1 and table 2, Stross and Bole, 1980, op. cit., pp. 847–848.

31. Ibid., p. 849.

32. Jonathan Lomas et al., "Opinion Leaders vs. Audit and Feedback to Implement Practice Guidelines," *Journal of the American Medical Association*, 265 (17), 1991, pp. 2202–2207.

33. R. G. Hiss, R. MacDonald, and W. R. David, op. cit., pp. 283–288.

34. J. K. Stross and G. G. Bole, op. cit.; R. G. Hiss, R. MacDonald and W. R. David, op. cit.; J. Avorn and S. Soumerai, "Improved Drug Therapy Through Educational Outreach: A Randomized Controlled Trial of Academically Based Detailing," *New England Journal of Medicine*, 308, 1983, pp. 1457–1463.

35. See table 3, Lomas et al., p. 2206.

36. Ibid., p. 2206.

37. Dorothy Leonard-Barton, "Experts as Negative Opinion Leaders in the Diffusion of a Technological Innovation," *Journal of Consumer Research*, 11, 1985, pp. 914–926.

38. The American College of Prosthodontics and The American Society of Prosthodontics.

39. Ibid., p. 925.

40. Booth and Babchuk, op. cit., p. 94.

41. Op. cit., p. 522.

42. Stephen B. Soumerai and Jerry Avorn, "Economic and Policy Analysis of University-based Drug 'Detailing,' " *Medical Care*, 24(4), 1986, pp. 313–331.

43. Ray, Schaffner, and Federspiel, op. cit.

44. June E. Osborn, "The AIDS Epidemic: Multidisciplinary Trouble," *The New England Journal of Medicine*, 314, 1986, pp. 779–782.

45. Karolynn Siegel, "Public Education to Prevent the Spread of HIV Infection," *New York State Journal of Medicine*, 88, 1988, pp. 642–646.

46. Ibid., p. 642.

47. Ibid., p. 645.

Part 4

1. Katz suggested a similar categorization of the critics, referring to them as the "institutional," "critical," and "technological" alternatives. See Elihu Katz, "Communication Research Since Lazarsfeld," *Public Opinion Quarterly*, 51, 1987, pp. s25–s45.

Chapter 14

1. Todd Gitlin, "Media Sociology: The Dominant Paradigm," *Theory and Society*, 6, 1978, pp. 205–253.

2. Ibid., pp. 205–206.

3. Ibid., p. 224 and p. 231.

4. In Gitlin's metaphor, "It is as if one were studying the influence of streets on mortality rates during an enormous flood. A street is a conduit, not a cause of drowning," ibid., p. 218.

5. In his discussion of the dominant paradigm and its rivals, Katz, op. cit., pp. 30–33.

6. Joseph T. Klapper, *The Effects of Mass Communication*, Glencoe, Illinois: The Free Press, 1960.

7. Katz, op. cit., p. 31.

8. M. Horkheimer and T. Adorno, "The Culture Industry: Enlightment as Mass Deception," in *The Dialetics of Enlightment*, London: Allen Lane, 1973.

9. Stuart Hall, "Encoding and Decoding in Television Discourse," in Hall et al. (eds.), *Culture, Media, Language*, London: Hutchinson, 1973, pp. 128–138.

10. On the "marketing orientation" of Lazarsfeld, see Steven H. Chaffee and John L. Hochheimer, "The Beginnings of Political Communication Research in the United States," in Everett M. Rogers and Francis Balle (eds.), *The Media Revolution in America and Western Europe*, Norwood: Ablex, 1982, pp. 263–283.

11. Gitlin, op. cit., p. 251.

12. T. W. Adorno, "Scientific Experiences of a European Scholar in America," in Donald Fleming and Bernard Bailyn (eds.), *The Intellectual Migration: Europe and America, 1930–1960*, Cambridge, Mass.: Harvard University Press, 1969, p. 343.

13. Katz, op. cit., p. 25.

14. Bruce Westley, "Communication and Social Change," *American Behavioral Scientist*, 14, 1971, pp. 719–742.

15. Paul Deutschmann and Wayne Danielson, "Diffusion of Knowledge of the Major News Story," *Journalism Quarterly*, 37, 1960, pp. 345–355.

16. Bradely S. Greenberg, "Person-to-person Communication in the Diffusion of News Events," *Journalism Quarterly*, 41, 1964, pp. 489–494.

17. Richard Hill and Charles M. Bonjean, "News Diffusion: A Test of the Regularity Hypothesis," *Journalism Quarterly*, 41, 1964, pp. 336–342.

18. Irving L. Allen and J. David Colfax, "The Diffusion of News of LBJ's March 31 Decision," *Journalism Quarterly*, 45, 1968, pp. 321–324.

19. John B. Adams and James J. Mullen, "Diffusion of the News of a Foreign Event," *Journalism Quarterly*, 46, 1969, pp. 545–557.

20. For example, Elmo Roper, *Trends in Public Attitudes Toward Television and Other Mass Media 1959–1974*, New York: Television Information Office, 1975.

21. John P. Robinson, "Interpersonal Influence in Election Campaigns: Two-step Flow Hypotheses," *Public Opinion Quarterly*, 40, 1976, pp. 304–319.

22. John P. Robinson, "The Press as Kingmaker," *Journalism Quarterly*, 51, 1974, pp. 587–594.

23. Robinson, 1976, op. cit., p. 305.

24. Verling C. Troldahl and Robert Van Dam, "Face-to-face Communication About Major Topics in the News," *Public Opinion Quarterly*, 29, 1965, pp. 626–634.

25. Charles Wright and Muriel Cantor, "The Opinion Seeker and Avoider: Steps Beyond the Opinion Leader Concept," *Pacific Sociological Review*, 10, 1967, pp. 33–43.

26. Robinson, 1976, op. cit., pp. 304–319.

27. Ibid., p. 311.

28. Ibid., pp. 305–306.

29. On this type of flow, see Gabriel Weimann, "On the Importance of Marginality: One More Step into the Two-step Flow of Communication," *American Sociological Review*, 47, 1982, pp. 764–773.

30. Nan Lin, *The Study of Human Communication*, Indianapolis, Indiana: Bobbs-Merrill Company, 1971, p. 203.

31. Troldahl and Van Dam, op. cit., pp. 626–634.

32. Chaffee and Hochheimer, op. cit., p. 272, emphasis added.

33. A. W. Van Den Ban, "A Revision of the Two-step Flow of Communication," *Gazette*, 10, 1964, pp. 237–250.

34. Weimann, op. cit., pp. 767–770.

35. Lloyd R. Bostian, "The Two-step Flow Theory: Cross-cultural Implications," *Journalism Quarterly*, 47, 1970, pp. 109–117.

36. Chaffee and Hochheimer, op. cit., pp. 277–278.

37. Elihu Katz and Paul F. Lazarsfeld, *Personal Influence*, New York: Free Press, 1955, p. 160.

38. Gitlin, op. cit., p. 221, emphasis added.

39. These were: 1. "Have you recently tried to convince anyone of your political ideas?" and 2. "Has anyone recently asked you for your advice on a political question?"

40. Katz and Lazarsfeld, op. cit., p. 142., emphasis in original.

41. Gitlin, op. cit., p. 220.

42. Herbert Menzel and Elihu Katz, "Social Relations and Innovations in the Medical Profession: The Epidemiology of a New Drug," *Public Opinion Quarterly*, 19, 1955, pp. 337–352, p. 352, emphasis added.

43. Robinson, 1976, op. cit., pp. 308–309.

44. Ibid., p. 306.

45. N. Lin, op. cit.; and G. Weimann, 1982, op. cit., p. 764–773.

46. Carl A. Sheingold, "Social Networks and Voting: The Resurrection of a Research Agenda," *American Sociological Review*, 38, 1973, pp. 712–720.

47. Ibid., p. 714.

48. For a review of such attempts, see Gabriel Weimann, "Social Networks and Communication," in M. Asante and W. B. Gudykunst (eds.), *Handbook of International and Intercultural Communication*, Beverly Hills: Sage, pp. 186–203. Illustrative examples are provided by Rogers and Kincaid, op. cit.

49. Mark S. Granovetter, "The Strength of Weak Ties," *American Journal of Sociology*, 78, 1973, p. 1360.

50. For a review, see Michael Schenk, "Massenkommunikation und Interpersonale Kommunikation," *Kölner Zeitschrift fur Soziologie und Sozialpsychologie*, 30, 1989, pp. 406–417; Michael Schenk, "Politische Meinungsfuhrer," *Publizistik*, 30, 1985, pp. 7–16; and Michael Schenk and Uwe Pfenning, "Opinion Leadership Reconsidered: A Social Network Approach," paper presented at the European Conference on Social Network Analysis, Paris, June 1991.

51. Weimann, 1982, op. cit. pp. 767–770.

52. Diana Crane, *Invisible Colleges*, Chicago: The University of Chicago Press, 1972.

53. G. Zaltman and J. Blau, "A Note on an International Invisible College in Theoretical High Energy Physics," unpublished report, Northwestern University, 1969, quoted in Crane, ibid., p. 53.

54. Schenk and Pfening, op. cit., table 1.

55. Bernard Berelson, Paul F. Lazarsfeld and William N. McPhee, *Voting*, Chicago: Chicago University Press, 1954, p. 112.

56. For example, Mark R. Levy, "Opinion Leadership and Television News Uses," *Public Opinion Quarterly*, 42, 1978, pp. 402–406; N. Lin, 1973, op. cit.; Robinson, 1976, op. cit., pp. 312–313.

57. Virginia P. Richmond, "The Relationship between Opinion Leadership and Information Acquisition," *Human Communication Research*, 4, 1977, pp. 38–43.

58. Ibid., p. 42.

59. Mark R. Levy, 1978, op. cit., pp. 402–406.

Chapter 15

1. On the development of the scale, see Elisabeth Noelle-Neumann, *Spiegel Dokumentation: Personlichkeitsstarke*, Hamburg: Spiegel Verlag, 1983; and Elisabeth Noelle-Neumann, "Identifying Opinion Leaders," paper presented at 38th ESOMAR Conference, Wiesbaden, September 1985, pp. 3–12.

2. Noelle-Neumann, 1985, ibid., pp. 3–7.

3. They are included in the Allensbach Institute Archives, and reported in Elisabeth Noelle-Neumann and Mihaly Csikszentmihalyi, "Personality

Strength: A New Variable for Opinion-Attitude Research," paper presented at the WAPOR Conference, St. Petersburg Beach, Florida, May 1992.

4. Gabriel Weimann, "The Influentials: Back to the Concept of Opinion Leaders?," *Public Opinion Quarterly*, 55, 1991, pp. 267–279.

5. "The first factor seems to measure strength, which has an "internal" origin, whereas the second describes a relatively less autonomous "reflected" strength derived from comparison with other people," Elisabeth Noelle-Neumann, Mihaly Csikszentmihalyi, and Friedrich Tennstaedt, "The Measurement of Personality Strength and Its Correlates," unpublished manuscript, p. 7.

6. For a detailed review of these studies, see Gabriel Weimann, "On the Importance of Marginality: One More Step into the Two-step Flow of Communication," *American Sociological Review*, 47, 1982, pp. 764–773; Gabriel Weimann, "On the Strength of Weak Conversational Ties," *Social Networks*, 5, 1983, pp. 245–267; and a review by Mark S. Granovetter, "The Strength of Weak Ties: a Network Theory Revisited," in P. V. Marsden and N. Lin (eds.), *Social Structure and Network Analysis*, Beverly Hills: Sage, 1982.

7. For a description of the items, see Weimann, 1982, op. cit., pp. 767.

8. William D. Richards, "A Manual for Network Analysis," mimeo, Stanford: Stanford University, Institute for Communication Research, 1972; William D. Richards, "Network Analysis Methods: Conceptual and Operational Approaches," paper presented at the Fourth Annual Colloquium on Social Networks, Honolulu, University of Hawaii, 1977. For a detailed example of this procedure, see Everett M. Rogers and Laurence M. Kincaid, *Communication Networks: Toward New Paradigm for Research*, New York: Free Press, 1981, pp. 163–182.

9. Noelle-Neumann, 1985, op. cit., table 10.

10. For example, Nan Lin, *The Study of Human Communication*, Indianapolis: Bobbs-Merrill, 1973.

11. The media use of the influentials will be discussed in the following chapter. Basically, there were no significant differences among the PS levels in terms of amount of watching television or listening to the radio (see Noelle-Neumann, 1985, op. cit., table 18). In the Israeli study, the higher levels of PS did not report more exposure to newspapers, television, or radio. However, in both studies, some indication of the different quality of media consumption was revealed, especially when PS ratings were related to reading certain newspapers and specific contents of the papers and magazines (see Noelle-Neumann, 1983, op. cit., tables 27l, 27m, and 27n).

12. Elihu Katz, himself, when revising his two-step flow model noted: "Opinion leaders, though more exposed to the media than non-leaders, nevertheless reported personal influence as the major factor in their decisions," Elihu Katz, "The Two-step Flow of Communication: An Up-to-date Report on an Hypothesis," *Public Opinion Quarterly*, 21, 1957, p. 76. Several studies related different patterns and forms of media consumption to opinion leadership. For example, Lyman Ostlund, "Interpersonal Communication Following McGovern's Eagleton Decision," *Public Opinion Quarterly*, 37, 1973, pp. 601–610;

Mark R. Levy, "Opinion Leadership and Television News Uses," *Public Opinion Quarterly*, 42, 1978, pp. 402–406; and Virginia P. Richmond, "The Relationship Between Opinion Leadership and Information Acquisition," *Human Communication Research*, 4, 1977, pp. 38–43.

13. For example, Alan Booth and Nicholas Babchuck, "Informed Medical Opinion Leadership Among the Middle Aged and Elderly," *Public Opinion Quarterly*, 36, 1972, pp. 87–94; Herbert Hamilton, "Dimensions of Self-designated Opinion Leadership and Their Correlates," *Public Opinion Quarterly*, 35, 1971, pp. 266–274; John W. Kingdon, "Opinion Leaders in the Electorate," *Public Opinion Quarterly*, 34, 1970, pp. 256–261.

14. To be discussed in the following chapter. Also, see Noelle-Neumann, 1985, op. cit., p. 47.

15. Alan S. Marcus and Raymond A. Bauer, "Yes: There Are Generalized Opinion Leaders," *Public Opinion Quarterly*, 28, 1964, pp. 628–632.

16. Charles W. King and John O. Summers, "Overlap of Opinion Leadership Across Consumer Product Categories," *Journal of Marketing Research*, 7, 1970, pp. 43–50; David B. Montegomery and Alvin J. Silk, "Clusters of Consumer Interests and Opinion Leaders' Spheres of Influence," *Journal of Marketing Research*, 8, 1971, pp. 317–321; James H. Myers and Thomas S. Robertson, "Dimensions of Opinion Leadership," *Journal of Marketing Research*, 4, 1972, pp. 41–46.

Chapter 16

1. Elisabeth Noelle-Neumann, *Spiegel Dokumentation: Personlichkeitsstarke*, Hamburg: Spiegel Verlag, 1983; Elisabeth Noelle-Neumann, "Identifying Opinion Leaders," paper presented at 38th ESOMAR Conference, Wiesbaden, September 1985, pp. 3–12; and Elisabeth Noelle-Neumann and Mihaly Csikszentmihalyi, "Personality Strength: A New Variable for Opinion-Attitude Research," paper presented at the WAPOR Conference, St. Petersburg Beach, Florida, May 1992.

2. Gabriel Weimann, "The Influentials: Back to the Concept of Opinion Leaders?" *Public Opinion Quarterly*, 55, 1991, pp. 267–279.

3. Unpublished report. We gratefully acknowledge the access to the findings granted by Mihaly Csikszentmihalyi.

4. For example, more Israelis than Germans report membership in a union, explained by the dominance of the *Histadrut*, the Israeli workers' union, in the country's economic system.

5. This comparison and the following ones were reported by Noelle-Neumann, *Spiegel Dokumentation: Personlichkeitsstarke*, op. cit., and in several unpublished reports prepared by the Allensbach Institute.

6. The report was not published but we gratefully acknowledge the access to the analyses and findings provided by Mihaly Csikszentmihalyi, The University of Chicago.

7. See, Noelle-Neumann, *Spiegel Dokumentation: Personlichkeitsstarke*, op. cit., on "Berufliche Prioritaten" (work-related priorities).

8. Table based on the data provided in tables 27L, 27N, and 27M, in Noelle-Neumann, 1983, op. cit.

9. Data based on table 27N, ibid.

10. In the Israeli sample, higher PS was related to higher viewership of programs such as *Mabat* (the news bulletin), *Mabat Sheni* (documentaries), *Moked* (political panel), and *Roim Olam* (news from around the world).

11. Table based on data presented in tables 15 and 34, Noelle-Neumann, 1985, op. cit.

12. Louis Guttman developed this modified version of factor analysis, suggesting that ordering the relationships among the correlations between variables results in a *Simplex*, or a mapping on a straight line. The distance between pairs of points are inversely related to the correlation coefficients. For a review of Guttman's work, the SSA procedure and program, see the collection of essays in Samuel Shye (ed.), *Theory Construction and Data Analysis in the Behavioral Sciences*, San Francisco: Jossey-Bass, 1978, and especially pp. 11–15.

13. Noelle-Neumann, 1985, op. cit., p. 16.

14. Bernard Cohen, *The Press and Foreign Policy*, Princeton: Princeton University Press, 1963, p. 13, emphasis added.

15. For updated review of the research on agenda-setting, see D. Protess and M. McCombs (eds.), *Agenda-Setting: Reading on Media, Public Opinion and Policymaking*, Hillsdale, New Jersey: Lawrence Erlbaum Associates, 1991; Maxwell McCombs, Edna Einsiedel, and David Weaver, *Contemporary Public Opinion: Issues and the News*, Hillsdale, New Jersey: Lawerence Erlbaum Associates, 1991; and E. M. Rogers and J. W. Dearing, "Agenda-setting Research: Where Has It Been, Where Is It Going?" in J. A. Anderson (ed.), *Communication Yearbook 11*, Newbury Park, California: Sage, 1988, pp. 555–594.

16. McCombs, Einsiedel, and Weaver, op. cit., p. 7, emphasis added.

17. Rogers and Dearing, op. cit., p. 557.

18. Maxwell McCombs, "The Agenda-setting Approach," in D. D. Nimmo and K. R. Sanders (eds.), *Mass Communication Review Yearbook 2*, Newbury Park, California: Sage, 1981, p. 121.

19. Maxwell McCombs and Donald Shaw, "The Agenda-setting Function of Mass Media," *Public Opinion Quarterly*, 36, 1972, pp. 176–184.

20. Hans-Bernd Brosius and Hans Mathias Kepplinger, "The Agenda-setting Function of Television News: Static and Dynamic Views," *Communication Research*, 17, 1990, pp. 183–211.

21. The salience of an issue is relative to that of other issues, as noted by Gladys Lang and Kurt Lang, "Watergate: An Exploration of the Agenda-setting Process," in G. C. Wilhoit and H. DeBock (ed.), *Mass Communication Review Yearbook 2*, Newbury Park, California: Sage, pp. 447–468. For example, the existence of "killer issues" was suggested by Hans-Bernd Brosius and Hand Mathias Kepplinger, "In Search of Killer Issues: Issue Competition in the Agenda-setting

Process," paper presented at the annual conference of the American Association for Public Opinion Research (AAPOR), May 1992, St. Petersburg Beach.

22. Shanto Iyengar, and D. R. Kinder, *News That Matters: Television and American Opinion*, Chicago: University of Chicago Press, 1987; and Shanto Iyengar, *Is Anyone Responsible?* Chicago: Chicago University Press, 1991.

23. Rogers and Dearing, op. cit., pp. 573–574.

24. An interesting exception is Stephen D. Reese, "Setting the Media's Agenda: A Power Balance Perspective," in J. A. Anderson, *Communication Yearbook 14*, Newbury Park, California: Sage, 1991, pp. 309–340.

25. Charles Whitney, "Agenda-setting: Power and Contingency," in J. A. Anderson, *Communication Yearbook 14*, Newbury Park, California: Sage, 1991, pp. 347–356.

Bibliography

Abelson, Herbert L., and Donald W. Rugg, "Self-designated Influentiality and Activity," *Public Opinion Quarterly*, 22, 1959, pp. 566–567.

Adams, John B., and James J. Mullen, "Diffusion of the News of a Foreign Event," *Journalism Quarterly*, 46, 1969, pp. 545–557.

Adorno, Theodor W., "Scientific Experiences of a European Scholar in America," in Donald Fleming and Bernard Bailyn (eds.), *The Intellectual Migration: Europe and America, 1930–1960*, Cambridge, Massachusetts: Harvard University Press, 1969.

Alba, Richard D., and Charles Kadushin, "The Introduction of Social Circles: A New Measure of Social Proximity in Networks," *Sociological Methods and Research*, 5, 1976, pp. 77–102.

Alpert, R. and R. H. Haber, "Anxiety in Academic Achievement Situations," *Journal of Abnormal and Social Psychology*, 61, 1960, pp. 207–215.

Andersen, Peter A. and John P. Garrison, "Media Consumption and Population Characteristics of Political Opinion Leaders," *Communication Quarterly*, 26, 1976, pp. 40–50.

Anderson, Bo, "Opinion Influentials and Political Opinion Formation in Four Swedish Communities," *International Social Sciences Journal*, 14(2), 1962, pp. 320–326.

Anspach, Karlyne, *The Why of Fashion*, Ames, Iowa: The Iowa State University Press, 1967.

Armstrong, Gary M., and Laurence P. Feldman, "Exposure and Sources of Opinion Leaders," *Journal of Advertising Research*, 16, 1976, pp. 21–27.

Arndt, John, "Role of Product-related Conversations in the Diffusion of a New Product," *Journal of Marketing Research*, 4, 1967, p. 291–295.

Arnold, David O., *The Sociology of Subcultures*, Berkeley, California: Glendasary Press, 1970.

Attah, E. B., "An Analysis of Polymorphic Opinion Leadership in Eastern Nigerian Communities," Master's thesis, 1968, East Lansing: Michigan State University.

Avorn, Jerry, and Stephen B. Soumerai, "Improving Drug-therapy Decisions Through Educational Outreach: A Randomized Controlled Trial of Academically Based Detailing," *The New England Journal of Medicine*, 308(24), 1983, pp. 1457–1463.

Ayonrinde, Akolawole, and Alayiwola A. Erinosho, "The Development of a Community Psychiatric Program at Igbo-Ora, Nigeria," *International Journal of Social Psychiatry*, 26 (3), 1980, pp. 190–195.

Bass, B. M., *Stogdill's Handbook of Leadership*, New York: Free Press, 1981.

Bass, Frank M., "A New Product Growth Model for Consumer Durables," *Management Science*, 15, 1969, pp. 215–227.

Bates, Erica, "Opinion Leaders in a Psychiatric Hospital Community," *Social Science and Medicine*, 5, 1971, pp. 615–620.

Bauer, Raymond A., "Source Effect and Persuability: A New Look," in Donald F. Cox (ed.), *Risk Taking and Information Handling in Consumer Behavior*, Boston: Harvard Business School, 1967, pp. 559–578.

Baumgarten, Steven A., "The Innovative Communicator in the Diffusion Process," *Journal of Marketing Research*, 12, 1975, pp. 12–18.

Beal, George M., and Everett M. Rogers, "Informational Sources in the Adoption Process of New Fabrics," *Journal of Home Economics*, 49, 1957, pp. 630–634.

Bearden, William O., and Michael J. Etzel, "Further Validation of the Consumer Susceptibility to Interpersonal Influence Scale," *Advances in Consumer Research*, 17, 1990, pp. 770–776.

Bearden, William O., and Michael J. Etzel, "Reference Group Influence on Product and Brand Purchase Decisions," *Journal of Consumer Research*, 9, 1982, pp. 183–194.

Bearden, William O., Richard G. Netemeyer, and Jesse E. Teel, "Measurement of Individual Susceptibility to Interpersonal Influence," *Journal of Consumer Research*, 15, 1989, pp. 473–481.

Beck, Paul Allen, "Voters' Intermediation Environment in the 1988 Presidential Contest," *Public Opinion Quarterly*, 55, 1991, pp. 371–394.

Bell, Quentin, *On Human Finery*, New York: A. A. Wyn Inc., 1949.

Bellenger, Danny N., and Elizabeth C. Hirschman, "Identifying Opinion Leaders by Self-report," in B. A. Greenberg and D. N. Bellenger (eds.), *Contemporary Marketing Thought*, Chicago: American Marketing Association, 1977, pp. 341–344.

Berelson, Bernard, "On Family Planning Communication," *Demography*, 1, 1964, p. 94–105.

Berelson, Bernard, Paul F. Lazarsfeld, and William N. McPhee, *Voting*, Chicago: University of Chicago Press, 1954.

Bhowmik, K. L., and Atrayee Bhowmik, "Orientation of Opinion Leaders and Followers in Rural West Bengal," *Society and Culture*, 7, 1976, pp. 49–61.

Bineham, Jefferey, L., "A Historical Account of the Hypodermic Model in Mass Communication," *Communication Monographs*, 55 (3), 1988, pp. 230–246.

Bienenstock, Elisa Jayne, Philip Bonacich, and Melvin Oliver, "The Effects of Network Density and Homogeneity on Attitude Polarization," *Social Networks*, 12, 1990, pp. 153–172.

Black, John S., "Opinion Leaders: Is Anyone Following?" *Public Opinion Quarterly*, 46, 1982, pp. 169–176.

Bloch, Peter H., and Marsha L. Richins, "A Theoretical Model for the Study of Product Importance Perceptions," *Journal of Marketing*, 47, 1983.

Blumer, Herbert, "Fashion: From Class Differentiation to Collective Selection," *Sociological Quarterly*, 10, 1969, pp. 275–291.

Blumer, Herbert, *The Movies and Conduct*, New York: Macmillan, 1933.

Bockman, Sheldon, and William F. Gayk, "Political Orientation and Political Ideologies," *Pacific Sociological Review*, 20(4), 1977, pp. 536–552.

Bogue, Donald J., "Hypotheses for Family Planning Derived from Recent and Current Experience in Asia," *Studies in Family Planning*, 3, 1964, pp. 6–8.

Booth, Alan, and Nicholas Babchuk, "Informal Medical Opinion Leadership Among the Middle Aged and Elderly," *Public Opinion Quarterly*, 36, 1972, pp. 87–94.

Bose, A. B., and P. C. Saxena, "Opinion Leaders in a Village in Western Rajasthan," *Man In India*, 46 (2), 1966, pp. 121–129.

Bostian, Lloyd R., "The Two-step Flow Theory: Cross-cultural Implications," *Journalism Quarterly*, 47, 1970, pp. 109–117.

Brett, Joyce E., and Anne Kernaleguen, "Perceptual and Personality Variables Related to Opinion Leadership in Fashion," *Perceptual and Motor Skills*, 40, 1975, pp. 775–779.

Brickell, Bettina, Robert Huckfeldt, and John Sprague, "Gender Effects on Political Discussion: The Political Networks of Men and Women," paper presented at the annual meeting of the American Political Science Association, Washington, D.C., 1988.

Brinberg, David, and Linda Plimpton, "Self-monitoring and Product Conspicuousness on Reference Group Influence," *Advances in Consumer Research*, 13, 1986, pp. 297–300.

Bristor, Julia M. "Enhanced Explanations of Word of Mouth Communications: The Power of Relationships," *Research in Consumer Behavior*, 4, 1990, pp. 51–83.

Broom, Leonard, and Philip Selznick, *Sociology*, 2nd edition, Evanston, Illinois: Row and Peterson, 1959.

Brosius, Hans-Bernd, and Hans Mathias Kepplinger, "The Agenda-setting Function of Television News: Static and Dynamic Views," *Communication Research*, 17, 1990, pp. 183–211.

Brosius, Hans-Bernd, and Hans Mathias Kepplinger, "In Search of Killer Issues: Issue Competition in the Agenda-setting Process," paper presented at the annual conference of the American Association for Public Opinion Research (AAPOR), May 1992, St. Petersburg Beach.

Burnham, Walter Dean, *Critical Elections and the Mainsprings of American Politics*, New York: Norton, 1970.

Bylund, Bruce H., and David L. Sanders, "Validity of High Scores on Certain Self-evaluation Questions," *Rural Sociology*, 32, 1967, pp. 346–351.

Campbell, Angus, Gerald Gurin, and Warren E. Miller, *The Voter Decides*, Westport, Connecticut: Greenwood Press, 1971.

Campbell, Bruce A., "Patterns of Change in the Partisan Loyalties of Native Southerners: 1952–1972," *Journal of Politics*, 39, 1977, pp. 730–761.

Carmody, John, Denise Lardner Carmody, and Robert L. Cohn, *Exploring the Bible*, Englewood Cliffs, New Jersey: Prentice Hall, 1988.

Carter, Roy E., and Peter Clarke, "Public Affairs Opinion Leadership Among Educational Television Viewers," *American Sociological Review*, 27, 1962, pp. 792–799.

Chaffee, Steven H., and John L. Hochheimer, "The Beginnings of Political Communication Research in the United States," in Everett M. Rogers and Francis Balle (eds.), *The Media Revolution in America and Western Europe*, Norwood: Ablex, 1982, pp. 263–283.

Chan, Kenny K., and Shekhar Misra, "Characteristics of the Opinion Leader: A New Dimension," *Journal of Advertising*, 19 (3), 1990, pp. 53–60.

Childers, Terry L., "Assessment of the Psychometric Properties of an Opinion Leadership Scale," *Journal of Marketing Research*, 23, 1986, pp. 184–188.

Cobb, J. C., et al., "Pakistan: The Medical Social Research Project at Luiliani," *Studies in Family Planning*, 1 (8), 1965, pp. 11–16.

Cohen, Bernard, *The Press and Foreign Policy*, Princeton: Princeton University Press, 1963.

Cohn, Robert L., *The Shape of Sacred Space: Four Biblical Studies*. Chico, California: Scholars Press, 1981.

Coleman, James, et al., "The Diffusion of Innovation Among Physicians," *Sociometry*, 20, 1957, pp. 253–270.

Coleman, James, Elihu Katz, and Herbert Menzel, *Medical Innovation: A Diffusion Study*, 1966, Indianapolis: Bobbs-Merrill.

Converse, Philip E., and Roy Pierce, "Measuring Partisanship," *Political Methodology*, 11, 1987, pp. 143–166.

Corey, Lawrence G., "People Who Claim To Be Opinion Leaders: Identifying Their Characteristics by Self-report," *Journal of Marketing*, 35, 1971, pp. 48–53.

Crane, Diana, *Invisible Colleges*, Chicago: The University of Chicago Press, 1972.

Crawford, S., *Informal Communication Among Scientists in Sleep and Dream Research*, unpublished Doctoral dissertation, University of Chicago, 1970.

Darden, William R., and Fred D. Reynolds, "Predicting Opinion Leadership for Men's Apparel Fashions," *Journal of Marketing Research*, 9, 1972, pp. 324–328.

Dasgupta, Satadal, "Innovation and Innovators in Indian Villages," *Man In India*, 43 (1), 1963, pp. 29–34.

Davis, Leslie L., and Sharron J. Lennon, "Self-monitoring, Fashion Opinion Leadership, and Attitudes Toward Clothing," in Michael R. Solomon (ed.), *The Psychology of Fashion*, Lexington, Massachusetts: Lexington Books, 1985, pp. 177–182.

Debruyn, M., "Women and AIDS in Developing Societies," *Social Science and Medicine*, 34, 1992, pp. 249–262.

DeFleur, Melvin L., "The Emergence and Functioning of Opinion Leadership: Some Conditions of Informal Transmission," pp. 257–278 in Norman F. Washburne (ed.), *Decisions, Values, and Groups*, Vol. 2, 1962, New York: Macmillan.

DeFleur, Melvin L., *Theories of Mass Communication*, New York: David McKay, 1970.

Deutschmann, Paul, and Wayne Danielson, "Diffusion of Knowledge of the Major News Story," *Journalism Quarterly*, 37, 1960, pp. 345–355.

Dickerson, Mary Dee, and James W. Gentry, "Characteristics of Adopters and Non-Adopters of Home Computers," *Journal of Consumer Research*, 10, 1983, pp. 225–235.

Dodd, C. H., Homophily and Heterophily in Diffusion of Innovations: A Cross-cultural Analysis in an African Setting, paper presented at the Speech Communication Association Convention, New York, November 1973.

Dubey, Dinesh C., and Harvey M. Choldin, "Communication and the Diffusion of the IUD: A Case Study of Urban India," *Demography*, 4, 1967, pp. 601–614.

Eagleton, Terry, *Literacy Theory: An Introduction*, Minneapolis: University of Minnesota Press, 1983.

Eco, Umberto, *A Theory of Semeiotics*, Bloomington: Indiana University Press, 1979.

Emery, Frederick, and Oscar Oeser, *Information, Decision and Action: A Study of the Psychological Determinants of Changes in Farming Techniques*, New York: Cambridge University Press, 1958.

Engel, James F., David T. Kollat, and Roger D. Blackwell, *Consumer Behavior*, (2nd edition), New York: Holt, Rinehart, and Winston, 1973.

Eulau, Heinz, "The Columbia Studies of Personal Influence," *Social Science History*, 4, 1980, pp. 207–228.

Fawcett, J. T., et al., "Thailand: An Analysis of Time and Distance Factors at an IUD Clinic in Bangkok," *Studies in Family Planning*, 1 (19), 1967, pp. 3–12.

Feick, Lawrence F., and Linda L. Price, "The Market Maven: A Diffuser of Marketplace Information," *Journal of Marketing*, 51, 1987, pp. 83–97.

Feick, Lawrence F., Linda L. Price, and Robin A. Higie, "People Who Use People: The Other Side of Opinion Leadership," *Advances in Consumer Research*, 13, 1986, pp. 301–305.

Fenton, James S. and Thomas R. Leggett, "A New Way to Find Opinion Leaders," *Journal of Advertising Research*, 11, 1971, pp. 21–25.

Festinger, Leon, "A Theory of Social Comparison Processes," *Human Relations*, 7, 1954, pp. 117–140.

Fiah, Solomon, "Training for Rural Development," *Community Development Journal*, 22, 1987, pp. 322–332.

Finkel, Steven E., Edward N. Muller, and Karl-Dieter Opp, "Personal Influence, Collective Rationality, and Mass Political Action," *American Political Science Review*, 83(3), 1989, pp. 885–903.

Fischer, Claude S., et al., *Networks and Places: Social Relations in the Urban Setting*, New York: Free Press, 1977.

Fleishman, E. A., *Manual for Leadership Opinion Questionnaire*, Chicago, Illinois: Science Research Associates, 1969.

Freedman, Ronald, and John Y. Takeshita, *Family Planning in Taiwan*, New Jersey: Princeton University Press, 1969.

Gaikwad, V. R., B. L. Tripathi, and G. S. Bhatnagar, *Opinion Leaders and Communication in Indian Villages*, Ahmedabad: Indian Institute of Management, 1972.

Gaston, J., *Big Science in Britain: A Sociological Study of the High Energy Physics Community,* unpublished Doctoral dissertation, Yale University, 1969.

Gatignon, Hubert and Thomas S. Robertson, "A Propositional Inventory for New Diffusion Research," *Journal of Consumer Research*, 11, 1985, pp. 849–867.

Gibb, Cecil A., "Leadership," in Gardner Lindzey and Elliot Aronson (eds.), *Handbook of Social Psychology,* Vol. 4, Reading, Massachusetts: Addison-Wesley, 1969, pp. 205–282.

Gitlin, Todd, "Media Sociology: The Dominant Paradigm," *Theory and Society,* 6, 1978, pp. 205–253.

Glock, Charles Y., and Francesco M. Nicosia, "Sociology and the Study of Consumers," *Journal of Advertising Research,* 3, 1963, pp. 21–27,

Goldsmith, Elizabeth B., and Ronald E. Goldsmith, "Dogmatism and Confidence as Related Factors in Evaluation of New Products," *Psychological Reports,* 47, 1980, pp. 1068–1070.

Goldsmith, Ronald E., and Rene Desborde, "A Validity Study of a Measure of Opinion Leadership," *Journal of Business Research,* 22, 1991, pp. 11–19.

Goldsmith, Ronald E., Melvin T. Stith, and J. Dennis White, "Race and Sex Differences in Self-identified Innovativeness and Opinion Leadership," *Journal of Retailing,* 63, 1987, pp. 411–425.

Granovetter, Mark S., "The Strength of Weak Ties," *American Journal of Sociology,* 73, 1973, pp. 1360–1380.

Granovetter, Mark S., "The Strength of Weak Ties: A Network Theory Revisited," in R. Collins (ed.), *Sociological Theory,* San Francisco: Jossey-Bass, 1983, pp. 201–233.

Greenberg, Bradley S., "Person-to-person Communication in the Diffusion of News Events," *Journalism Quarterly,* 41, 1964, pp. 489–494.

Griffith, B. C., and A. J. Miller, "Networks of Informal Communication Among Scientifically Productive Scientists." In C. Nelson and D. Pollock (eds.), *Communication Among Scientists and Engineers,* Lexington, Massachusetts: D.C. Heath, pp. 125–154.

Grindereng, Margaret P., "Fashion Diffusion," *Journal of Home Economics,* 59, 1967, pp. 171–174.

Grossbart, Sanford L., Robert A. Mittelstaedt, and Gene W. Murdock, "Nearest Neighbor Analysis," *Advances in Consumer Research*, 5, 1977, pp. 1140–1148.

Gunn, Bruce, Kenneth L. Koonce, and David M. Robinson, "A Survey Design for Isolating Opinion Leaders in the Open Marketplace," *Economic and Business Bulletin*, 24, 1972, pp. 27–34.

Gur-Arie, Oded, Richard M. Durand, and Subhash Sharma, "Identifying Moderating Variables Using Moderated Regression Analysis," in R. S. Franz, R. M. Hopkins and A. G. Toma (eds.), *Proceedings: Southern Marketing Association*, Lafayette: Southern Marketing Association, 1979, pp. 189–192.

Gur-Arie, Oded, Richard M. Durand, and William O. Bearden, "Attitudinal and Normative Dimensions of Opinion Leaders and Non-leaders," *The Journal of Psychology*, 101, 1979, pp. 305–312.

Hall, Stuart, "Encoding and Decoding in Television Discourse," in Hall et al. (eds.), *Culture, Media, Language*, London: Hutchinson, 1973, pp. 128–138.

Hamilton, Herbert, "Dimensions of Self-designated Opinion Leadership and Their Correlates," *Public Opinion Quarterly*, 35, 1971, pp. 266–274.

Harik, Iliya F., "Opinion Leaders and the Mass Media in Rural Egypt: A Reconsideration of the Two-step Flow of Communication Hypothesis," *American Political Science Review*, 65, 1971, pp. 731–740.

Havens, Eugene A., "Social Psychological Conditions Affecting the Adoption of Farm Innovations," unpublished Ph.D. dissertation, Columbus, Ohio State University, 1962.

Heath, M. R. and S. J. Bekker, *Identification of Opinion Leaders in Public Affairs, Educational Matters, and Family Planning in the Township of Atteridgeville*, Pretoria: Human Sciences Research Council, 1986.

Hellevik, Ottar, and Tor Bjorklund, "Opinion Leadership and Political Extremism," *International Journal of Public Opinion Research*, 3, 1991, pp. 157–181.

Hill, R., J. Stycos, and K. Back, *The Family and Population Control*, Chapel Hill: University of North Carolina Press, 1959.

Hill, Richard, and Charles M. Bonjean, "News Diffusion: A Test of the Regularity Hypothesis," *Journalism Quarterly*, 41, 1964, pp. 336–34.

Hirschman, Elizabeth C., "American Jewish Ethnicity: Its Relationship to Some Selected Aspects of Consumer Behavior," *Journal of Marketing*, 45, 1981, pp. 102–110.

Hirschman, Elizabeth C., and W. O. Adcock, "An Examination of Innovative Communicators, Opinion Leaders, and Innovators for Men's Fashion Apparel," *Advances in Consumer Research*, 5, 1978, pp. 303–314.

Hiss, R. G., R. MacDonald, and W. R. Davis, "Identification of Physician Educational Influentials in Small Community Hospitals," *Research in Medical Education*, 17, 1978, pp. 283–288.

Ho, Y. C., Homophily in the Diffusion of Innovations in Brazilian Villages, Master's thesis, 1969, East Lansing: Michigan State University.

Holland, Paul, and Samuel Leinhardt, "A Method for Detecting Structure in Sociometric Data," *American Journal of Sociology*, 76, 1970, pp. 492–513.

Homans, George C., *Social Behavior: Its Elementary Forms*, London, Routledge, 1961.

Horkheimer, Max, and Theodor Adorno, "The Culture Industry: Enlightment as Mass Deception," in *The Dialetics of Enlightment*, London: Allen Lane, 1973.

Hovland, Carl, et al., *Communication and Persuasion*, New Haven: Yale University Press, 1953, pp. 99–133.

Huckfeldt, Robert, and John Sprague, "Networks in Context: The Social Flow of Political Information," *American Political Science Review*, 81 (4), 1987, pp. 1197–1216.

Hunt, D. E., L. F. Butler, J. E. Noy, and M. E. Rosser, *Assessing Conceptual Level by a Paragraph Completion Method*, Toronto: The Toronto Institute for Studies in Education, 1978.

Hurt, Thomas H., Katherine Joseph, and Chester D. Cook, "Scales for the Measurement of Innovativeness," *Human Communication Research*, 4, 1977, pp. 58–65.

Hyman, Herbert H., "The Psychology of Status," *Archives of Psychology*, 38, 1942, No. 269.

Iyengar, Shanto, *Is Anyone Responsible?* Chicago: Chicago University Press, 1991.

Iyengar, Shanto and D. R. Kinder, *News That Matters: Television and American Opinion*, Chicago: University of Chicago Press, 1987.

Jacoby, Jacob, "Personality and Innovation Process," *Journal of Marketing Research*, 8, 1971, pp. 244–247.

Jacoby, Jacob, "The Construct Validity of Opinion Leadership," *Public Opinion Quarterly*, 38, 1974, pp. 81–89.

Jennings, Kent M., "Gender Roles and Inequalities in Political Participation: Results from Wight-Nation Study," *Western Political Quarterly*, 36, 1983, pp. 364–385.

Kadushin, Charles C., "The Friends and Supporters of Psychotherapy; On Social Circles in Urban Life," *American Sociological Review*, 31, 1966, pp. 786–802.

Kadushin, Charles C., "Power, Influence, and Social Circles: A New Methodology for Studying Opinion Makers," *American Sociological Review*, 33, 1968, pp. 685–699.

Katona, George, and Eva Mueller, "A Study of Purchasing Decisions," in Lincoln H. Clark (ed.), *Consumer Behavior: The Dynamics of Consumer Reaction*, New York: New York University Press, 1955, pp. 30–87.

Katz, Elihu, "The Two-step Flow of Communication: An Up-to-date Report on an Hypothesis," *Public Opinion Quarterly*, 21, 1957, pp. 61–78.

Katz, Elihu, "Communication Research Since Lazarsfeld," *Public Opinion Quarterly*, 51, 1987, pp. s25–s45.

Katz, Elihu, and Paul F. Lazarsfeld, *Personal Influence*, New York: The Free Press, 1955.

Katz, Elihu, et al., "Traditions of Research on the Diffusion of Innovations," *American Sociological Review*, 28, 1963, pp. 237–253.

Keith Simonton, Dean, "Intelligence and Personal Influence in Groups: Four Nonlinear Models," *Psychological Review*, 92, 1985, pp. 532–547.

Kelly, Jeffrey A., et al., "HIV Risk Behavior Reduction Following Intervention with Key Opinion Leaders of Population: An Experimental Analysis," *American Journal of Public Health*, 81, 1991, pp. 168–171.

Kerby, Joe Kent, *Consumer Behavior: Conceptual Foundations*, New York: Dun-Donnellewy, 1975.

Kerr, John R., and Bruce Weale, "Collegiate Clothing Purchasing Patterns and Fashion Adoption Behavior," *Southern Journal of Business*, 5, 1970, pp. 126–133.

Key, V. O. Jr., *Public Opinion and American Democracy*, New York: Knopf, 1961; *The Responsible Electorate*, Cambridge, Massachusetts: Harvard University Press, 1966.

Key, V. O. Jr., and Frank Munger, "Social Determinism and Electoral Decision: The Case of Indiana," pp. 281–299 in Eugene Burdick and Arthur J. Brodbeck (eds.), *American Voting Behavior*, Glencoe, Illinois: Free Press.

King, Charles, W. "Fashion Adoption: A Rebuttal to the Trickle-down Theory," in Stephen A. Greyser (ed.), *Toward Scientific Marketing*, Chicago: American Marketing Association, 1963, pp. 108–125.

King, Charles W. and John O. Summers, "Dynamics of Interpersonal Communication: The Interaction Dyad," in Donald F. Cox (ed.), *Risk Taking and Information Handling in Consumer Behavior*, Boston: Graduate School of Business Administration, Harvard University, 1967, pp. 240–264.

King, Charles W., and John O. Summers, "Overlap of Opinion Leadership Across Consumer Product Categories," *Journal of Marketing Research*, 7, 1970, pp. 43–50.

King, Charles W., and John O. Summers, "Technology, Innovation, and Consumer Decision-making," in Reed Moyer (ed.), *Consumer, Corporate and Government Interfaces*, Chicago: American Marketing Association, 1967, pp. 63–68.

Kingdon, John W., "Opinion Leadership in the Electorate," *Public Opinion Quarterly*, 34, 1970, pp. 256–261.

Klapper, Joseph T., *The Effects of Mass Communication*, Glencoe, Illinois: The Free Press, 1960.

Kornhauser, William, *The Politics of Mass Society*, Glencoe, Illinois: Free Press, 1953.

Kraus, Sidney, and Dennis Davis, *The Effects of Mass Communication on Political Behavior*, University Park: Pennsylvania State University Press, 1976.

Kuhn, Thomas, *The Structure of Scientific Revolutions*, Chicago: University of Chicago Press, 1962.

Labay, Duncan G., and Thomas C. Kinnear, "Exploring the Consumer Decision Process in the Adoption of Solar Energy Systems," *Journal of Consumer Research*, 8, 1981, pp. 271–278.

Lang, Gladys, and Kurt Lang, "Watergate: An Exploration of the Agenda-Setting Process," in G. C. Wilhoit and H. DeBock (ed.), *Mass Communication Review Yearbook* 2, Newbury Par, California: Sage, pp. 447–468.

Langeard, E., M. Crousillat, and R. Weiss, "Exposure to Cultural Activities and Opinion Leadership," *Advances in Consumer Research*, 5, 1977, pp. 606–610.

Lasswell, Harold L., *Propaganda Technique in the World War*, New York: Alfred A. Knopf, 1927.

Laumann, Edward O., *Bonds of Pluralism: The Form and Substance of Urban Social Networks*, New York: Wiley, 1973.

Laumann, Edward O., "Friends of Urban Man: an Assessment of Accuracy in Reporting Their Sociometric Attributes," *Sociometry*, 32, 1969, pp. 54–59.

Laumann, Edward O., "Network Analysis in Large Social Systems: Some Theoretical and Methodological Problems," pp. 379–402 in P. Holland S. Leinhardt (eds.), *Perspectives on Social Networks Research*, New York: Academic Press, 1979.

Laumann, Edward O., and Franz U. Pappi, *Networks of Collective Action: A Perspective on Community Influence*, 1976, New York: Academic Press.

Lazarsfeld, Paul F., Bernard Berelson, and Hazel Gaudet, *The People's Choice*, New York: Duell, Sloan, and Pearce, 1944.

Lazarsfeld, Paul F., and Herbert Menzel, Mass Media and Personal Influence, in Wilbur Schramm (ed.), *The Science of Human Communication*, New York: Columbia University Press, 1963.

Leinhardt, Samuel (ed.), *Social Networks*, New York: Academic Press, 1977.

Lennon, Sharron J., and Leslie L. Davis, "Individual Differences in Fashion Orientation and Cognitive Complexity," *Perceptual and Motor Skills*, 64, 1987, pp. 327–330.

Leonard-Barton, Dorothy, "Experts as Negative Opinion Leaders in the Diffusion of a Technological Innovation," *Journal of Consumer Research*, 11, 1985, pp. 914–926.

Lerner, Daniel, *The Passing of Traditional Society: Modernizing the Middle East*, New York: Free Press, 1958

Lerner, Max (ed.), *The Portable Veblen*, edited by Max Lerner, New York: Viking Press, 1948.

Leventhal, H., and P. D. Cleary, "The Smoking Problem: A Review of the Research and Theory in Behavioral Risk Modification," *Psychological Bulletin*, 88, 1980, pp. 370–405.

Levy, Mark R., "Opinion Leadership and Television News Uses," *Public Opinion Quarterly*, 42, 1978, pp. 402–406.

Lievrouw, Leah A., Everett M. Rogers, Charles U. Lowe, and Edward Nadel, "Triangulation as a Research Strategy for Identifying Invisible Colleges Among Biomedical Scientists," *Social Networks*, 9, 1987, pp. 217–248.

Lin, Nan, *The Study of Human Communication*, Indianapolis: Bobbs-Merrill, 1971, pp. 149–150.

Lingwood, D., "Interpersonal Communication, Scientific Productivity, and Invisible Colleges: Studies of Two Behavioral Science Research Areas," paper presented to the Colloquium on Improving the Social and Communication Mechanisms of Educational Research, The American Educational Research Association, Washington, D.C., November 1968.

Lionberger, Herbert F., *Adoption of New Ideas and Practices*, Ames, Iowa: Iowa University Press, 1960.

Lomas, Jonathan, et al., "Opinion Leaders vs Audit and Feedback to Implement Practice Guidelines," *Journal of the American Medical Association*, 265 (17), 1991, pp. 2202–2207.

Lowe, Francis E., and Thomas C. McCormick, "A Study of the Influence of Formal and Informal Leaders in an Election Campaign," *Public Opinion Quarterly*, 20, 1956, pp. 651–662.

Lowery, Shearon A., and Melvin L. DeFleur, *Milestones in Mass Communication Research*, New York: Longman, 1988 (2nd edition).

Lurie, Alison, *The Language of Clothes*, New York: Random House, 1981.

Mahajan, Vijay, Eitan Muller, and Roger A. Kerin, "Introduction Strategies for New Products with Positive and Negative Word-of-mouth," *Management Science*, 30, 1984, pp. 68–79.

Mancuso, Joseph R., "Why Not Create Opinion Leaders for New Product Introductions?" *Journal of Marketing*, 33, 1969, pp. 20-25.

Mann, Richard D., "A Review of the Relationships Between Personality and Performance in Small Groups," *Psychological Bulletin*, 56, 1959, pp. 241-270.

March, Robert M., and Margaret W. Tebbutt, "Housewife Product Communication Activity Patterns," *Journal of Social Psychology*, 107, 1979, pp. 63-69.

Marcus, Alan S., and Raymond A. Bauer, "Yes, There Are Generalized Opinion Leaders," *Public Opinion Quarterly*, 28, 1964, pp. 628-632.

Marsden, Peter V., "Core Discussion Networks of Americans," *American Sociological Review*, 52, 1987, pp. 122-131.

Martilla, John A., "Word-of-mouth Communication in the Industrial Adoption Process," *Journal of Marketing Research*, 8, 1971, pp. 173-178.

McCleneghan, Sean J., "A Longitudinal Study of High School Opinion Leaders for USAF Panel," *Journalism Quarterly*, 54, 1977, pp. 357-361.

McCombs, Maxwell E., "The Agenda-setting Approach," in D. D. Nimmo and K. R. Sanders (eds.), *Mass Communication Review Yearbook 2*, Newbury Park, California: Sage, 1981, pp. 121-140.

McCombs, Maxwell E., and Donald Shaw, "The Agenda-Setting Function of Mass Media," *Public Opinion Quarterly*, 36, 1972, pp. 176-184.

McCombs, Maxwell E., Edna Einsiedel, and David Weaver, *Contemporary Public Opinion: Issues and the News*, Hillsdale, New Jersey: Lawerence Erlbaum Associates, 1991.

McConnel, T. S., A. H. Cushing, A. D. Bankhurst, J. A. Healy, P. A. McIlvenna, and B. J. Skipper, "Physician Behavior Modification Using Claims Data," *Western Journal of Medicine*, 137, 1982, pp. 448-450.

McCraken, Grant D. "The Trickle-down Theory Rehabilitated," in Michael R. Solomon (ed.), *The Psychology of Fashion*, Lexington, Massachusetts: Lexington Books, 1985, pp. 39-54.

McCroskey, James C., "Validity of the PRCA as an Index of Oral Communication Apprehension," *Communication Monographs*, 45, 1978, pp. 192-203.

McGuire, William J., "An Information Processing Model of Advertising Effectiveness," in H. L. Davis and A. J. Silk (eds.), *Behavior and Management Sciences in Marketing*, New York: Wiley, 1978, pp. 156–180.

McGuire, William J., "Personality and Susceptibility to Social Influence," in E. F. Borgatta and W. W. Lambert (eds.), *Handbook of Personality Theory and Research*, New York: Rand McNally, 1968, pp. 1130–1187.

Mendelsohn, Harold, and Irving Crespi, *Polls, Television, and the New Politics*, San Francisco: Chandler, 1970, pp. 297–298.

Menzel, Herbert, and Elihu Katz, "Social Relations and Innovation in the Medical Profession," *Public Opinion Quarterly*, 19, 1955, pp. 337–352.

Merton, Robert K., "Patterns of Influence," in Paul F. Lazarsfeld and Frank N. Stanton (eds.), *Communications Research*, New York: Harper and Brothers, 1949, pp. 180–219.

Merton, Robert K., *Social Theory and Social Structure*, Glencoe, Illinois: Free Press, 1957.

Midgley, David F., and Graham R. Dowling, "Innovativeness: The Concept and Its Measurement," *Journal of Consumer Research*, 4, 1978, pp. 229–242.

Miller, Warren E., "Party Identification, Realignment, and Party Voting: Back to the Basics," *American Political Science Review*, 85(2), 1991, pp. 557–568.

Mitchell, Arnold, *The Nine American Lifestyles*, New York: Macmillan, 1983.

Montgomery, David B., and Alvin J. Silk, "Clusters of Consumer Interests and Opinion Leaders' Spheres of Influence," *Journal of Marketing Research*, 8, 1971, pp. 317–321.

Moreno, Jacob, L., *Who Shall Survive?*, Beacon, New York: Beacon House, 1953.

Munson, Michael J., and W. Austin Spivey, "Product and Brand-User Stereotypes Among Social Classes: Implications for Advertising Strategy," *Journal of Advertising Research*, 21, 1981, pp. 37–46.

Myers, James H., and Thomas S. Robertson, "Dimensions of Opinion Leadership," *Journal of Marketing Research*, 4, 1972, pp. 41–46.

Niemi, Richard G., Roman Hedges, and M. Kent Jennings, "The Similarity of Husbands' and Wives' Political Views," *American Politics Quarterly*, 5, 1977, pp. 133–148.

Noda, M., "Contraception in Japan: Problems of Motivation and Communication," in C. V. Kiser (ed.), *Research in Family Planning*, New Jersey: Princeton University Press, 1962, pp. 551–569.

Noelle-Neumann, Elisabeth, "The Spiral of Silence: A Theory of Public Opinion," *Journal of Communication*, 24, 1974, pp. 43–51.

Noelle Neumann, Elisabeth, *Spiegel Dokumentation: Personlichkeitsstarke*, Hamburg: Spiegel Verlag, 1983.

Noelle-Neumann, Elisabeth, *The Spiral of Silence: Public Opinion: Our Social Skin*, Chicago: University of Chicago Press, 1984.

Noelle-Neumann, Elisabeth, "Identifying Opinion Leaders," paper presented at 38th ESOMAR Conference, Wiesbaden, September 1985, pp. 3–12.

Noelle-Neumann, Elisabeth, "Advances in Spiral of Silence Research," *Communication Review*, 10, 1989, pp. 3–34.

Noelle-Neumann, Elisabeth, "The Theory of Public Opinion: The Concept of the Spiral of Silence," *Communication Yearbook*, 14, 1991, pp. 256–287.

Noelle-Neumann, Elisabeth and Mihaly Csikszentmihalyi, "Personality Strength: A New Variable for Opinion-Attitude Research," paper presented at the WAPOR Conference, St. Petersburg Beach, Florida, May 1992.

Omura, Glenn S., and W. Wayne Talarzyk, "Shaping Public Opinion: Personal Sources of Information on a Major Political Issue," *Advances in Consumer Research*, 10, 1982, pp. 484–489.

Osborn, June E., "The AIDS Epidemic: Multidisciplinary Trouble," *The New England Journal of Medicine*, 314, 1986, pp. 779–782.

Ostlund, Lyman E., "Interpersonal Communication Following McGovern's Eagleton Decision," *Public Opinion Quarterly*, 37, 1973, pp. 601–610.

Palmore, James A., "The Chicago Snowball: A Study of the Flow and Diffusion of Family Planning Information," in Donald J. Bogue (ed.), *Sociological Contributions to Family Planning Research*, Chicago: University of Chicago Press, 1967, pp. 272–363.

Palmore, James A., "Awareness Sources and Stages in the Adoption of Specific Contraceptives," *Demography*, 5, 1968, pp. 960–972.

Palmore, James A., and D. M. Monsees, "The Eastern Kentucky Private Physician-Plus-Education Program: First Evaluation and Results," in Donald J. Bogue (ed.), *The Rural South Fertility Experiments*, Chicago: Community and Family Study Center, University of Chicago, Report 1, 1966, pp. 11–26.

Palmore, James A., Paul M. Hirsch, and Ariffin Marzuki, "Interpersonal Communication and the Diffusion of Family Planning in West Malaysia," *Demography*, 8, 1971, pp. 411–425.

Park, Whan C., and V. Parker Lessig, "Students and Housewives: Differences in Susceptibility to Reference Group Influences," *Journal of Consumer Research*, 4, 1977, pp. 102–110.

Payne, S. K. and M. J. Beatty, "Innovativeness and Cognitive Complexity," *Psychological Reports*, 51, 1982, pp. 85–86.

Peterson, Ruth C., and L. L. Thurstone, *Motion Pictures and the Social Attitudes of Children*, New York: Macmillan, 1933.

Placek, Paul J., "Direct Mail and Information Diffusion: Family Planning," *Public Opinion Quarterly*, 39, 1975, pp. 548–561.

Plaut, Gunther W., (ed.), *The Torah: A Modern Commentary*, New York: Union of American Hebrew Congregations, 1981.

Polegato, Rosemary, and Marjorie Wall, "Information Seeking by Fashion Opinion Leaders and Followers," *Home Economics Research Journal*, 8, 1980, pp. 327–338.

Pomper, Gerald M., "From Confusion to Clarity: Issues and American Voters," *American Political Science Review*, 66, 1972, pp. 415–428.

Pontius, Steven K., "The Communication Process of Adoption: Agriculture in Thailand," *The Journal of Developing Areas*, 18, 1983, pp. 93–118.

Price, D. J., *Little Science, Big Science*, New York: Columbia University Press, 1963.

Price, Linda L., and Nancy M. Ridgway, "Development of a Scale to Measure Use Innovativeness," *Advances in Consumer Research*, 10, 1983, pp. 679–684.

Protess, David L., and Maxwell E. McCombs (eds.), *Agenda-Setting: Reading on Media, Public Opinion and Policymaking*, Hillsdale, New Jersey: Lawrence Erlbaum Associates, 1991.

Puska, P., et al., "Use of Lay Opinion Leaders to Promote Diffusion of Health Innovations in a Community Program: Lessons from the North Karelia Project," *Bulletin of the World Health Organization*, 64(3), 1986, pp. 437–446.

Rao, Appa G., and Everett M. Rogers, "Caste and Formal Education in Interpersonal Diffusion of an Innovation in Two Indian Villages," *Indian Journal of Extension Education*, 16, 1980, pp. 1–9.

Rao, Sethu M. K., and C. Bhaskaran, "Application of Sociometric Techniques in Identifying Opinion Leaders in Two South Indian Villages," *Group Psychotherapy, Psychodrama and Sociometry*, 31, 1978, pp. 46–50.

Ray, Michael L., "Psychological Theories and Interpretations of Learning," in Thomas S. Robertson and Scott Ward (eds.), *Consumer Behavior: Theoretical Sources*, Englewood Cliffs, New Jersey: Prentice-Hall, 1973, pp. 45–117.

Ray, Michael L., *Advertising and Communications Management*, Englewood Cliffs, New Jersey: Prentice-Hall, 1982, pp. 34–55.

Ray, W. A., R. Fink, W. Schaffner, and C. F. Federspiel, "Improving Antibiotic Prescription in Outpatient Practice," *Medical Care*, 23, 1985, p. 1307.

Ray, W. A., D. G. Blazer, W. Schaffner, C. F. Federspiel, and R. Fink, "Reducing Long-term Diazepam Prescribing in Office Practice: A Controlled Trial of Educational Visits," *Journal of the American Medical Association*, 256, 1986, pp. 2536–2539.

Reese, Stephen D., "Setting the Media's Agenda: A Power Balance Perspective," in J. A. Anderson, *Communication Yearbook 14*, Newbury Park, California: Sage, 1991, pp. 309–340.

Requena, M., "Studies of Family Planning in The Quinta Normal District of Santiago," *Milbank Memorial Fund Quarterly*, 43, October 1965, pp. 69–99

Reynolds, Fred D., and William R. Darden, "Mutually Adaptive Effects of Interpersonal Communication," *Journal of Marketing Research*, 8, 1971, pp. 449–454.

Richards, William D., *A Manual for Network Analysis*, Mimeo, Stanford: Stanford University, Institute for Communications Research, 1975.

Richards, William D., "Network Analysis Methods: Conceptual and Operational Approaches," paper presented at the Fourth Annual Colloquium on Social Networks, Honolulu, University of Hawaii, 1976.

Richins, Marsha L., "An Analysis of Consumer Interaction Styles in the Marketplace," *Journal of Consumer Research*, 10, 1983, pp. 73–82.

Richins, Marsha L., "Negative Word-of-mouth by Dissatisfied Consumers: A Pilot Study," *Journal of Marketing*, 47, 1983, pp. 68–78.

Richins, Marsha L., and Peter H. Bloch, "After the New Wears Off: The Temporal Context of Product Involvement," *Journal of Consumer Research*, 13, 1986, pp. 280–285.

Richins, Marsha L., and Teri Root-Schaffer, "The Role of Involvement and Opinion Leadership in Consumer Word-of-mouth: An Implicit Model Made Explicit," *Advances in Consumer Research*, 15, 1988, pp. 32–36.

Richmond, Virginia P., "The Relationship Between Opinion Leadership and Information Acquisition," *Human Communication Research*, 4, 1977, pp. 38–43.

Richmond, Virginia P., "Monomorphic and Polymorphic Opinion Leadership within a Relatively Closed Communication System," *Human Communication Research*, 6(2), 1980, pp. 111–115.

Richmond, Virginia P. and James C. McCroskey, "Whose Opinion Do You Trust?" *Journal of Communication*, 25, 1975, pp. 42–50.

Rieken, Glen, and Ugur Yavas, "Internal Consistency Reliability of King and Summers' Opinion Leadership Scale: Further Evidence," *Journal of Marketing Research*, 20, 1983, pp. 325–326.

Rieken, Glen, and Ugur Yavas, "Seeking Donors Via Opinion Leadership," *Journal of Professional Services Marketing*, 2, 1986, pp. 109–116.

Robertson, Thomas S., *Innovative Behavior and Communication*, New York: Holt, Rinehart and Winston, 1971.

Robertson, Thomas S., and James H. Myers, "Personality Correlates of Opinion Leadership and Innovative Buying Behavior," *Journal of Marketing Research*, 6, 1969, pp. 164–168.

Robertson, Thomas S., and Scott Ward, "Consumer Behavior Research: Promise and Prospects," in T. S. Robertson and S. Ward (eds.), *Consumer Behavior: Theoretical Sources*, Englewood Cliffs, New Jersey: Prentice-Hall, 1973, pp. 3–42.

Robertson, Thomas S., Joan Zielinski, and Scott Ward, *Consumer Behavior*, Glenview, Illinois: Scott, Foresman, and Company, 1984.

Robinson, John P., "The Press as Kingmaker," *Journalism Quarterly*, 51, 1974, pp. 587–594.

Robinson, John, P., "Interpersonal Influence in Election Campaigns: Two Step Flow Hypotheses," *Public Opinion Quarterly*, 40, 1976, pp. 304–319.

Rogers, Everett M., *Social Change in Rural Sociology*, New York: Appelton-Century-Crofts, 1960.

Rogers, Everett M., "Characteristics of Innovators and Other Adopter Categories," *Ohio Agricultural Experiment Station Research Bulletin*, 882, 1961.

Rogers, Everett M., *Diffusion of Innovations*, New York: The Free Press, 3rd edition, 1983.

Rogers, Everett M., and David G. Cartano, "Methods of Measuring Opinion Leadership," *Public Opinion Quarterly*, 26, 1962, pp. 435–441.

Rogers, Everett M., and Lynne Svenning, *Modernization Among Peasants: The Impact of Communication*, New York: Holt, Rinehart, and Winston, 1969.

Rogers, Everett M., and Floyd F. Shoemaker, *Communication of Innovations: A Cross-Cultural Approach*, New York: Free Press, 1971.

Rogers, Everett M., and Lawrence D. Kincaid, *Communication Networks: Toward a New Paradigm for Research*, New York: Free Press, 1981.

Rogers, Everett M., and James W. Dearing, "Agenda-setting Research: Where Has It Been, Where Is It Going?" in J. A. Anderson (ed.), *Communication Yearbook 11*, Newbury Park, California: Sage, 1988, pp. 555–594.

Roper, Elmo, *Trends in Public Opinion Toward Television and Other Mass Media 1959–1974*, New York: Television Information Office, 1975.

Rosario, Florangel Z., "The Leader in Family Planning and the Two-step Flow Model," *Journalism Quarterly*, 48, 1971, pp. 288–297.

Rosenberg, Morris, *Society and the Adolescent Self-image*, Princeton, New Jersey, 1965, Princeton University Press.

Ross M. W. and J. A. Carson, "Effectiveness of Distribution of Information on AIDS: A National Study of Six Media in Australia," *New York State Journal of Medicine*, 88, 1988, pp. 239-241.

Rotter, Julian B., "General Expectancies for Internal versus External Control of Reinforcement," *Psychological Monographs*, 6, 1966, pp. 91-92.

Ryan, Bryce, and Neal C. Gross, "The Diffusion of Hybrid Seed Corn in Two Iowa Communities," *Rural Sociology*, 8, 1943, pp. 15-24.

Sackett, D. L., and R. B. Hynes (eds.), *Compliance with Therapeutic Regimens*, Baltimore: Johns Hopkins University Press, 1976.

Saunders, John, J., Michael Davis, and David M. Monsees, "Opinion Leadership in Family Planning," *Journal of Health and Social Behavior*, 15(3), 1974, pp. 217-227.

Schaffner, W., W. A. Ray, C.F. Federspiel, and W. O. Miller, "Improving Antibiotic Prescribing in Office Practice: A Controlled Trial of Three Educational Methods," *Journal of the American Medical Association*, 250, 1983, pp. 1728-1732.

Schenk, Michael, "Politische Meinungsfuhrer," *Publizistik*, 30, 1985, pp. 7-16.

Schenk, Michael, "Massenkommunikation und Interpersonale Kommunikation," *Kölner Zeitschrift fur Soziologie und Sozialpsychologie*, 30, 1989, pp. 406-417.

Schenk, Michael, and Uwe Pfenning, "Opinion Leadership Reconsidered: A Social Network Approach," paper presented at the European Conference on Social Network Analysis, Paris, June 1991.

Schiffman, Leon G., and Vincent Gaccione, "Opinion Leaders in Institutional Markets," *Journal of Marketing*, 38, 1974, pp. 49-53.

Schott, Thomas, "Interpersonal Influence in Science: Mathematicians in Denmark and Israel," *Social Network*, 9, 1987, pp. 351-374.

Schramm, Wilbur, *Mass Communication*, Urbana, Illinois: University of Illinois Press, 1960.

Schrank, Holy L., and D. Lois Gilmore, "Correlates of Fashion Opinion Leadership: Implications for Fashion Process Theory," *The Sociological Quarterly*, 14, 1973, pp. 534-543.

Scorer, N., *The Social System of Science*, New York: Holt, Rinehart and Winston, 1966.

Sen, L. K., "Opinion Leadership in India: Diffusion of Innovations." Research Report 22, Department of Communication, 1969, East Lansing: Michigan State University.

Sen, L. K., *Opinion Leadership in India: A Study of Interpersonal Communication in Eight Villages*, Hyderbad: National Institute of Communication Development, 1969.

Sengupta, T., "Opinion Leaders in Rural Communities," *Man In India*, 48, 1968, pp. 156–166.

Sheingold, Carl A., "Social Networks and Voting: The Resurrection of a Research Agenda," *American Sociological Review*, 38, 1973, pp. 712–720.

Sheth, Jagdish N., "Word-of-mouth in Low-risk Innovations," *Journal of Advertising Research*, 11, 1971, pp. 15–18.

Shye, Shmuel (ed.), *Theory Construction and Data Analysis in the Behavioral Sciences*, San Francisco: Jossey-Bass, 1978.

Siegel, Karolynn, "Public Education to Prevent the Spread of HIV Infection," *New York State Journal of Medicine*, 88, 1988, pp. 642–646.

Silk, Alvin J. "Overlap Among Self-designated Opinion Leaders: A Study of Selected Dental Products and Services," *Journal of Marketing Research*, 3, 1966, pp. 255–259.

Silk, Alvin J. "Response Set and the Measurement of Self-Designated Opinion Leadership," *Public Opinion Quarterly*, 35, 1971, pp. 382–397.

Simmel, Georg, "Fashion," *International Quarterly*, 10, 1904, pp. 130–155.

Simon-Miller, Francoise, "Commentary: Signs and Cycles in the Fashion System," in Michael R. Solomon (ed.), *The Psychology of Fashion*, Lexington, Massachusetts: Lexington Books, 1985, pp. 71–81.

Sma, Hossain, and B. R. Crouch, "Patterns and Determinants of Adoption of Farm Practices: Some Evidence from Bangladesh," *Agricultural Systems*, 38, 1992, pp. 1–15.

Snyder, Mark, "Self-monitoring Processes," in L. Berkowitz (ed.), *Advances in Experimental Social Psychology*, New York: Academic Press, 1979, pp. 85–128.

Snyder, Mark, and Thomas C. Monson, "Persons, Situations, and the Control of Social Behavior," *Journal of Personality and Social Psychology*, 32, 1975, pp. 637–644.

Sola Pool, Ithiel de, "TV: A New Dimension in Politics," in E. Burdick and A. J. Brodbeck (eds.), *American Voting Behavior*, Glencoe, Illinois: Free Press, 1959, pp. 239–242.

Sollie, Carlton R., "A Comparison of Reputational Techniques for Identifying Community Leaders," *Rural Sociology*, 31, 1966, pp. 301–309.

Soumerai, Stephen B., and Jerry Avorn, "Economic and Policy Analysis of University-based Drug 'Detailing'," *Medical Care*, 24(4), 1986, pp. 313–331.

Soumerai, Stephen B., and Jerry Avorn, "Principles of Educational Outreach ('Academic Detailing') to Improve Clinical Decision Making," *Journal of the American Medical Association*, 263, 1990, pp. 549–556.

Soumerai, Stephen B., Thomas J. McLauglin, and Jerry Avorn, "Improving Drug Prescribing in Primary Care: A Critical Analysis of the Experimental Literature," *The Milbank Quarterly*, 67, 1990, pp. 268–317.

Sperber, Irwin, *Fashions in Science: Opinion Leaders and Collective Behavior in the Social Sciences*, Minneapolis: University of Minnesota Press, 1990.

Sproles, George B., *Fashion: Consumer Behavior toward Dress*, Minneapolis: Burgess, 1979; George B. Sproles (ed.), Perspectives of Fashion, Minneapolis: Burgess, 1981.

Sproles, George B., "Behavioral Science Theories of Fashion," in Michael R. Solomon (ed.), *The Psychology of Fashion*, Lexington, Massachusetts: Lexington Books, 1985, pp. 15–28.

Stern, Barbara B. and Stephen J. Gould, "The Consumer as Financial Opinion Leader," *Journal of Retailing Banking*, 10, 1988, pp. 43–52.

Stewart, John B., *Repetitive Advertising in Newspapers: A Study of New Products*, Boston: Harvard University Division of Research, Graduate School of Business Administration, 1964.

Stone, Gregory P., "Appearances and the Self," in Arnold R. Rose, (ed.), *Human Behavior and Social Interaction*, Boston: Houghton Mifflin, 1962, pp. 86–118.

Straits, Bruce C., "Bringing Strong Ties Back: Interpersonal Gateways to Political Information and Influence," *Public Opinion Quarterly*, 55, 1991, pp. 432–448.

Strong, E. K., *The Psychology of Selling*, New York: McGraw-Hill, 1920.

Stross, J. K. and G. G. Bole, "Continuing Education in Rheumatoid Arthritis for the Primary Care Physician," *Arthritis Rheum*, 22, 1979, pp. 787–791.

Stross, J. K. and G. G. Bole, "Evaluation of a Continuing Education Program in Rheumatoid Arthritis," *Arthritis Rheum*, 23, 1980, pp. 846–849.

Stycos, Mayone J., "The Potential Role of Turkish Village Opinion Leaders in a Program of Family Planning," *Public Opinion Quarterly*, 29, 1965, pp. 120–130.

Summers, John O., "The Identity of Women's Clothing Fashion Opinion Leadership," *Journal of Marketing Research*, 7, 1970, pp. 178–185.

Szybillo, George J., "A Situational Influence on the Relationship of a Consumer Attribute to New-Product Attractiveness," *Journal of Applied Psychology*, 60, 1975, pp. 652–655.

Tarde, Gabriel, *The Laws of Imitation* (translated from French), New York: Henry Holt, 1903.

Taylor, James W., "A Striking Characteristic of Innovators," *Journal of Marketing Research*, 14, 1977, pp. 104–107.

Thomas, John S., "Leadership, Innovativeness, and Centrality in a Mexican Ejido," *Human Organization*, 40 (4), 1981, pp. 349–352.

Thomas, Veronica G., and Lawrence W. Littig, "A Typology of Leadership Style: Examining Gender and Race Effects," *Bulletin of The Psychonomic Society*, 23 (2), 1985, pp. 132–134.

Tigert, Douglas J., and Stephen J. Arnold, *Profiling Self-designated Opinion Leaders and Self-designated Innovators Through Life Style Research*, Toronto: School of Business, University of Toronto, 1971.

Tigert, Douglas J., Charles W. King and L. Ring, "Fashion Involvement: A Cross-cultural Comparative Analysis," *Advances in Consumer Research*, 7, 1979, pp. 17–21.

Trivedi, D. N., "Modernization, Opinion Leaders and their Instrumental Information Seeking Behavior," *Indian Journal of Sociology*, 3, 1972, pp. 69–78.

Troldahl, Verling C., and Robert Van Dam, "Face-to-face Communication about Major Topics in the News," *Public Opinion Quarterly*, 29, 1965, pp. 626–634.

Troldahl, Verling C., and Robert Van Dam, "A New Scale for Identifying Public-affairs Opinion Leaders," *Journalism Quarterly*, 42, 1965, pp. 655–657.

Van Den Ban, A. W., "A Revision of the Two-step Flow of Communication Hypothesis," *Gazette*, 10, 1964, pp. 237–249.

Veblen, Thorstein, *The Theories of the Leisure Class*, New York: Macmillan, 1915.

Veblen, Thorstein, *What Veblen Taught: Selected Writings of Thorstein Veblen*, New York: A. M. Kelly, 1936.

Venkatraman, Meera P., "Opinion Leadership, Enduring Involvement and Characteristics of Opinion Leaders: A Moderating or Mediating Relationship?" *Advances in Consumer Research*, 17, 1990, pp. 60–67.

Weatherford, Stephen M., Interpersonal Networks and Political Behavior," *American Journal of Political Science*, 26(1), 1982, pp. 117–142.

Weimann, Gabriel, "On the Importance of Marginality: One More Step into the Two-step Flow of Communication," *American Sociological Review* 47 (6), 1982, pp. 764–773.

Weimann, Gabriel, "The Strength of Weak Conversational Ties in the Flow of Information and Influence," *Social Networks*, 5, 1983, pp. 245–267.

Weimann, Gabriel, "Social Networks and Communication," in M. Asante and W. B. Gudykunst (eds.), *Handbook of International and Intercultural Relations*, Los Angeles: Sage, 1989, pp. 186–203.

Weimann, Gabriel, "The Influentials: Back to the Concept of Opinion Leaders?" *Public Opinion Quarterly*, 55, 1991, pp. 267–279.

Weiss, Walter, "Effects of the Mass Media of Communication," in Gardner Lindzey and Elliot Aronson (eds.), *Handbook of Social Psychology*, Vol. 5, 1969, Boston: Addison-Wesley, pp. 77–195.

Westbrook, Robert A., and Claes Fornell, "Patterns of Information Source Usage Among Durable Goods Buyers," *Journal of Marketing Research*, 16, 1979, pp. 303–312.

Westley, Bruce, "Communication and Social Change," *American Behavioral Scientist*, 14, 1971, pp. 719–742.

Whitney, Charles, "Agenda-setting: Power and Contingency," in J. A. Anderson, *Communication Yearbook* 14, Newbury Park, California: Sage, 1991, pp. 347–356.

Whyte, William H. "The Web of Word-of-mouth," *Fortune*, 50, November 1954, p. 140.

Wilkening, Eugene, Joan Tully, and Hartley Presser, "Communication and Acceptance of Recommended Farm Practices Among Dairy Farmers of Northern Victoria," *Rural Sociology*, 27, 1962, pp. 116–119.

Wilson, Stan Le Roy, *Mass Media/Mass Culture*, (2nd edition), New York: McGraw-Hill, 1992, pp. 321–324.

Witteman, H. R. and P. A. Andersen, The Polymorphic Opinion Leadership Test: Development and Validation, paper presented to the Western Speech Communication Association Convention, 1976, San Francisco.

Wright, Charles R., and Muriel Cantor, "The Opinion Seeker and Avoider: Steps Beyond the Opinion Leader Concept," *Pacific Sociological Review*, 10, 1967, pp. 33–43.

Yadav, D. P., Communication Structure and Innovation Diffusion in Two Indian Villages, Ph.D. dissertation, 1967, East Lansing: Michigan State University.

Yavas, Ugur, and Glen Rieken, "Extensions of King and Summers' Opinion Leadership Scale: A Reliability Study," *Journal of Marketing Research*, 19, 1982, pp. 154–155.

Zaltman, G. and J. Blau, "A Note on an International Invisible College in Theoretical High Energy Physics," unpublished report, Northwestern University, 1969.

Index of Names

Index of Subjects